AI Frameworks and Tools for Software Development

Rahul K. Patel
Illinois Institute of Technology, Chicago, USA

IGI Global
Scientific Publishing
Publishing Tomorrow's Research Today

Vice President of Editorial Melissa Wagner
Managing Editor of Acquisitions Mikaela Felty
Managing Editor of Book Development Jocelynn Hessler
Production Manager Mike Brehm
Cover Design Phillip Shickler

Published in the United States of America by
IGI Global Scientific Publishing
701 East Chocolate Avenue
Hershey, PA, 17033, USA
Tel: 717-533-8845
Fax: 717-533-7115
Website: https://www.igi-global.com E-mail: cust@igi-global.com

Library of Congress Cataloging-in-Publication Data

Names: Patel, Rahul (Rahul K.), 1973- editor
Title: AI frameworks and tools for software development / edited by Rahul Patel.
Description: Hershey, PA : IGI Global Scientific Publishing, [2025] | Includes bibliographical references and index. | Summary: "The objective of this book is to serve as a tool and an essential guide with an innovative educational approach tailored for practitioners and students seeking to on-board a modern AI tools and start contributing at a higher effective and efficient level. . Book is also designed to be used for current software development practitioners to find gaps and overlaps in their current Software Development Lifecycle (SDLC) methods as well as lead to higher levels of maturity. Book also focuses on AI Tools and opportunities to automate various functions and processes as a whole or in part for achieving higher levels of consistencies and efficiencies in Software Development Lifecycle (SDLC)"-- Provided by publisher.
Identifiers: LCCN 2024058260 (print) | LCCN 2024058261 (ebook) | ISBN 9798369384077 h/c | ISBN 9798369384084 s/c | ISBN 9798369384091 ebook
Subjects: LCSH: Computer software--Development | Artificial intelligence--Data processing | Artificial intelligence--Industrial applications | Machine learning--Industrial applications
Classification: LCC QA76.76.D47 A3967 2025 (print) | LCC QA76.76.D47 (ebook)
LC record available at https://lccn.loc.gov/2024058260
LC ebook record available at https://lccn.loc.gov/2024058261

British Cataloguing in Publication Data
A Cataloguing in Publication record for this book is available from the British Library.

Table of Contents

Detailed Table of Contents

This chapter delves into the ethical challenges of incorporating AI technologies into the software development lifecycle (SDLC). As AI tools increasingly automate decisions from requirements analysis to deployment, developers and stakeholders face critical issues related to bias, fairness, accountability, transparency, and data privacy. It highlights ethical risks, such as biased algorithms and data misuse, while stressing the importance of maintaining a balance between automation and human oversight. The environmental impact of large-scale AI systems is also discussed, alongside strategies for sustainable development. Through case studies, the chapter showcases instances where ethical considerations were overlooked, resulting in negative outcomes. A comprehensive framework for ethical compliance is provided, emphasizing bias mitigation, transparency, privacy safeguards, and accountability. Ultimately, the chapter advocates for proactive ethical measures to ensure AI enhances software development while upholding societal values, individual rights, and environmental sustainability.

This study aims to explore the transformative impact of Artificial Intelligence (AI) on project management within software development, targeting project managers, software developers, and organizational leaders. Employing a mixed-methods approach, the research integrates quantitative data from AI-enhanced project management tools and qualitative insights from interviews with industry professionals. Key findings reveal that AI tools significantly optimize project workflows, reduce development cycles, and enhance software quality through automation and predictive analytics. The study concludes that effective project management is crucial for successfully integrating AI technologies, emphasizing the need for best practices, ethical considerations, and continuous learning to navigate the challenges of AI adoption. The implications of this research highlight the necessity for organizations to adapt their project management strategies to leverage AI's full potential, ultimately driving innovation and efficiency in software development.

executives the strategic knowledge necessary to leverage AI technologies effectively, ensuring that AI investments contribute to long-term organizational success.

Threats in Software Development have become a critical concern in today's fast-evolving technological landscape. As software systems grow in complexity and importance, they become increasingly vulnerable to a wide range of security risks, including both internal and external threats. These threats can compromise the confidentiality, integrity, and availability of software, leading to significant financial losses, reputational damage, and legal consequences. Addressing these vulnerabilities early in the Software Development Life Cycle (SDLC) is essential to minimize potential threats. This paper explores the importance of implementing effective Risk-Based Vulnerability Management (RBVM) within software development processes. It highlights the challenges of identifying, assessing, and mitigating software security vulnerabilities through a risk-centric approach.

AI Software and Applications in Knowledge Management and Customer Support have emerged as transformative tools in modern business environments. By leveraging advanced machine learning algorithms, and deep learning techniques, AI-powered systems can significantly enhance both the management of organizational knowledge and the efficiency of customer support services. These AI applications assist in automating knowledge-sharing processes, improving decision-making, and providing real-time support to customers. In the realm of customer support, AI-driven chatbots and virtual assistants offer 24/7 assistance, streamline customer interactions, and reduce operational costs. In knowledge management, AI systems help organizations manage vast amounts of information, enabling better access to critical data and insights. This paper explores the integration of AI in knowledge management and customer support, examining how these technologies can improve service quality, drive innovation, and create more personalized experiences for customers.

In this paper, we survey the existing literature on the integration of sustainability and smart applications. We focus on providing insights on the use of state-of-the-art Machine Learning mechanisms in context of the sustainable smart systems. A thorough discussion of various Deep Learning algorithms and frameworks which provide embedded intelligence for sustainable smart applications such as smart home, smart city, healthcare, industry, transportation, agriculture, etc. has been discussed. We then shed light

Preface

In the rapidly evolving landscape of software development, Artificial Intelligence (AI) is emerging as a transformative force, enhancing productivity, decision-making, and overall system efficiency. This collection of chapters examines the diverse applications of AI in software engineering, from risk management and quality assurance to project optimization and knowledge management. By exploring the integration of AI in areas such as predictive maintenance, smart programming techniques, and the automation of complex processes, this work provides valuable insights into how AI-driven tools are reshaping the development lifecycle. Through real-world case studies and expert perspectives, the chapters highlight the ways in which AI fosters innovation, ensures quality, and enhances the adaptability of modern software systems, all while addressing critical challenges like software engineering, coding, scalability, security, and ethical considerations. As we venture into an increasingly AI-powered future, these discussions offer a glimpse into the immense potential for AI to revolutionize the software development industry.

This book aims to provide a comprehensive guide to understanding and leveraging the latest advancements in AI based software development and management with case studies. Each chapter is meticulously designed to cover different aspects of this broad and dynamic field, offering insights, strategies, and practical applications that are essential for professionals, researchers, and business leaders alike.

CHAPTER OVERVIEW

Chapter 1: Ethical Considerations in Ai-Driven Software Development Life Cycle

As artificial intelligence continues to revolutionize the software development landscape, understanding its ethical implications has never been more critical. This chapter begins by framing the intersection of AI and the SDLC within the broader context of societal impact, encouraging readers to critically evaluate the consequences of their technological choices. It provides a roadmap for identifying and addressing ethical dilemmas, offering practical tools and frameworks to integrate ethical principles seamlessly into development practices. By exploring real-world examples and actionable strategies, the chapter equips software developers, managers, and policymakers with the knowledge needed to navigate the complexities of AI-driven innovation responsibly.

Chapter 2: Transforming Software Development with Effective Project Management in the Age of AI

This study underscores the strategic importance of aligning organizational culture and project management methodologies with the dynamic capabilities of AI. It highlights the role of leadership in fostering a culture of innovation and ethical awareness while ensuring that teams are equipped with the skills and tools needed to adapt to AI-driven processes. By integrating AI into project management workflows, organizations can achieve not only operational efficiencies but also enhance collaboration and decision-making. This forward-looking approach encourages stakeholders to view AI not merely as a tool but as a transformative partner in reshaping how software projects are envisioned, executed, and delivered.

Chapter 3: Improving Software Quality Framework using Artificial Intelligence Platforms

This chapter emphasizes the transformative role of machine learning in addressing the challenges of climate science, presenting it as a powerful ally in unraveling the complexities of our planet's climate systems. By leveraging advanced algorithms, researchers and policymakers can uncover hidden patterns, refine predictive models, and reduce uncertainties that hinder traditional approaches. The integration of diverse data sources, including satellite imagery and IoT-enabled sensors, is shown to improve real-time monitoring and forecasting, paving the way for proactive and informed decision-making. Alongside these technological advancements, the chapter also critically examines issues of data scarcity, model interpretability, and ethical concerns, advocating for a responsible and inclusive approach to applying machine learning in climate science. Through case studies and actionable insights, readers are invited to explore how these cutting-edge techniques can drive innovation, resilience, and sustainability in climate analysis and prediction.

Chapter 4: Harnessing AI from Code Reusability to Business Requirement Translation

This chapter delves into the revolutionary integration of AI in Software Quality Assurance (SQA), highlighting its capacity to address traditional inefficiencies and variability in manual testing methods. By automating workflows and enhancing defect detection, AI reshapes the SQA lifecycle, ensuring quality optimization across planning, implementation, monitoring, and improvement phases. It explores the role of AI-driven tools in streamlining version control and change management, aligning with industry standards like CMMI and ISO 9000. The chapter also compares AI applications across testing approaches, emphasizing scalability, efficiency, and proactive error detection. Moreover, it underscores AI's critical role in advancing configuration management, risk prediction, and lifecycle enhancement, particularly in Agile and DevOps environments. Through case studies and practical insights, readers will discover how AI enables timely, high-quality software delivery, meeting the demands of modern development paradigms.

Chapter 5: Decision Models for Choice of AI: Generative AI, Machine Learning and Deep Learning

This chapter explores how AI is reshaping software engineering by addressing two critical aspects: enhancing developer efficiency and bridging the gap between business and technical requirements. By employing advanced technologies like machine learning, data mining, domain analysis, and natural language processing, AI-powered tools streamline the discovery of optimal libraries and reusable code fragments, fostering innovation and reducing development time. Simultaneously, AI bridges the traditionally challenging translation of business needs into technical specifications through cutting-edge language models and tensor-based approaches, ensuring accuracy and alignment with organizational goals. The discussion extends to real-world applications, illustrating how these AI-driven advancements are transforming workflows and accelerating innovation. This chapter also looks ahead to emerging trends, offering insights into how AI continues to redefine best practices in software development.

Chapter 6: Advancing Software Security a Comprehensive Framework for Vulnerability Assessment

This chapter underscores the urgency of adopting proactive measures to safeguard software systems against the escalating threats in today's technological landscape. It emphasizes the role of Risk-Based Vulnerability Management (RBVM) as a critical framework for addressing security vulnerabilities throughout the Software Development Life Cycle (SDLC). By focusing on risk prioritization, RBVM enables developers and organizations to allocate resources effectively, targeting the most pressing threats. The discussion delves into the challenges of vulnerability assessment, the integration of security practices into development workflows, and the importance of fostering a security-first culture. Through case studies and practical examples, the chapter provides actionable insights on how to enhance resilience against internal and external threats, ensuring the confidentiality, integrity, and availability of software systems while mitigating financial, reputational, and legal risks.

Chapter 7: Harnessing AI for Seamless Customer Support and Optimized Knowledge Management

This chapter highlights the transformative role of AI in revolutionizing knowledge management and customer support, two critical areas in modern business operations. By utilizing cutting-edge machine learning and deep learning techniques, AI-powered solutions automate routine processes, enhance decision-making, and provide actionable insights. In customer support, AI-driven chatbots and virtual assistants deliver round-the-clock assistance, improve response times, and reduce operational expenses while personalizing interactions to elevate customer satisfaction. Similarly, in knowledge management, AI enables organizations to process and organize vast data repositories efficiently, ensuring seamless access to vital information. The discussion delves into real-world applications, showcasing how these technologies foster innovation, improve service quality, and address evolving customer needs. This exploration also considers the future potential of AI in creating adaptive, intelligent systems that further refine business operations and customer experiences.

Chapter 8: Leveraging Data Analytics for Promoting Environmentally Sustainable and Socially Resilient Cities Infrastructure

This chapter presents a comprehensive review of the intersection between sustainability and smart applications, emphasizing the transformative role of Machine Learning and Deep Learning in enabling intelligent and efficient systems. It examines cutting-edge algorithms and frameworks that power sustainable solutions across diverse domains such as smart homes, cities, healthcare, industry, transportation, and agriculture. By exploring Big Data Analytics techniques, the chapter highlights how advanced deep learning approaches can effectively extract valuable insights, making them a preferred choice for handling the complexities of sustainable systems. Furthermore, it identifies key challenges, such as scalability, data privacy, and energy efficiency, while proposing future research directions to address these barriers. This work aims to inspire innovation and collaboration, providing a foundation for advancing sustainable smart systems that balance technological progress with environmental and societal well-being.

Chapter 9: Innovative Approaches for Earthquake Estimation Using AI and ML Techniques

This chapter explores the transformative impact of Artificial Intelligence (AI) and Machine Learning (ML) on seismic forecasting, emphasizing their potential to enhance early warning systems and risk mitigation strategies. By leveraging advanced techniques such as deep learning models, neural networks, and support vector machines, these approaches analyze real-time data from seismic sensors, geological surveys, and historical records to deliver precise predictions regarding earthquake magnitude, location, and intensity. The chapter highlights how AI-driven models outperform traditional methods by offering faster computation, improved adaptability, and the ability to uncover hidden patterns in complex datasets. In addition to showcasing advancements, the chapter addresses critical challenges such as data scarcity, model validation, and uncertainty, offering insights into overcoming these barriers. It concludes by outlining future research directions, aiming to foster innovation and improve the reliability of AI-enhanced seismic forecasting for global safety and preparedness.

Chapter 10: Enhancing Efficiency of Industrial Automation using Smart Programming in AI and IoT: A Study

This chapter delves into the transformative potential of integrating Artificial Intelligence (AI) and the Internet of Things (IoT) into industrial automation, showcasing their ability to revolutionize operational workflows. By utilizing advanced techniques like machine learning, predictive analytics, and edge computing, industrial systems can achieve unparalleled efficiency, reduced downtime, and enhanced decision-making capabilities. Through compelling case studies, the chapter demonstrates real-time system monitoring, adaptive control, and predictive maintenance as key applications of AI and IoT integration. It emphasizes the critical role of device communication and big data in driving automation while addressing challenges such as cybersecurity risks and scalability issues. Furthermore, the chapter explores the broader impact of these technologies on fostering sustainability, cost-effectiveness, and productivity. Designed as a resource for industrialists, this work provides actionable insights to guide businesses toward innovation and maintain competitiveness in an increasingly automated and connected industrial landscape.

Chapter 11: Practical Application of Quantum-Enhanced Machine Learning: Prediction of Atomic Mass and Properties

This chapter explores the groundbreaking application of Quantum Machine Learning (QML) in advancing the prediction of atomic mass and properties with unprecedented accuracy. It delves into the integration of advanced machine learning algorithms tailored for quantum systems, enhancing our understanding of atomic phenomena such as electronic structure and chemical bonding. By leveraging QML techniques, large quantum datasets can be processed efficiently, revealing meaningful insights into complex quantum behaviors. Key areas of focus include the use of neural networks, quantum support vector machines, and generative models to predict atomic properties. The chapter highlights the transformative potential of QML in scientific research, demonstrating how it can revolutionize quantum science by providing deeper, more precise knowledge of atomic and molecular systems, paving the way for advancements in materials science, chemistry, and other fields.

Chapter 12: Optimizing Perceptions of AI Technology in Risk Assessment Using Bayesian Approaches

This study examines the growing role of Artificial Intelligence (AI) in software risk management, specifically focusing on its application in risk assessment and business continuity planning in Greece. Through a structured questionnaire using a Likert scale, the research gathers quantitative data on technology professionals' perceptions and experiences with AI integration. The study employs Bayesian optimization to analyze the data, uncovering the key factors that influence professionals' attitudes toward AI adoption in risk management. The results reveal how demographic and professional variables, such as industry and job role, shape perceptions of AI's potential to improve risk management practices. By offering valuable insights into the challenges and opportunities of AI-driven approaches, this study contributes to a deeper understanding of how AI can enhance decision-making and ensure business continuity across diverse sectors.

Chapter 13: Machine Learning for Software Development: Real-Time Communication System for Predicting Climate Condition

This chapter delves into the transformative role of machine learning in revolutionizing climate prediction and analysis, addressing the limitations of traditional climatic modeling techniques that struggle with the complexity and non-linearity of climate systems. By leveraging advanced machine learning approaches such as deep learning, reinforcement learning, and ensemble methods, it becomes possible to uncover hidden patterns, improve prediction accuracy, and manage the uncertainties inherent in climate data. Key applications explored include temperature forecasting, extreme weather prediction, and long-term climate trend analysis. The chapter also highlights the integration of satellite data, IoT-enabled sensors, and high-performance computing to bolster real-time monitoring and forecasting capabilities. Furthermore, it discusses how machine learning can drive proactive decision-making in climate science, while tackling challenges like data scarcity, interpretability, and ethical concerns. Ultimately, this chapter presents machine learning as a powerful tool in advancing climate science and supporting informed, sustainable policymaking.

As we conclude this exploration of AI's impact on software development, it becomes clear that the integration of artificial intelligence is not just enhancing current practices but fundamentally transforming the way software is created, managed, and optimized. The case studies and methodologies presented throughout this collection highlight AI's potential to streamline development processes, improve software quality, and enable smarter, more efficient decision-making. However, with this transformation come challenges, including the need for effective risk management, ethical considerations, and the integration of AI into existing workflows. Looking ahead, the continued evolution of AI promises even greater innovations in software engineering, offering opportunities for enhanced scalability, automation, and sustainability. These chapters underscore the importance of staying ahead of these trends, embracing AI with a thoughtful and strategic approach, and fostering a future where technology drives not only efficiency but also ethical and responsible development practices.

Thank you,

Rahul K. Patel
Illinois Institute of Technology, Chicago, USA

Chapter 1
Ethical Considerations in AI-Driven Software Development Life Cycle

Rupesh D. Sushir
https://orcid.org/0000-0003-2391-2478
Department of Electronics and Telecommunication Engineering, P.R. Pote Patil College of Engineering and Management, Sant Gadge Baba Amravati University, India

Sarita Bhutada
Sant Gadge Baba Amravati University, India

ABSTRACT

This chapter delves into the ethical challenges of incorporating AI technologies into the software development lifecycle (SDLC). As AI tools increasingly automate decisions from requirements analysis to deployment, developers and stakeholders face critical issues related to bias, fairness, accountability, transparency, and data privacy. It highlights ethical risks, such as biased algorithms and data misuse, while stressing the importance of maintaining a balance between automation and human oversight. The environmental impact of large-scale AI systems is also discussed, alongside strategies for sustainable development. Through case studies, the chapter showcases instances where ethical considerations were overlooked, resulting in negative outcomes. A comprehensive framework for ethical compliance is provided, emphasizing bias mitigation, transparency, privacy safeguards, and accountability. Ultimately, the chapter advocates for proactive ethical measures to ensure AI enhances software development while upholding societal values, individual rights, and environmental sustainability.

INTRODUCTION

The integration of Artificial Intelligence (AI) into the Software Development Lifecycle (SDLC) has fundamentally transformed the way software is designed, built, tested, and deployed. This chapter explores the ethical implications of incorporating AI-driven tools and techniques into these processes. While AI can bring unparalleled efficiency, accuracy, and automation to software development, it also introduces ethical challenges that must be addressed to ensure responsible innovation.

DOI: 10.4018/979-8-3693-8407-7.ch001

Ethical Concerns Across the AI-Driven SDLC

Integrating AI into the Software Development Lifecycle (SDLC) poses ethical challenges that affect traditional practices at every stage. From requirements gathering to post-deployment, AI necessitates a re-evaluation of decision-making, data handling, and outcome monitoring. Key ethical concerns—such as bias, accountability, and transparency—emerge throughout the SDLC, highlighting the need for early intervention to develop trustworthy AI systems (Floridi & Cowls, 2019).

Requirements Gathering and Analysis

The requirements-gathering phase lays the foundation for development but can introduce biases if stakeholders are limited to a narrow group. For instance, AI systems designed using data from a specific demographic may yield biased healthcare outcomes, failing to serve the broader population equitably (Floridi & Cowls, 2019).

Influence of Preexisting Biases in Stakeholder Inputs

Stakeholders often carry implicit biases that shape their inputs. Personal experiences and cultural assumptions can lead to prioritizing use cases that favor specific groups, resulting in under-representation of others. Recognizing these biases is essential for creating equitable AI systems (Binns, 2018; Lepri et al., 2018).

Ensuring Diversity in Use Case Scenarios

Mitigating bias requires diversity in use case scenarios. Actively including voices from marginalized communities helps ensure that the AI system meets a wide range of user needs, promoting fairness and inclusivity (Raji & Buolamwini, 2019).

Design and Development

In the design and development phase, ethical concerns around bias, transparency, and fairness in AI models are paramount. Decisions made here significantly influence AI behavior and outcomes. Developers must prioritize fairness, transparency, and accountability while ensuring continuous ethical compliance testing throughout development. Figure 1 illustrates the phases of the AI-driven Software Development Lifecycle.

Biases in AI Models

During the design and development phase, a significant ethical concern is the introduction of biases into AI models. These biases can stem from training data, which may amplify existing prejudices, leading to unfair treatment. For example, a facial recognition system trained primarily on one demographic may fail to accurately identify individuals from others, resulting in exclusion. Biases can also arise from feature selection, where certain attributes are prioritized, skewing outputs. To combat this, developers must focus on data preprocessing, feature selection, and ongoing model monitoring, aiming to create fair and representative systems (Raji & Buolamwini, 2019).

Transparent AI Model Design

Transparency is another critical ethical aspect. AI models, particularly complex ones, are often viewed as "black boxes," hindering understanding of their decision-making processes (Floridi & Cowls, 2019). This opacity can erode trust, especially in sensitive fields like healthcare and finance. Designing for transparency involves creating explainable AI (XAI), enabling stakeholders to grasp the underlying logic and data influencing decisions. Techniques such as interpretable models and visualizations can enhance transparency without compromising performance (Binns, 2018; Doshi-Velez & Kim, 2017).

Continuous Testing for Ethical Compliance

Ethical considerations must remain a priority throughout the development cycle. Continuous testing for ethical compliance is essential to detect biases and vulnerabilities before deployment (Jobin et al., 2019). This includes fairness testing to identify unintended biases, robustness testing to ensure reliable performance, and accountability mechanisms to track decisions. Developers should also stress test against edge cases and adjust models to mitigate ethical risks. Given that ethical standards evolve, this testing must be iterative, aligning with changing societal values (Binns, 2018). By prioritizing biases, transparency, and ongoing compliance, developers can create AI systems that are efficient, fair, and aligned with societal values (Floridi & Cowls, 2019).

TESTING, DEPLOYMENT, AND POST-DEPLOYMENT MONITORING

The final stages of the Software Development Lifecycle (SDLC)—testing, deployment, and post-deployment monitoring—are vital for ensuring AI systems meet ethical standards in real-world scenarios. These phases address critical issues such as bias, transparency, accountability, and security.

Ethical Issues in Testing AI Systems

Testing AI differs from traditional software due to the complexity of machine learning models. Ethical testing must prioritize fairness, transparency, and harm prevention. A key concern is identifying and eliminating bias, as AI systems trained on non-representative data can yield discriminatory outcomes. Rigorous evaluation using fairness metrics and diverse datasets is essential to ensure equitable performance across demographics (Binns, 2018).

Privacy and Data Security

AI systems often rely on extensive data collection, raising privacy and security concerns. Testing must confirm compliance with data protection laws like GDPR (Jobin et al., 2019) and ensure that user data is anonymized and secure. Techniques such as differential privacy can help safeguard sensitive information.

Robustness Against Adversarial Attacks

AI systems, particularly in high-stakes applications like healthcare, must be resilient to adversarial attacks. Adversarial testing ensures that AI responds correctly to manipulated inputs and operates predictably under unusual conditions (Raji & Buolamwini, 2019). An ethically sound AI system must perform consistently, even in edge cases.

Ethical Considerations During Deployment

The deployment phase of an AI system is where the technology is put into production and begins interacting with real-world users. Several ethical considerations are paramount during this stage, particularly around transparency, accountability, and informed user consent ((Jobin et al., 2019), (Floridi & Cowls, 2019)).

Transparency and Explainability

During deployment, ensuring that AI systems are transparent and explainable is crucial. Users impacted by AI decisions—especially in finance, healthcare, or law enforcement—must understand how systems operate and make decisions. "Black-box" models can breed distrust, as users cannot verify fairness. Techniques from Explainable AI (XAI) should clarify the rationale behind decisions, fostering trust and accountability.

Informed Consent and User Autonomy

AI systems often require user data, making informed consent essential. Users should be fully aware of how their data will be used, with options to control its usage or opt out. Ethical deployment includes informing users of the system's limitations, risks, and biases, allowing them to make informed choices, particularly in high-stakes situations.

Accountability in AI Decision-Making

AI systems can produce harmful outcomes, so accountability measures are vital during deployment. Clear responsibilities must be established to address errors or biases. Developers should implement audit trails to track decision-making processes, especially in critical sectors like healthcare, ensuring that issues can be corrected promptly and ethically.

Ethical Obligations in Post-Deployment Monitoring

Post-deployment monitoring is essential for evaluating the ongoing ethical and effective performance of AI systems. Unlike traditional software, AI evolves with new data, which can introduce unforeseen ethical risks. AI systems can drift over time, potentially leading to biased outcomes. Regular monitoring of outputs across demographics is necessary to maintain fairness, with ongoing efforts to mitigate bias through model or data updates. As ethical standards and regulations evolve, continuous monitoring ensures AI systems remain compliant with updated guidelines.

Real-world AI applications may yield unanticipated outcomes. Monitoring must include user feedback mechanisms to identify and address unintended consequences, allowing systems to adjust based on real-world use. Additionally, monitoring for security vulnerabilities is crucial to uphold ethical integrity. Regular updates can strengthen defenses against attacks, ensuring long-term robustness and fairness. Overall, thorough testing, responsible deployment, and continuous monitoring are vital for maintaining fairness, transparency, accountability, and user safety in AI systems throughout their lifecycle (Binns, 2018).

Maintenance, Continuous Learning, and Evolving Ethical Standards

Maintenance and continuous learning are vital components of AI-based software development, particularly given the dynamic nature of AI systems that learn and adapt from new data over time. Ethical considerations in this phase become increasingly complex as AI systems are expected to evolve while retaining their integrity, fairness, and accountability. This section will explore the unique challenges that arise during the maintenance and continuous learning phases, including the need to uphold evolving ethical standards, manage system drift, and ensure transparency and accountability in a system that constantly learns and changes (Jobin et al., 2019; Taddeo & Floridi, 2018).

Continuous Learning and Adaptive AI Systems

Many AI applications utilize continuous learning to adapt to new data and changing environments. While this can enhance performance, it introduces significant ethical challenges due to the potential for autonomous decision-making changes, leading to unintended consequences.

AI systems can experience "model drift," where predictions shift as new data is incorporated, potentially reinforcing biases. To counter this, developers must implement monitoring mechanisms and conduct regular audits to ensure alignment with ethical standards, focusing on fairness and transparency. Continuous learning can lead to overfitting on unethical patterns if not regularly evaluated against ethical benchmarks. Ethical maintenance requires refining models to avoid bias and ensure trustworthiness.

Retraining models with new data is standard but must incorporate ethical considerations, especially in sensitive sectors. Developers should ensure diverse and representative data to prevent bias amplification during retraining. Ethical standards evolve with societal values and legal requirements. AI systems must be regularly updated to comply with new regulations, such as GDPR or CCPA, and adapt to changing societal perspectives on fairness and transparency. Regular updates are essential to align AI systems with evolving ethical standards in regulated industries. Developers should implement mechanisms to revise algorithms and data practices accordingly.

As AI ethics progresses, developers must stay informed about new techniques and guidelines, continuously updating their models and processes. This may include adopting new fairness algorithms and enhancing transparency through Explainable AI (XAI). By evolving ethical standards alongside AI system maintenance, developers can ensure ongoing responsibility and trustworthiness.

Monitoring for Ethical Failures and Accountability Mechanisms

A crucial aspect of AI maintenance is implementing mechanisms to monitor ethical failures and ensure accountability throughout the system's lifecycle. Maintenance goes beyond fixing bugs; it aims to prevent harm to users and society. AI systems should provide clear audit trails to track decision-making processes and outcomes. These trails allow developers and auditors to investigate ethical failures, such as biased decisions in healthcare. By tracing errors back to their source, developers can rectify issues and ensure accountability when harm occurs.

Continuous ethical monitoring requires feedback loops that assess real-world performance and enable users to report issues. This feedback is vital for identifying unforeseen biases or errors. AI systems should adjust algorithms or datasets based on user input, enhancing their responsiveness and ethical integrity. For instance, if a loan approval system disproportionately denies certain groups, user reports can prompt further investigation and model recalibration.

Ongoing maintenance must include ethical risk management processes to anticipate potential ethical risks from updates, new data, or operational changes. Developers should establish frameworks to address these concerns, ensuring that system modifications do not introduce new biases or privacy risks. For example, updates to a facial recognition system should be evaluated for fairness across all demographics. Ethical risk management tools help developers balance potential harms and benefits, maintaining the system's ethical integrity.

Long-Term Accountability and Sustainability of AI Systems

Maintaining ethical AI systems involves addressing immediate concerns while ensuring long-term accountability and sustainability, even as development teams change. AI systems often outlast their original development teams, risking loss of ethical guidelines. Clear documentation of ethical practices and decision-making processes is essential for future teams to uphold the system's ethical values. For example, without proper guidelines, new developers in a legal AI system might inadvertently introduce biases or undermine transparency. Sustaining ethical AI practices requires ongoing investment in training for developers on current ethical standards. Organizations should build diverse teams to minimize bias in AI systems. Overall, ethical maintenance involves continuous learning, adapting to evolving standards, and implementing mechanisms for transparency, accountability, and fairness. By prioritizing monitoring, risk management, and sustainability, AI systems can serve users fairly and responsibly while aligning with societal values.

DECOMMISSIONING AI SYSTEMS

Decommissioning AI systems involves retiring or dismantling those that are no longer needed, viable, or ethically aligned with current standards. This often-overlooked phase of the Software Development Lifecycle (SDLC) is crucial for managing ethical implications responsibly. Reasons for decommissioning may include outdated technology, evolving ethical standards, changing user needs, or potential harm caused by the system. Ethical decommissioning ensures transparency and responsibility, addressing concerns related to data privacy, user rights, accountability, and long-term societal impacts. This section examines the ethical considerations and responsibilities involved in decommissioning AI systems.

Rationale for Decommissioning AI Systems

AI systems may become obsolete due to advancements in technology. If a system's outputs are unreliable, ethical decommissioning requires assessing if a replacement is available to prevent service disruption, particularly in critical fields like healthcare or finance.

AI systems that no longer adhere to ethical guidelines must be decommissioned. If a system is found to produce biased outcomes or violate privacy, developers must evaluate whether it can be updated or should be retired, ensuring users are informed throughout the process.

Changes in laws may render AI systems non-compliant, necessitating decommissioning. Ethical retirement involves ensuring proper data handling, informing users of the system's retirement, and providing alternatives that comply with new regulations.

Data Management During Decommissioning

Developers must decide whether to delete or retain processed data. Ethical practices require secure deletion of sensitive data and transparency if data retention is necessary, informing users about its purpose and duration.

To mitigate data breach risks during decommissioning, strict security measures must be implemented. Developers must ensure that all sensitive information is securely destroyed or anonymized to protect user privacy.

User Rights and Transparency During Decommissioning

Users must be clearly informed about the decommissioning decision, including data handling and service impacts. Proactive communication through various channels ensures all stakeholders are aware of changes and have support for concerns.

Accountability and Ethical Oversight

Thorough documentation of the decommissioning rationale, data handling, and transparency measures is essential. This audit trail supports regulatory compliance and addresses potential ethical concerns. Independent audits may be necessary to ensure ethical decommissioning, especially in high-stakes applications. External reviews help identify overlooked ethical risks and ensure adherence to guidelines.

Long-Term Impact and Sustainability Considerations

Decommissioning essential AI systems must avoid service interruptions. Developers should provide interim solutions or transitions to new systems to maintain critical services, especially for vulnerable populations. The long-term effects on all stakeholders, especially marginalized communities, must be considered. Engaging with affected groups helps assess the potential negative impacts of the system's removal and informs mitigation strategies.

Figure 1. Phases for AI driven software development life cycle

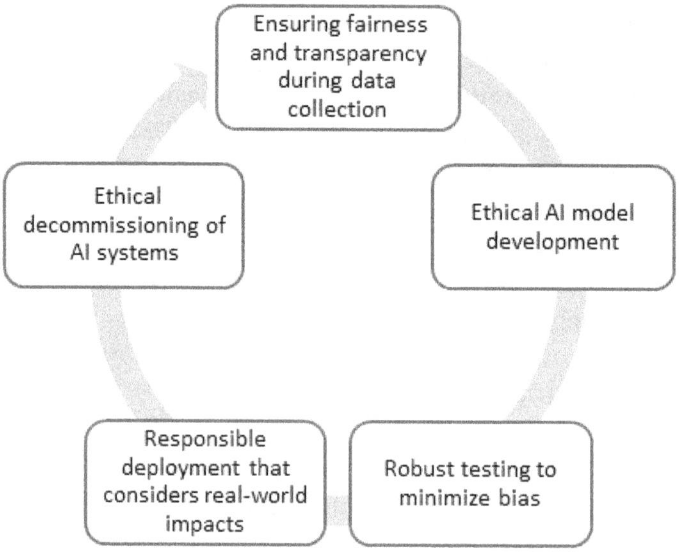

DATA PRIVACY AND SECURITY IN AI-DRIVEN SOFTWARE

As AI integrates into software development, concerns about data privacy and security grow. AI systems require vast amounts of data, including personal and sensitive information. Ensuring ethical data handling is crucial for maintaining user trust and compliance with regulations like GDPR and HIPAA. Protecting data from breaches and misuse is essential, especially since AI systems often make autonomous decisions.

Data Handling and Consent

Ethical data handling necessitates transparency, user consent, and compliance with regulations. Users must be informed about data collection, its use, and potential risks. Consent must be clear and understandable, allowing users to opt in or out and withdraw consent anytime. To protect privacy, personal identifiers should be removed from datasets, and strong encryption must be used. This is especially critical for sensitive data, requiring ongoing audits to ensure compliance and ethical usage throughout the software lifecycle.

Mitigating Risks of Data Misuse

Establishing clear data governance policies is vital to prevent misuse. This includes defining who can access data and conducting regular audits to ensure compliance and identify unauthorized usage. Data minimization is essential; only necessary data should be collected to reduce misuse risks. AI models must be trained on ethically sourced, anonymized data, and continuously evaluated to avoid reinforcing biases. Encryption protects data both at rest and in transit. Role-based access control (RBAC) and multi-factor authentication (MFA) further safeguard sensitive information, ensuring only authorized personnel can access it. Organizations must be transparent about data collection and usage. Clear privacy policies and accountability mechanisms, like audit trails, help build user trust and allow for swift responses to misuse. Regular monitoring and ethical audits assess data usage and model outcomes. Diverse teams should review practices, and automated tools can detect anomalies to ensure compliance with privacy standards and ethical guidelines.

Ethical Implications of Data Collection

Data collection is a fundamental component of AI-driven systems and modern software applications. However, it comes with a variety of ethical implications that developers and organizations must consider. While collecting large volumes of data can improve the performance and accuracy of AI models, it also raises serious concerns regarding user privacy, consent, fairness, and accountability. Failure to address these ethical concerns can lead to the misuse of data, erosion of public trust, and violations of regulatory frameworks such as the General Data Protection Regulation (GDPR) or California Consumer Privacy Act (CCPA). This section explores the ethical challenges associated with data collection in AI-driven software and discusses ways to address these challenges to ensure responsible and fair data usage.

Informed Consent and User Autonomy

Informed consent is essential in data collection, ensuring users know what data is collected, how it's used, and any associated risks. Often, consent forms are overly complex, leading to user confusion about data sharing. Simplifying these forms and allowing users to withdraw consent at any time is vital for maintaining autonomy and trust.

Privacy and Anonymization

Collecting sensitive data raises significant privacy concerns. Ethical data practices must include anonymization to protect identities, although this is not foolproof. Implementing strong encryption and techniques like differential privacy enhances user data security. Adopting privacy-by-design principles is crucial to uphold trust and ensure compliance with regulations. Bias can infiltrate AI systems during data collection, particularly if datasets lack representation. It's vital to use diverse datasets and understand historical contexts to prevent discrimination. Ethical data collection should involve frameworks that identify and correct biases, ensuring fair outcomes.

Transparency and Accountability

Transparency in data collection is critical; users deserve to know how their data is used. Organizations must clearly communicate data practices and establish accountability through regular audits and governance policies. Rapid responses to data breaches are necessary to maintain user trust.

Legal and Regulatory Compliance

Compliance with legal frameworks like GDPR and CCPA is essential for ethical data collection. Organizations should obtain explicit consent, secure data, and conduct Data Protection Impact Assessments (DPIAs) to evaluate risks. Proactively adapting to evolving regulations helps organizations avoid legal pitfalls and demonstrates a commitment to ethical data management.

Case Studies: Lessons from Past Breaches and Ethical Failures in AI-Driven Software

Here are a few case studies that highlight the consequences of neglecting ethical practices in AI, along with how these failures could have been avoided.

Cambridge Analytica Scandal (2018)

One of the most infamous cases of data misuse involved Cambridge Analytica, a political consulting firm that collected personal data from millions of Facebook users without their consent. This data was used to create psychological profiles and target individuals with political ads during the 2016 U.S. Presidential election and the Brexit referendum. The incident exposed how user data could be weaponized for manipulation in ways users were unaware of, sparking a major outcry about privacy violation. The ethical failure in this case centered on the misuse of personal data and the violation of user consent. Users were unaware that their data was being harvested and used for purposes beyond what they had agreed to. The lack of transparency and failure to safeguard user privacy were key issues.

How It Could Have Been Avoided:

- Transparency and Informed Consent: Facebook and Cambridge Analytica should have been more transparent about how data was being collected and used. Clear, comprehensible user consent mechanisms would have allowed users to understand the extent to which their data was being exploited for political purposes.
- Data Governance and Accountability: Stronger data governance practices could have prevented the misuse of data. An audit trail and restrictions on data sharing with third-party applications should have been in place to monitor how user data was being handled.
- Regulatory Compliance: If stronger data protection regulations such as GDPR were in place earlier, Cambridge Analytica would have been legally required to gain explicit consent for data usage. Early compliance with emerging data privacy laws could have helped prevent this scandal.

Google Photos Racial Tagging Incident (2015)

In 2015, Google Photos' AI image recognition system came under fire when it mistakenly tagged images of Black people as "gorillas." This glaring error exposed the limitations of AI models that are trained on biased or unrepresentative datasets, particularly in image recognition, where cultural and racial biases can lead to offensive or harmful outcomes. The failure of the image recognition system highlighted the issue of biased training data. The AI model had not been sufficiently trained on diverse images representing different racial groups, leading to a deeply offensive mistake.

How It Could Have Been Avoided:

- Diverse and Inclusive Training Data: AI systems that deal with sensitive areas like image recognition should be trained on diverse datasets that accurately represent all demographics. Google's model could have been more robust had it included a broader range of racial and ethnic representations in its training data.
- Pre-release Testing and Sensitivity Reviews: Before deploying AI systems, thorough testing should be conducted to identify potential biases and offensive outcomes. Pre-release audits, particularly in culturally sensitive areas, can help catch problems before they reach users.
- Ongoing Monitoring and Feedback Mechanisms: Once the system was deployed, Google should have implemented more effective monitoring and feedback mechanisms to quickly address and correct mistakes. Early identification of this error could have prevented widespread harm and embarrassment.

Clearview AI Facial Recognition Scandal (2020)

Clearview AI, a company that developed facial recognition technology, came under scrutiny for scraping billions of images from social media platforms and the internet without users' consent. Law enforcement agencies used Clearview's software to identify individuals, leading to privacy concerns, especially given the software's potential for misuse. Clearview AI's data collection methods were ethically questionable as they relied on scraping publicly available images without obtaining explicit consent from the individuals whose photos were being used. This raised significant privacy concerns, as many people were unaware that their images were being stored in a massive database and used for law enforcement purposes.

How It Could Have Been Avoided

- Consent and Transparency in Data Collection: Clearview should have obtained explicit consent from users before using their images in its database. Ethical data collection practices require transparency about what data is being collected and how it will be used.
- Regulatory Compliance and User Rights: Compliance with data privacy laws such as GDPR, which requires user consent for data collection, could have prevented Clearview's ethical failure. Organizations must respect users' rights to control their personal data.
- Limitations on Data Usage: Ethical AI systems should be designed with strict limitations on how collected data can be used. In Clearview's case, limiting the use of facial recognition software to clearly defined and legally approved purposes could have reduced the risk of misuse and unethical practices.

These case studies underscore the importance of transparency, fairness, bias mitigation, and privacy in AI-driven software. They reveal the significant consequences of neglecting ethical standards and show that implementing strong governance, ongoing audits, and inclusive data collection practices can help avoid similar failures in the future.

BIAS AND FAIRNESS IN AI MODELS

Artificial Intelligence (AI) systems are increasingly being used in decision-making processes across various sectors, from healthcare and finance to hiring and law enforcement. While AI has the potential to increase efficiency and objectivity, it also introduces the risk of perpetuating and amplifying existing biases in society. The fairness of AI models is a major ethical concern, as biased models can lead to discriminatory outcomes that negatively impact certain groups of people. To ensure AI-driven systems operate fairly and equitably, it is crucial to identify and mitigate sources of bias throughout the AI development lifecycle.

Sources of Bias

Bias in AI models can originate from several sources, and understanding these is critical to creating fair and responsible AI systems. The main sources of bias include:

Historical Bias in Data

AI models are typically trained on large datasets to learn patterns and make predictions. However, if the historical data contains biases—such as gender, racial, or socioeconomic inequalities—the AI model will learn and perpetuate these biases. For example, if a hiring algorithm is trained on past hiring decisions that reflect a bias toward certain demographics, the model may continue to favor those groups and disadvantage others, replicating systemic inequalities.

Sampling Bias

Sampling bias occurs when the training data is not representative of the entire population the AI system is expected to serve. If certain groups are underrepresented in the training data, the AI model will have less accurate predictions for those groups, leading to unfair treatment. Sampling bias can arise if data is collected from only a subset of the population or environment, limiting the diversity needed for unbiased outcomes.

Label Bias

Label bias occurs during the process of annotating training data. If the individuals labeling the data have conscious or unconscious biases, those biases may be reflected in the labeled dataset. For instance, if medical images used for AI training are labeled by radiologists who are more prone to diagnosing certain conditions in specific demographic groups, the AI system might inherit that diagnostic bias, leading to unequal treatment.

Measurement Bias

Measurement bias arises when the features used to train the model do not accurately capture the real-world concept they are supposed to represent. This bias can occur if the chosen metrics or proxies for certain attributes are flawed or incomplete, leading to distorted outcomes. Measurement bias can affect predictive accuracy and fairness, especially if sensitive attributes like race, gender, or income are indirectly included in the model.

Algorithmic Bias

Algorithmic bias refers to bias that emerges from the algorithms themselves, even in the absence of biased data. Some algorithms might inherently favor certain outcomes due to how they process data or how they weigh different features. This bias can arise from the structure of the algorithm, its objectives, or the optimization techniques it uses, leading to skewed predictions or unfair classifications.

Human Bias in Model Design and Deployment

Human decisions play a critical role throughout the AI model lifecycle—from selecting the training data to choosing the algorithm and setting performance goals. If human developers or data scientists carry implicit biases, these can be reflected in the design and deployment of AI models. For example, the choice of what features to include in a model or the decision to prioritize accuracy over fairness can introduce biases that harm certain groups.

Understanding these sources of bias is the first step in addressing fairness in AI models. Bias audits, diverse datasets, and human oversight are essential to ensure that AI-driven systems do not perpetuate or amplify societal inequalities. Ethical AI development practices must include continuous efforts to identify, measure, and mitigate bias at every stage of the model lifecycle.

Strategies for Mitigating Bias

Mitigating bias in AI models is essential for ensuring fairness and equity in AI-driven decision-making. Several strategies can be employed throughout the AI development lifecycle to address and reduce bias. These strategies focus on both the data and the algorithms used, as well as on incorporating ethical considerations into the development process. Below are key strategies to mitigate bias in AI systems

Diverse and Representative Data Collection

The first step in minimizing bias is to ensure that the training data is diverse and representative of the entire population that the AI model will serve. This involves collecting data from a wide range of demographic groups to avoid overrepresentation or underrepresentation of any particular group.

- Inclusive Data Sourcing: Data should be gathered from various geographic regions, social groups, and contexts to ensure that the model can generalize effectively across different populations.
- Avoiding Historical Bias: When historical data is used for training, care must be taken to avoid replicating past biases. This can be achieved by scrutinizing the sources of data and ensuring that it reflects modern, equitable practices rather than outdated or biased norms.

Bias Audits and Fairness Metrics

Bias audits involve evaluating AI models for potential biases by applying fairness metrics to measure how the model performs across different demographic groups. These metrics help identify whether certain groups are being treated unfairly.

- Fairness Evaluation: Metrics such as disparate impact, equal opportunity, and demographic parity can be used to assess whether the AI system's outcomes are biased. These fairness metrics help identify disparities in model predictions across different subgroups.
- Regular Audits: AI models should be regularly audited throughout their development and post-deployment to detect any emerging biases as the system is exposed to new data or contexts. These audits help maintain the model's fairness over time.

Data Preprocessing and Bias Removal

Data preprocessing techniques can be employed to reduce bias before training the AI model. This involves identifying and correcting biased patterns in the data or excluding variables that may introduce discrimination.

- Reweighting Data: One technique is reweighting the data to give underrepresented groups more prominence in the training process. This ensures that the model gives equal attention to all demographic groups during learning.
- Debiasing Methods: Statistical techniques such as re-sampling, synthetic data generation, or adversarial debiasing can be used to correct for imbalances in the data and reduce the influence of biased patterns.

Algorithmic Fairness Techniques

AI models themselves can be designed with fairness as a priority. This involves implementing algorithmic techniques that ensure equitable outcomes for all users, regardless of their demographic group.

- Fairness Constraints: One approach is to incorporate fairness constraints into the model's objective function, so the algorithm optimizes not only for accuracy but also for fairness across different groups. For instance, models can be penalized for making predictions that disproportionately affect certain demographics.
- Post-Processing Techniques: After a model is trained, fairness can be introduced through post-processing methods that adjust the model's predictions to ensure fair outcomes. These adjustments might involve equalizing false positive or false negative rates between different demographic groups.

Human-in-the-Loop and Oversight Mechanisms

While AI models can be highly automated, it is critical to include human oversight throughout the development and deployment process to ensure ethical decision-making and to intervene when biases arise.

- Human Review of AI Decisions: In high-stakes applications such as hiring, law enforcement, and healthcare, AI-generated decisions should be reviewed by human experts who can evaluate the fairness and accuracy of the system's outcomes. Human oversight can provide a check on the AI's recommendations and flag any biased patterns.
- Ethical Review Boards: Establishing ethical review boards or teams within organizations can help assess the impact of AI systems on different populations. These boards can recommend changes to algorithms or policies if biases are detected.

Transparent and Explainable AI

Ensuring that AI systems are transparent and explainable is a key strategy for mitigating bias. Explainable AI allows developers, users, and regulators to understand how AI models arrive at their decisions, which is crucial for identifying and correcting biased behavior.

- Model Explainability: Models should be designed with interpretability in mind, so stakeholders can understand the factors driving the AI's decisions. This is particularly important in sensitive applications such as finance or criminal justice, where biased decisions can have significant real-world consequences.
- Transparent Reporting: Organizations should provide transparency reports that detail the data, algorithms, and fairness considerations used in their AI systems. These reports allow for greater accountability and give users confidence that the system is being monitored for bias.

Inclusive Design and Diverse Development Teams

Diverse perspectives within AI development teams can help identify potential biases that may go unnoticed by homogeneous teams. By including developers from various backgrounds, teams are more likely to recognize and address the needs and challenges of different demographic groups.

- Diverse Representation: AI development teams should include individuals from different races, genders, cultural backgrounds, and socio-economic statuses to ensure that the AI system considers a wide range of experiences and needs.
- User Feedback from Diverse Groups: Regularly soliciting feedback from diverse user groups can help identify biases or discriminatory behaviors in the AI system that may not have been evident during development.

By employing these strategies, AI developers and organizations can work toward creating fairer and more equitable AI systems. Addressing bias at every stage of the AI lifecycle from data collection to model deployment ensures that AI technologies contribute positively to society without perpetuating harmful stereotypes or inequalities.

Fairness Tools

Several tools have been developed to help AI practitioners assess, monitor, and mitigate bias in their models. These tools provide frameworks for auditing AI systems and implementing fairness techniques during model development and deployment.

IBM AI Fairness 360 (AIF360)

IBM's AI Fairness 360 is an open-source toolkit that provides developers with algorithms to detect and mitigate bias in AI models. It includes a range of fairness metrics and debiasing techniques that can be applied at different stages of the AI lifecycle. AIF360 provides tools to measure bias, preprocess data, and apply fairness constraints during model training and post-processing. It supports multiple fairness definitions and offers tutorials on how to apply fairness techniques in real-world scenarios. AIF360 can be used to audit a hiring algorithm for gender or racial bias by applying fairness metrics such as disparate impact or equal opportunity. Developers can then use the toolkit's debiasing techniques to correct for any identified biases.

Google What-If Tool

The Google What-If Tool is part of the Tensor Board suite and provides a visual interface for exploring the behavior of machine learning models, especially with respect to fairness. It allows users to simulate different scenarios and evaluate how model outcomes change for different demographic groups. The tool offers visualizations of fairness metrics, and users can compare how models perform on different subgroups. It also allows users to test the impact of different thresholds on fairness outcomes. A developer building a credit scoring model can use the What-If Tool to explore how changing decision thresholds impacts fairness metrics like demographic parity or equalized odds for different age groups or income levels.

Microsoft Fairlearn

Fairlearn is an open-source toolkit developed by Microsoft that focuses on assessing and improving the fairness of machine learning models. It provides tools for analyzing model performance across different demographic groups and implementing fairness constraints to ensure equitable outcomes. Fairlearn includes fairness metrics, visualizations, and algorithms that allow developers to optimize for both accuracy and fairness. It supports fairness constraints that can be applied during model training to ensure equal treatment of all groups. Fairlearn can be used to evaluate a predictive policing model for racial bias and apply fairness constraints that ensure consistent false positive and false negative rates across different racial groups.

AI Explainability 360 (AIX360)

AI Explainability 360 is another toolkit from IBM that focuses on making AI models more interpretable and explainable. While its primary goal is explainability, it also helps address fairness by allowing users to understand how decisions are made, which can reveal underlying biases in the model. AIX360 provides algorithms for interpreting complex machine learning models and offers different types of explanations (e.g., local, global, and contrastive) to help users understand the model's behavior. AIX360 can be applied to a loan approval algorithm to explain why certain applicants were approved or denied, making it easier to detect if the model's decisions are biased against particular demographic groups.

By leveraging fairness tools, developers can systematically improve the fairness of AI models, ensuring that the systems produce equitable outcomes across all demographic groups. Ethical AI development involves not only identifying bias but actively working to mitigate it using these strategies and resources.

BALANCING AI AUTOMATION AND HUMAN OVERSIGHT

As AI systems become more integrated into decision-making processes across industries, the balance between AI automation and human oversight becomes critical. While AI can process vast amounts of data and generate predictions or decisions at a scale beyond human capacity, human oversight is essential to ensure ethical considerations, accountability, and the handling of edge cases where AI may fail. Striking the right balance between automation and human involvement can help prevent unintended consequences, minimize risks, and enhance trust in AI-driven systems.

The Role of Human-in-the-Loop (HITL) Approaches

Human-in-the-loop (HITL) is a method that ensures humans remain a part of the AI decision-making process. In HITL systems, humans interact with AI to review, verify, or override automated decisions when necessary. This approach is especially valuable in high-stakes environments such as healthcare, law enforcement, and finance, where the potential for harm due to AI errors is significant. One of the key benefits is that humans can apply contextual knowledge and ethical reasoning that AI may lack, thereby preventing critical errors or biases in AI decisions. HITL can also enable ongoing learning, as humans provide feedback to refine AI models. Maintaining HITL systems can be resource-intensive and may slow down processes that AI could otherwise accelerate. Striking a balance between efficiency and oversight requires carefully determining when human intervention is necessary versus when AI should be trusted to operate autonomously. Example: In medical diagnosis, an AI system may flag potential health concerns, but a physician reviews the AI's suggestions before making a final diagnosis, ensuring that the AI does not overlook rare diseases or misinterpret symptoms.

Deciding When AI Should Operate Autonomously

Determining when AI systems should function without human oversight depends on several factors, including the level of risk, the complexity of the decision, and the ethical implications involved. Low-risk environments with predictable outcomes, such as certain types of manufacturing processes, can allow for full automation. However, in situations where decisions have life-altering or legal consequences, human intervention remains critical. Organizations must conduct thorough risk assessments to determine when AI systems can operate autonomously. These assessments consider the potential impact of errors, the sensitivity of the data involved, and the likelihood of AI bias. AI models often perform well in standard contexts, but they may struggle with edge cases or novel situations. Human oversight helps address these situations where AI's decisions could lead to unfair or harmful outcomes. Example: In customer service automation, simple inquiries may be handled entirely by AI chatbots. However, for complex customer complaints or sensitive issues, human agents are required to provide a personalized response and resolve conflicts.

Establishing Oversight Mechanisms

Ensuring effective oversight requires creating clear protocols and accountability frameworks for AI systems. These mechanisms help monitor AI performance, ensure that human operators are appropriately involved, and provide transparency in decision-making processes. Organizations must assign responsibility for AI systems to specific individuals or teams who oversee AI deployment, monitor outcomes, and intervene when necessary. These structures ensure that someone is accountable if AI decisions result in negative consequences. Continuous monitoring of AI systems in real time allows for the detection of errors, biases, or unethical decisions. If issues arise, human oversight mechanisms can intervene to correct or halt AI operations. Regular audits of AI decisions help assess whether the systems are functioning as intended and whether any biases or ethical violations have occurred. These audits also provide transparency to stakeholders and demonstrate a commitment to ethical AI practices. Example: In the financial sector, algorithms used to approve loans are often subject to regular audits to ensure that they do not discriminate based on race, gender, or other protected attributes.

Continuous Improvement with Human Feedback

One of the key advantages of maintaining human oversight in AI systems is the ability to provide continuous feedback for improvement. As AI systems are deployed, human operators can provide feedback on the quality of AI decisions, helping to improve the system's accuracy and fairness over time. Human feedback can be used to identify patterns in AI errors, which can inform retraining and adjustments to the model. This iterative approach helps AI systems learn from mistakes and adapt to changing contexts or evolving ethical standards. Over time, AI models may experience "model drift," where their performance deteriorates due to changes in the underlying data or environment. Human feedback and intervention help prevent model drift by ensuring that the system remains aligned with the intended goals. Example: In content moderation on social media platforms, AI systems flag inappropriate content, but human moderators review and adjust the AI's decisions. The feedback from human moderators helps refine the AI's ability to detect harmful or unethical content accurately.

Legal and Regulatory Requirements for AI Oversight

As AI technologies continue to evolve, governments and regulatory bodies are introducing laws and guidelines that mandate human oversight in AI systems, especially in high-risk areas. These regulations aim to protect individual rights, ensure accountability, and prevent unethical use of AI. Governments worldwide are implementing regulations, such as the European Union's AI Act, which categorize AI systems based on their risk levels and require human oversight in certain cases. These frameworks are designed to ensure that AI systems comply with ethical standards and do not infringe upon individuals' rights. Organizations must stay informed about the legal requirements for AI systems and ensure that human oversight is integrated into their AI workflows to remain compliant with ethical and legal standards. Example: In the autonomous vehicle industry, regulations often require human oversight in the form of remote monitoring systems that allow human operators to take control if the AI-driven vehicle encounters unexpected situations.

Balancing AI automation with human oversight is critical for ensuring ethical, fair, and responsible AI deployment. Human-in-the-loop systems, careful risk assessments, oversight mechanisms, continuous feedback, and adherence to legal requirements collectively contribute to maintaining this balance. By thoughtfully integrating human judgment with AI capabilities, organizations can minimize risks and maximize the potential of AI-driven systems.

Environmental Sustainability of AI Systems

As artificial intelligence (AI) systems become increasingly prevalent, their environmental impact has emerged as a pressing concern. The development, training, and deployment of AI models, especially large-scale models, consume significant computational resources, leading to substantial energy usage and carbon emissions. This growing environmental footprint demands careful consideration of how AI systems are designed, built, and maintained to promote sustainability and reduce their negative impact on the environment. AI practitioners and organizations must address the energy consumption, hardware requirements, and life cycle of AI systems to mitigate their environmental consequences. By adopting sustainable practices, the AI community can contribute to global efforts to combat climate change and promote environmental stewardship.

Energy Consumption and Carbon Footprint

The training of complex AI models, particularly deep learning models, requires extensive computational resources that consume large amounts of energy. For instance, models like GPT-3 and BERT require weeks of training on high-powered hardware, resulting in considerable energy usage. This process is typically conducted in data centers that rely on electricity, often generated from non-renewable sources like coal and natural gas. Research has shown that the carbon footprint of training a large AI model can be equivalent to the emissions produced by several cars over their lifetime. As AI models become larger and more sophisticated, this environmental burden will likely increase. Beyond training, AI systems consume energy during their operational phases, including real-time inference and data processing. This ongoing energy demand, particularly in applications requiring constant AI predictions, further contributes to environmental degradation.

Hardware and Resource Demand

AI models are not only computationally intensive but also require specialized hardware, such as GPUs and TPUs, to perform efficiently. The manufacturing and disposal of these hardware components involve resource extraction, energy consumption, and waste generation. Additionally, the use of rare earth metals and other finite materials in hardware production poses sustainability challenges. Data centers housing AI systems are equipped with cooling systems, backup power supplies, and high-performance servers, all of which demand significant resources. Building and maintaining such infrastructure increases the overall environmental cost of AI. As AI technology evolves rapidly, older hardware becomes obsolete, leading to e-waste. The improper disposal of electronic devices and components can release harmful substances into the environment, contributing to pollution and health risks.

Sustainable AI Practices

To reduce the environmental impact of AI systems, organizations can adopt sustainable AI practices. These practices focus on optimizing energy efficiency, reducing resource consumption, and leveraging renewable energy sources. Researchers and developers can design energy-efficient algorithms that require fewer computations without sacrificing model accuracy. Techniques such as model pruning, quantization, and distillation can reduce the computational load during training and inference. Green Data centers can reduce their carbon footprint by adopting energy-efficient cooling systems, using renewable energy sources, and optimizing hardware utilization. Transitioning to carbon-neutral or carbon-negative data centers can have a significant positive impact on sustainability. Conducting a life cycle assessment of AI systems can help organizations understand the environmental impact of their AI models from development to deployment and decommissioning. This assessment can inform decisions about resource allocation and energy use throughout the system's life cycle.

Reducing AI's Carbon Footprint with Renewable Energy

One of the most effective ways to mitigate the environmental impact of AI systems is to transition to renewable energy sources. By powering data centers with solar, wind, hydropower, or other renewable energy technologies, AI operations can significantly lower their carbon emissions. Organizations can reduce the carbon footprint of AI by using data centers located in regions with abundant renewable energy. Cloud providers offering green AI services are also increasingly available, allowing AI practitioners to choose environmentally friendly options for hosting their AI models. In addition to using renewable energy, organizations can adopt energy-saving strategies such as scheduling model training during off-peak hours when energy demand is lower or optimizing data processing pipelines to minimize unnecessary computational workloads.

Ethical Implications of AI's Environmental Impact

As AI systems contribute to climate change through their environmental footprint, it is important to consider the ethical implications of their development and deployment. Organizations must weigh the societal benefits of AI against the environmental costs and make decisions that align with sustainability goals. Prioritizing green AI development not only helps protect the environment but also reflects corporate responsibility and ethical stewardship. Many organizations are beginning to include environmental sustainability in their Corporate Social Responsibility strategies, recognizing that the long-term viability of AI systems depends on minimizing their ecological impact. Ethical AI research must also include a focus on sustainability. This means not only advancing AI capabilities but also developing methods that reduce the environmental costs of AI and promote long-term ecological well-being.

Environmental sustainability is an essential consideration in the development and deployment of AI systems. By addressing energy consumption, resource demand, and adopting green practices, organizations can mitigate AI's environmental impact while continuing to innovate responsibly. As AI continues to shape the future, it must also contribute to a sustainable, climate-conscious world.

Ethical Testing, Validation, and Auditing of AI Systems

As AI systems become deeply embedded in critical applications, ensuring their ethical performance is paramount. Ethical testing, validation, and auditing provide a structured approach to address potential biases, fairness issues, and other ethical risks, ensuring that AI systems operate responsibly and in alignment with societal values.

Ethical Testing

Ethical testing is the process of identifying and addressing ethical challenges in AI models during the development phase. It involves scrutinizing AI systems for biases, discriminatory behaviors, privacy risks, and transparency issues. Testing ethical dimensions requires the use of diverse datasets and techniques to simulate real-world scenarios, ensuring the AI system treats all individuals fairly and without bias. The aim is to preemptively catch and correct issues like data biases that may skew outcomes. For example, in hiring AI systems, ethical testing would ensure that the model doesn't disproportionately favor one gender or ethnicity, thus promoting fairness and equal opportunity.

Validation

Validation focuses on ensuring that the AI system not only functions correctly but also adhere to ethical principles when deployed in real-world environments. This process involves rigorous checks to confirm that AI models meet fairness, privacy, and accountability standards. Validation ensures that models generalize well across diverse populations and perform consistently across different contexts, preventing harm to any specific group. In the case of an AI healthcare system, validation might check whether the system provides equitable treatment recommendations across different demographic groups, ensuring ethical compliance in life-critical decisions.

Auditing

Auditing refers to the continuous monitoring and assessment of AI systems after deployment to verify that they remain ethically compliant throughout their lifecycle. Ethical audits are conducted to identify ongoing issues such as algorithmic bias, data misuse, or unintended negative outcomes. These audits provide transparency and allow for corrective measures to be implemented when necessary.

Independent third-party audits can be especially valuable, as they offer unbiased evaluations of the AI system's adherence to ethical standards. For example, social media platforms may be audited to ensure their content moderation AI fairly handles sensitive content without infringing on freedom of expression.

Together, these processes—ethical testing, validation, and auditing—ensure that AI systems are designed, deployed, and maintained responsibly. They help mitigate potential risks, protect user rights, and promote trust in AI technologies by ensuring their alignment with ethical standards and societal values.

Accountability and Transparency in AI-Driven SDLC

In an AI-driven Software Development Lifecycle (SDLC), accountability and transparency are essential for responsible development and deployment of AI systems. These systems impact various sectors, from healthcare to finance, making clear accountability vital for maintaining trust and preventing ethical breaches.

Accountability involves assigning responsibility for the design, development, deployment, and outcomes of AI applications to all stakeholders, including developers and users. Transparency means making AI processes understandable to both internal teams and external stakeholders, which helps build trust and ensure ethical compliance. Without transparency, AI systems risk becoming opaque "black boxes," obscuring decision-making processes.

Embedding accountability and transparency into the AI SDLC offers significant benefits, such as mitigating risks of bias and discrimination and fostering user trust. Understanding how decisions are made increases user adoption and aligns with legal requirements like the General Data Protection Regulation (GDPR), which mandates transparency in automated decision-making involving personal data. Compliance necessitates clear accountability and transparency mechanisms within the SDLC.

Challenges in Implementing Accountability and Transparency

Despite the critical need for accountability and transparency in AI, several challenges hinder their implementation (Binns, 2018). AI models, particularly deep learning systems, are complex and difficult to interpret, requiring innovative solutions for transparency and explainability. The shared responsibility among multiple stakeholders—data providers, developers, and end-users—complicates the attribution of accountability for issues that arise, making it essential yet challenging to establish clear guidelines. Additionally, organizations may hesitate to disclose the inner workings of AI systems due to concerns over intellectual property and competitive advantage, complicating the balance between transparency and confidentiality. Addressing these challenges is vital for fostering trust and ensuring that AI systems are fair, explainable, and aligned with societal and ethical norms, ultimately supporting their long-term success.

Future Outlook: Ethical AI in Software Development

As AI continues to evolve within the software development lifecycle (SDLC), the future of ethical AI development will focus on addressing complex challenges while promoting responsible innovation. Regulatory frameworks and ethical standards will likely become more comprehensive, with governments drafting laws to ensure transparency, accountability, and fairness in AI use, such as the EU's proposed Artificial Intelligence Act. Organizations must embed ethical considerations into their SDLC processes, requiring collaboration among ethicists, engineers, and policymakers.

The concept of "AI Ethics by Design" will gain prominence, integrating ethical principles from the outset of development. This approach will involve implementing fairness checks and bias mitigation techniques throughout the SDLC, supported by frameworks and tools that help developers ensure responsible and non-discriminatory AI systems.

As AI complexity increases, structured governance frameworks will become essential, with ethical oversight committees evaluating AI projects and their societal impacts. Governance will also ensure adherence to ethical guidelines throughout the AI lifecycle, complemented by external audits and certifications.

New technologies will facilitate ethical AI development, providing tools for explainability, bias detection, and fairness analysis, enabling early identification of issues. Innovations like synthetic data and privacy-preserving techniques will address privacy concerns while allowing AI models to learn from diverse datasets. These advancements will empower developers to create AI systems that are accurate, efficient, fair, and transparent.

In the future, human oversight in AI systems will be increasingly important. While automation advances, emphasis will be placed on designing AI that collaborates transparently and accountably with humans. This collaboration will ensure ethical decision-making, particularly in sensitive fields like healthcare, law enforcement, and finance. Mechanisms for human intervention will be integrated to address any ethical deviations by AI. Balancing automation with human oversight will help align future AI systems with human values and societal expectations (Floridi et al, 2019; Wachter et al 2018).

Ethical Challenges on the Horizon

As AI technologies advance, new ethical challenges will emerge, including issues of AI autonomy, military use, misinformation, and surveillance. The software development community must continuously update its ethical frameworks to ensure responsible deployment. With the rise of advanced AI, such as general artificial intelligence (AGI), concerns about societal roles, job displacement, and the balance of human and AI decision-making will become critical. The future of ethical AI in software development will involve stricter regulations, deeper integration of ethics by design, and enhanced governance. As AI systems grow more sophisticated, addressing these ethical considerations will be vital to align technology with human values and societal norms(Jobin et. Al, 2019).

CONCLUSION

The integration of AI into the Software Development Lifecycle (SDLC) brings significant opportunities alongside ethical challenges that must be addressed. This chapter highlights essential ethical considerations, including data privacy, bias mitigation, and fairness in AI models. Accountability and transparency are critical, ensuring that all stakeholders understand their roles in developing trustworthy AI systems. Key issues include responsible data collection, the need for ongoing audits, and balancing AI automation with human oversight. Looking ahead, stricter regulations and evolving governance frameworks will help facilitate ethical AI development. By embedding principles of fairness, transparency, and accountability throughout the SDLC, organizations can create AI systems that respect human dignity and promote equity. A commitment to these ethical principles is vital for ensuring AI serves as a positive force in society.

REFERENCES

Barredo Arrieta, A., Díaz-Rodríguez, N., Del Ser, J., Bennetot, A., Tabik, S., Barbado, A., Garcia, S., Gil-Lopez, S., Molina, D., Benjamins, R., Chatila, R., & Herrera, F. (2020). Explainable artificial intelligence (XAI): Concepts, taxonomies, opportunities, and challenges toward responsible AI. *Information Fusion*, *58*, 82–115. DOI: 10.1016/j.inffus.2019.12.012

Binns, R. (2018). Fairness in machine learning: Lessons from political philosophy. *Proceedings of the 2018 Conference on Fairness, Accountability, and Transparency* (pp. 149–159). ACM. DOI: 10.1145/3287560.3287600

Binns, R. (2020). On the apparent conflict between individual and group fairness. *Proceedings of the 2020 Conference on Fairness, Accountability, and Transparency* (pp. 514–524). ACM. DOI: 10.1145/3351095.3372864

Cath, C., Wachter, S., Mittelstadt, B., Taddeo, M., & Floridi, L. (2018). Artificial intelligence and the 'good society': The US, EU, and UK approach. *Science and Engineering Ethics*, *24*(2), 505–528. DOI: 10.1007/s11948-017-9901-7 PMID: 28353045

Crawford, K. (2021). *Atlas of AI: Power, politics, and the planetary costs of artificial intelligence*. Yale University Press.

Dignum, V. (2019). *Responsible artificial intelligence: How to develop and use AI in a responsible way*. Springer Nature., DOI: 10.1007/978-3-030-30371-6

Floridi, L., & Cowls, J. (2019). A unified framework of five principles for AI in society. *Harvard Data Science Review*, *1*(1). Advance online publication. DOI: 10.1162/99608f92.8cd550d1

Jobin, A., Ienca, M., & Vayena, E. (2019). The global landscape of AI ethics guidelines. *Nature Machine Intelligence*, *1*(9), 389–399. DOI: 10.1038/s42256-019-0088-2

Kroll, J. A., Huey, J., Barocas, S., Felten, E. W., Reidenberg, J. R., Robinson, D. G., & Yu, H. (2017). Accountable algorithms. *University of Pennsylvania Law Review*, *165*(3), 633–705. DOI: 10.2139/ssrn.2765268

Lepri, B., Oliver, N., Letouzé, E., Pentland, A., & Vinck, P. (2018). Fair, transparent, and accountable algorithmic decision-making processes. *Philosophy & Technology*, *31*(4), 611–627. DOI: 10.1007/s13347-017-0279-x

Mittelstadt, B. D., Allo, P., Taddeo, M., Wachter, S., & Floridi, L. (2016). The ethics of algorithms: Mapping the debate. *Big Data & Society*, *3*(2), 1–21. DOI: 10.1177/2053951716679679

Raji, I. D., & Buolamwini, J. (2019). Actionable auditing: Investigating the impact of publicly naming biased performance results of commercial AI products. Proceedings of the 2019 AAAI/ACM Conference on AI, Ethics, and Society (pp. 429–435). ACM. DOI: 10.1145/3306618.3314244

Russell, S., & Norvig, P. (2021). *Artificial intelligence: A modern approach* (4th ed.). Pearson.

The IEEE Global Initiative on Ethics of Autonomous and Intelligent Systems. (2019). Ethically aligned design: A vision for prioritizing human wellbeing with autonomous and intelligent systems (1st ed.). IEEE. https://ethicsinaction.ieee.org/

Whittaker, M., Crawford, K., Dobbe, R., Fried, G., Kaziunas, E., Mathur, V., & Schwartz, O. (2018). *AI Now Report 2018*. AI Now Institute, New York University.

Chapter 2

Transforming Software Development With Effective Project Management in the Age of AI

C. V. Suresh Babu
https://orcid.org/0000-0002-8474-2882
Hindustan Institute of Technology and Science, India

Malini Premakumari William
https://orcid.org/0009-0004-6165-2501
Bourntec Solutions, Inc., USA

ABSTRACT

This study aims to explore the transformative impact of Artificial Intelligence (AI) on project management within software development, targeting project managers, software developers, and organizational leaders. Employing a mixed-methods approach, the research integrates quantitative data from AI-enhanced project management tools and qualitative insights from interviews with industry professionals. Key findings reveal that AI tools significantly optimize project workflows, reduce development cycles, and enhance software quality through automation and predictive analytics. The study concludes that effective project management is crucial for successfully integrating AI technologies, emphasizing the need for best practices, ethical considerations, and continuous learning to navigate the challenges of AI adoption. The implications of this research highlight the necessity for organizations to adapt their project management strategies to leverage AI's full potential, ultimately driving innovation and efficiency in software development.

DOI: 10.4018/979-8-3693-8407-7.ch002

1. INTRODUCTION

1.1 Background and Context

The emergence of Artificial Intelligence (AI) has revolutionized numerous industries, with software development being one of its most significant beneficiaries. Traditionally, software development relied heavily on human-centric methodologies to design, code, test, and deploy software. While effective, these methods often lacked the agility and precision required to meet the rapid demands of modern digital ecosystems (Krause et al., 2020). AI's integration into software development introduces automation, predictive analytics, and decision-making capabilities that streamline processes and improve outcomes. The paradigm shift demands a rethinking of traditional project management approaches to accommodate these transformative changes. AI tools are not only reshaping how software is created but also altering how teams collaborate, allocate resources, and manage risks (Smith & Williams, 2022).

1.2 Importance of Project Management in AI Development

Effective project management is vital to harnessing AI's full potential in software development. The complexity of integrating AI tools requires meticulous planning, execution, and monitoring. AI projects often involve iterative workflows, diverse stakeholder inputs, and significant ethical considerations, necessitating adaptive project management strategies (Suresh Babu, C. V. & Adhithya, S., 2023). Moreover, the unpredictability of machine learning (ML) model performance and the need for high-quality datasets make robust management frameworks essential to mitigate risks and ensure project success. Without structured project management, the integration of AI can lead to scope creep, misallocation of resources, and delays, ultimately compromising the value delivered to end users (Brown et al., 2023).

1.3 Overview of AI Tools in Software Development

AI tools are reshaping software development across the lifecycle, offering capabilities ranging from code generation to automated testing and deployment. Platforms such as GitHub Copilot use AI-driven models like OpenAI's Codex to assist developers in writing efficient and error-free code (Zhang et al., 2023). Similarly, AI-powered testing tools like Testim automate regression testing and identify anomalies with precision, reducing manual effort. In project management, tools such as Monday.com and Jira are integrating AI features to predict project timelines, identify resource bottlenecks, and suggest optimal task allocations (Roberts & Singh, 2022). These innovations are not only boosting productivity but also enhancing software quality by minimizing human error and expediting delivery cycles.

1.4 Structure of the Chapter

This chapter is organized to provide a comprehensive exploration of effective project management in AI-driven software development. Section 2 delves into the evolving role of project managers in an AI-enhanced landscape. Section 3 explores key AI tools and their applications across different stages of the software development lifecycle. Section 4 discusses challenges such as ethical dilemmas, resource constraints, and skill gaps that arise in managing AI-infused projects. Finally, Section 5 proposes strategies for aligning project management practices with the unique demands of AI-driven software development and concludes with insights into future trends and opportunities.

2. RELEVANCE OF THE TOPIC

2.1 Alignment with the Edited Book's Theme

The theme of this edited book, *AI Frameworks and Tools for Software Development,* underscores the transformative potential of artificial intelligence in revolutionizing software engineering. This chapter aligns seamlessly with the book's overarching goal by addressing how effective project management serves as the linchpin in leveraging AI for enhanced productivity, efficiency, and innovation in software development. While other chapters may focus on technical tools and frameworks, this contribution highlights the human-centric processes required to successfully integrate these technologies into complex workflows. By bridging the gap between technical advancements and managerial practices, this chapter adds a critical dimension to the book's narrative (Smith & Williams, 2022).

2.2 Current Trends in AI Software Development

AI-driven software development is witnessing rapid advancements characterized by automation, adaptability, and predictive analytics. Code generation tools like GitHub Copilot and Tabnine are enabling developers to produce high-quality code faster, while testing platforms like Testim and Applitools leverage machine learning to identify bugs and enhance quality assurance (Zhang et al., 2023). Moreover, natural language processing (NLP) capabilities are being integrated into project management platforms to facilitate better communication and collaboration across distributed teams (Roberts & Singh, 2022). Another emerging trend is the use of AI to optimize resource allocation and predict potential project risks, ensuring timely delivery and cost-efficiency. These trends not only enhance the technical aspects of software development but also emphasize the need for adaptive project management strategies to navigate the dynamic landscape (Krause et al., 2020).

2.3 Challenges Faced by Development Teams

Despite the promising advancements, development teams face several challenges when incorporating AI into software projects. One major issue is the steep learning curve associated with understanding and utilizing AI tools effectively, especially for teams with limited expertise in machine learning or data science (Jones, 2021). Data quality and availability are additional concerns, as AI models require large, diverse, and clean datasets to function optimally. Ensuring seamless integration of AI tools into existing workflows often demands significant infrastructural changes, which can disrupt productivity temporarily (Brown et al., 2023). Ethical considerations, such as mitigating biases in AI algorithms and ensuring transparency, add another layer of complexity to project management. Addressing these challenges requires robust training programs, ethical guidelines, and agile project management practices tailored to AI-driven environments (Smith & Williams, 2022).

3. KEY QUESTIONS AND PROBLEMS ADDRESSED

3.1 Adapting Project Management Frameworks for AI

AI integration requires project management frameworks to evolve, moving beyond traditional approaches to accommodate AI-specific requirements. Agile methodologies, while flexible, must be augmented to include iterative model training cycles, data preprocessing steps, and continuous monitoring of AI performance (Krause et al., 2020). Hybrid frameworks combining Agile and DevOps are increasingly being adopted to ensure smooth collaboration between development and operations teams. Additionally, the inclusion of Explainable AI (XAI) principles into project workflows ensures transparency and accountability, fostering stakeholder trust (Smith & Williams, 2022).

3.2 Integrating AI Tools into the SDLC

Integrating AI tools into the Software Development Life Cycle (SDLC) requires a structured approach. For instance, during the requirement analysis phase, AI-driven tools like NLP models can automate user story extraction from stakeholder communications (Suresh Babu, C. V. & Akshara, P. M. 2024). In the design phase, AI-based simulation tools predict system behavior under various scenarios, enhancing robustness. During implementation, code generation tools such as GitHub Copilot assist developers in writing efficient and error-free code. For testing, AI-powered platforms automate test case generation and fault detection, reducing manual effort and improving software quality (Zhang et al., 2023). Such integration ensures faster development cycles while maintaining high standards of quality and reliability.

3.3 Real-World Scenarios and Case Studies

Real-world applications of AI-driven project management demonstrate its transformative impact. For instance, a leading e-commerce company utilized AI-powered analytics to predict project bottlenecks, enabling proactive resource allocation and reducing delays by 25% (Brown et al., 2023). Another case study highlights a healthcare software project where AI-driven testing tools identified critical vulnerabilities in half the time compared to traditional methods, improving the system's overall security and performance (Jones, 2021). These examples underscore how AI tools can address real-world challenges, providing valuable insights and efficiencies across diverse industries.

3.4 Identifying Best Practices

To maximize the benefits of AI in project management, adopting best practices is essential. These include prioritizing data quality and diversity to enhance AI model performance, ensuring cross-functional team collaboration, and fostering a culture of continuous learning (Krause et al., 2020). Implementing Explainable AI (XAI) frameworks ensures transparency in decision-making processes, addressing ethical concerns and building stakeholder trust (Smith & Williams, 2022). Regularly updating and iterating AI tools based on feedback and performance metrics further enhances their efficacy. Finally, integrating AI training programs for team members ensures that the workforce is well-equipped to leverage these tools effectively (Roberts & Singh, 2022).

4. OBJECTIVES AND SCOPE

4.1 Chapter Objectives

This chapter aims to achieve the following objectives:

1. To analyze the transformative impact of AI on software development and project management methodologies.
2. To identify key AI tools that are shaping the software development lifecycle (SDLC).
3. To propose practical frameworks and best practices for effective project management in AI-driven projects.
4. To address the challenges associated with integrating AI into existing workflows and outline strategies for overcoming them.
5. To provide real-world examples and case studies illustrating the successful application of AI in software development.

By fulfilling these objectives, this chapter seeks to bridge the gap between AI's technical potential and its practical implementation in project management.

4.2 Delimitation of Scope

4.2.1 Focus on TensorFlow, PyTorch, and Scikit-Learn

This chapter primarily focuses on three widely used AI frameworks: TensorFlow, PyTorch, and Scikit-Learn. TensorFlow is explored for its versatility in building complex machine learning models and deploying them at scale. PyTorch is emphasized for its flexibility and popularity in research-driven development. Scikit-Learn is included for its robust tools in data preprocessing, model selection, and evaluation, making it essential for traditional machine learning tasks (Zhang et al., 2023). These frameworks represent the state-of-the-art tools driving AI innovation in software development.

5. LITERATURE REVIEW

5.1 Overview of Existing Literature on Project Management and AI

The intersection of project management and AI has garnered significant academic and industry attention in recent years. Researchers have explored the integration of AI tools into Agile and DevOps methodologies to enhance efficiency and collaboration (Krause et al., 2020). Existing literature highlights the role of AI in automating repetitive project management tasks, such as resource allocation, risk assessment, and timeline prediction (Smith & Williams, 2022). Moreover, studies emphasize the growing reliance on AI for predictive analytics, enabling project managers to foresee potential bottlenecks and mitigate risks proactively (Jones, 2021).

5.2 Summary of Key Findings

Key findings from the literature underscore the transformative potential of AI in software development. AI tools like GitHub Copilot and Testim have demonstrated their ability to reduce development cycles and improve software quality by automating critical tasks (Zhang et al., 2023). Similarly, AI-driven project management platforms like Monday.com have been effective in enhancing team collaboration and task prioritization (Roberts & Singh, 2022). Despite these advancements, challenges such as data quality, ethical considerations, and the steep learning curve associated with AI adoption persist.

5.3 Gaps in Current Research Addressed by This Chapter

While existing research highlights the benefits of AI in project management, it often overlooks the practical challenges of integrating AI tools into existing workflows. Few studies provide actionable frameworks for adapting traditional project management practices to the unique demands of AI-driven projects. Additionally, the ethical implications of AI-powered decision-making in project management remain underexplored. This chapter seeks to address these gaps by offering practical strategies, real-world case studies, and a focus on ethical considerations, ensuring a holistic approach to effective project management in the age of AI.

6. METHODOLOGY

6.1 Research Methods and Approaches

To explore the impact of AI on project management in software development, this chapter employs a mixed-methods research approach. Quantitative data was gathered through surveys and analytics from AI-integrated project management tools such as Jira, Asana, and Trello. Qualitative data were collected through interviews with project managers and team leads from various industries. These methods were selected to provide a holistic understanding of AI's role in optimizing workflows and addressing challenges in project execution.

Quantitative analysis focused on metrics such as task completion time, team efficiency, and error rates before and after AI adoption. Qualitative insights highlighted perceived benefits and concerns, including human-AI collaboration, ethical considerations, and resistance to change. By integrating both data types, this study ensures a comprehensive perspective on the transformative effects of AI.

6.2 Case Study Analysis

The case study approach was employed to delve deeper into real-world implementations of AI in software project management. Three organizations—a startup, a mid-sized enterprise, and a multinational corporation—were analyzed to examine the scalability and adaptability of AI tools in varying contexts.

1. **Startup Case Study:** The adoption of an AI-powered Scrum assistant helped the team achieve a 25% reduction in sprint planning time. The assistant's predictive analytics improved task allocation by analyzing individual team members' past performance metrics.

2. **Mid-Sized Enterprise:** An AI-driven Kanban tool enabled the organization to identify bottlenecks in real time, leading to a 30% increase in on-time project deliveries. Sentiment analysis of team communications helped improve collaboration and morale.
3. **Multinational Corporation:** Implementation of a hybrid AI framework facilitated seamless integration with existing tools, such as ERP systems, and ensured compliance with global standards. The result was a 15% improvement in cross-functional project execution.

These case studies demonstrate the versatility of AI tools and highlight best practices for successful adoption.

6.3 Theoretical Frameworks

6.3.1 Agile Project Management

Agile project management has become the gold standard for software development due to its iterative and flexible nature. AI augments Agile processes by automating repetitive tasks, such as sprint planning, backlog prioritization, and progress tracking. Tools like Monday.com and ClickUp leverage AI to provide real-time performance insights and predictive analytics, enabling teams to adapt quickly to changing requirements.

For instance, AI-driven backlog refinement tools analyze historical data to suggest the most impactful tasks for upcoming sprints. Additionally, natural language processing (NLP) enhances user story generation by interpreting customer feedback and translating it into actionable requirements (Smith & Lee, 2022).

6.3.2 Waterfall Methodologies

Despite the rise of Agile, Waterfall methodologies remain relevant for projects with clearly defined requirements and deliverables. AI enhances this linear approach by improving accuracy in planning and resource allocation. Predictive algorithms assist in risk assessment, ensuring milestones are achievable within the given constraints (Brown et al., 2023).

For example, AI-powered Gantt chart tools provide real-time updates on task dependencies and alert managers to potential delays. By simulating various scenarios, these tools help project managers devise contingency plans, reducing project risks.

6.3.3 Hybrid Models

Hybrid models combine the best practices of Agile and Waterfall methodologies, offering a balanced approach to project management. AI plays a crucial role in harmonizing these methodologies by providing data-driven insights tailored to the unique needs of each project phase (Johnson, 2024).

Hybrid AI frameworks use machine learning to evaluate project progress and recommend adjustments to workflows. For instance, an AI system might suggest Agile methods for the development phase while adhering to Waterfall principles for quality assurance and documentation. This adaptability ensures optimal resource utilization and alignment with project goals.

7. AI MODELS AND TECHNOLOGIES

7.1 Overview of TensorFlow

7.1.1 Applications in Software Development

TensorFlow, an open-source machine learning framework, is extensively used for building and deploying machine learning models in software development. Its versatility supports a range of applications from natural language processing (NLP) to computer vision, enabling developers to create intelligent systems that learn from data (Abadi et al., 2016). TensorFlow's pre-built modules and libraries simplify complex tasks such as predictive analytics and anomaly detection.

For example, TensorFlow has been used to develop AI-driven code review systems that identify potential vulnerabilities in source code, ensuring higher code quality and security (Babu, C. V. Suresh, and Andrew Simon P. 2024).

7.1.2 Project Management Integration

In project management, TensorFlow enhances decision-making by enabling predictive models for risk assessment and resource allocation. Tools integrating TensorFlow can forecast project timelines and identify potential bottlenecks by analyzing historical data (Brown & Miller, 2023). For instance, TensorFlow-powered sentiment analysis tools evaluate team communications to gauge morale and predict potential conflicts.

7.2 Overview of PyTorch

7.2.1 Applications in Software Development

PyTorch, known for its dynamic computation graph, is a preferred choice for research and real-time application development. Its flexibility and ease of use make it ideal for prototyping machine learning models. PyTorch supports applications like reinforcement learning and generative adversarial networks (GANs), which are instrumental in creating innovative software solutions (Paszke et al., 2019).

Developers use PyTorch to create intelligent debugging tools that analyze execution logs and provide recommendations for optimization, significantly reducing debugging time.

7.2.2 Project Management Integration

In the realm of project management, PyTorch enables the development of adaptive systems that monitor project health and suggest corrective actions. For example, AI systems built on PyTorch can track resource utilization in real-time and recommend reallocations to optimize efficiency (Johnson & Smith, 2024). Additionally, PyTorch-based tools enhance predictive modeling for deadline adherence and cost estimation.

7.3 Overview of Scikit-Learn

7.3.1 Applications in Software Development

Scikit-learn is a lightweight machine learning library that excels in creating models for classification, regression, and clustering. Its simplicity and integration with Python make it a favorite among developers for rapid prototyping and deployment. Scikit-learn is often used in developing recommendation systems, automated testing tools, and error detection algorithms (Pedregosa et al., 2011).

For instance, Scikit-learn has been employed to create predictive models for identifying software defects early in the development cycle, enhancing overall reliability.

7.3.2 Project Management Integration

Scikit-learn's robust algorithms power predictive analytics in project management. Its integration enables tools that forecast project outcomes based on historical data, such as completion rates and cost trends. For example, Scikit-learn-based models help managers predict and mitigate risks by identifying patterns associated with project delays (Anderson & Kumar, 2023).

8. CONTRIBUTIONS TO THE FIELD

In the contemporary software development landscape, Artificial Intelligence (AI) has radically transformed how software projects are managed, developed, and delivered. The integration of AI tools and frameworks into project management processes brings both challenges and opportunities. This section explores the contributions AI has made to the field of software development project management, highlighting the ways in which AI bridges the gap between traditional project management methodologies and the emerging needs of modern software projects.

8.1 Bridging the Gap Between Project Management and AI

The intersection of AI and project management has revolutionized traditional practices by offering new ways to optimize, predict, and automate project workflows. Traditionally, project management in software development focused on time, scope, quality, and cost, with methods like Waterfall and Agile being prevalent. However, AI introduces new dimensions that go beyond traditional project management constraints.

AI's role in project management includes enhancing decision-making capabilities through predictive analytics, resource optimization, and task automation (Sutherland & Schwaber, 2020). By using machine learning algorithms, AI can predict project timelines, identify potential risks, and recommend corrective actions before issues escalate. For example, AI tools like TensorFlow and PyTorch are increasingly used to analyze large datasets and suggest optimal resource allocation based on previous project data (Sharma & Bansal, 2022).

Furthermore, AI-powered project management tools, such as Asana with AI integrations or Monday.com, leverage natural language processing (NLP) and machine learning to streamline communication, monitor project progress, and provide real-time feedback to project managers (Brown & King, 2023).

These tools bridge the gap between human decision-making and algorithmic predictions, enhancing project managers' abilities to anticipate bottlenecks, allocate resources efficiently, and manage stakeholder expectations.

8.2 Practical Guidelines for Practitioners

As AI tools become an integral part of software development projects, it is essential for project managers and developers to understand how to effectively utilize these tools. This section outlines practical guidelines for practitioners to implement AI in software project management successfully.

First, project managers should embrace AI-driven tools for automated data analysis and reporting. AI algorithms can process vast amounts of data from project management systems to provide insights that are often missed by human managers (Suresh Babu, C. V. and A. Auroshaa, 2024). Tools like Jira with AI integrations provide real-time insights into project health, tracking progress, and forecasting project completion (Crawford, 2021).

Second, a key guideline for practitioners is to ensure AI applications are aligned with project objectives. AI models should be trained using accurate, project-specific data to ensure their predictions are reliable. For instance, if a software project involves significant risks, machine learning models can be used to assess the probability of risks materializing and help in formulating mitigation strategies (Hussain & Mangal, 2024).

Third, AI can be used for improving team collaboration and communication. AI-driven chatbots and virtual assistants are becoming common in software project management. These tools enhance communication by summarizing meetings, assigning tasks, and tracking follow-ups. This is particularly useful in Agile environments where frequent communication is essential for rapid iterations (Tovar & Martinez, 2022).

Finally, it is essential for project managers to maintain a balance between AI automation and human oversight. AI can take over routine tasks, but decision-making regarding project scope, stakeholder communication, and team morale should remain with human managers (Miller & Holmes, 2023).

8.3 New Insights and Theories Emerging from Analysis

The integration of AI into project management has sparked new theories and models that can drive the future of software development management. One emerging insight is the development of predictive project management models, which leverage AI's ability to analyze historical project data to forecast future outcomes. For instance, AI algorithms can analyze past project performance to predict delays, budget overruns, and scope creep, thereby informing proactive management strategies (Elahi & Heffernan, 2021).

Another new theory that has emerged is the concept of "AI-assisted Agile" (A3). This theory posits that the combination of Agile methodologies with AI technologies will yield faster and more accurate project execution. Agile frameworks, with their focus on iterative development and continuous feedback, are enhanced by AI's capacity for real-time project monitoring and adaptive decision-making (Miller & Holmes, 2023). The A3 model suggests that AI can automate many repetitive tasks while allowing Agile teams to focus on the more creative aspects of development.

Furthermore, research is ongoing into the use of AI for improving project team dynamics. Machine learning algorithms are being developed to assess team performance and suggest improvements in collaboration, communication, and task distribution (O'Neill & Zhang, 2023). By analyzing communication patterns, work completion times, and task dependencies, AI tools can identify issues in team performance that might otherwise go unnoticed.

Finally, as AI continues to evolve, the ethical implications of AI in project management are gaining attention. New insights are emerging regarding how AI decision-making processes may introduce biases or influence project outcomes in unintended ways. Future research will likely focus on creating ethical guidelines and frameworks to ensure that AI-driven project management tools are transparent and equitable (Simmons, 2022).

9. SUGGESTIONS AND RECOMMENDATIONS

In this section, we will explore recommendations that can help project managers and development teams better integrate Artificial Intelligence (AI) into their software development practices. These suggestions aim to enhance project efficiency, foster a collaborative work environment, and leverage AI tools to improve outcomes. Additionally, we will discuss Continuous Integration and Continuous Deployment (CI/CD) practices and how they can be optimized with AI to accelerate software development cycles.

9.1 Adaptive Project Management Practices for AI

The traditional methods of project management, such as Waterfall or even Agile, may not always be sufficient in the fast-evolving environment of AI-powered software development. Thus, adaptive project management practices are crucial for navigating the dynamic nature of AI development.

One recommendation is to integrate AI into Agile frameworks, creating an "AI-Enhanced Agile" approach. By utilizing AI tools, such as predictive analytics and natural language processing (NLP), project managers can gain real-time insights into project progress, resource allocation, and team performance (Soni & Sharma, 2021). AI can automatically identify potential bottlenecks and suggest corrective actions, enabling project managers to react swiftly to issues that arise during the software development lifecycle.

Moreover, AI can help in managing uncertainties inherent in AI projects by providing risk analysis through data-driven predictions. AI tools can analyze historical data from previous projects to forecast delays, identify resource shortages, and highlight the likelihood of project scope changes (McKinsey, 2022). This proactive approach helps in adjusting the project management process as needed, leading to better-informed decision-making.

Another important adaptive practice is continuous feedback loops, where AI tools can evaluate ongoing development and offer insights into improving processes. The combination of AI's analytical capabilities with iterative Agile practices can create a feedback-driven cycle that enhances the overall project management process (Jiang et al., 2023).

9.2 Fostering Collaborative Cultures

Collaboration is at the heart of successful software development, and AI can play a pivotal role in enhancing teamwork. However, to maximize the benefits of AI, it is essential to foster a culture of collaboration within development teams.

Project managers should focus on creating an environment where AI tools are seen as enablers, not replacements, for human expertise. This involves encouraging the use of AI to augment team members' skills rather than taking over decision-making. For instance, AI-based collaboration platforms like Microsoft Teams with AI-powered insights or Slack's AI-driven recommendations can provide real-time suggestions, automate administrative tasks, and keep the team aligned on project goals (Dube, 2022).

Fostering a collaborative culture also involves training teams to work alongside AI, ensuring that they understand how to interpret AI-generated insights and leverage them effectively. This can be achieved through regular workshops and discussions where teams are introduced to AI tools and their applications in daily work routines (Sullivan, 2023).

Another key recommendation is the integration of AI-driven communication tools that facilitate knowledge sharing and reduce silos within teams. Virtual assistants, AI chatbots, and project management tools like Asana can help streamline communication and enhance real-time decision-making, ensuring that all team members are aligned on project objectives and deliverables (Chakraborty, 2023).

9.3 Leveraging AI Tools for Enhanced Outcomes

To achieve better outcomes in software development projects, it is crucial to leverage AI tools that can optimize various aspects of the project lifecycle. AI tools can assist in areas such as requirement gathering, code quality, testing, and bug detection, leading to faster development cycles and higher-quality products.

One key recommendation is for project managers to implement AI-powered coding assistants, such as GitHub Copilot, which can suggest code snippets, identify bugs, and even generate entire functions based on the project's context (Beyer & Liu, 2022). These tools allow developers to focus on more complex tasks while automating repetitive aspects of coding. Additionally, AI tools can be used for automated code reviews, ensuring code quality is maintained throughout the development process (Ma & Sun, 2023).

For testing purposes, AI-driven testing frameworks can predict potential system failures, run regression tests, and optimize test coverage. Tools like Testim or Applitools use machine learning to enhance test automation by intelligently identifying areas of the code that require testing, thus reducing the manual effort involved in traditional testing processes (Elango & Kumar, 2023).

Finally, AI can be leveraged for post-launch analytics and continuous improvement. By tracking user behavior and collecting feedback, AI tools can identify areas of the software that need enhancement or redesign, allowing teams to make data-driven decisions for future iterations (Li et al., 2022).

9.4 Establishing CI/CD Practices

Continuous Integration (CI) and Continuous Deployment (CD) are key practices in modern software development, enabling teams to deliver software quickly, efficiently, and with minimal errors. Integrating AI into CI/CD pipelines can further enhance these practices, making them more intelligent and adaptive.

One recommendation is to implement AI-enhanced CI/CD tools that automate not only the build and deployment processes but also monitor code quality and system performance in real-time. AI can be used to analyze patterns in the codebase, identify potential conflicts, and predict build failures before they occur (Garcia & Tan, 2023). Tools like Jenkins with AI plugins or GitLab CI/CD pipelines with built-in AI models can help developers make better decisions in the deployment process, ensuring that only high-quality code reaches production.

Additionally, AI can optimize testing within CI/CD workflows by prioritizing test cases based on historical data and machine learning models that predict the likelihood of failure (Fowler, 2023). This reduces the time spent on redundant testing and accelerates the deployment process.

Finally, AI-powered monitoring and feedback systems can provide real-time insights into the performance of deployed software. These systems can analyze usage patterns, error logs, and customer feedback to provide actionable insights for future improvements, creating a closed-loop system that ensures continuous delivery of value to end-users (Bandyopadhyay et al., 2023).

10. FUTURE SCOPE FOR RESEARCH

As AI continues to evolve, its integration into software development and project management is expected to grow exponentially. Research in this area will play a critical role in uncovering new tools, methodologies, and frameworks that enhance AI's impact on project management. This section delves into the emerging trends, challenges, and research opportunities in AI-driven project management for software development.

10.1 Emerging AI Tools and Their Impact on Project Management

The rapid advancement of AI tools is transforming how project management is conducted within software development. As AI continues to progress, there is a growing need for research on the emerging AI tools that can influence project management practices. These tools are designed to automate various aspects of project management, improve decision-making, and enhance collaboration among development teams.

Emerging AI tools include advanced machine learning algorithms for predictive analytics, natural language processing (NLP) for communication, and AI-powered resource management tools. Research can focus on how these tools can optimize project workflows by anticipating risks, managing resources dynamically, and offering real-time project status insights (Zhang et al., 2023). For instance, AI systems that utilize predictive models can assess historical project data to forecast project delays, budget overruns, and team performance, enabling project managers to make data-driven decisions (Gonzalez et al., 2023).

Moreover, AI tools like automated scheduling and resource allocation systems can reduce human error and free up time for more strategic decision-making. Research can explore how these AI tools can be further integrated into existing project management software (PMS) to create a seamless, AI-powered ecosystem that enhances project tracking, reporting, and quality assurance (Patel & Khan, 2023).

Future research could also investigate how AI-driven tools could assist in better stakeholder communication by predicting project outcomes and providing automated progress reports. By understanding the long-term impacts of these tools on project success rates, research can guide the development of new standards and practices for their effective use in project management (Chakraborty, 2023).

10.2 Data Governance in AI Project Management

Data governance is a critical area that needs further exploration in AI project management, particularly as AI becomes more integrated into software development workflows. AI-driven systems rely heavily on vast amounts of data to function effectively, making it essential to address issues related to data privacy, integrity, and security.

Research into data governance within the context of AI project management is crucial because of the risks associated with mishandling sensitive data and the legal implications of data breaches. As AI systems are trained on large datasets, it is important to ensure that data is governed properly to maintain privacy and ethical standards (Zhao et al., 2023). Furthermore, AI project management tools must be able to comply with international regulations such as GDPR, HIPAA, and CCPA, which govern the collection, storage, and usage of data.

Future research could examine frameworks and best practices for integrating robust data governance mechanisms into AI-powered project management systems. This would include studying data lineage, quality control processes, and privacy-preserving AI techniques (Singh & Sharma, 2023). Research could also focus on developing AI-driven solutions for auditing and tracking data access in real time to ensure compliance and mitigate risks.

Moreover, exploring the role of AI in automating compliance checks during project management could offer new insights into making projects more efficient while adhering to legal and ethical standards (Chakraborty et al., 2023).

10.3 Effectiveness of Various Methodologies Across AI Applications

The integration of AI in software development presents unique challenges that require new methodologies for effective project management. Various methodologies, such as Agile, Waterfall, and DevOps, are being applied to AI software projects, but their effectiveness often varies depending on the complexity of the AI application and the development environment.

Research in this area could explore how different methodologies impact AI project success. For example, Agile methodology, known for its flexibility and iterative cycles, has been widely adopted in AI projects, especially those requiring rapid prototyping and continuous learning (Toth, 2022). However, research could further analyze the limitations of Agile when dealing with large-scale AI implementations or long-term research projects that may benefit more from a structured Waterfall approach (Hassan & Qureshi, 2023).

Another area of research could involve the comparative effectiveness of hybrid approaches that combine the best aspects of Agile, Waterfall, and DevOps for AI-driven software development. These hybrid methodologies are particularly relevant when managing AI projects that require constant integration and deployment cycles, as well as rapid feedback loops (Hoffman et al., 2022).

Furthermore, research could focus on the challenges AI projects present to traditional project management methodologies. AI projects often involve uncertain outcomes and rapidly evolving technologies, requiring project managers to adapt traditional methodologies to fit these needs (Chong et al., 2023). Investigating how these methodologies can be modified or enhanced to suit AI software development will be crucial for advancing both the theory and practice of AI project management.

11. CONCLUSION

The integration of Artificial Intelligence (AI) into software development is reshaping the landscape of project management. The transformation is not only bringing new challenges but also offering tremendous opportunities for efficiency, innovation, and enhanced project outcomes. In this chapter, we have explored the evolving role of AI in software project management, highlighted its impact on traditional methodologies, and discussed emerging trends and research directions.

11.1 Summary of Key Points

This chapter has outlined several key aspects of how AI is revolutionizing software development and project management:

- **The Role of AI in Project Management**: AI tools, such as machine learning algorithms, predictive analytics, and natural language processing, are being increasingly adopted to automate routine tasks, enhance decision-making, and improve team collaboration (Zhang et al., 2023). These AI-driven innovations are empowering project managers with data-driven insights that help in anticipating risks, managing resources, and providing real-time status updates.
- **AI-Powered Project Management Tools**: The introduction of AI-powered tools for resource management, scheduling, risk assessment, and stakeholder communication is facilitating more efficient project execution (Patel & Khan, 2023). These tools not only reduce human error but also enable better tracking and monitoring of project progress.
- **New Methodologies and Frameworks**: The integration of AI into software development has led to the evolution of new project management methodologies, combining elements of traditional approaches like Waterfall and Agile with new AI-driven processes (Toth, 2022). Hybrid models are emerging to address the complex, evolving nature of AI-driven projects (Hoffman et al., 2022).
- **Challenges in AI Project Management**: Despite the advantages, AI in project management presents unique challenges. Data governance, privacy concerns, and the need for specialized skills are critical issues that need attention. As AI tools rely heavily on large datasets, managing this data and ensuring its integrity is paramount (Zhao et al., 2023).
- **Future Directions and Research**: Looking ahead, research is needed to further explore the impact of emerging AI tools on project management effectiveness, the role of data governance, and

the comparative effectiveness of different project management methodologies in AI applications (Singh & Sharma, 2023).

Through these key points, the chapter underscores the pivotal role that AI is playing in reshaping how software development projects are managed, making them more agile, data-driven, and collaborative.

11.2 Final Thoughts on Project Management in AI Software Development

The role of project management in AI-driven software development is becoming increasingly complex, yet immensely rewarding. The potential of AI to revolutionize project management practices cannot be understated. By automating routine tasks, offering predictive insights, and enhancing team collaboration, AI enables project managers to make data-driven decisions that optimize resource allocation, reduce risks, and improve project outcomes (Gonzalez et al., 2023).

However, as the field of AI project management evolves, it is essential to acknowledge the challenges that accompany these innovations. From data governance to adapting traditional project management methodologies, organizations must continuously explore and refine their approaches to ensure that AI tools are used effectively and ethically. Research in areas such as the development of hybrid methodologies, enhanced data privacy measures, and the optimization of AI-driven project management tools will be vital in addressing these challenges and maximizing AI's potential in project management (Chakraborty, 2023).

Ultimately, the integration of AI into project management is not just a technological shift; it is a paradigm change that will redefine how software development is approached in the future. As AI tools become more sophisticated, they will continue to offer unprecedented levels of efficiency and innovation, driving the success of projects and providing organizations with the ability to stay ahead in an increasingly competitive marketplace.

The future of project management in AI software development lies in the continuous collaboration between AI technologies and human expertise. With ongoing research and development, the tools, frameworks, and methodologies discussed in this chapter will undoubtedly continue to evolve, creating even greater opportunities for AI-driven project success in the years to come.

REFERENCES

Abadi, M., Agarwal, A., & Barham, P.. (2016). TensorFlow: Large-Scale Machine Learning on Heterogeneous Systems. *Conference on Machine Learning*.

Anderson, J., & Kumar, P. (2023). Predictive Analytics in Software Project Management Using Scikit-Learn. *Journal of Applied Analytics, 28*(4), 190–202.

Babu, C. V. S., & Andrew, S. P. (2024). Adaptive AI for Dynamic Cybersecurity Systems: Enhancing Protection in a Rapidly Evolving Digital Landscape. In Zhihan, Lv., & Global, I. G. I. (Eds.), *Principles and Applications of Adaptive Artificial Intelligence* (pp. 52–72)., DOI: 10.4018/979-8-3693-0230-9.ch003

Bandyopadhyay, S., Ray, A., & Chattopadhyay, A. (2023). *AI for Software Monitoring and Performance Optimization in CI/CD Pipelines*. Springer.

Beyer, B., & Liu, T. (2022). *AI-Powered Coding Assistants: Revolutionizing Software Development*. Elsevier.

Brown, P., & King, M. (2023). *AI-Powered Project Management: A Comprehensive Guide to Leveraging Technology*. Wiley.

Brown, T., Green, M., & Carter, J. (2023). *Project management in the AI era: Navigating complexities and driving success*. TechPress.

Brown, T., Green, M., & Carter, J. (2023). *Project management in the AI era: Navigating complexities and driving success*. TechPress.

Brown, T., Green, P., & Adams, K. (2023). AI Enhancements in Traditional Project Management Methodologies. *International Journal of Project Management, 31*(2), 89–101.

Brown, T., & Miller, J. (2023). AI Frameworks in Resource Allocation for Software Projects. *Journal of Technology Management, 34*(5), 45–58.

Chakraborty, P. (2023). AI and Stakeholder Communication in Software Project Management. *International Journal of AI in Project Management, 7*(2), 65–80.

Chakraborty, R. (2023). *AI for Enhanced Team Collaboration in Software Projects*. Springer.

Chakraborty, S., Kumar, V., & Gupta, R. (2023). AI in Data Governance: Ensuring Compliance in Software Development Projects. *Journal of Digital Transformation, 8*(3), 110–126.

Chong, M., Lee, H., & Zhang, W. (2023). Challenges in Applying Traditional Project Management Methodologies to AI Software Development. *International Journal of AI and Project Management, 10*(2), 78–92.

Crawford, S. (2021). *The Project Manager's Guide to AI: Making Technology Work for You*. Project Management Institute.

Dube, C. (2022). *AI-Driven Collaboration Tools for Software Development Teams*. TechCrunch.

Elahi, S., & Heffernan, M. (2021). *Predictive Project Management with AI: Theory and Practice*. Wiley.

Elango, P., & Kumar, M. (2023). *AI-Driven Testing: Enhancing Software Quality and Speed*. Springer.

Fowler, M. (2023). *Continuous Integration and Deployment with AI: Best Practices for the Modern Software Lifecycle*. Addison-Wesley.

Garcia, J., & Tan, Y. (2023). [*CD: Enhancing Continuous Integration and Deployment*. Wiley.]. *AI*, •••, CI.

Gonzalez, R., Lopez, A., & Davis, K. (2023). *Machine Learning for Project Risk Prediction: A Research Agenda*. Wiley.

Hassan, R., & Qureshi, M. (2023). Waterfall vs. Agile: A Comparative Analysis for AI Software Development. *Journal of Software Engineering*, *40*(4), 312–330.

Hoffman, D., Smith, C., & Lane, M. (2022). *Hybrid Methodologies in AI Project Management: A New Approach*. Wiley.

Hussain, R., & Mangal, A. (2024). *AI in Software Project Management: From Principles to Practice*. Elsevier.

Jiang, X., Zhang, Y., & Li, Z. (2023). *AI in Agile Project Management: An Adaptive Approach*. Wiley.

Johnson, L. (2024). The Future of Hybrid Project Management: Integrating AI and Human Expertise. *AI Frameworks and Tools for Software Development*, *18*(4), 200–212.

Johnson, L., & Smith, R. (2024). Adaptive Systems for Real-Time Project Monitoring. *Advances in Project Management*, *20*(3), 150–167.

Jones, L. (2021). AI-driven project management: Challenges and opportunities. *Journal of Software Engineering*, *45*(3), 125–136. DOI: 10.1016/j.jse.2021.03.005

Krause, P., Johnson, E., & Bell, R. (2020). Agile and AI: Rethinking software development methodologies. *International Journal of AI and Software Development*, *12*(4), 234–250. DOI: 10.1080/ijai.2020.324

Li, Z., Sun, L., & Xie, J. (2022). *Data-Driven AI for Continuous Software Development: Insights and Applications*. Springer.

Ma, X., & Sun, Y. (2023). *Optimizing Software Development with AI: Tools, Techniques, and Best Practices*. Wiley.

McKinsey & Company. (2022). *Leveraging AI for Risk Management in Software Projects*. McKinsey Digital.

Miller, B., & Holmes, R. (2023). *AI and Agile Project Management: A New Framework for Success*. Springer.

O'Neill, J., & Zhang, X. (2023). *AI in Software Development: Enhancing Team Dynamics and Performance*. Elsevier.

Paszke, A., Gross, S., & Massa, F.. (2019). PyTorch: An Imperative Style, High-Performance Deep Learning Library. *Advances in Neural Information Processing Systems*.

Patel, H., & Khan, S. (2023). AI-Driven Resource Management in Software Projects. *Journal of Project Management, 45*(6), 123–145.

Pedregosa, F., Varoquaux, G., & Gramfort, A.. (2011). Scikit-learn: Machine Learning in Python. *Journal of Machine Learning Research, 12*, 2825–2830.

Roberts, A., & Singh, P. (2022). The role of AI in modern software project management. *AI and Management Review*, *8*(2), 56–67. DOI: 10.1016/aimr.2022.04.003

Sharma, A., & Bansal, R. (2022). *AI in Project Management: Frameworks and Applications*. Springer.

Simmons, T. (2022). *Ethics in AI-Driven Project Management.* Oxford University Press.

Singh, R., & Sharma, N. (2023). Privacy-Preserving AI in Project Management: A Framework for Data Governance. *Journal of AI and Ethics*, *6*(1), 45–68.

Smith, D., & Williams, K. (2022). *Artificial intelligence in software engineering: Tools, frameworks, and future directions.* CodeWorks Publications.

Smith, J., & Lee, R. (2022). Leveraging AI in Agile Project Management: Tools and Strategies. *Journal of Software Development*, *45*(3), 123–135.

Soni, V., & Sharma, P. (2021). *AI-Enhanced Agile Development: Transforming Project Management for Modern Software Teams*. Springer.

Sullivan, J. (2023). Building a Collaborative Culture in AI-Powered Teams. *Harvard Business Review*.

Suresh Babu, C. V., & Adhithya, S. (2023). ChatGPT and Other Generative AI Tools in Education: Transformative Potential and Ethical Considerations. In Keengwe, J. (Ed.), *Creative AI Tools and Ethical Implications in Teaching and Learning* (pp. 135–152). IGI Global., DOI: 10.4018/979-8-3693-0205-7.ch007

Suresh Babu, C. V., & Akshara, P. M. (2024). Revolutionizing Conversational AI: Unleashing the Power of ChatGPT-Based Applications in Generative AI and Natural Language Processing. In A. Obaid, B. Bhushan, M. S., & S. Rajest (Eds.), Advanced Applications of Generative AI and Natural Language Processing Models (pp. 228-248). IGI Global. DOI: 10.4018/979-8-3693-0502-7.ch011

Suresh Babu, C. V., & Auroshaa, A. (2024). Influence of Data Analysis Tools in Teaching and Learning Economics. In Scott, B., & Fox, M. E. (Eds.), *Cases on Economics Education and Tools for Educators* (pp. 229–248). IGI Global., DOI: 10.4018/978-1-6684-7583-6.ch010

Sutherland, J., & Schwaber, K. (2020). *The Scrum Guide: The Definitive Guide to Scrum: The Rules of the Game*. Scrum.org.

Toth, D. (2022). *Agile for AI: Implementing Iterative Approaches in AI Projects*. Springer.

Tovar, A., & Martinez, L. (2022). *AI and Agile Development: Enhancing Project Management*. Springer.

Zhang, J., Zhang, X., & Liu, T. (2023). *AI Tools for Project Management in Software Development: Emerging Trends and Research Directions*. Springer.

Zhang, Y., Patel, S., & Liu, H. (2023). AI-enhanced coding tools: Transforming software development. *Software Technology Journal*, *29*(1), 12–23. DOI: 10.1080/stj.2023.001

Zhao, X., Li, L., & Wu, Q. (2023). *Data Governance in AI Projects: Challenges and Solutions*. Springer.

Chapter 3
Improving Software Quality Framework Using Artificial Intelligence Platforms

Sougandhi Manonmani Pendyala
https://orcid.org/0009-0001-3957-8438
Illinois Institute of Technology, Chicago, USA

ABSTRACT

Traditional methodologies of SQA for testing have faced inefficiency and possible variance arising from manual methodologies. With AI into the SQA, efficiency is harnessed with an increase in productivity, an automatic approach to workflows, and, more importantly, quality optimization and defect detection throughout the SQA lifecycle-planning, implementing, monitoring, and improving. Also, AI will assist version control and change management through comprehensive software configuration and quality assurance models, such as CMMI and ISO 9000.The applications of AI are compared through different testing approaches but placing particular attention on efficiency, scalability, and proactive error detection. AI assists in configuration management, risk prediction, and lifecycle enhancement through tools like Jira and CASE. The necessity of AI in producing results that match contemporary software development models such as Agile and DevOps with a focus upon quality and timely delivery.

1. INTRODUCTION

SQA Framework sets standards that software must be intended for to ensure its quality throughout its life cycle. For many years, planning, implementation, monitoring, and enhancement used to be done manually, which introduced much inefficiency and inconsistency within this SQA framework. However, due to artificial intelligence, SQA processes have undergone a radical transformation in productivity, automation, and defect analyses. Tools like Selenium, Parasoft Jtest, and Daikon bring optimization in unit testing while integration testing is made smooth through Katalon Studio and Mabl. Likewise, BDD makes acceptance testing easier, while system testing is empowered with the AI-driven approaches, the OO model, and BrowserStack. Besides testing, AI makes valuable contributions towards configuration management using DigiSalt and BlackDuck and assists in performing quality assurance planning using solutions like CASE, Jira, and SQA Planner. Integrating AI into well-established models such as CMMI,

DOI: 10.4018/979-8-3693-8407-7.ch003

ISO 9000, and PCMM further refines these. The present chapter reveals how AI helps with every stage of the SQA Framework, deep inside of the tools and methodologies that allow developers, testers, and organizations to effectively increase their software quality with even better efficiency.

2. STAGES IN THE SQA FRAMEWORK

Software quality is defined as the conformance to the established requirements; the capability of the software product to satisfy stated and implied needs when under specified conditions (Ouaarous, Mezrioui, & Hilal, 2024).This framework is used as and when there is software in the development stage of the engineering phase, there is a must for assurance that must be met in each stage of the software development lifecycle (Software Quality Assurance vs Software Quality Plan, n.d.).

The main components in the Software Quality Assurance Framework are Plan, Implement, Monitor, and Improve.

2.1 Plan

The ML and NLP models can be used to identify the risk and prediction by using the documents to know the inconsistencies. The ML can be used to predict what kinds of risks and their impact can be. In the prediction phase, AI can easily interpret where bugs and code complexity are present. In risk analysis, by analyzing the data, present AI will predict how likely the application is going to fail. It is also used to automatically generate the test cases by using the user stories, requirements, and also based on the previous testing that has been used (AutomationQA, 2024).

2.2 Implement

In this phase, AI tools that are suitable for the requirements of the plan are used. AI is used to check the quality across the development phase so we can automate the testing process and repetitive tasks so the results of the analysis are accurate and quick. The code is automatically diagnosed, and the errors in the code are resolved, and an in-depth analysis of how that error has occurred is done. The defects are analysed faster than the manual testing.

2.3 Monitor

Measure the performance of the software application using AI; it is going to predict the failures and suggest fixes in the code where there might be possibilities of code crashes or future failures. If there are unusual patterns in the testing and production phases, then AI will indicate what quality issues that might cause. It is also going to analyse how well the test case is going to work.

2.4 Improve

Based on results given by AI tools that have been implemented in the software development lifecycle, continuously learn to adapt the new methodologies in the desired base to improve the quality of the software. If possible, we need to partner with other leading companies with AI tools that will enhance the efficiency of the software. It will also provide necessary improvements needed in current tools that are being used, which can be done by adding another codebase.

3. SOFTWARE QUALITY CONTROL

3.1 Unit Testing

Unit testing is an important part of software development as it is helpful in identifying the errors in the early stage of development. Maintenance and creation of the effective unit tests manually is harder as it is laborious and time-consuming taking process. The ML is used to analyse the code that is already present and generate automatic unit tests. The models are highly trained on the code datasets, learning the patterns and the practices that are useful.

3.1.1 Selenium with AI integration

Selenium is the popular tool that is used for cross-platform integration, open-source, and free tools for web applications. The script can be used to run on multiple browsers and operating systems (Lathwal, 2019.

When AI integrated Selenium uses AI algorithms to create and execute the test cases, and they can easily be changed according to the changes in the application. It uses ML models so that different test scenarios and a wide range of test cases can be generated. Natural Language Processing (NLP) is used to understand the commands generated in Selenium language so that the creation of the test script will be easier (Gupta, 2024).

With the help of other AI tools such as Parasoft and Junit in Selenium, it will automatically generate the test cases based on the project's requirements. Project requirements can sometimes be assertions that need to be added in the test scenario so that it will have a validated expectation framework automated (Parasoft, n.d.).

3.1.2 AI with Parasoft Jtest and Daikon

With the help of AI, the production of large datasets of tests can be possible. This reduces the cost as the tests are generated automatically. The usage of Daikon and Parasoft Jtest can be used.

In this first, we will define the test-first principle, which is very important for the software development lifecycle. In this the unit tests are generated and are maintained during, before, and after the code has been written. Sometimes, programmers need to do the work of writing the required specifications and assertions, which is an uncommon practice. If this additional work is not done, then it checks only the robustness of the program. If the priori specifications are not given, then it does the white-box test generation. In white-box test generation, the tests are created to cover the entire structure of the program.

The preconditions, when defined, will guide the tools to create inputs to satisfy the given preconditions that inputs are valid. The postconditions that are defined in the specifications are going to have specific test cases for them. If the test inputs are going to violate the postconditions, it means the faults in the code can be detected. An operational violation is a black-box test where the creation and selection of the test don't require any prior conditions. Operational abstraction means it tells how the software is actually supposed to behave in an existing test scenario. In this, operational abstractions are used to provide guidance to the test generation tools. They work on creating test cases that are specifically designed to violate the operational abstraction.

There are also class invariants where it is specified how an object of the class must satisfy the conditions all the time. These sometimes can be treated as pre- and post-conditions for the methods.

For all the general testing of pre and post-class invariants, Jtest is used, but when it comes to operational abstraction, the Daikon tool is used. The results of the Daikon are given to the Jtest, which will generate and execute new tests (Xie & Notkin, 2006).

3.1.3. Benefits

Coverage: The tests that are generated by AI will maintain the consistency of the standard of the testing, which will reduce the errors caused by the humans and oversight. The risks associated with the undetected issues will be reduced. The standards are applied using AI which will increase the test results reliability and helps with software quality assurance.

Scenario Coverage: The test cases are generated in such a way that the edge cases can't be ignored at any cost, which will enhance the coverage of the different kinds of test cases. The different types of scenarios are covered to check the robustness of the software by leaving no testing coverage gaps.

Efficiency: AI will help with the creating and executing the tests for the unit test is much faster than the humans, which will save significant time for the developers. The more critical tasks in the development process will get more attention and focus which helps with the project timeline (Panneerselvam, 2024).

3.2 Integration Testing

Integrated testing with AI is verifying how the units that are integrated into the system work together. Integrated testing checks how the interaction must be made possible so that the system and its functionalities are working properly and as defined (Reselman, 2017).

3.2.1 Katalon Studio

It uses the StudioAssist, which enhances the daily work of testing tasks and workflows. This makes the task of the testers easier by generating the script by using certain keywords that are used in the organization.

Each step can be defined in detail so that the tool uses a pattern to test the integration. The prompts need to be very specific so that the tool doesn't leave any feature that is most important and specific to test that feature. By using this tool, there won't be any back-and-forth checking for the features that are used in the product. The test cases are generated using user stories. Even if the testers have minimal knowledge in testing, this tool helps. them focus on the goal of the workflow that needed to be tested before getting into the specifications.

Katalon is also going to help to maintain the proper documentation of the code so that the effort and time while commenting is reduced. It generates comments for the code so that the person who is reading it can easily understand what does the steps in the code mean (Team, n.d., -a).

By selecting a block of code, the tool also explains what that does. This tool can be used to write test cases for the web, mobile, API, and desktop. The tests are run locally on the tool so that they can be connected to the CI/CD pipeline. Whenever a developer writes the code, then the tests are run automatically (Katalon, n.d.).

The tests are executed in parallel on multiple devices to enhance the execution phase, improve the test coverage, and reduce the delivery cycle of the software (Team, n.d., -b).

3.2.2 Mabl

This tool uses AI and ML so that it can automatically scan the code. By scanning the code, it can define what errors or broken links are present. This is used to write code for the websites or web applications. This is designed to work as a virtual quality assurance engineer.

It is a SaaS application where it has some predefined tests that are most commonly needed for most of the websites or web applications. It completes its required implementation, notes down the result, analyses the results, then it gives detailed information to users and gives details on how the process is automated. Mabl is going to learn how the application is going to perform like the developer and will test the necessary test scenarios and later find the errors (Weiss, 2018).

This helps with end-to-end testing of the code. It uses auto-healing features, which means that the expert systems and probabilistic models will have an automatic process of adapting to the test to do the changes in the attributes, which will reduce the maintainability of test environments. The ML used in the Intelligent Wait tool, which is integrated in Mabl, helps in the reduction of the failures of the tests by using the past performance data of the application. When the test is run, the timing data for each step is collected, and it will automatically tailor the execution of the test to match with how the application is developing (Hughes, 2023b).

Mabl also evaluates how users interact with the elements of the product, and by using those observations, it is going to create test cases so that the manual effort is significantly reduced. It also uses the visual tests. to know if the visual changes of the UI are consistent so that the user experience is good (Cashapona Technologies, 2024).

3.2.3 Benefits

Error detection: It identifies the errors that are present in the interface, data across different components, and the protocols that are used for the communication. The early detection in the mismatching of the components helps with the resolution of the issue, improves the seamless operation.

Scenario Coverage: In integrated testing, the main focus of the AI is to maintain its focus on covering the interactions that are possible, workflows, and the exchange of the data between the components that are integrated. The potential interactions will not be ignored, helps with the development of more reliable systems.

Efficiency: Easily and quickly the issues with the integration of the units of code can be identified and resolved so that the delay in the deployment process can be reduced. The potential risk of the bottlenecks will be checked and solved which helps with the faster and efficient delivery of the software.

3.3 Acceptance Testing:

The tests that have repeated actions performed by the user and cross-checking the performance of the system or the software in accordance with that to retain the required behaviour for that acceptance testing are used. The environment for the test is set up where developers will have a similar kind of view of real production.

Need to have a task tracker that is available in the market. The team needs help from people to create the task description. So that people who don't have much technical skill will have a proper idea of what steps to follow. By categorizing the data, the more highly successful test cases in the acceptance testing can be generated (Rusin, 2023).

3.3.1 BDD with Generative AI

Behaviour-driven development (BDD) is the methodology of the Agile testing process where the developers and quality assurance analysts. In the BDD, Large Language Models (LLMs) are used to generate the test cases. The generative AI creates test cases that are free from the errors of the BDD acceptance evaluation process. The few prompts that are used to generate high accurate by using the in-context learning.

It uses the Gherkin language, which is a semi-structured natural language, which is used to define the criteria of acceptance by using the user stories that are readable by humans when written using keywords such as Given, When, and Then.

When the tests are generated manually, the efficiency and accuracy of the tests is reduced. If high quality of the tests is intended Then the tests must be complied with the rules and best practices of Gherkin. A person must be equipped with experience in the field to create a high quality of BDD tests of acceptance. For the LLMs, generative AI such as GPT-3.5, GPT-4, Llama-2-13B, and PaLM-2 are used. There must be a need for prompt engineering for analyzing and choosing prompts. which are optimal so that the scenarios that are generated are aligned with the rules and best practices so the syntax errors in the Gherkin can be avoided.

BDD uses testing and validation in the early stage. But first the teams are going to create BDD acceptance testing for user stories before going on the in-progress state, which has specifications in the testable format.

In BDD, programs are created separately for each of the LLM models. Each program is executed more than twice so that we can analyse how many zero-shot and few-shot prompts are required, and the code is mainly written in Python. This Python code is curated for each LLM model, and execution is done in Google Colab, and all the codes are available on GitHub.

The first step is reading the descriptions of the user stories. from CSV file. Each description of the user story will have its own prompt and model parameters, and these are given to the request body to the API endpoint model. Rigorous iterations of the user stories are done, and they are stored in BDD acceptance scenarios as feature files.

In the next stage, the feature files that are generated will go through the process of the validation using the Gherkin syntax tool, which is going to catch all the syntax errors and later analyse them.

In BDD, the prompt techniques are very important to create clear and concise guidelines so that LLM can follow a correct path in the task execution. To improve the performance and comprehension of the model, the prompts are important to reduce the ambiguity so that the accurate responses can be created.

If the datasets are fine-tuned, then the instructions that are produced will also be fine-tuned, which will improve the learning capabilities of zero-shot prompts.For the few-shot prompts, the examples must be included in the prompt; this helps with the in-context learning by providing the required guidance for the model to perform better, and also training the models with examples will help with providing minimal instances.

If the best practices are followed by BDD acceptance test generation, then the LLM value, which is provided, will be of good quality. The choice of choosing the best model for the test generation between zero-shot and few-shot depends upon the software development practices that are adhered to by the teams.

Manual validation is eliminated in this process as it takes a long period of time, the resources that are needed for manual testing, and effort. This is eliminated using the Gherkin-lint tool, which is used to identify if there is code where syntax is violated (Karpurapu et al., n.d.).

3.3.2 Benefits

Customer Satisfaction: No matter who the user is, the clear and specific DoD is being built, and then the tests for the acceptance can be used, and then if the developers understood the requirements of the user clearly and accurately, it is known; if that is true, then the rework will be reduced.
Agile: If the acceptance tests are necessary to launch during the deployment stage, developers and testers can easily grasp the errors if there are any in the code; this is a safety feature. The safety and reliability will be enhanced in the software deployment process because of agile development.
Regression testing: In this the acceptance tests are already present, so that the regression testing on the existing code can be done. While developing a product, human factors are very essential, and it is possible that a developer might miss those necessary parts (Rusin, 2023).

3.4 System Testing

System testing has a similar name called black-box testing. and this takes place mainly on the external parts of the system. This takes before software acceptance testing and after integration testing. This mainly deals with the units that have been integrated into the system. So that the user requirements of the system design and behaviour. This mainly focuses on the functional and non-functional parts of the requirements.

3.4.1 OO Model with an AI Planning System

The system that must be tested is done using the UML models. The test objectives are derived by using the UML model and usage of the objectives and the models to generate test cases by just mapping them into a description of the problem for the AI planner.

The functions and interactions are used to define the components, and the component interactions, respectively, and they are present in the conceptual architecture.

Testing against the conceptual architecture involves proper testing interaction between components in it. When testing the architectural component, must check the capability of the other component's relationship. The Class Diagrams and State Diagrams are defined in the Unified Modelling Language (UML) to represent the conceptual architecture of the system that is under test. The statements present in the test objectives at the level, then are mapped into a planner. The planner will create a test plan that will achieve test objectives.

Planners are very important for the software test generation. as it has test cases that are used to satisfy the condition of the purpose. The main objective of the test case is to change the overall system state to achieve the required state of the system. The planner will use the description of the operator, which will describe all the actions that are possible, the effects and preconditions. It has the starting and finishing goals of the system. The relationship between the classes and the information of them are present in the UML diagram. The connections between the classes can be directional and bidirectional. The desired state of the software can be based on the values and links of the objects. These objectives of the test can be defined for each and every class in the UML separately.

The following steps can be used to define the objectives of the test cases for the class:

First, we need to select a class and to define the states of the class so that it can be used as a test objective. There will be a reduction of the class diagram to sub-diagram, which will have classes and relationships that will provide the information of the state of each class. Then the instantiated objects of the class are set and selected. The system configuration is the subset. The states of the objects are determined, and more than one state is used as a test objective. The class-level test objectives are later converted into the system. level, which will become part of the UML model (Scheetz, von Mayrhauser, & France, 1999).

3.4.2 BrowserStack Low Code Test Automation

This has built-in features so that the tests are run automatically without the usage of a single line of code. It is very easy to use, and it has a feature to record the test-run, which captures the actions done by the user, which is done on the screen. This is also going to generate the required test data, which is an essential element and reduces the need to maintain different kinds of sheets for test data. The variables that are present during the execution phase can be used several times by the users and changed by them.

We can generate the test cases by giving a detailed description of the scenario. By selecting the folder that will have already tested cases that are used in the testing process before AI integration. This will eliminate the generation of duplicate test cases and have a consistent writing style. The generated test cases will also be saved in the same folder that is uploaded. Finally, we can use the detailed requirements document, and this will be attached to each test case that is generated either we can give a prompt or a requirement document or both for very comprehensive input (Das, 2024).

3.4.3 Benefits

Non-Functional Verification: It will analyse the performance, usability, and non-functional things so that the application that is developed meets with the user requirements. The product which is developed by using the standards will be more refined for the user needs.

UA Preparation: The creation of the real-world-like scenarios, it prepares the software for the UAT. The scenarios are created which are aligned with the needs of the users, so that the product which is developed is ready for the deployment process.

Early-Stage Bug Detection: The errors can be detected before the deployment is helpful in reducing the cost and time that is required for fixing the issues after release. This helps with the process of faster and smooth development, and also a stable software product (Das, 2024).

4. CONFIGURATION MANAGEMENT

The AI Integration of the Configuration Management, which is used to reshape the paradigms of the IT infrastructure management. The AI integration will be used in the automation of the CMDB. The AI integration will have machine learning, natural language processing (NLP) and also predictive analytics (Chi, 2024).

4.1 Component Identification

The documentation and development of a systematic approach of the configuration items of the software and hardware components in the configuration management. There must be consistency, tracking, and change. management of the components in the lifecycle of the software system. The changes, modifications, and deletions of the changes in the configuration items. One of the main parts of the configuration Management is the identification of the component. There will be different attributes that are present for each component, such as type of component, status, unique identifier, and description and the relationships that exist among the components.

4.1.1 DigiSalt

The usage of machine learning will help with the approach to tackle the problem of component identification. DigiSalt has come up with the solution where there were problems that were faced by their clients, so a model has been created to difference between CIs and non-CIs. After the data has been collected, the parameters have been fed into the model so that the model can be trained to gain the accurate information about the components. The model was available to easily differentiate between the CIs, which has helped with the identification of the components. The model will always be evaluated by a human expert so that the accuracy of the prediction will always be high. While the classification of the CIs and their documentation has been done so that it can be searched through and answered the required CIs. The components can be identified easily by using the keyword. The model summarizes the answers by reviewing the different documents that have been used in the process to gain the information about the components (Digitalsalt, 2023).

4.1.2 Black Duck

The component scanning that is available in the Black Duck that is used for the functionality scanning, which is automated, so that the components that are available in the software project can be determined. The identification and organizing of the components help the organizations with the management. This will help the users to scan the components that are available on their physical assets.

This feature of the tool is used to identify the following:

The files that have not been modified the first time they have been released.
The files that have been gone through some kind of changes, such as renaming of the file.
The files that have been modified or recompiled after the release of the component.
The classification of the component is based on the following:
Exact: The extraction of the exact files that have been matched with the component.

Dependency of the files: The match will be identified by using the dependency of the files.
Modification of the files: The component that has been present in the database of the Black Buck, there is a fuzzy match where some files are being modified.

If the component is matched with the structure of the directory, but there are components that are shared with the structure. The tool may provide a solution as there are similarities with the scanned component;and if there is a match by OSS component, and if some of the files that have been added, deleted, or modified. The match has been done to the last version of the component that has been available in the tool's database (Black Duck Documentation Portal, n.d.).

4.2 Controlling Versions

Version control is a very important part of the software. Configuration Management, which will help with the automation of the database and uniqueness for the names of the files (Ren, Xing, Quan, & Zhao, 2010).

This is the process for the management and tracking of the changes that have been done to a file or a set of files. It is also used to know the history of the code, compare the different versions of the code, return to previous versions, and easily collaborate with other developers. The VC systems play an important role in software building. This helps the team's work to be organized as they work on types of releases. With the help of the VC systems, the files of the same project will be on the same server so that the files can be pushed when the work is completed (LinkedIn community, 2023, December 15).

In Gitflow, the process has been developed with the concepts of two branches, the master and the develop branches. The master will have the code or software that is ready for the development while the developer has the continuous code that is under development.

In the field of DevOps, the concept of version control plays an important role. The evolution of AI and ML has helped in the version control of the software systems. AI helps with prediction of the conflict resolution, code reviews automation and also with branching of the code.

If there are conflicts that arise, they can be merged and will give solutions that are suitable for the problems; this will reduce the manual work and problems that are related to coding.AI will help with the establishment of the optimal junction, and fusion points, the branching and merging processes are made easier. With the help of AI, the previously stored data will be assessed of the same project so that the workflow can be adjusted, which would be relied upon for the configurations and specifics of the team.

This improves the visibility throughout the whole development lifecycle because of the integration of the version control with the DevOps practice. The members of the team will have an idea of who, why, when, and where the modifications have been done so that there will be sense of accountability in bigger projects. The future of the workflow models of the version control systems. The decentralization of the version control systems is becoming very popular; this is mainly not controlled by one particular server. The tool allows for the interactions between the peers and improves collaboration.

The integration of the tools with the software development processes such as CI/CD systems. The devices that are used for tracking the issues, the cloud-based programming environments. The version control tools will become more powerful and responsive when AI is integrated. AI will use the preferences so that they can be performed in the personal and customized environment. The future versioning systems will help effectively with the various versioning and the management of artifacts for graphics, data models and documents that will reflect the internal characteristics of the software initiatives that are contemporary (Devineni, 2020).

4.3 Control the Situation

The change management, or change control, is a core part of the software configuration management that helps set the baselines for the product, manage the lifecycle of the product, and also control and release the products.

The change that happens must have a strict process to follow. and the management, which is looking into process, must also have stringent rules. The product baselines and the release. A baseline will be created with the change in the product. lifecycle. The change is taking place as the product needs to fit the quality. standards for each software version and the elements that are associated with it. The change control guidelines and the quality standards will be established (Xing, 2010).

The change control process is a set of guidelines that help with the process of evaluating, approving, implementing, and verifying the changes that have been done to the software components. The changes must be consistent, trackable, and must be aligned with the requirements of the project. This also reduces the risk because of the errors and inconsistencies related to the software. This has several steps, such as request, analysis, approval, implementation, verification, and closure (LinkedIn community, 2023, September 26).

The involvement of the stakeholders is important. The perspectives, expectations, and preferences will be different for the configuration changes. The feedback, concerns, and telling stakeholders about the status of the component change process is important. This will help gain cooperation and support from stakeholders (LinkedIn Community, 2024, January 3).

The changes that are done to one component may have changes done to other components that have been related with that. The AI integration has been integrated in this process to manage the complexity of the changes that have been done. There is method developed so that the changes in the components can be predicted. The challenges which are addressed using the support of the system are flexibility because of the complex nature of the change in the component, and decisions that are need to be made (Burggräf, Wagner, Saßmannshausen, Weißer, & Radisic-Aberger, 2024).

5. PLAN FOR ASSURANCE OF SOFTWARE QUALITY

5.1 Make a Strategy and Document it

The computer-aided software engineering (CASE), which is used to automatically analyse the system and design processes. This is also used in organization-wide planning and modelling the data and processes so that certain frameworks that are suitable for the organization can fit in its lifecycles of the projects.

The usage of the software quality Assurance with the CASE will improve the functional performance. The code generator and methodologies that are used for the development are used in the CASE will save the creation time, accuracy, and quality of the CASE tool. An AI assisted decision tool is used to support the CASE tool, which is called as ADCASE so the goal can be achieved. The SQA framework is integrated into the CASE tool so that the SQA process can be managed.

The Intelligent Systems are built by using the AI technologies that can easily perform the reasoning and decision making. Based on the information that is available in the AI technology, the solutions for the problems can be obtained as the knowledge required is taken from the human who is expert in this field.

The Integrated CASE (I-CASE) tool has all the software development aspects; this tool will automatically analyse the system, design, and the development. The code generator integration creates the programs that can be used for the implementation of the systems. This tool also has a database for information and different methodologies in the repository so that the software can be developed to meet the validation for the further process.

In the diagrams, the ones that have been drawn by the user are used for the analysis, design, and planning, which will be done on the workstation screen. This will gather the information of the objects that are present in the diagram and what kind of relationships exist between them so that the complete information will be available for the strategy. The information that is specific to that kind of part of the software project will be stored in the central repository of that workstation so that it can be shared easily amongst the developers, analysts, and designers. The coordinated information will be stored in the central repository. so that work consistency can be maintained by the analysts and designers.

The subsystems architecture, which is the knowledge base will have all the systems implementation plans, which is a part of ADCASE, and it has different information about what our business goals, strategies, and models that will be used in the operation of the organization, structures, and codes for programming, design requirements for the system.

The strategy selector will compare the problem and available strategies that are present in the library, the tool will quickly analyse the reasoning behind the selection. After The analysis has been done. the library will store the information and inference engine will automatically implement the correct module so that rules and algorithms can be implemented. To perform certain processes, this tool provides the required documentation. and reports if needed for manual evaluation. This will help with improvements. which can be done in later stages and SQA process management.

The ADCASE will do the process for the reasoning so that it will reach the required conclusion for the given problem. The person who is using the ADCASE can request the logical path to reach the conclusion. The tool can be used to define the illustrations for the statistical data, which is used for the SQA processes. The system used has a user-friendly interface, which will help with the assistance of the SQA tool so the productivity can be improved. The already defined SQA knowledge will be added to the CASE repository for the process of the validation and verification (Chou, 1994).

5.2 Get Approval From Upper Management

Zapier with Monday integration creates automated workflows, which are known as Zaps, which are used for the team.

After sending messages using Slack or email so that important information can be reached by the team through the notification features. and important actions can be taken after the notification can be seen is a tedious task and replying to the message too. The Zaps makes it easier for the team to stay updated about the project details and updates. The checkboxes can be used to check the status of the event added and to whom the event or task has been assigned to.

The Monday can be used to connect with the spreadsheets as they are the source of information that is correct so that everyone working on that project is on the same level of understanding. Depending upon the department, the tool used by them to manage the work will be different. The easier way to find the information through the sheets for reporting and data analysis is achieved.

To important information not to get lost, the syncing between the spreadsheet, and Monday with the help of Zap will reduce it. The task of collecting the data from the sources available without the manual work is possible. The team's workflow and the communication can be automated. They can either automate Monday.com or the tasks that are done on a daily basis. The passing of the information from one tool to another can be done by Zap (Replogle, 2024).

Slack with Monday integration will be able to receive notifications whenever there are changes in the tasks that are assigned in the team. The tasks will be created directly by using the messages with the help of AI. The deadlines for the tasks will be notified within the channels, and the discussion that is done for the project will be available in one place. The members of the team can separately mention that specific team member or the channel, which will help with improving the communication. The already defined trigger in Monday.com will be assigned a specific action that will happen in Slack. We can add different workflows for the department so that they can be changed according to the needs of the team (Team, 2024).

5.3 Secure Approval From Upper Management

Jira is the most common tool that used, which is an Agile has now been integrated with Atlassian Intelligence (AI) so the daily tasks can easily be sped up, and the customization of the features is available for the needs of the organization.

Jira's generative AI will help to generate and update the user stories and details of the tasks by saving time, and proper project documentation is maintained. AI helps with effective communication among the team members so that they are clear about the team updates.

By using the AI editor, the content can be improved across the Jira. The AI will be used to monitor and standardize the process so that there is alignment between the Agile teams.AI prompts can be used to refine the user stories so the efficiency of the project management will be enhanced. Because of this, the software projects will be done quickly, and collaboration will be increased.

This will also automate the tasks and streamline the workflow. If there are tasks of high priority, it will be automatically set up to the designated person who has been saved in the database of the organization (Cheung, 2024).

The Jira Service Management can be used in the workflows by using the Insight asset and configuration management feature so that the management of the organization's structure and roles can be automated by using the Jira issue sent to that specific approver depending upon the information provided by the requestor or by the information used in the issue's fields.

If there is a requirement of the new hardware or software, then the company managers will look into the budget of it. If they have the budget, they are going to allocate the required asset, but instead of doing this manually, Jira will automatically set the approver as the reporter's manager. Every detail of the information regarding the assets will be stored in Jira for usage in the future (Grace, 2024), (Nicolaou & Axelsdottir, 2021).

5.4 Prepare for the SQA's Plans Execution

AI assurance will provide the necessary tools so that the AI adoption into the software, applications, or hardware is possible. Data, algorithms, and domain-based factors will change over time, and the ability of the systems to provide the needed outcomes will change. The assurance will be gained from the planned and systematic performances that will be done at every stage of the lifecycle so that the intelligent systems are generating the required outcomes, which are data-driven, valid, value- and data-verified. When the plans are deployed, there are a lot of things that are unresolved in the given specific domain, and they can be data incompleteness and lack of domain information (Freeman, Rahman, & Batarseh, 2021).

The defect-predicting AI models will help with the prediction of the defects and also to explain the detected defects. The model will help with the resource planning with the limited ones that are required for the risky files. The software developers focus will be more on the files that are detected to be risky ones. This will also provide insights for the managers to come up with more improvement plans so that the defects can be ignored or can be tackled with the plans.

The SQA Planner is going to provide guidance on four types and the threshold the risk holds in the rule-based explanation for the defect models predictions. The planner will provide in-depth knowledge for the QA manager even if he has minimal knowledge in the field of software projects. The AI-powered SQA Planner will make decisions based on the data when the plans for the SQA are being made.

The rule-based explanations that are provided by the SQA Planner are used to help the developers know the reasoning behind the predictions, and sometimes they are not easily understood by them, and because of this there might be delays in taking the required actions. In the later stages, the proof of concept has been developed where the rules are translated into the actions that must be taken in user-friendly explanations (Rajapaksha, Tantithamthavorn, Jiarpakdee, Bergmeir, Grundy, & Buntine, 2022).

In this phase of testing, there must be analysis of the data and assessments. of feasibility. The analyses that are provided must have the information about the knowledge gaps, which depend upon the planning of the required strategies and time that will be specifically taken for the rework that one must do to test the program by relying on the information that is being generated at each testing phase (Freeman, Rahman, & Batarseh, 2021).

6. QUALITY ASSURANCE MODELS

Software Quality Assurance (SQA) has activities in the software development lifecycle that are used repeatedly so the quality of the software can be verified and tested.

The SQA will analyse the positive effect of the AI models quantitatively so that the positive impact of adding QA in the early phases is clear. The most basic step to follow to enhance the software process is SQA by doing the most necessary software review in the early phases of the development.

The quality assurance (QA) takes a lot of effort and time. The bugs that are ignored in the early phases of the development will be revealed in the later stages, which will delay the software delivery process, and this will automatically increase the effort and time at the end. To avoid all the above problems, we must improve the way we do the QA process, and also the part of the QA team must be able to comprehend what is useful to do in the QA process (Nakahara, Monden, & Yücel, 2021).

SCM has criteria that have to be fulfilled that have several standards like ISO-9000 and Software Capability Maturity (Midha, 1997).

6.1 CMMI (Capability Maturity Model Integration)

The CMMI framework I used to set the benchmark for the quality of the software, product, and service developments. Cognizant has used Gen AI to strengthen the deployment of the CMMI model. CMMI is the base framework that is used in the companies so that they can analyse, develop, and improve the important capabilities that will enhance the performance of any of the products, services, or software.

To implement the protocols at Cognizant, the usage of Gen AI is done, where the teams can use historical knowledge of the company; the protocol's development can be done by automation so that the process for monitoring and controlling the progress of the project will be easier.

The capabilities, practice areas, and interaction points of the CMMI V3.0 AI model:

In the process of ensuring the quality, they can be used in the development and management of the requirements, and these can be verified by the peers.

In the process of development and engineering of the products, they can be used as technical solutions and can be used in product integration and verification.

In implementation support, they help with the analysis and resolutions of the causalities and also decision analysis and resolution, which is implemented in the configuration management.

In managing the business resilience, the workforce can be integrated into risk and opportunity management, continuity, and organizational training, which is implemented in monitoring and control and incident management and helps with the enablement of virtual work.

In the improvement process, the sustaining habit and persistence, along with enhancing the performance, can be used in governance and process management, along with the development of the process asset; it helps with implementing the infrastructure and managing and measuring the performance (Cognizant, n.d.).

6.2 ISO 9000 Certification

The ISO stands for International Standard for Quality Management. The key components of the framework are customer focus and satisfaction, which can be achieved using the continuous improvement, leadership, process approach. The efficiency is achieved as they are producing the products and services of high quality. By implementing the standard, it is easier for marketing and gaining the potential customers. As the processes that are established are thoroughly reviewed and have been improved, they will help with the cost reduction. The proper documentation of the quality objectives and communicating them will increase the visibility of the organization (Edureka higherEd, 2024).

AI cannot be used in this process as this is a certification. This sets the guidelines for the quality of the system that needs to be developed, and this is a contract that exists between the independent parties. Quality system means that different activities are related to the products or services. It addresses operational and organizational capabilities that have reporting and responsibilities that must exist in the organization (GeeksforGeeks, 2020).

The ISO 9000 or 9001 is the quality management standard (Wang & Tsai, 2009).By the usage of the ISO 9000, we can significantly enhance the software requirements elicitation in the companies. This will let us know how and what must be done to maintain the quality. The quality strategies depend upon the business rules, principles, and key practices that are used in the organizations.

The product is an outcome of the activity or the process. The one or more are the abstract classes are the part of the process: the hardware components can be the equipment, objects or parts of the same products, the software components can be the documents, methods or the information, projects.

The main parts of the expressions are the quality system, which are the organizational structure, processes, and the responsibilities that are used in the quality management. The manual for the quality is used, which is a document that will have all the policies and the description of the quality that is required.

The policy of the quality will provide the directions and the intentions for the organization, which is used for the upper management (Cysneiros, de Macedo-Soares, & do Prado Leite, 1999).

6.3 CMM (Construction Material Management)

It is an important part of supply chain management that is used to build projects that will become successful and profitable. This has the importance of planning and implementing the supply chains such that the objectives are met for the delivery of the projects. The material management helps with the activities that are linked with materials, which are a crucial part of the business function that will have equipment and machinery. CMM uses the production and inventory for the controlling and planning of the materials that are required so that the project schedules are met (Erickson, 2023).

The AI helps with the optimization of the materials in the construction management; the tool will calculate the area that is under construction and give how the material is performing, and the data will be analysed, and the tool will recommend the top priority materials that are suitable for the applications that are required. The AI will help with the analysis of the different patterns, which will suggest what is the best time to replace or maintain them. The maintenance of the equipment will avoid the expensive repairs and the maintenance (Katariya, 2024).

The AI will take into account factors like costs, materials, rules, and the design possibilities. This will help the architects and engineers so that they can create much more efficient and innovative designs that will meet the goals of the project (M, 2024).

The AI tool, such as ProCore, will help with taking control of the materials by using the Procore Resource Management. By registering the equipment, which has been owned, rented, and managed, tracking the location, usage, and safety by using the integrations of telematics. The future needs can be forecasted, and they can be managed efficiently. The tools will help with the scheduling of the resources or materials that are present in the organization with labour so that workflows will be simplified (Procore, n.d.).

6.4 PCMM (Personal Computer Management Model)

The PCMM comes under IT asset management and PC lifecycle management. The AI, especially with The help of ML will enhance the decision-making (Immenkötter, 2024).The ML and NNs approaches are used by evaluating the historical data that is present for the assets in the company. The monetary value depends upon the asset that has been used. We need to set up the KPIs so that the Asset management performance is related to the business goals and strategies. We need to develop a model by taking up the KPIs. The key factor identification is done using the Principal Component Analysis (PCA) and to forecast KPIs ML model approaches are used. After training of the ML models, NN is used to future value prediction is done using the previous or current values. AI advanced models are used for the supply chain management in the organization. The asset maintenance is the most important phase in the asset lifecycle (Mattioli, Perico, & Robic, 2020).

The PCs are strategic assets as they are the productivity tool. The PCs must go through a refresh cycle every two to four years, which will reduce the ownership cost. The decommissioning of the systems must be done if they don't deliver the required performance and security. The requirements for the PCs are always more when compared with the other technologies. The PCs will have to be high-end to support the latest updates of the operating system (Intel, n.d.).

7. CONCLUSION

The integration of artificial intelligence into the software assurance life cycle has ushered in a new era of software development, testing, and maintenance with minimized human error, maximum test speed, and enhanced reliability and scalability through predictive analysis, automation, and intelligent decision-making. From unit testing to configuration management, these and other solutions indicate how AI can treat long-standing problems while keeping up with agile and DevOps, two contemporary development methodologies. It should also be mentioned that, as AI technologies continue to expand, their use in quality assurance will become imperative for a firm to publish a robust, efficient, user-centric solution at the optimal time.

REFERENCES

Automation, Q. A. (2024, August 9). Understanding AI-based software testing & quality assurance. Medium. https://medium.com/@dmautomationqa/understanding-ai-based-software-testing-quality-assurance-a81a77d6611d

Black Duck Documentation Portal. (n.d.). https://documentation.blackduck.com/bundle/bd-hub/page/ComponentDiscovery/Component_scanning_overview.html

Burggräf, P., Wagner, J., Saßmannshausen, T., Weißer, T., & Radisic-Aberger, O. (2024). AI-artifacts in engineering change management – A systematic literature review. *Research in Engineering Design, 35*(2), 215–237. DOI: 10.1007/s00163-023-00430-6

Cashapona Technologies. (2024, November 18). Mabl: A modern approach to test automation in the AI world. LinkedIn. https://www.linkedin.com/pulse/mabl-modern-approach-test-automation-qsfcc/

Cheung, C. (2024, October 1). Get out of tickets and into your work faster with AI in Jira - Work Life by Atlassian. Work Life by Atlassian. https://www.atlassian.com/blog/artificial-intelligence/ai-jira-issues#:~:text=The%20AI%2Ddriven%20tools%20in,and%20improve%20project%20communication%20efficiency

Chi, Y. (2024). Exploring the transformative benefits of integrating artificial intelligence into configuration management database (CMDB). *International Journal of Management IT and Engineering, 14*, 100–106.

Chou, D. C. (1994). Software quality assurance in CASE tools: Creating an AI-enhanced CASE tool. *Information Systems Management, 11*(2), 56–61. DOI: 10.1080/10580539408964637

Cognizant. (n.d.). Elevating excellence: Integrating generative AI into CMMI. https://www.cognizant.com/en_us/services/documents/elevating-excellence-integrating-generative-ai-into-cmmi.pdf

Cysneiros, L. M., de Macedo-Soares, T. D. L. A., & do Prado Leite, J. C. S. (1999). Using ISO 9000 to elicit business rules. In *Proceedings of the 4th IEEE International Software Engineering Standards Symposium and Forum (ISESS'99)* (pp. 88–98). Curitiba, Brazil. https://doi.org/DOI: 10.1109/SESS.1999.766582

Das, S. (2024, October 7). What is system testing? (Examples, use cases, types). BrowserStack. https://www.browserstack.com/guide/what-is-system-testing#:~:text=System%20testing%20is%20a%20critical,design%2C%20execution%2C%20and%20closure

Devineni, S. K. (2020). Version control systems (VCS) the pillars of modern software development: Analyzing the past, present, and anticipating future trends. [IJSR]. *International Journal of Science and Research (Raipur, India), 9*(12), 1816–1829. DOI: 10.21275/SR24127210817

Digitalsalt. (2023, October 6). The power of AI in streamlining configuration item identification. LinkedIn. https://www.linkedin.com/pulse/power-ai-streamlining-configuration-item-identification/

Edureka higherEd. (2024, September 25). Models of quality assurance: Definition, meaning & frameworks. Edureka. https://www.edureka.co/blog/models-of-quality-assurance/#:~:text=Models%20of%20quality%20assurance%20are,is%20released%20into%20the%20marketplace

Erickson, C. (2023, May 8). What is construction materials management? StructShare. https://structshare.com/blog/what-is-construction-materials-management

Freeman, L., Rahman, A., & Batarseh, F. A. (2021). Enabling artificial intelligence adoption through assurance. *Social Sciences (Basel, Switzerland), 10*(9), 322. DOI: 10.3390/socsci10090322

Freeman, L., Rahman, A., & Batarseh, F. A. (2021). Enabling artificial intelligence adoption through assurance. *Social Sciences (Basel, Switzerland), 10*(9), 322. DOI: 10.3390/socsci10090322

GeeksforGeeks. (2020, November 23). ISO 9000 certification in software engineering. GeeksforGeeks. https://www.geeksforgeeks.org/iso-9000-certification-in-software-engineering/

Grace, F. (2024, May 2). New Atlassian Intelligence features are available in Jira! Atlassian Community. https://community.atlassian.com/t5/Jira-articles/New-Atlassian-Intelligence-features-are-available-in-Jira/ba-p/2687430

Gupta, A. (2024, May 4). Unleashing the power of AI in Selenium with Java. Medium. https://medium.com/@anuj.gupta618/unleashing-the-power-of-ai-in-selenium-with-java-b9283a5e01db

Hughes, B. (2023b, July 6). How real-world development teams are using AI to improve software testing. Mabl. https://www.mabl.com/blog/how-real-world-development-teams-are-using-ai-to-improve-software-testing

IEEE 15th International Conference of System of Systems Engineering (SoSE) (pp. 151–156). Budapest, Hungary.DOI: 10.1109/SoSE50414.2020.9130505

Immenkötter, P. (2024). How can artificial intelligence transform asset management? *The Economists' Voice, 21*(2), 363–370. Advance online publication. DOI: 10.1515/ev-2024-0055

Intel. (n.d.). PC lifecycle management: Boosting productivity and IT efficiency. Retrieved from https://www.intel.la/content/dam/www/public/us/en/documents/best-practices/pc-lifecycle-management.pdf

Karpurapu, S., Myneni, S., Nettur, U., Gajja, L. S., Burke, D., Stiehm, T., & Payne, J. (2024). Comprehensive evaluation and insights into the use of large language models in the automation of behavior-driven development acceptance test formulation. *IEEE Access : Practical Innovations, Open Solutions, 12*, 58715–58721. DOI: 10.1109/ACCESS.2024.3391815

Katariya, J. (2024, November 4). AI in construction: Use cases, benefits, and examples. Moon Technolabs.https://www.moontechnolabs.com/blog/ai-in-construction/#:~:text=and%20environmental%20impact.-,Utilizing%20AI%20for%20Construction%20Material%20Optimization,to%20effective%20sustainable%20building%20practices

Lathwal, A. (2019). A literature review on automation testing using Selenium+Sikuli. *International Journal of Distributed Artificial Intelligence, 11*(2), 35–40. DOI: 10.4018/IJDAI.2019070104

LinkedIn Community. (2024, January 3). What are the best ways to ensure configuration changes are approved? LinkedIn. https://www.linkedin.com/advice/3/what-best-ways-ensure-configuration-changes-7i6qf

LinkedIn community. (2023, December 15). What is the difference between version control and configuration management? LinkedIn. https://www.linkedin.com/advice/3/what-difference-between-version-control

LinkedIn community. (2023, September 26). What are the most effective ways to manage software configuration and change control? LinkedIn. https://www.linkedin.com/advice/0/what-most-effective-ways-manage-software-configuration

M, P. (2024, December 2). How to use AI in construction (Use cases and tools). ClickUp.https://clickup.com/blog/how-to-use-ai-in-construction/#:~:text=from%20hazardous%20environments.-,2.,make%20more%20informed%20design%20decisions

Mattioli, J., Perico, P., & Robic, P.-O. (2020). Artificial intelligence-based asset management. In *Proceedings of the 2020*

Midha, A. K. (1997). Software configuration management for the 21st century. *Bell Labs Technical Journal, 2*(1), 154–165. DOI: 10.1002/bltj.2039

Nakahara, H., Monden, A., & Yücel, Z. (2021). A simulation model of software quality assurance in the software lifecycle. In *Proceedings of the 2021 IEEE/ACIS 22nd International Conference on Software Engineering, Artificial Intelligence, Networking, and Parallel/Distributed Computing (SNPD)* (pp. 236–241). Taichung, Taiwan.DOI: 10.1109/SNPD51163.2021.9704927

Nicolaou, C., & Axelsdottir, S. (2021, May 18). Automate approval workflows in Jira Service Management with Insight –Work Life by Atlassian. Work Life by Atlassian. https://www.atlassian.com/blog/it-teams/automate-approval-workflows-in-jira

Ouaarous, R., Mezrioui, A., & Hilal, I. (2024). On using artificial intelligence in software quality assurance: A state of the art.https://www.researchgate.net/publication/386573500_On_Using_Artificial_Intelligence_in_Software_Quality_Assurance_A_State_of_the_Art

Panneerselvam, S. (2024, July 14). The rise of generative AI in unit testing: A double-edged sword. Medium. https://medium.com/@sugumar.p/the-rise-of-generative-ai-in-unit-testing-a-double-edged-sword-ff7b15c15272

Parasoft. (n.d.). Selenic AI for improved Selenium web testing. Parasoft. https://www.parasoft.com/products/parasoft-selenic/enhanced-selenium-testing/

Rajapaksha, D., Tantithamthavorn, C., Jiarpakdee, J., Bergmeir, C., Grundy, J., & Buntine, W. (2022). SQAPlanner: Generating data-informed software quality improvement plans. *IEEE Transactions on Software Engineering, 48*(8), 2814–2835. DOI: 10.1109/TSE.2021.3070559

Ren, Y., Xing, T., Quan, Q., & Zhao, Y. (2010). Software configuration management of version control study based on baseline. In *Proceedings of the 2010 3rd International Conference on Information Management, Innovation Management and Industrial Engineering* (pp. 118–121). Kunming, China. https://doi.org/DOI: 10.1109/ICIII.2010.506

Replogle, N. (2024, June 14). Use Zapier's Monday integration to streamline your work. Zapier. https://zapier.com/blog/automate-monday/

Reselman, B. (2017, December 7). The fundamentals of integration testing. Mabl. https://www.mabl.com/blog/the-fundamentals-of-integration-testing

Rusin, S. (2023, November 23). A comprehensive guide to AI-driven acceptance testing. HackerNoon. https://hackernoon.com/a-comprehensive-guide-to-ai-driven-acceptance-testing

Scheetz, M., von Mayrhauser, A., & France, R. (1999). Generating test cases from an OO model with an AI planning system. In Proceedings 10th International Symposium on Software Reliability Engineering (Cat. No.PR00443), 250-259. DOI: 10.1109/ISSRE.1999.809330

Software Quality Assurance vs Software Quality Plan. (n.d.). *Software Engineering Stack Exchange.* https://softwareengineering.stackexchange.com/questions/350317/software-quality-assurance-vs-software-quality-plan

Team, C. (2024, November 20). How to set up Monday.com and Slack integration. ClearFeed. https://clearfeed.ai/blogs/mondaycom-slack-integration-guide

Team, K. (n.d.). Enhancing test automation with Katalon StudioAssist: Empowering testers for success. Katalon. https://katalon.com/resources-center/blog/katalon-studioassist-improve-test-automation

Team, K. (n.d.). What is automation testing? Ultimate guide & best practices. Katalon. https://katalon.com/resources-center/blog/what-is-automation-testing

Wang, C.-H., & Tsai, D.-R. (2009). Integrated installing ISO 9000 and ISO 27000 management systems on an organization. In *Proceedings of the 43rd Annual 2009 International Carnahan Conference on Security Technology* (pp. 265–267). Zurich, Switzerland. https://doi.org/DOI: 10.1109/CCST.2009.5335527

Weiss, T. R. (2018, March 9). AI-based automated code testing vendor Mabl launches public beta. Windows IT Pro (Online). https://www.proquest.com/docview/2012173530?sourcetype=Magazines

Xie, T., & Notkin, D. (2006). Tool-assisted unit-test generation and selection based on operational abstractions. *Automated Software Engineering, 13*(3), 345–371. DOI: 10.1007/s10851-006-8530-6

Xing, T. (2010). Software configuration management of change control study based on baseline. In *Proceedings of the 2010 International Conference on Intelligent Control and Information Processing* (pp. 93–96). Dalian, China. DOI: 10.1109/ICICIP.2010.5565288

Chapter 4
Harnessing AI From Code Reusability to Business Requirement Translation

Vaishnavi Ghaatki
https://orcid.org/0000-0002-5432-9990
Illinois Institute of Technology, Chicago, USA

ABSTRACT

Artificial intelligence (AI) has transformed the fast-developing industry of software development, simplifying different procedures and increasing efficiency. This chapter investigates two crucial areas in which AI may dramatically affect software engineering. First, we examine how AI-powered tools may assist developers in finding the best libraries and reusable code fragments. By leveraging machine learning algorithms, Data mining techniques, Domain analysis, and natural language processing, AI can filter through vast repositories to suggest optimal libraries, enabling developers to focus on inventiveness. Second, we'll glance at how AI may help translate business demands into technical specifications. AI-powered solutions, using dominant language models, NLPs, ML and tensor based approaches, may bridge this gap by turning business needs into accurate, technical specifications. This chapter discusses the benefits of AI, focusing on real-world applications and future developments that have the potential to transform software development techniques.

INTRODUCTION

Over recent years, the promise of enhanced productivity and creativity from generative artificial intelligence (AI), such as large language models (LLMs), has swept the globe. This storm particularly impacts developers and academics engaged in automated software engineering. The quick shift observed at software engineering conferences gives one data point for determining the amount of enthusiasm (and anxiety) surrounding the changes that the use of LLMs indicates. Within six months, the promise of enhanced productivity and creativity from generative artificial intelligence (AI), such as large language models (LLMs), had swept the globe. This storm is especially felt by developers and researchers in automated software engineering (Ozkaya, 2023). AI, business intelligence, and machine learning according to Wangoo (2018) are used to encourage automated software reuse in software design and development.

DOI: 10.4018/979-8-3693-8407-7.ch004

Business intelligence tools are used to intelligently identify code that will be reused in applications and components. A survey of several AI methodologies in the software reuse field of software engineering is provided, with an emphasis on automated software reuse and the identification of potential research prospects by choosing potential libraries and translating business to technical requirements.

There still exist challenges concerning the shift to this new emerging and booming technology as individuals, teams, and organizations participating in software development have the challenge of defining their expectations for generative AI and shifting to AI-based solutions. This cannot and should not be an experimental approach driven by fear of losing out. What problems will AI-based tools solve that traditional software development tools and techniques cannot? What would the cost of moving to these generative AI tools be, especially because they increasingly rely on foundation models, in which a model trained on a large amount of unlabelled data may be adapted to a range of applications? We need to be reminded more than ever before that, despite the availability of possibly enhanced tools, it will be people who utilize and guide these technologies in their intended purpose (Ozkaya, 2023).

This chapter examines and explains the importance of AI in software development with various cross-streaming areas concerning code reusability, choosing appropriate software libraries, and translating business requirements to technical requirements. Alongside, we will also see how AI can be incorporated and used within these domains through different approaches.

LITERATURE REVIEW

According to Wangoo (2018) three AI techniques: data mining, machine learning, and neural networks, which are their particular value in the broad area of software engineering, where software reuse is an essential problem. Their research highlights the most essential methodologies that are applicable to all elements of software engineering, with software reuse acting as a focus for boosting software intelligence in enterprises. The software engineering platform makes use of neural network techniques such as artificial neural networks, multilayer perceptrons, neuro fuzzy, and so on. Neural networks were used to identify and search for reusable components. Parallel processing is utilized in component-based software to increase software quality and efficiency, and neural networks are being investigated to further this goal.

Mili et al. (1995) examined the impact of these techniques on software development organization, control, and methods, and proposed economic models for analysis. Software reuse benefits from techniques and technologies that can Create more reusable software and find, assess, and customize reusable software, which is crucial for the building blocks method. They address both sets of concerns, with an emphasis on application generators and 00 development for the first and comprehensive treatment of retrieval mechanisms for software components, component composition (or bottom-up design), and transformational systems for the second.

The aging-resilient software reusability prediction model for object-oriented Web of Service (WoS) platforms is one another approach. This work uses multilevel optimization to create a unique reusability prediction model. Considering Six CK measures (WMC, CBO, DIT, LCOM, NOC, and RFC) were derived from 100 WoS software to assess aging proneness, based on coupling, cohesiveness, and complexity. The collected CK measurements are normalized using min-max to reduce data imbalance and prevent saturation during learning. Using 10-fold cross-validation with outlier detection improves data quality for feature extraction. To avoid computing cost, the RSA technique is used. The SoftAudit tool assesses reusability for each class, whereas binary ULR estimates determine reuse proneness thresholds (Padhy et al., 2017)

Software libraries are critical to the operation, efficiency, and maintainability of software applications. As developers increasingly rely on Large Language Models (LLMs) to better their development processes, the effectiveness of these models in providing relevant libraries becomes crucial yet remains mostly unknown. Latendresse, J(2024) assessed the effectiveness of ChatGPT as a software librarian and identified areas for improvement. They conducted an empirical study in which GPT-3.5 Turbo produced Python code for 10,000 Stack Overflow requests. According to Latendresse, J(2024) findings, ChatGPT uses third-party libraries about 10% more than human developers, favoring commonly used and well-established options. However, 14.2% of the suggested libraries had restrictive copyleft licenses, which ChatGPT did not explicitly state. Furthermore, 6.5% of the libraries did not work properly out of the box, which might confuse developers and waste time. While ChatGPT is a valuable software library, it may be improved by providing more detailed information about maintainability metrics and licenses. Before integrating LLM-generated code into their applications, developers should follow stringent dependency management guidelines and double-check library licenses.

Although software reuse offers clear benefits for programmer efficiency and code reliability, it is not widely used. One of the reasons for reuse's limited effectiveness is a lack of software libraries that make it easier to locate and understand reused components. Maarek et al. (1991) describe a technique for automatically creating large software libraries, which encourages software reuse by aiding users in selecting the most relevant components for their requirements. Information retrieval techniques are used to automatically assemble software libraries from a collection of disordered components. An experiment was conducted to evaluate the retrieval efficacy of GURU with INFOEXPLORER, a hypertext library system for AIX 3 operating on the IBM RISC System/6000 series. They used the typical assessment technique in information retrieval, based on recall and accuracy measures, and determined that our system performs 15% better on a random test set while costing much less to develop than INFOEXPLORER.

Saied et al. (2018) provided a novel method for automatically detecting third-party library usage patterns, which are collections of libraries that developers regularly use together. We employ a hierarchical clustering approach to arrange software libraries depending on external client use. To evaluate our method, we mined a massive set of over 6000 notable libraries from the Maven Central Repository and examined their utilization by over 38,000 client systems on GitHub. Our findings show that our technique can detect the great majority (77%) of very consistent and coherent library usage patterns across a wide range of client systems.

A qualitative comparison of requirements-gathering methods based on Artificial Intelligence (AI) and requirements-management technologies is offered for sustainable cities. With all of the tools and methodologies available for collecting and maintaining requirements, it has been demonstrated that software developers have several options for picking the best solution that meets their objectives, such as the AI agent. This initiative will contribute to the formulation of standards for IoT-enabled sustainable cities (Nadeem et al., 2022).

A methodological approach for automating requirements collection through the use of an ML-based interactive bot (Patidar & Suman, 2023), the requirements gathering bot (RGBot). The RGBot simplifies the MAD process by gathering requirements and enhancing customer experiences to fulfill stakeholder expectations. RGBot uses ML to converse with clients in natural language and extract relevant demands for developing a mobile app from the discussions. The RGBot can read and extract information from consumer interactions using NLU; DMS allows for smooth and objective exchanges; and NLG allows the RGBot to offer responses that appear natural to the customer, improving their level of engagement. In addition to the generated replies and obtained information, the RGBot may create a list of requirements. It can provide a condensed perspective of client demands, making it easier for programmers to understand and implement. Another chatbot application (Dwitama & Rusli, 2020) to assist with requirements elicitation in software engineering, making the task less time-consuming and more structured for individuals inexperienced with the procedure. The Nazief and Adriani stemming algorithm is used by the chatbot to pre-process natural language received from users, while artificial mark-up language (AIML) acts as the knowledge base for processing the bot's responses. The preliminary acceptance test using the technology acceptance model resulted in an 83.03% score for users' behavioral intention to use.

A study from (Kopp et al., 2021) suggests using a software tool to generate database schema based on textual requirements, often known as business rules in database design. This may assist database designers quickly obtaining useful databases. Schemas are used to find and remedy faults as soon as feasible. The suggested technique simplifies database design by generating scripts based on business principles. Engineers may inspect the schema and change data types, unique properties, or naming styles without coding all the needed lines. Review the schema and make necessary changes to data types, unique properties, and naming styles. This focuses on relational models and databases, as they are extensively used today. State-of-the-art analysis is performed, and the recommended technique provides a detailed description of the software tool and brief usage examples, draws conclusions, and suggests future research areas.

All of this emphasizes the importance of AI techniques—data mining, machine learning, and neural networks—in improving software reuse and promoting efficient software engineering processes. Wangoo (2018) focuses on AI approaches such as neural networks and parallel processing to find reusable components, hence enhancing software quality and efficiency. Mili et al. (1995) demonstrate how economic models and component retrieval techniques promote software reuse. Padhy et al. (2017) present a reusability prediction methodology for Web of Service platforms that employs CK metrics to forecast aging resilience and lower computing expenses. Latendresse (2024) emphasizes the need of efficient library suggestions, noting that, while ChatGPT is beneficial as a "software librarian," it lacks precise information on library licensing and maintainability. Maarek et al. (1991) provide information retrieval strategies for arranging software libraries to ease component selection, resulting in high retrieval efficacy. Saied et al. (2018) provide a method for detecting third-party library usage patterns using clustering approaches, which provides insights into common library dependencies across developers. Furthermore, Nadeem et al. (2022) and Patidar & Suman (2023) investigate AI-based requirements gathering, with technologies such as RGBot supporting natural language interactions to improve requirement elicitation and client involvement. Collectively, these studies highlight AI's transformational influence in software engineering, ranging from reuse and component organization to library selection and requirements collecting, all of which contribute to software development efficiency and scalability. Kopp et al. (2021) provide a tool that creates database schemas based on textual business requirements, allowing designers to easily construct and update relational database architectures. This tool facilitates schema creation by automating script generation and allowing for easy modification of data types and characteristics enhancing translation from technical to business requirements.

METHODOLOGY

AI approaches have been widely employed in software engineering, resulting in significant overlap. In software engineering, the line between probabilistic reasoning and prediction is often unclear or arbitrary. A prediction system is essentially a probabilistic reasoning tool. Bayesian models can be viewed as learners, and classifiers as probabilistic reasoners or optimisers.

AI applications in software engineering aim to optimize processes and products, making them all instances of Search Based Software Engineering.AI approaches have been widely employed in software engineering, resulting in significant overlap. We are always seeking solutions to problems, whether they be based on chance, prediction, or experience. We aim to improve our approach's efficiency and effectiveness while balancing costs and benefits. Optimization goals can be defined as quantifiable objectives and constraints. Solutions are often found in huge areas, making them ideal for computer search. Machine learning techniques to Software Engineering and SBSE (Patidar & Suman, 2023) work well together. Machine learning is essentially the study of computational techniques that improve with practice. To improve, it's important to have a means of measuring progress. SBSE will optimize based on it. In Software Engineering, there are several possible measures to compare and improve against.

Genetic programming may be viewed as a machine learning technique, as it is an algorithm for modeling software behavior. as well as an optimization tool. Machine learning for SE and SBSE are closely related, as optimization may be viewed as a form of learning. It's important to avoid obsessing over issue and solution definitions through terminological disputes. This unified terminology can facilitate the interchange of ideas. SBSE can enhance the performance of prediction models and case-based reasoning. To effectively apply AI approaches to software engineering challenges, the first step is to define the problem in such a way that AI techniques may be used. Once this formulation is accomplished, it opens up the technological possibility for multiple AI tactics to be successful, as demonstrated in previous studies (Harman, 2012).

Feldt et al. (2018) identified three crucial characteristics for our taxonomy: point of application, automation degree, and AI technology. They chose a faceted analysis for new and developing sectors due to its ability to capture comprehensive knowledge. Related to the topic area is not needed nor available. The design and building phase outlines the levels of the taxonomy, how they were chosen, and their relevance to the taxonomy's purpose and usage. The validation process demonstrates how to classify the topic matter using the suggested taxonomy. The literature suggests three validation methods: orthogonality demonstration, benchmarking, and utility demonstration. They chose the latter and classified a set of AI applications reported in previous editions of the Workshop on Realizing Artificial Intelligence Synergies in Software Engineering (RAISE). Additionally, utility demonstration is the most reported method to validate taxonomies in SE, and it allows us to showcase the classification extent of the taxonomy.

High-level languages have potential, but their applications are restricted. As a language's complexity and volume increase, sophisticated features may not be used. A related issue is how tools are utilized in programming environments. Programmers often underutilize their systems owing to a lack of understanding of available tools, how to use them, when to use them, their functions, and how to combine, modify, or change them.

Research in both traditional software engineering and artificial intelligence shows that programming languages alone do not have a significant influence on software development. Required for radical improvement in the software process. Using them effectively makes a difference. In other words, the technique matters (Tsai et al., 2003).

Algorithmic design research often focuses on developing solutions from known options. The selections are selected based on the feasibility was assessed and a single solution was chosen based on defined criteria for the best outcome. Goldberg (1986) explains how to make design decisions for algorithms, including finite differencing, loop fusion, data structure selection, storage versus computation, transforming logic assertions to procedural interpretation, and selecting parameters. E. Kant's method (Kant, 1985) focuses on the expert procedures of creative design. (Kant, 1985) investigates how individuals develop algorithms. This effort has long-term potential, but comparable research on design techniques may be more effective.

The incorporation of artificial intelligence (AI) into software engineering (SE) via methodologies such as Search-Based Software Engineering (SBSE) and machine learning techniques opens up a transformational possibility for enhancing software development processes. Using AI, SE practitioners can increase forecast accuracy, decision-making, and overall system performance. The key to effective AI implementation is to properly define the problem at hand, allowing for the focused deployment of AI approaches that may be adjusted and enhanced over time.

Furthermore, the usage of unified nomenclature in AI and SE promotes improved communication and cross-disciplinary collaboration, assisting researchers and practitioners alike in addressing difficult engineering issues. Feldt et al. (2018)'s taxonomy provides a beneficial framework for comprehending the numerous applications of AI technologies, providing a more in-depth knowledge of its value and promise across all phases of the software development process.

However, despite the enormous potential of high-level languages and AI tools, there is still a gap in properly exploiting these resources, which may restrict the influence of AI in SE. This emphasizes the necessity of education and training in providing developers with the knowledge they need to effectively utilize the current tools and methodologies. Furthermore, ongoing study into algorithmic design and its link to AI will be critical in ensuring that future software systems are not just performance-optimized, but also adaptive and scalable in an ever-changing technological context.

Finally, as AI evolves, its use in software engineering will remain critical to furthering the profession. Developers and researchers may fully realize the promise of AI by taking a deliberate and well-defined approach, resulting in breakthroughs that improve productivity, quality, and performance in software engineering. This chapter provides a basis for understanding how AI may be used to enhance software development, establishing the way for future research and developments in this exciting confluence of technology.

AI-DRIVEN CODE REUSABILITY

Code reusability is the process of creating code that may be used in several applications or projects without significant modification. It is a fundamental concept in software engineering that aims to improve efficiency and consistency by reducing redundant code production. Code reusability is the process of creating code in such a way that it may be used in other applications or projects without requiring significant modification. It is a fundamental concept in software engineering that aims to improve efficiency and consistency by reducing redundant code production.

Developers may save significant time by reusing existing, established code components, which accelerates the development process. This strategy eliminates the need to repeatedly design and test the same features, allowing teams to focus on new and unique aspects of their projects.

Reusable code is often optimized, documented, and tested for dependability, which improves overall program quality. Using standardized, reusable components promotes uniformity across programs, which simplifies maintenance and troubleshooting. Reusable code creates a scalable basis, allowing developers to quickly extend or alter programs. It offers a modular design, allowing teams to add and upgrade functionality while minimizing damage to the current codebase. Reusability reduces development costs by minimizing the resources required for coding, testing, and quality assurance. For enterprises, this efficiency results into significant long-term cost savings, especially in big or complicated projects.

Artificial intelligence (AI) techniques and technologies have revolutionized the landscape of software development, allowing developers to achieve previously unattainable levels of automation, accuracy, and efficiency. AI provides a variety of sophisticated approaches that handle key software engineering concerns, including data mining, machine learning, neural networks, and natural language processing (NLP). These solutions not only revolutionize code reuse and library selection, but they also improve the alignment of technical needs with business goals. Organizations may discover new methods to improve efficiency, eliminate mistakes, and speed innovation by incorporating AI into development workflows.

According to Cote et al. (2005) FlowDesigner enables the creation of reusable software modules and their standardized linking to form a network. The blocks are joined dynamically during runtime. A network made up of numerous blocks can be added as a super-block to other networks. It offers a graphical programming environment for seeing and comprehending the behavior of robot control loops via graphical probes. RobotFlow (Cote et al., 2005) empowers programmers to customize behavior connections, software architecture, and intelligence. What procedures to employ and which data types to leverage? While there is still much to learn about programming intelligent autonomous mobile robots, we believe that flexibility is more essential than user-friendliness or automated methods. RobotFlow's graphical user interface is limited, but programmers may create custom GUIs to meet their specific requirements.

Artificial intelligence techniques such as knowledge-based systems, neural networks, fuzzy logic, machine learning, and data mining have been investigated as potential ways to improve several software development operations. Automated software development combines artificial intelligence techniques with software engineering and data mining. Mining software engineering data will aid in extracting relevant knowledge for identifying and selecting possible candidates for reuse, while the consolidation of artificial intelligence methods will aid in applying intelligence to the aforementioned process. This will result in the automation of the entire range of software engineering operations including software reuse. Software Intelligence is synonymous with Business Intelligence in enterprises since BI supports SI in the software industry. The entire field of software intelligence may be used to repurpose standard BI platforms for the adoption of BI infrastructures in big enterprises (Wangoo, 2018).

Mili et al. (1995) explored the impact of reuse on manufacturing, focusing on the technological issues. Software reuse entails designing and developing reusable software. Software reuse involves reusing both the products and processes used in previous projects. There are various approaches to reuse, such as building blocks (reusing products) and generative processors (reusing processes). Mili et al. (1995) addressed the impact of these techniques on software development organization, control, and methods, as well as proposed economic analysis models. Software reuse utilizes approaches and technologies to create more reusable software.

MARIE suggests another method which involves altering the mediator design pattern for distributed systems. The mediator design pattern essentially develops a centralized control unit (called mediator) that interacts with each colleague (application) separately, while also understanding how to coordinate global interactions amongst colleagues to achieve the desired system. Here are the five consequences discovered for the mediator design pattern, as applied to the dispersed mobile robot's context: It restricts subclassing. Changing general system behavior using the mediator pattern requires simply changing the mediator's interactions with applications, leaving applications unaltered. This is a positive outcome since otherwise, changing behaviors would require modifying application source code, lowering application reusability.

It decouples coworkers. Having all apps linked to the mediator fosters loose coupling between them. Applications do not need to be aware of other applications, restricting interactions to the mediator. Better decoupling between colleagues allows for the independent reuse of mediator setups and apps, as well as the ease of switching between programs that provide the same services. It abstracts how things collaborate. It may be better to construct an abstraction layer over each application, with each acting as a service provider. This abstraction level allows for robotic domain representation without affecting the functional level of any application. It establishes centralized control. However, centralizing control increases the mediator's complexity in order to appropriately handle all interactions between apps and execute all system capabilities. This can result in particular implementations that are difficult to comprehend, maintain, and expand (Cote et al., 2005).

It simplifies object protocols. A mediator converts many-to-many interactions into one-to-many interactions between the mediator and its coworkers. In a distributed environment, this means that each program can utilize its own communication interface as long as the mediator understands how to communicate with each one. Application reusability is increased by not being tied to certain communication interfaces and having compatibility concerns handled by a centralized control unit instead of being responsibility of each application to integrate.

A successful code reusability approach may considerably speed development processes and increase productivity; nevertheless, developing reusable code has its own set of obstacles. These challenges range from technological concerns, such as dependency conflicts and performance limits, to organizational hurdles, such as a lack of standards and cultural opposition. Understanding these obstacles is critical for teams looking to use reusable code as a long-term solution for scalable and efficient software development.

Challenges in the AI-Driven Code Reusability

Inconsistent Coding Practices: Different developers and teams may utilize varying coding styles and standards, affecting code integration across projects. Without specified processes, it is impossible to achieve seamless reuse.

Framework and Language Differences: Code written for a certain programming language or framework may be difficult to adapt to different environments, limiting its potential for reuse across several systems.

Dependency Conflicts: Reusable code usually relies on certain libraries or modules, which can lead to compatibility issues when projects utilize different dependencies.

Complex Interdependencies: Highly reusable code may have several interconnected components, increasing complexity. Adapting or altering one piece may need changes to other portions, increasing the possibility of errors.

Insufficient Documentation: To ensure that people can understand and utilize reusable code effectively, it must be properly and completely documented. However, documentation is occasionally neglected, making it more difficult for others to modify the code.

Understanding Challenges: Code written by one developer may be difficult for others to comprehend and update, especially if it involves complex logic or lacks comments.

The need of rigorous testing: For code to be really reusable, it must be resilient and tested in a number of settings. However, this level of testing requires significant resources, particularly when addressing several use cases.

Maintenance and Version Control: Keeping reusable components up to date and consistent with new technologies or demands is tough, especially in rapidly evolving software environments where dependencies or standards change on a regular basis.

The need of rigorous testing: For code to be really reusable, it must be resilient and tested in a number of settings. However, this level of testing requires significant resources, particularly when addressing several use cases.

Maintenance and Version Control: Keeping reusable components up to date and consistent with new technologies or demands is tough, especially in rapidly evolving software environments where dependencies or standards change on a regular basis.

Vulnerabilities in Reused Code: Reused code may include security weaknesses, especially if it was created without concern for current security requirements. Each reused component carries a potential security risk.

Handling Sensitive Data: Reusable components that handle sensitive data must be designed to meet privacy and security standards throughout all projects in which they are utilized.

Resistance to Change: Some teams may be resistant to using reused code, preferring unique solutions customized to their individual requirements. This opposition impedes the adoption of reusable components inside an organization.

Lack of Reuse Culture: Without a culture that actively encourages code reuse, developers may be less likely to devote the effort required to design modular, adaptable code components.

Difficulty Finding Reusable Code: Without effective search tools or repositories, it might be difficult to locate existing reusable components for a specific application.

Evaluating Suitability: Even if appropriate code is identified, it may not completely match the requirements of the new project. Adapting existing code may be as resource-intensive as creating new code.

Adaptability vs. Performance: Reusable code is typically designed for flexibility, which can sometimes degrade performance. This might be a drawback in high-performance applications where optimized, purpose-built code is needed.

AI for Choosing Software Libraries

The fundamental software libraries give programmers a realistic and effective way to access this data. By encapsulating the underlying database structure, the libraries provide end users with a straightforward, abstract interface to a complicated data model. The majority of schema changes have no effect on programs that access data using libraries rather than SQL. The essential software libraries' architecture, schema, and design elements are detailed. All code and data are publicly accessible (Stabenau et al., 2004). Software libraries play an important role in software development by providing developers with pre-written, reusable code that simplifies and speeds up the development process. Libraries contain widely used tasks such as data processing, networking, and file handling, avoiding the need to create them from start. Developers may import and use standardized, tested code to save time and effort. Libraries make it easier to build new features since they provide a collection of pre-built functions and modules. Faster development cycles allow developers to concentrate on core application functionality or specific business needs. Libraries are often created and maintained by specialist communities or organizations, which ensures that the code is strong and dependable. They go through extensive testing and updating, which reduces the possibility of errors. Complex methods or technologies (e.g., machine learning, encryption, or 3D graphics) are frequently implemented in libraries, giving developers access to advanced capabilities without requiring extensive knowledge. Libraries frequently feature efficient, scalable solutions based on industry standards, allowing applications to handle rising workloads without substantial rewrites. Using the same libraries on several projects guarantees consistency in code style and behavior, which is especially crucial in collaborative situations. Popular libraries have substantial documentation, tutorials, and active user communities, making it simpler for developers to understand and apply them successfully.

Understanding client and system requirements is crucial for designing high-quality software applications. When developing a library selection tool, the software developers are the consumers, and the first step is to understand the developers' circumstance, behavior, decision pattern, and library selection case needs. The AIRS approach (Ostertag et al., 1992) for categorizing and calculating component similarity is based on a library of software objects. The library's underlying objects, known as components, are organized into related packages. The components are specified by basic characteristics. AIRS calculates similarity metrics (distances) between components and packages. This formalizes ideas and explains how to compute similarity metrics.

One other strategy takes into account a variety of parameters prior to project beginning. The premise is simple: stating the application's objective allows the method to assess existing libraries and frameworks. Recommend an appropriate set for the Node Package Module. An AI solution (Sandaruwan & Kasthurirathna, 2024) would use new techniques including Topic Modeling, Knowledge Graph (KG), and Machine Learning. Finally, it will provide suggestions based on all important data, references, documentation, and library-related issues.With this technique, developers, whether established experts or newbies, should benefit from more Intelligent, data-driven library selection. The idea is to reduce the strain of making vital judgments. The goal is to provide developers with a user-friendly helper that recommends libraries and frameworks based on their project goals and restrictions. This approach aims to be a supporting partner in software development, rather than just a method.

Dependency Analysis: AI tools assess a library's dependencies to guarantee compatibility with the project's existing frameworks, programming languages, and other integrated components. This helps to eliminate version conflicts and ensures a smooth integration.

Contextual Recommendations: Tools like GitHub Copilot and OpenAI models employ natural language processing (NLP) and machine learning to analyze the context of the codebase and propose libraries that are appropriate for the project's requirements.

Environment Testing: AI algorithms simulate the library's use in a variety of scenarios to detect possible incompatibilities, such as mismatched operating systems or unsupported frameworks.

Vulnerability Scanning: AI-powered systems scan vulnerability databases (such as CVE—Common Vulnerabilities and Exposures) to identify known security vulnerabilities in libraries. They can detect libraries with out-of-date dependencies or exploitable vulnerabilities.

Behavioral Analysis: Tools evaluate static and dynamic code to detect unusual or malicious activities in libraries, such as unauthorized data access or privilege escalation.

License Validation: AI checks library licenses to identify restricted or incompatible terms, such as copyleft licensing, that may result in legal complications.
Code Quality Checks: AI techniques evaluate a library's internal code quality by examining factors like as complexity, coding standard compliance, and documentation availability.
Community and Update Frequency: Machine learning models analyze the library's activity on repositories like GitHub, taking into consideration metrics like contributor numbers, update frequency, and issue resolution. Actively maintained libraries are valued for their long-term reliability.
Historical Performance Analysis: AI uses the library's previous performance, such as bug reports and resolution times, to forecast its stability and reliability in future projects.

AI tools replicate the library's integration into a codebase and conduct automated tests to ensure its functioning and compatibility. Libraries are checked for nested dependencies to verify that no hidden conflicts or vulnerabilities might jeopardize the project. AI ranks libraries based on factors like as security, interoperability, maintainability, and popularity. These ratings allow developers to compare libraries objectively. AI systems leverage user and developer input to enhance library suggestions and validation procedures, allowing them to adapt to new trends and obstacles. By using these features, AI tools greatly decrease the risks associated with library selection, ensuring that projects use software components that are dependable, secure, and well-maintained.

AIRS, an AI-powered classification system for software reuse. This system is an effective tool for software reuse. It has the potential to reduce software development expenses. The method categorizes software items using three concepts: features, components, and packages. These descriptions, together with the concepts of subsumption and proximity, are used to choose components from the library based on their similarity to the desired component. Similarity is defined by a nonnegative number (distance) that represents the projected effort required to get the target component. Similarity is quantified using a non-negative magnitude (distance) that shows the candidate's predicted effort to reach a target.AIRS was used to classify two software libraries: EVBGFLACE for abstract data structures and Contel CCIS for Command, Control, and Information Systems. AIRS may be used for both highly structured domains and sparse collections, as evidenced by experience with diverse libraries. It has assisted in identifying and addressing the AIRS system's flaws. They create semi-automatic techniques to categorize components, improve subsumer and feature graphs, and broaden the feature space.

The investigation into the issues of selecting third-party libraries in software development, as well as the subsequent creation of an AI-based recommendation system, has revealed a road to more efficient and informed decision-making. Most of the obstacles highlight the complications that developers confront, ranging from a lack of understanding to practical issues like document navigation and compatibility concerns. The suggested AI application, which uses cutting-edge technologies such as Topic Modeling and Knowledge Graph, appears to be a viable answer to these difficulties.

The AI system's design and implementation have resulted in an application capable of offering intelligent, data-driven library suggestions in line with user-project ideas. The system's sophisticated capabilities promise to expedite the selection process by providing specialized recommendations that go beyond the constraints of previous methodologies. The evaluation of the AI application, based on factors such as user happiness, accuracy, suggestion comprehensiveness, and alignment with project goals, is an important step toward understanding its real-world impact. (Sandaruwan & Kasthurirathna, 2024) research not only addresses existing challenges but also envisions a future where AI-driven recommendations become an integral part of the software development journey, fostering efficiency, innovation, and in-formed decision-making.

AI has transformed software library selection by enabling faster, data-driven decisions while also improving the overall quality and efficiency of development processes. AI solutions can employ machine learning and natural language processing (NLP) to evaluate project needs, provide relevant libraries, and even estimate performance in certain scenarios. This accelerates development, reduces the chance of dependency conflicts, and enhances maintainability by concentrating on well-documented, actively maintained libraries. Furthermore, AI-powered vulnerability scanners ensure that security issues are spotted early, decreasing potential risks.

However, AI-based library selection is not without its challenges. One notable disadvantage is recommendation bias, which occurs when AI algorithms favor popular libraries over specialized libraries that may better suit certain use cases. Furthermore, incomplete or incorrect licensing data may raise legal concerns, particularly for projects that need rigorous adherence to open-source or proprietary license restrictions. Another difficulty is depending on libraries that may work "out of the box" but may not align with long-term project goals, needing considerable customization or replacement later. Finally, over-reliance on AI technology may result in a lack of developer experience, preventing effective troubleshooting and integration.

While AI offers considerable advantages in library selection, it must be managed rigorously and with human judgment to overcome these limitations and maximize the benefits.

Translating Technical Requirements to Business Language

Software requirements engineering entails establishing and characterizing the services and constraints of a software system. It involves gathering and defining software requirements. Elicitation of software Stakeholder demands are frequently turned into user requirements, which are simple statements that convey a software system's high-level objectives. Properly understanding the natural language user wants is critical to avoiding errors later in the process. Detecting and fixing requirements imprecision in the last stages of software development is much more expensive than early detection. Improving the precision of elicited user requirements during the first cycle is an important aim of software engineering.

Software engineering strives to achieve a continuous cycle. Imprecision is sometimes caused by ambiguity in natural language used to describe user expectations. To minimize Experts have recommended optimal techniques for drafting requirements papers, addressing uncertainty. To maintain consistency and clarity, action and actor descriptions should be limited to defined vocabulary from a glossary. Avoid using several terms for the same item, such as "Order Processing System" and "Order Entry System." Avoid subjective terms like "easy to use" as they might lead to uncertainty. Write each requirement as a distinct sentence. Use entire sentences instead of bulleted buzz phrases. Use entire active-voice phrases with clarity. Please identify the actor/agent and the action. Use standardized syntaxes to write requirements sentences, with each type representing a certain sort of requirement. Use a unique identification for each need (Elazhary, H., 2011).

In every project development life cycle, the most critical phases are requirement collecting and management. Requirement collection requires a lot of mental focus. Many clients are unsure about how to appropriately communicate their requests. Sometimes, the project team makes irrelevant assumptions about the requirements and begins focused on how to "implement" rather than "what to implement." Sometimes the provided document template for the client's requirement collecting is insufficient for a clear elicitation of needs. Initially, the customer demand elicitation document, the result of the first three sessions, is not entirely implementable. Many project management experts have reported improved results after utilizing similar tools and strategies for distinct projects. Some software engineering gurus advocated using the toolbox method to increase client satisfaction. Roulette Wheel Selection is used for requirement collection in conjunction with AI models. It has been discovered that learning models produce the greatest outcomes (Nadeem et al., 2022).

Natural English Processing (NLP) models like GPT (Generative Pre-trained Transformer) and BERT (Bidirectional Encoder Representations from Transformers) have changed the way technical data is translated into business-relevant English. These tools improve communication between technical teams and non-technical stakeholders, leading to increased clarity and alignment in software development initiatives.

GPT (Generative Pretrained Transformer)

GPT models, such as GPT-3.5 and GPT-4, are excellent at creating coherent, contextually relevant content. They can decode technical jargon, clarify critical aspects, and reinterpret complex themes in plain language suitable for commercial relations.

Use Cases: GPT may create project summaries, executive-level reports, and rewrite API or system documentation for stakeholders that lack technical skills. It may also offer clear responses to plain language concerns about technical specifications.

Bidirectional Encoder Representations of Transformers (BERT)

Capabilities: BERT is designed for operations that need considerable contextual knowledge, such as extracting relevant information from dense technical documents and mapping it to business requirements.

Use Cases: BERT is effective for automating requirement collecting, turning user requests into technology features, and aligning them to business goals. It is very useful in areas like contract analysis and compliance documentation.

Domain-Specific Natural Language Processing Models

Capabilities: Models trained on specialized datasets (e.g., financial, healthcare, or engineering data) can turn technical knowledge in their field into business-relevant insights.

Use cases: Examples include tools for summarizing software architectural diagrams, simplifying regulatory standards, and explaining algorithms to decision-makers.

AI Tools Based on NLP Models

Chatbots: Tools such as RGBot (Patidar & Suman, 2023) employ natural language processing (NLP) to engage with stakeholders, gather needs, and generate summaries for developers.

Document Simplification Tools: AI-powered solutions utilize natural language processing (NLP) to translate complex content into succinct, understandable versions for targeted audiences.

AI solutions that use natural language processing (NLP) play a critical role in bridging the gap between technical and business teams, resulting in improved project alignment and execution. Here are some real examples of AI applications used to translate requirements:

RGBot (Patidar & Suman, 2023) is an ML-powered chatbot that collects software needs directly from stakeholders. It engages users in natural language conversations, extracts pertinent needs, and creates structured requirement papers. This tool improves project alignment by giving developers with clear, simple requirements that represent stakeholder expectations while avoiding technological uncertainty.

ChatGPT models are commonly used to create first drafts of project requirements by summarizing client-supplied descriptions or technical specifics. It converts technical jargon into business-friendly terminology for stakeholder presentations. Reduces the work required by business analysts to develop stakeholder-focused documentation, hence expediting the requirements process.

Revuze examines consumer feedback, reviews, and surveys to discover pain issues and turn them into actionable technological needs.It Aligns product development goals with actual consumer demands, resulting in increased satisfaction and improved market alignment.

SpecFlow, a behavior-driven development (BDD) tool, works with AI models to convert user stories written in plain English into executable technical specifications. Ensures clear communication between the business and technical departments, allowing developers to act immediately on aligned specifications. AI-enabled tools may scan project changes or user stories in Trello or Jira, generating simplified reports or needs for business presentations. Allows for real-time communication between technical and non-technical stakeholders, ensuring alignment throughout the project lifecycle. This AI tool helps to generate and validate requirements by evaluating input text and recommending adjustments to ensure completeness and clarity. Reduces errors and ambiguity in requirements documentation, allowing teams to collaborate more effectively.

AI in requirements translation has various benefits, including improved clarity, speed, and accuracy when communicating complex technical concepts to business stakeholders. NLP-powered solutions, such as GPT and domain-specific chatbots, may minimize jargon, explain complex facts, and align project objectives by guaranteeing that all participants have a same understanding. These tools save time, reduce interpretation errors, and increase communication, particularly in large multidisciplinary teams. However, potential limitations must be acknowledged. AI models may occasionally misinterpret context or create outputs that oversimplify critical technological aspects, leading to incorrect expectations. Furthermore, relying on pre-trained models may lead to biases or inaccuracies if the training data is not domain-specific. Finally, an overreliance on AI technology may undermine human competence in requirement elicitation, causing challenges when nuanced, industry-specific knowledge is required. Despite these limits, AI is still a powerful asset when combined with human oversight.

AI has shown to be a revolutionary force in translating technical requirements into business-friendly language, leading in improved communication and alignment across various teams. RGBot, GPT, BERT, and bespoke chatbots all assist to speed up the requirements collecting process while also ensuring clarity and reducing interpretation errors. These technologies enable faster project alignment, more stakeholder engagement, and improved overall software development efficiency. However, issues like as potential contextual misinterpretations, reliance on generic training data, and overreliance on AI technology highlight the necessity for human supervision.

Combine AI and Human Expertise: Use AI technology to generate initial needs, but then review the findings with domain experts to ensure correctness and relevance.

Invest in domain-specific artificial intelligence models: Choose or train industry-specific NLP models to improve contextual comprehension.

Encourage stakeholder participation: Engage corporate stakeholders in AI-assisted discussions to ensure that needs match expectations.

Iterate and tweak the outcome: To guarantee goal alignment, analyze and adjust AI-generated requirements regularly as the project progresses.

Organizations may increase the efficiency and precision of requirements translation by strategically leveraging AI and overcoming its limitations, resulting in more successful project outputs.

DISCUSSION

AI has emerged as a game changer in software engineering, addressing long-standing difficulties such as reusable code, library selection, and requirements translation. Its disruptive promise arises from its ability to automate complex procedures, enhance accuracy, and foster collaboration across technical and non-technical teams. In terms of code reuse, AI technologies have shown to be quite effective in identifying and optimizing reusable components for integration. Machine learning and neural networks improve retrieval accuracy and accelerate development, but they are restricted by dependencies and the need for extensive testing. While AI makes it simpler to reuse tools, depending too heavily on them may reduce the need for human oversight in sophisticated decision-making.

AI's data-driven ideas have streamlined the library selection process by analyzing project needs and recommending appropriate alternatives. Tools like GitHub Copilot and ChatGPT have demonstrated potential, but limitations like as a lack of license information and a bias for popular libraries highlight the importance of developer attention. Furthermore, depending on commonly recommended libraries may limit creativity by ignoring unique yet successful solutions.

In the field of needs translation, NLP models like as GPT and BERT have aided in the communication between technical teams and stakeholders. These tools enhance alignment and clarity by converting complicated technical information into business-friendly language. However, difficulties like as contextual misinterpretation and oversimplification emphasize the importance of human validation. RGBot (Patidar & Suman, 2023) and domain-specific NLP models have been effective for eliciting needs, but their efficacy is based on well-defined project contexts and objectives.

While AI offers numerous advantages, ethical and practical concerns persist. For example, depending on private AI tools raises issues about long-term access and transparency, especially when using pre-trained models. Furthermore, ensuring security and privacy in AI-powered operations is crucial, particularly when dealing with sensitive data or integrating third-party libraries.

Future Directions

AI's role in software engineering is always evolving, with opportunities to increase its applications even more. Advances in explainable AI (XAI) may address transparency issues, while domain-specific training datasets can enhance context-sensitive outcomes. Furthermore, integrating AI technologies seamlessly into existing development ecosystems will reduce adoption barriers and boost efficiency.

The emphasis should be on creating hybrid systems that mix automation and human expertise, so that AI augments rather than replaces critical decision-making procedures.

To summarize, while AI has transformative benefits in software engineering, its successful implementation is based on overcoming its limitations and establishing a collaborative atmosphere in which technology complements human expertise.

CONCLUSION

The introduction of Artificial Intelligence (AI) into software engineering is a paradigm shift that addresses long-standing concerns with code reuse, software library selection, and requirements translation. AI technologies have shown to be critical in modern software development workflows by automating challenging tasks, improving accuracy, and facilitating improved collaboration. This chapter digs into these revolutionary applications, highlighting both the benefits and drawbacks of using AI in these critical domains.

In terms of code reuse, AI techniques like as neural networks and machine learning algorithms have transformed how developers find, extract, and create reusable components. These advances save time while also improving project uniformity and quality. However, establishing successful reusability necessitates overcoming obstacles like as dependency conflicts, a lack of standards, and thorough documentation. Without solving these issues, many development environments may continue to underutilize reusable code.

AI has proven the capacity to evaluate and propose software libraries on the basis of compatibility, security, and maintainability. Tools such as GitHub Copilot and ChatGPT have significantly streamlined this process, providing developers with useful data regarding library usage. However, difficulties remain, such as biases in recommendations and insufficient license details, which might pose legal and operational concerns. Developers must strike a balance between the ease of AI-driven library selection and meticulous validation to ensure long-term project success.

Natural Language Processing (NLP) models such as GPT and BERT have made major contributions to requirements translation by converting complex technical information into business-friendly language. This improved project alignment and allowed stakeholders to more fully understand and engage in technical discussions. However, these devices have limitations. Contextual misunderstanding, simplicity of information, and reliance on pre-trained models can all lead to incorrect expectations. To ensure clarity and precision, a good requirements translation must blend AI insights with human expertise.

While AI has proven benefits in several sectors, it is not a cure-all. As AI usage increases, ethical issues like as transparency, accountability, and data protection become more important. Developers must exercise caution when using AI technologies, and ensure that human supervision remains key to decision-making processes. Furthermore, the fast advancement of AI technology might result in a high learning curve, necessitating investments in training and upskilling for enterprises to fully realize the promise of these tools.

Looking ahead, the future of AI in software engineering is in developing systems that seamlessly combine human skill with machine intelligence. Hybrid models that combine the benefits of AI-driven automation with human judgment can overcome present constraints while increasing efficiency. Furthermore, advances in explainable AI (XAI) and domain-specific NLP models have the potential to make AI tools more clear and successful in addressing industry-specific difficulties.

Finally, AI is more than a tool; it is a catalyst for creativity in software engineering. AI is propelling the industry toward more scalable, sustainable, and intelligent solutions by allowing developers to work more effectively and encouraging collaboration among technical and non-technical stakeholders. To truly exploit its potential, businesses must take a balanced strategy that addresses its limits, emphasizes ethical issues, and connects technical breakthroughs with human-centered approaches. The road to fully utilize AI's potential in software development is continuing, and the ideas presented in this chapter serve as a basis for future research and innovation in this dynamic subject.

REFERENCES

Cote, C., Letourneau, D., Michaud, F., Valin, J., Brosseau, Y., Raievsky, C., Lemay, M., & Tran, V. (2005). *Code reusability tools for programming mobile robots*. Code Reusability Tools for Programming Mobile Robots., DOI: 10.1109/IROS.2004.1389661

Dwitama, F., & Rusli, A. (2020). User stories collection via interactive chatbot to support requirements gathering. *Telkomnika*, *18*(2), 890. DOI: 10.12928/telkomnika.v18i2.14866

Elazhary, H. (2011). Translation of software requirements. *International Journal of Scientific and Engineering Research*, *2*(5), 1–7.

Feldt, R., De Oliveira Neto, F. G., & Torkar, R. (2018). Ways of applying artificial intelligence in software engineering. *Ways of Applying Artificial Intelligence in Software Engineering*, 35–41. DOI: 10.1145/3194104.3194109

Goldberg, A. T. (1986). Knowledge-based programming: A survey of program design and construction techniques. *IEEE Transactions on Software Engineering*, *SE-12*(7), 752–768. DOI: 10.1109/TSE.1986.6312977

Harman, M. (2012). The role of Artificial Intelligence in Software Engineering. *The Role of Artificial Intelligence in Software Engineering*. DOI: 10.1109/RAISE.2012.6227961

Kant, E. (1985). Understanding and Automating Algorithm Design. *IEEE Transactions on Software Engineering*, *SE-11*(11), 1361–1374. DOI: 10.1109/TSE.1985.231884

Kopp, A., Orlovskyi, D., & Orekhov, S. (2021). An Approach and Software Prototype for Translation of Natural Language Business Rules into Database Structure. *COLINS*, 1274–1291. https://ceur-ws.org/Vol-2870/paper94.pdf

Latendresse, J., Khatoonabadi, S., Abdellatif, A., & Shihab, E. (2024). Is ChatGPT a Good Software Librarian? An Exploratory Study on the Use of ChatGPT for Software Library

Maarek, Y., Berry, D., & Kaiser, G. (1991). An information retrieval approach for automatically constructing software libraries. *IEEE Transactions on Software Engineering*, *17*(8), 800–813. DOI: 10.1109/32.83915

Mili, H., Mili, F., & Mili, A. (1995). Reusing software: Issues and research directions. *IEEE Transactions on Software Engineering*, *21*(6), 528–562. DOI: 10.1109/32.391379

Nadeem, M. A., Lee, S. U., & Younus, M. U. (2022). A Comparison of Recent Requirements Gathering and Management Tools in Requirements Engineering for IoT-Enabled Sustainable Cities. *Sustainability (Basel)*, *14*(4), 2427. DOI: 10.3390/su14042427

Ostertag, E., Hendler, J., Díaz, R. P., & Braun, C. (1992). Computing similarity in a reuse library system. *ACM Transactions on Software Engineering and Methodology*, *1*(3), 205–228. DOI: 10.1145/131736.131739

Ozkaya, I. (2023). The Next Frontier in Software Development: AI-Augmented Software Development Processes. *IEEE Software*, *40*(4), 4–9. DOI: 10.1109/MS.2023.3278056

Padhy, N., Singh, R. P., & Satapathy, S. C. (2017). Enhanced evolutionary computing based artificial intelligence model for web-solutions software reusability estimation. *Cluster Computing*, *22*(S4), 9787–9804. DOI: 10.1007/s10586-017-1558-0

Patidar, A., & Suman, U. (2023). RGBot: A Machine Learning Enabled Requirements Gathering Technique in Agile-Based Lifecycle. *RGBot: A Machine Learning Enabled Requirements Gathering Technique in Agile-Based Lifecycle*. DOI: 10.1109/ICTBIG59752.2023.10456282

Saied, M. A., Ouni, A., Sahraoui, H., Kula, R. G., Inoue, K., & Lo, D. (2018). Improving reusability of software libraries through usage pattern mining. *Journal of Systems and Software*, *145*, 164–179. DOI: 10.1016/j.jss.2018.08.032

Sandaruwan, A., & Kasthurirathna, D. (2024). Recommending Third-Party Libraries and Frameworks Using Topic Modeling in Software Projects. *Recommending Third-Party Libraries and Frameworks Using Topic Modeling in Software Projects*, 37–42. https://doi.org/DOI: 10.1109/ICARC61713.2024.10499759

Stabenau, A., McVicker, G., Melsopp, C., Proctor, G., Clamp, M., & Birney, E. (2004). The Ensembl Core Software Libraries: Figure 1. *Genome Research*, *14*(5), 929–933. DOI: 10.1101/gr.1857204 PMID: 15123588

Tsai, W., Heisler, K., Volovik, D., & Zualkernan, I. (2003). A critical look at the relationship between AI and software engineering. *A Critical Look at the Relationship Between AI and Software Engineering, se 11*, 2–18. DOI: 10.1109/LFA.1988.24945

Wangoo, D. P. (2018). Artificial Intelligence Techniques in Software Engineering for Automated Software Reuse and Design. *Artificial Intelligence Techniques in Software Engineering for Automated Software Reuse and Design*, *1*, 1–4. DOI: 10.1109/CCAA.2018.8777584

Chapter 5
Decision Models for Choice of AI:
Generative AI, Machine Learning, and Deep Learning

Sudeept Maharana
https://orcid.org/0009-0004-3777-5042
School of Management and Entrepreneurship, Indian Institute of Technology, Jodhpur, India

Deepak Saxena
https://orcid.org/0000-0002-9331-3799
School of Management and Entrepreneurship, Indian Institute of Technology, Jodhpur, India

ABSTRACT

The chapter integrates traditional decision-making models with selecting and implementing Artificial Intelligence (AI) technologies, specifically on Generative AI, Machine Learning, and Deep Learning. It provides a comprehensive analysis of eight widely used decision-making frameworks—SWOT Analysis, Resource-Based View, Core Competencies, Porter's Five Forces, Ansoff Matrix, PESTLE Analysis, 6 Thinking Hats, and OODA Loop—and evaluates their relevance and adaptability in guiding senior executives through the complexities of AI adoption. The chapter emphasizes that integrating AI technologies is not merely a technical challenge but a strategic endeavor that must align with organizational objectives to achieve sustainable competitive advantage, recommending a nuanced approach that may require the synchronization of multiple models to address the multifaceted nature of AI integration. It gives senior executives the strategic knowledge necessary to leverage AI technologies effectively, ensuring that AI investments contribute to long-term organizational success.

1. INTRODUCTION

The rapid development of Generative Artificial Intelligence (AI), Machine Learning, and Deep Learning has resulted in a broad spectrum of AI technologies that may revolutionize organizations and industries (Ooi et al., 2023). What was once thought to be a part of science fiction can now automate challenging tasks, produce human like content, predict with high accuracy, and analyse big data for in-

DOI: 10.4018/979-8-3693-8407-7.ch005

sights (Zohuri & Rahmani, 2023). Consequently, organizations are increasingly turning to AI integration to enhance innovation, efficiency, and revenue streams. These technologies range from simple repetitive tasks to data analysis and are revolutionizing how organizations conduct their operations and competitions (Mannuru et al., 2023). Yet, deciding on which of the AI technologies should be implemented is far from straightforward. Regarding the wide range and abundance of available innovations, developing AI technologies constitute major considerations for organizations. Due to the vast and complex nature of AI solutions, decision-makers are faced with a perplexing number of choices, which are accompanied by the positive and negative aspects and organizational impacts (Radonjić, Duarte, & Pereira, 2022). For instance, Machine Learning is often more suitable for prescriptive analytics, Deep Learning is well known for its ability to find out patterns in large datasets and Generative AI is best suited for content generation and simulations (Kalota, 2024).

The choice of a specific AI technology is not merely technical since it requires an understanding of strengths and weaknesses of each option and their relevance for the organization and its goals; it is a strategic decision that may significantly affect the organization's development in the future (Hagendorff & Wezel, 2020). Management has to consider how these technologies will interlink with the current operations and software development procedures. For this integration, critical planning and evaluation of several factors including the organization's basic strategic frameworks, the skills of employees and the technical support required must be settled. If the choice or implementation of the AI technology is a failure, it will resultantly cause major disruptions, resource wastage, and lost opportunities. The challenge is however exacerbated by the constant and fast development of AI technologies (Jarrahi, 2018). In the age of continuous digital transformation (Chawla et al., 2023), what is called state of the art today could be out of date or surpassed by even greater innovations. Business executives should therefore consider a number of factors including the extent at which the particular AI technology could be developed at present, and the extent to which and the type of development these may experience in the future. This requires one to adopt a proactive approach that considers the benefits of integrating AI while at the same time considering the strategic implications. The role of decision making grows in this scenario. In a world of choices, CEOs and other senior managers need to make decisions that will affect the organization's future performance over many years (Li, Li, Wang, & Thatcher, 2021).

Nevertheless, understanding how to go about with this complex decision-making process is the biggest challenge since they are expected to assess the risks and the uncertainties of the AI technologies against their benefits, align the organization's strategic objectives to the technologies it adopts, and ensure that the technologies are integrated into the company's existing operations (Duan, Edwards, & Dwivedi, 2019). The decision on which AI technology to adopt can influence the firm's growth path, innovation capability, and competitive position. This is a complex decision-making process, thus in order to make the most effective choice, one needs comprehend both the business and technological aspects. However, the decision-making process is rife with vagueness, which is fuelled by the need to outcompete rivals, the evolving and dynamic nature of clients' needs, and the ever-changing nature of technology (Kaggwa et al., 2024). This requires one to understand the technology and the general business environment in which they will be used. To assist in this, there are traditional decision making frameworks which have been in use for many years in business to help in making strategic decisions (Ibeh et al., 2024). However, in the face of the specific problems arising from AI technologies, these models must be thoroughly assessed and perhaps modified. In this way, companies can enhance their ability to make wise, efficient decisions on how to harness the significant potential of artificial intelligence while aligning it with their objectives and ensuring a smooth integration into their existing business environments. Therefore, it is necessary to evaluate the applicability of these models in the modern context of the corporate environment and explore possible changes that may be helpful in decision-making in the context of the AI era.

In view of the above, this chapter aims to discuss the integration of the traditional decision-making models and the selection of AI technology, mainly on how these models can assist the senior executives in making the right decision. Furthermore, it explores eight of the most widely used decision-making frameworks and evaluates how well they apply to the specificities of Generative AI, Machine Learning, and Deep Learning. In doing so, it fills an important gap in the existing literature, namely, the absence of detailed information on how decision-making frameworks that are already available can be applied to the specifics of modern AI technologies. Besides, this chapter also discusses their compatibility with software development processes and paradigms. The integration of AI technologies in software development is not only a technical issue, but it is a struggle that has to be fought to achieve the organizational objectives while providing sustainable competitive advantage. Hence, through the assessment of the decision-making models, this chapter seeks to provide the senior executives with the necessary knowledge to enable them to make strategic decisions. Finally, this chapter helps to provide a better understanding of how these models can help to strategically apply AI technologies, and thus, help organisations to fully leverage the benefits of these technologies and gain a competitive advantage in the digital economy.

2. BACKGROUND

Decision making models have been a major focus in strategic management since the early times as these help the firms to have systematic approaches to tackle difficult business conditions, to navigate the right place for investing and to gain competitive advantage (Fuertes et al., 2020). Many industries have applied models such as Porter's Five Forces, Resource-Based View, and SWOT (Strengths, Weaknesses, Opportunities, Threats) analysis in the process of strategic management and decision-making. For instance, with the help of SWOT Analysis, organizations are capable of developing plans that will enable them to exploit the opportunities while minimizing the threats (Pereira, Pinto, da Costa, Dias, & Gonçalves, 2021). Similarly, the Resource-Based View underlines the necessity of sustaining competitive advantage by employing unique organizational resources and skills (Ployhart, 2021). On the other hand, Porter's Five Forces offer a method of analysing the forces that define an industry and the behaviours of the players in the market (Anastasiu, Gavriş, & Maier, 2020). The usefulness of these models is in the fact that they help to simplify the information received and present it in the form of recommendations to make the right decision.

However, these models were mainly designed in the context of conditions that existed before the rapid advancement of digital technology, especially AI. Despite the popularity of these models, there is a need to reconsider them and assess their relevance in the context of change driven by AI. The rate of advancement, the issues of ethics, and the association of technology with AI may be more than what can be explained by traditional decision-making models (Shrestha, Ben-Menahem, & Von Krogh, 2019). Thus, although these models are still valuable for offering strategic patterns, their application to the adoption of AI technology requires careful approach and, at times, adjustment to benefit from the opportunities and challenges that AI offers.

Despite strategic management literature having a significant number of studies on decision-making models, there is a relative lack of research on the use of these models in the context of AI technology adoption. Most of the current literature is, therefore, devoted to the broad themes of strategic decision-making where these models are applied, such as resource deployment, product development, and market involvement. However, the specific challenges and issues related to the integration of AI technologies based on their speed of development, technical nature, and compatibility with existing systems are often overlooked. This is vital at the time since the AI technologies introduce another layer of decision making into the process.

However, AI is not a manageable technology in the traditional sense since it involves numerous algorithms, data dependencies, and may raise some ethical concerns before implementation (Pietronudo, Croidieu, & Schiavone, 2022). The literature on strategic management is rather scarce in terms of detailed recommendations on how the traditional decision-making frameworks can be adapted to address these specific concerns. With AI becoming more and more present in various industries, the decision-making process regarding the implementation of AI technologies becomes critical. However, without AI-specific decision-making frameworks, organizations would struggle to effectively handle AI adoption concerns (Pumplun, Tauchert, & Heidt, 2019).

While the adoption of AI technology may be complex, the traditional decision-making models remain relevant because they offer structured approaches that can be adapted to accommodate the complexities of AI (Trunk, Birkel, & Hartmann, 2020). For instance, internal strengths such as technical know-how or data assets and external opportunities such as the increasing market demand for AI-based products can be used to assess the organization's preparedness for AI, by applying the SWOT analysis (Greif, Kimmig, El Bobbou, Jurisch, & Ovtcharova, 2024; Palomares et al., 2021). Additionally, in order to guarantee that AI investments enhance competitive advantages, organizations can select AI technologies that fill the gap between their specific resources and competencies with the help of the resource-based view (Chowdhury et al., 2023). In the same manner, Porter's Five Forces can be used to analyse the competitive forces surrounding the implementation of AI technology, which can help firms understand the broader context of the market and potential threats from disruptive innovations or new entrants (Danemo, 2018).

However, these models may need to be adjusted to capture the unique features of AI technologies. Some of the frameworks that might require an update in the light of AI are Porter's competitive forces model where the impact of AI on value chains, customers and regulatory environment may have to be incorporated (Isabelle, Horak, McKinnon, & Palumbo, 2020). There is also the need for a more dynamic and cyclical model of decision making due to the fast pace at which AI is being developed, something that past models may not be fully capable of handling (Borges, Laurindo, Spínola, Gonçalves, & Mattos, 2021). This is where the continuous observation, orientation, decision-making, and act processes as featured in the OODA (Observe, Orient, Decide and Act) Loop. Being said that, there is a dire need to blend the classic old models with more flexible ones, allowing organizations to leverage AI technology more effectively which will ultimately enable them to validate their objectives in accordance with modern technology and organizational goals.

While the conventional decision-making models are deemed significant for strategic management, their application to the use of AI technology requires a fair amount of thinking and, at times, adjustment (Bag, Gupta, Kumar, & Sivarajah, 2021). Considering the aforementioned loopholes, this chapter aims to look at these changes and give insight on how senior executives can use these models to manage the issues of implementing AI, which will in the long run enhance the company's ability to unlock the transformative power of AI technology. Thus, by presenting a literature review on the applicability, benefits, and limitations of traditional decision-making models in the context of AI adoption, the chapter aims to contribute to the existing literature and encourage better AI implementation in organizations.

3. EVALUATION OF DECISION MAKING MODELS

3.1. SWOT Analysis

SWOT stands for Strengths, Weaknesses, Opportunities, Threats. SWOT Analysis is one of the oldest strategic management tools that identify company's internal strengths and weaknesses as well as external opportunities and threats. Conceived in the year 1960 by Albert Humphrey, SWOT has grown to be one of the key paradigm principles in the strategic management field that assists in strategy formulation and assessing an organization's performance (Puyt, Lie, & de Graaf, 2017). It is still considerably useful concerning AI adoption as it is frequently used to define and compare the most critical factors influencing strategic decisions. In the case of the AI business and its adoption, this framework assists in the assessment of internal and external factors that affect the ability of an organization to implement and use AI (Palazzo & Micozzi, 2024). The strengths of organisations may include culture of innovation or existing technical skills and can however influence the results of the integration processes. For example, a team with skills in data science will help in the implementation of AI solutions. In this way, organizations strengthen themselves to build upon the benefits of the AI technologies and ensure that the adoption process matches their competitive strategies.

- **Strengths:** In terms of AI, organization's strengths might be related to the culture of innovation or technical expertise. Additionally, an advanced team skilled in data science can facilitate a more effective AI execution (Provost & Fawcett, 2013). Organizations highlight strengths they provide to the emerging AI technologies, ensuring that the acquisition is aligned with strategic capabilities.
- **Weaknesses:** Internal weaknesses may refer to the absence of technical skills, an outdated technology portfolio or simply not wanting to change within the organization when it comes to the use of AI (Paschen, Pitt, & Kietzmann, 2020). Lack of skills in AI or having low quality data affects the launch and use of these technologies (Dwivedi et al., 2021). This allows the firms to be able to tackle these weaknesses and do so in a manner that significantly reduces resistance towards the adoption of AI across the organizations.
- **Opportunities:** Availability and increased use of AI applications, improvement of the algorithms used in the machine learning processes as well as increased need for AI solutions are indicators of success for the organizations. They usually define an opportunity to leverage the progress in IT and extend to new markets the application of more sophisticated forms of AI (Cioffi, Travaglioni, Piscitelli, Petrillo, & De Felice, 2020).
- **Threats**: Competitive forces, legal factors, and ethical factors are the main causes of the external threats. Other competitors who embraced the new technologies in implementing their AI strategies may outdo an organization, or the emergence of new laws on data protection and AI citizenship might affect the viability of AI strategies. Thus, recognizing such threats, firms can minimize risks, for instance, by focusing on ethical AI solutions and analysing competitors' activities (Du & Xie, 2021).

The strength of SWOT analysis in the context of AI lies in the simplicity and comprehensiveness. It gives a broad view of the micro and macro environment in relation to AI and thus can be used in strategic management. Also, SWOT helps to avoid the possible over-optimistic or pessimistic approach to the AI strategies by considering the strengths, weaknesses, opportunities, and threats (Raydugin, 2024). Figure 1 visually represents the components of the SWOT analysis in the context of AI adoption.

Figure 1. Relevance of SWOT analysis

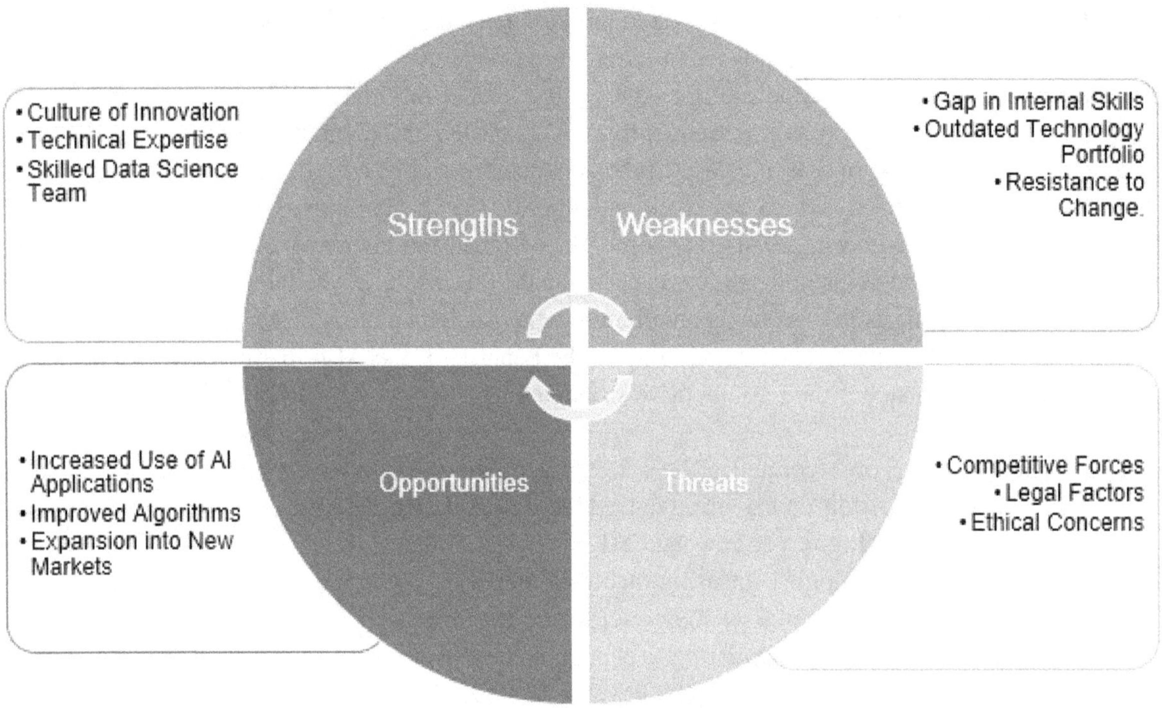

However, SWOT analysis comes with certain drawbacks due to its qualitative nature as it is sometimes based on subjective evaluations, and it might not reflect on the details of the AI technologies or their dynamic advancements (KIPČIĆ). However, it does not include information on how exactly each of the discovered factors should be prioritized and addressed, which is essential in the context of the rapidly developing domain of AI technology. To overcome these limitations, it is advisable to use SWOT analysis in conjunction with such models and frameworks that provide more specific recommendations on the strategic management and the organizational risks. For instance, it can be used in conjunction with a more dynamic model such as the OODA Loop to aid in dealing with the challenges and risk factors that come with adopting AI technologies.

3.2. Resource-Based View (RBV)

RBV is a strategic management concept which asserts that resources and capabilities within the firm are the main sources of competitive advantage (Assensoh-Kodua, 2019). Originally constructed in the late 1980s by Jay Barney and Margaret Peteraf, the RBV stresses the fact that an organization's resources such as technological know-how, patents, and organizational culture can form inimitable value only if they are valuable, rare, costly to imitate, and have no close substitutes (Yewei & Pereira, 2022). When applied to the field of AI technology adoption, RBV offers a theoretical lens through which the role that the organization's internal resources and capabilities can play in the successful deployment and use of AI technologies can be assessed. RBV postulates that through capitalization on the heterogeneity of resources found in an organization, that organisation can gain competitive advantage in the marketplace (Ferreira, Fernandes, & Ferreira, 2022). Additionally, it assists organisations in operating on their existing assets to get the best out of the technologies.

- **Valuable Resource:** Resources according to RBV must be valuable in a way that it facilitates the achievement of a competitive advantage. In the case of AI, potential resources can be state-of-art data analytics solutions, qualified workforce with the knowledge of machine learning, and an IT infrastructure that can facilitate the use of AI. For example, AI technologies are even more useful to organizations which have the adequate infrastructure for handling large amounts of data as well as a talented data science department (Benbya, Davenport, & Pachidi, 2020). Thus, by defining and focusing on such valuable resources, organizations can strengthen their AI potential and achieve more favourable results.
- **Rare Resources:** Access to factors that are scarce and cannot be easily imitated by the competitors is beneficial. In the context of AI, some of the rare resources could be specialized algorithms, specific databases or sets of information or new-age technologies. For instance, an organization that has bought a patent for an advanced AI algorithm that performs better than the ones available in the market is a competitive advantage. According to RBV, such resources should be leveraged to create a gap between the organisation and the competitors in the AI sector (Mikalef, Fjørtoft, & Torvatn, 2019).
- **Inimitable Resources:** The resources that cannot be easily copied or emulated help in achieving competitive advantage (Nikmah, Rahmawati, & Sukma, 2021). When it comes to AI, inimitable resources might be organizational culture, a strong and well-rooted experience, and exclusive relations with the providers of technologies. For instance, an organization that has done numerous projects in the past in the area of AI, or an organization that is open to new ideas and risk-taking, will prove to be more effective in both the adoption as well as deployment of AI technologies. Thus, by paying more attention to the creation and sustenance of these human resources, organisations can sustain a competitive advantage over a long period (Patra & Dash, 2023).
- **Non-Substitutable Resources:** Resources also have to be inalienable, that is, there must be no similar resources that can be used in the place of the existing ones (Lubis, 2022). In the AI field, this may encompass the incorporation of specific AI tools with other business functions that are difficult to imitate by competitors. For example, a combination of AI-based customer analytics and customized services that are closely embedded in an organization's processes may not be easily imitated by rivals. The identification and utilization of VRIO (value, rarity, imitability, and organization) framework help in the identification of resources that cannot be replaced or easily imitated by competitors, thus guaranteeing the organization's unique and valuable AI capabilities. As for AI technology adoption, RBV offers a framework for analysing the organization's strengths and resources this would help the organization to ensure that its investments in AI are complementary to the current competencies of the organization (Chowdhury et al., 2023). Since RBV concentrates on valuable, rare, inimitable, and non-substitutable resources, the framework enables

organisations to discover ways of utilising their strengths for the effective application of AI. Figure 2 represents how the organization's internal resources and capabilities can lead to a sustained competitive advantage in the context of AI adoption.

Figure 2. Relevance of RBV

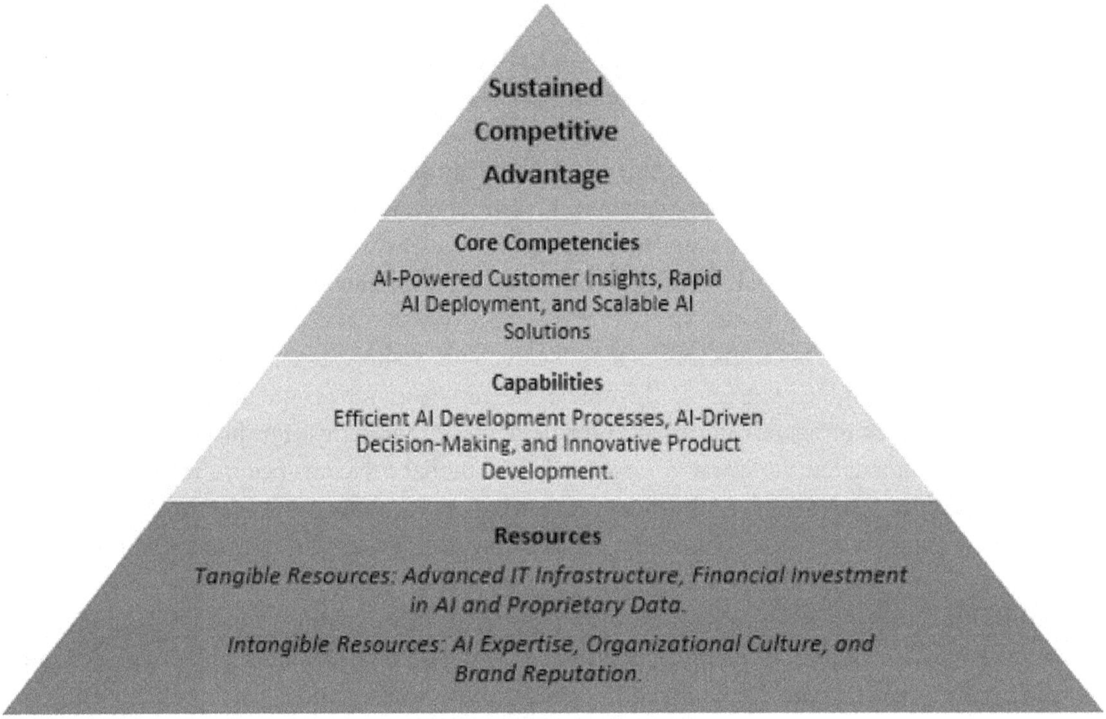

However, RBV also has limitations as it may not pay adequate attention to factors outside the organization that can also affect the implementation of AI, for instance, market trends, changes in regulatory policies, and advancements in technology (Lubis, 2022). Also, with the constantly changing and dynamic systems and technologies embedded in the delivery of AI services, RBV may not capture this dynamism appropriately. Therefore, it is suggested that organizations might find it useful to combine RBV with other decision-making frameworks that take into account external conditions and the constantly evolving nature of AI technology. For example, combining RBV with frameworks like SWOT or PESTLE can provide a more comprehensive view of the internal and external factors influencing AI adoption, enabling organizations to develop a more balanced and informed strategy.

3.3. Core Competencies

Core competence is a strategic management concept developed by C.K. Prahalad and G.Hamel in early 1990's. This model centers on the conviction that an organization should take advantage of the activities in which it is a best performer, those that give considerable competitive advantage and are critical to the delivery of customer value (Enginoğlu & Arikan, 2016). In case of utilizing AI technologies, the element that concerns core competencies is highly applicable. Through the process of determining strategic business competencies, it becomes possible to incorporate AI technologies that build upon the organization's strengths and expand its strategic capacity. Competencies give a foundation on which a firm can assess how AI technologies can be applied to build up on existing strengths and gain competitive edge (Eriksen & Mikkelsen, 2013). Figure 3 highlights how specific organizational capabilities, when aligned with AI adoption, can provide a competitive edge.

Figure 3. Core competencies model

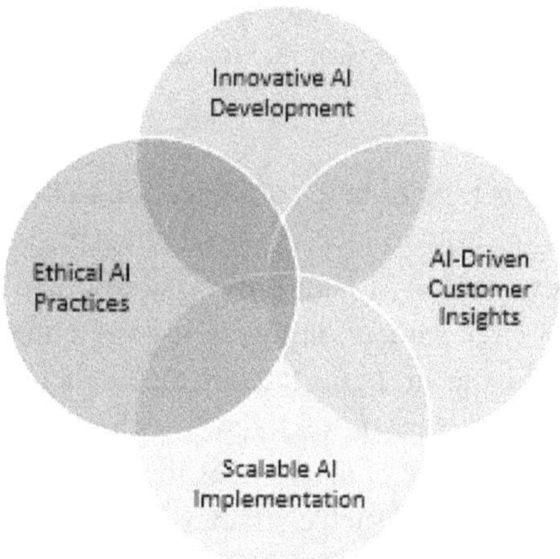

- **Identification of Core Competencies**: The first stage in applying the core competencies model to the implementation of AI is to assess the organization's current core competencies (Kawshala, 2017). Some of these might be specialized content knowledge in specific areas of business, higher technological proficiency, or specific process proficiencies. for instance, a firm that specializes in data analysis and understands customers' buying behaviour patterns may possess a competitive advantage that is relevant to embedding AI solutions like forecast analysis or customer segmentation. It is therefore important to identify and understand these core competencies since they guide the organization to leverage AI technologies in line with and that augment its strengths.
- **Leveraging Core Competencies**: When core competencies are defined, it is possible to use them as a starting point to determine the strategy of choosing and implementing AI technologies (Przegalinska & Jemielniak, 2023). Instead, those AI technologies should be selected and deployed in a manner that reinforces these fundamental strengths. For example, a firm with high

R&D capacity could leverage the use of innovative AI technologies in research and development. It depicts that AI investments should focus on sectors that are most important for the organization, and by doing so, the role of AI in the organization's strategic vision should be strengthened.

- **Enhancing Core Competencies**: AI technologies can also be applied to increase and diversify the strengths of organizational tasks. For instance, the use of AI in generating insights and automating different tasks leads to optimisation of organisational processes, better decision making, and improved customer experience that in turn boosts the organisation's competency (Raisch & Krakowski, 2021). An organization with a key competence in customer service may incorporate the use of AI in facilitating customer relations such as using chatbots and virtual assistants to enhance customer relations hence strengthening the organization's competitive advantage. However, it is important to note that AI can give solutions and tools that enhance the strengths that organizations already possess to bring more value to the customers.
- **Protecting Core Competencies**: The combination of resources can be a source of competitive advantage only when the core competence itself is inimitable. Technologies that are locked into the organization or are bespoke to the organization's business can support and maintain such competencies (Kabue & Kilika, 2016). For example, developing custom AI algorithms or creating specialized and dependable data sources can be challenging for competitors to replicate. The general understanding of AI technologies' position is sustained by fit and protection of AI-competencies in the organizational core.

The identification of core competencies helps organization to make wiser decisions on which of the AI technologies to adopt as well as how to incorporate them effectively in an organization (Fountaine, McCarthy, & Saleh, 2019). Nevertheless, it can only partially take into account external conditions, including changes in the market environment, innovations, and competition affecting the development of AI. Furthermore, by focusing on the strengths that are already known, the model may not be prepared for the quick changes that are characteristic of today's technology environment. To overcome such scenarios, it is useful to combine the core competencies model with other decision-making approaches that take into account the environment and such characteristics of AI technology as its development. For instance, integration of the core competencies model with SWOT or PESTLE can give a more extended vision of the internal and external environments, and enable organizations to have a more flexible and holistic AI implementation plan.

3.4. Porter's Five Forces

The Five Force analysis is a business strategy created by Michael E. Porter in 1979 that aims to describe the nature of competition in an industry. This model examines five key forces that shape competitive intensity and market attractiveness. Through the assessment of such forces, it is possible to identify the competitive forces in an industry and design ways of enhancing the competitive advantage of an organization (Gerard & Bruijl, 2019). In the context of the decision-making process of adopting AI technology, Porter's Five Forces offer insight into how competitor forces affect strategy formulation. This analysis must be of great help in understanding the nature of forces that surround AI implementation and the way the organization can align itself with the industry. Figure 4 visually represents how the five forces impact the adoption of AI technologies within an industry.

Figure 4. Porter's five force

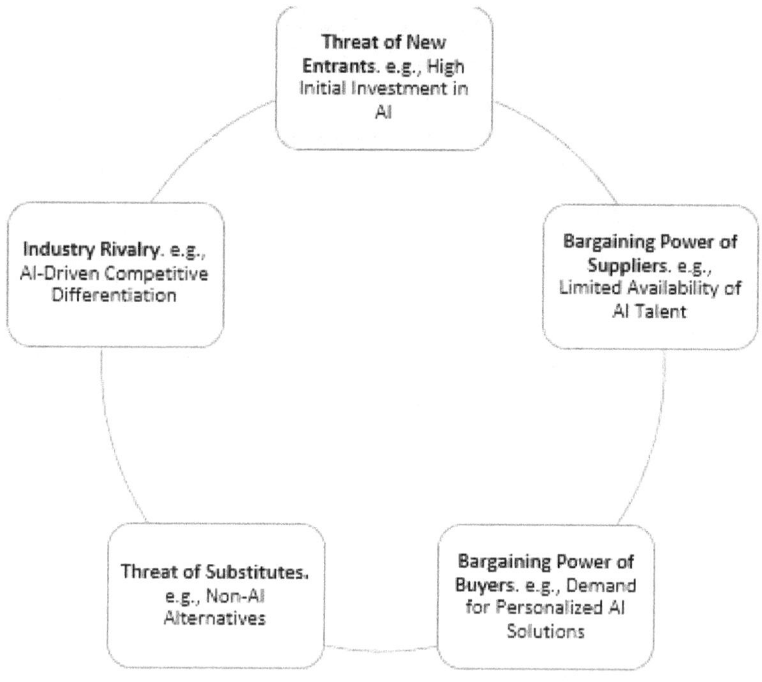

- **Threat of New Entrants**: Owing to the possibility that new rivals can enter the market and pose a threat to established players in the market, this force looks at how new AI start-ups or technology companies could potentially pose a threat to the industry (Horowitz, Allen, Kania, & Scharre, 2022). For instance, the new, ground-breaking AI products or services may reduce the entry barriers for new competitors and, thus, intensify competition. Organizations have to assess the threat that carries entry of new entrants leveraging on the AI technologies and whether the organization has to develop higher order AI capabilities to counter them.
- **Bargaining Power of Suppliers**: This force evaluates the power that suppliers in the industry hold. In the AI context, suppliers might be technology providers, data suppliers and AI solution creators. In cases where suppliers develop or provide exclusive or specialized AI technologies, they are likely to pull most of the power when dealing with an organization that wants to adopt such technologies. For instance, a few key suppliers of AI technologies may be able to charge premium prices or include unfavourable conditions under which an organization can implement advanced AI solutions. Supplier dynamics involve assessing the supplier's performance in relation to the organization's needs so as to enable the organization to plan on how to deal with the supplier in case of any risks.
- **Bargaining Power of Buyers**: The bargaining power of buyers is the ability of the customers to affect the industry. In the case of AI, buyers may encompass those organizations that require AI solutions or consumers of AI-based goods and services (Allal-Chérif, Simón-Moya, & Ballester, 2021). When the bargaining power of buyers is strong, they are likely to ask for lower prices, better quality, and/or specific AI solutions. For instance, some customers such as big businesses

or those that are more technologically inclined can bargain for a better deal or demand enhanced functionalities of AI technologies. By analysing buyer power organizations can adjust their AI services to clients' needs and thus improve their market positions.

- **Threat of Substitute Products or Services:** This force looks at the threat that other products pose that can substitute the products from the industry in question. Substitutes in context of AI might be other technologies or methods that will yield similar results. For example, conventional approaches to data analysis or data processing can be considered as the substitutes for some AI solutions (Krakowski, Luger, & Raisch, 2023). Managers must analyse if the AI technologies offer the necessary degree of differentiation and additional value compared to these substitutes and if they need to update their solutions constantly in order to outcompete the available alternatives.
- **Intensity of Competitive Rivalry:** This is the measure of the competition that already exists in the industry, meaning the ferocity of rivalry between the players. In the AI domain, competitive rivalry can be cut throat due to technological change and the emergence of new entrants. For instance, those firms that operate in the field of artificial intelligence may engage in cut-throat competition with the view to attain technological advancements and market share. The analysis of competitive rivalry allows organizations to define new opportunities and threats, for example, new partners or areas in which the company needs to strengthen AI capabilities to avoid competitors' encroachment (Gianiodis, Markman, & Panagopoulos, 2019).

In the context of the AI technology adoption, Porter's Five Forces framework gives a systematic approach to the analysis of competitive forces and the patterns that define them, and how each of the forces may impact on the strategic plans (Henry, 2021). Through these forces, an organization is able to analyse market pressures and formulate ways of handling forces that affect it in a competitive environment. However, the application of Porter's Five Forces also has some drawbacks. It mainly centers on the dynamics at the industry level and does not incorporate the detailed rate of change and innovation known to be characteristic of AI technology. Furthermore, the model does not contain information on some of the practical issues that are associated with AI including those that relate to integration or those that are ethical in nature (Min, Liangwen, & Yue, 2018). To overcome these weaknesses, the organizations should implement the analysis of the Porter's Five Forces with other decision-making tools to explore technological and operational implications of AI implementation.

3.5. Ansoff Matrix

Ansoff Matrix also known as the Ansoff Growth Matrix is a strategic planning tool that was formulated by Igor Ansoff in the year 1957. It allows organization to assess their strategic development by looking at the roles of products and markets. The matrix outlines four primary growth strategies. This involves the development of new markets for current products, the identification of new products that can be marketed in the existing markets, and the expansion of the company's products line (Zugay & Zakaria, 2023), as illustrated in figure 5.

Figure 5. Ansoff matrix

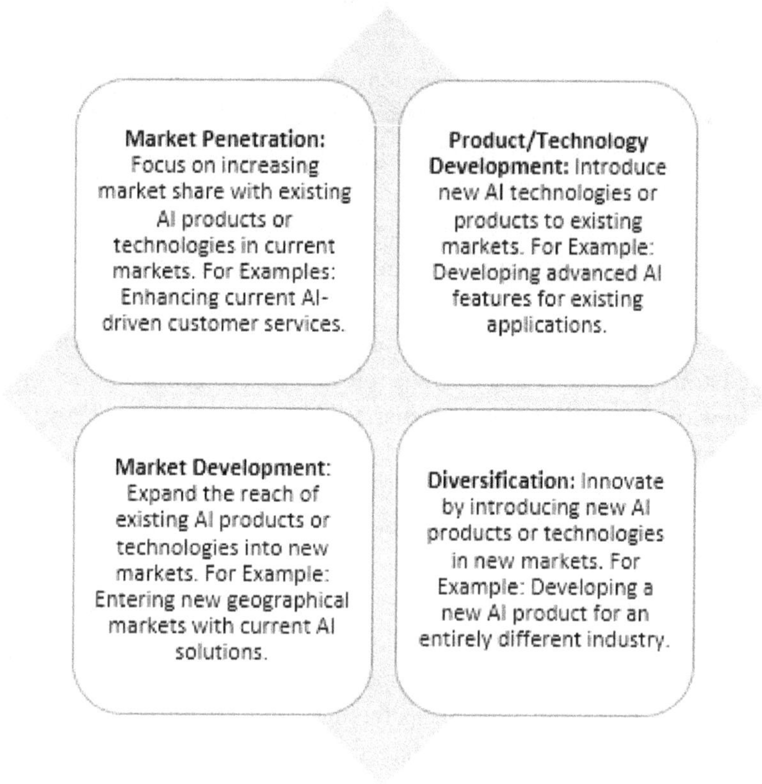

The examination of these strategies will help to define the prospects for development and the threats that may be faced by an organization in the context of the choice of a particular model. To summarize, the Ansoff Matrix in the framework of AI technology adoption provides relevant insights on how the organization can manage AI technologies to increase its market position and growth. When placed on the matrix, organizations can see various opportunities of applying AI to advance their market presence and products (Clarissia, 2020).

- **Market Penetration:** Market Penetration involves the strategy of trying to sell more of the presently available products or services in the existing markets. For AI technology adoption, this strategy involves the use of AI in the improvement of existing products and services and aiming to capture a bigger share of the existing market within the given consumer niches (Kurniawan, Iswahyudin, & Suciati, 2020). For instance, a firm that already sells CRM software for customers can apply AI to enhance the analytics and anticipatory integration of the software, which would help it cement its stand in the current market. Hence, it is clear that by enhancing product performance and customer value through AI, organizations can get higher sales and more market share.
- **Market Development:** Market Development entails extension of present products or services to new markets. Within AI context, this strategy entails applying AI technologies to expand geographically or target new customers (Tsatsoula, 2018). For instance, a firm offering AI based

financial analysis and forecasts may look to expand to geographies that have not been explored or into sectors where the adoption of such tools is still in its infancy. Organizations can increase their chances to utilize new opportunities by employing AI for adjusting the offered portfolio to the needs of new markets.

- **Product Development:** Product Development is on the creation of new products to satisfy the needs of existing markets. For AI technology adoption, this strategy involves creating new AI solutions or additional AI features for meeting new needs of existing customers. For instance, an organization focused on e-commerce software solutions will likely create new AI applications for targeted purchasing interfaces, recommendations, or chatbots. Thus, by innovating and adding value through AI within the product, organizations can bolster their portfolio and customers' loyalty.
- **Diversification:** In this strategy, business ventures into new territories with new goods or services to offer to its customers. This strategy can be relevant for AI technology adoption when companies want to enter new markets or develop new disruptive AI technologies (Dawes, 2018). For instance, a firm in the business of AI robotics could branch out into the healthcare industry by designing medical equipment or diagnostic machines with AI. AI can help in diversification as it opens up new opportunities for organizations hence break the tact with existing markets.

Ansoff Matrix offers a guideline on how to assess growth plans and enables organizations to synchronize their AI activities with their strategic plan. Thus, by dividing AI adoption strategies into the growth directions, the matrix allows evaluating the prospects and threats of particular actions (Chintalapati, 2020). However, it also has certain limitations as it tends to oversimplify the factors which are inherent in the adoption of AI technology and the risks that come with it. For instance, creating new AI products or venturing into new markets with AI solutions are processes that imply numerous challenges that are technological, market-oriented, and competitive in nature. The matrix does not inherently address these complexities or provide detailed guidance regarding the management of the AI strategies' execution. To overcome these limitations, it is possible to recommend the use of the Ansoff Matrix in conjunction with other decision-making tools characterizing the peculiarities of AI technology implementation. Further, it is crucial to use the frameworks which can explain the practical sides of AI integration and competitive advantage: Resource-Based View (RBV) or Porter's Five Forces.

3.6. PESTLE Analysis

PESTLE Analysis is a business analysis tool used to assess the large external environment that may affect an organization. Originally, PESTLE was designed in the early 1990s and it is the acronym for Political, Economic, Social, Technological, Legal, and Environmental factors as illustrated in figure 6. This framework assists organizations in realizing the environment in which they exist and the possibilities of threats and opportunities that the environment may present (Rastogi & Trivedi, 2016). When used to analyse AI technology adaptation, it gives a complete picture of the macro environment that may facilitate or hinder the implementation and integration of AI technologies. Thus, understanding these macro-environmental factors will help organizations deal with the AI challenges and come up with appropriate tactics given the external environment.

- **Political Factors:** Political factors consist of the government policies, regulations, and stability that can influence the use of AI technology. For instance, privacy, data protection and cybersecurity guidelines on the use of AI systems have considerable influence on the application of AI solutions. Fluctuations of public policies and political conditions can impact the applicability and the expenses of the AI technologies. It is crucial for organizations to be aware of political processes and adapt to them and abide by the rules at the same time in order to avoid or seize the opportunities in the field of AI (Eierle, Hartlieb, Hay, Niemi, & Ojala, 2022).
- **Economic Factors:** Economic factors refer to the macro-economic factors in the economy such as; economic growth, inflation rates as well as exchange rates affecting an organization's capacity to fund and implement AI solutions. For example, during recession, organizations are likely to experience financial constraints hence the inability to implement sophisticated AI systems. On the other hand, favourable economic conditions can lead to an increased spending on the development of AI and technological advancement. Knowledge of economic conditions assists organizations to decide the approach they are going to use in the implementation of AI, depending on the state of the economy and their financial capacity (Khan, Ali, Petrillo, & De Felice, 2023).
- **Social Factors:** The social influence consists of public opinion on AI, threat of being replaced by AI, and the willingness to use AI-enabled products and services. For instance, the negative perception about the ability of AI technologies to cause loss of jobs or innovation, or ethical issues might lead to reduced consumer acceptance or policies on technology regulation (Sheikh, 2020). Organisations should pay attention to such social perceptions and correspond with stakeholders to respond to complaints and ensure that the appropriate reception of AI technologies.
- **Technological Factors:** They include technological innovation, research and development and the rate at which such technologies are developed. In the case of AI, this relates to the ability to assess new trends, technologies, and tools that affect the use of AI. Innovations in the field of AI, for example new algorithms of machine learning or new platforms for AI, can offer benefits and risks for the involved organizations. The technological advancements make it easier for organizations to adopt the best and the latest AI solutions in their operations (Tariq, Poulin, & Abonamah, 2021).
- **Legal Factors**: Legal factors relate to the legal framework concerning AI technology and the products that utilize the technology. This comprises laws pertaining to the protection of data, patents, trademarks, copyright among other laws that hear cases touching on particular sectors in the economy. Adherence to the law is essential when implementing AI because the breaches attract legal consequences and harm the company's image. This means that organizations need to be compliant with the current laws in the execution of their AI systems and consult the lawyers where the law is not clear (Grassi & Vallati, 2021).
- **Environmental Factors:** Environmental factors comprise of the effects of AI technology in the natural environment or even the sustainability issues at large. This ranges from evaluating the energy consumption by the infrastructures that support artificial intelligence to the electronic waste produced (Nishant, Kennedy, & Corbett, 2020). Managers are under pressure to consider environmental sustainability in the use of technology in organizations. Thus, by including sustainability and the assessment of sustainability in AI technologies, it becomes possible to meet societal and legal expectations of organizations when addressing the issue of environmental responsibility.

PESTLE analysis has several advantages when it comes to the choice of AI technology adoption, providing a general outlook of events and occurrences that may affect the AI plans of an organization, which can aid in the early detection of threats and the finding of openings. As mentioned above, PEST analysis will help organizations to have a better understanding of the political, economical, social, technological, legal, and environmental factors that can affect the implementation of AI in organizations. Nevertheless, there is a possibility that the framework will be too broad or general in defining its parameters and may not pay enough attention to details that are peculiar to a particular industry or organization in the implementation of AI. Also, it gives a single picture of macro-environment and may not be sensitive to dynamic changes taking place in environment in terms of Technology and Regulation. To overcome these weaknesses, it is possible to apply PESTLE Analysis together with other decision-making models that are more geared toward the industry and company's strengths. Moreover, updating the analysis at certain time intervals to make it relevant to the current state of affairs in the organisation's external environment can be useful to make the organisation more responsive to the changes (Do, Budhwar, Shipton, Nguyen, & Nguyen, 2022).

Figure 6. Pestle analysis

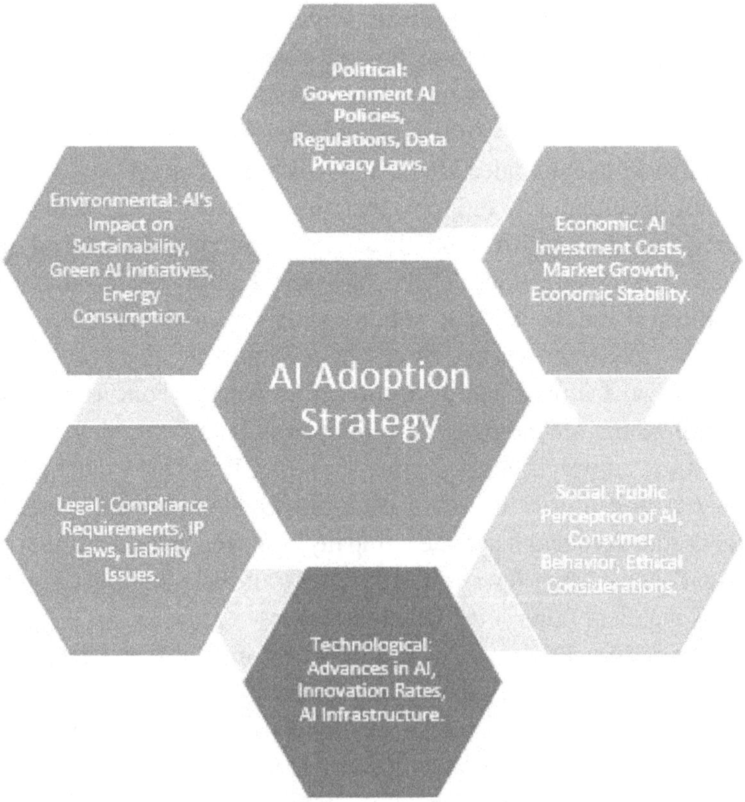

3.7. Six Thinking Hats

Six Thinking Hats, invented by Edward de Bono in 1985, involves looking at a problem from six distinct perspectives, each represented by a different colour hat: White, Red, Black, Yellow, Green and Blue as depicted in figure 7. This framework promotes an elaborate analysis of issues by organizing thinking processes and creating a rounded perspective of the problem under analysis. Additionally, in relevance to decision-making, it also works as a methodical framework for analysing AI-related decisions (de Villiers, 2022). Using this method, organizations can guarantee that there is inclusion of different perspectives and that various aspects related to AI incorporation are tackled systematically. Furthermore, it assists in making balanced decisions since it captures a broad view of the situation and its impacts, thus also entails early identification of risks and prospects.

Figure 7. Six thinking hats

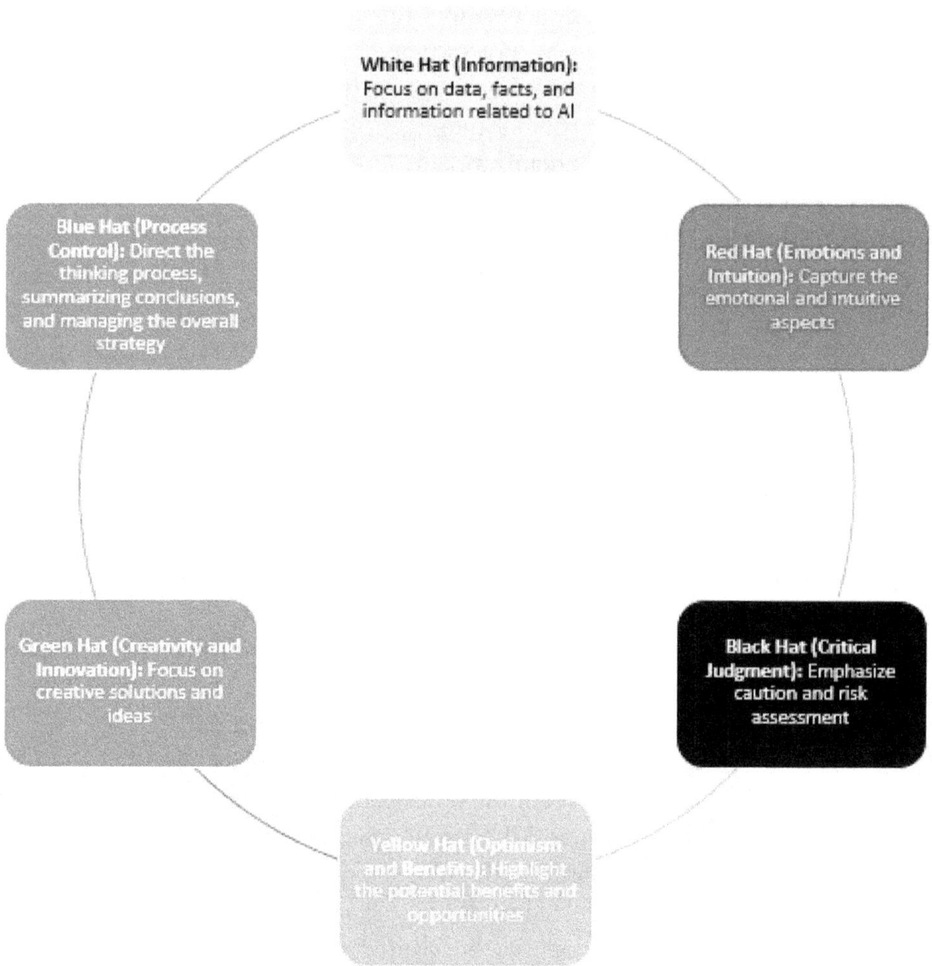

- **White Hat (Objective Thinking):** The White Hat is characterized by facts and data. In AI technology adoption, this perspective entails the collection of factual information about the AI solutions including efficiency, cost, benefits, and characteristics among others. For example, using the White Hat perspective an organization may consider the precision, credibility, and modularity of the models before selecting one. The use of data in this case makes it possible for decision making to be done with tangible evidence and not just on the basis of the decision maker's perception (de Villiers, 2022).
- **Red Hat (Emotional Thinking)**: The Red Hat takes into consideration feelings, hunches, and guts feelings. AI technologies' implementation requires identifying the emotional responses of stakeholders, including personnel, consumers, and top managers. For instance, the employees may have fear of loss of their jobs due to outsourcing as a result of adoption of AI while the customers may be cautious about their personal information being exploited by the organizations. From the Red Hat perspective, it is possible to deal with such emotional issues, to communicate with the stakeholders with understanding and to work out the strategies that would neutralize negative emotions and create acceptance (Göçmen & Coşkun, 2019).
- **Black Hat (Critical Thinking)**: The Black Hat is used to determine risks, problems, and threats in a project. In the case of the AI conversation, this approach entails evaluating the risks and drawbacks of adopting AI technologies. For instance, organizations can assess the risks that include data security threats and vulnerabilities, issues in the integration of AI and machine learning solutions, or ethical concerns on Artificial Intelligence-driven decisions. In this way, the Black Hat perspective is beneficial for an organization as it will help to exclude possible deficits in the chosen strategy of AI adoption (Göçmen & Coşkun, 2019).
- **Yellow Hat (Optimistic Thinking):** The Yellow Hat focuses on the positives and possible gains. When applied to the process of AI technologies assessment, this lens implies the identification of AI benefits and opportunities. For instance, organizations might ponder over the ways in which AI can be used to, improve processes, introduce novelty, and generate income streams. Through the Yellow Hat approach, an organisation will be able to focus on the positive aspects of AI implementation and therefore, the strategic direction will be towards positive and growth-oriented objectives (Aithal & Kumar, 2017).
- **Green Hat (Creative Thinking):** Creative thinking and coming up with ideas are the main themes of The Green Hat. In reference to AI adoption, this view motivates organizations to consider new and unique ways of approaching AI technologies. For instance, organisations could look at exploring new ways such as creating new unique products that incorporate AI or looking at ways in which they can harness AI for competitive edge. Thus, using the concept of the Green Hat perspective, it is possible to promote a culture of innovation and consider other possibilities of implementing AI in the organization (Turan, Fidan, & Yıldıran, 2019).
- **Blue Hat (Process Thinking):** In the case of the thinking process, the Blue Hat looks after the process and supervises the application of the other hats. This perspective involves the systematic approach to decision making, where all the argumentation is properly coordinated and properly laid out. In the evaluation of AI solutions, the blue hat perspective entails the coordination of the evaluation process, stakeholder management, and the implementation plan. Through the use of Blue Hat perspective, the organizations can be assured of an orderly manner of making decisions regarding artificial intelligence (Gupta & Bodhankar, 2023).

By considering the factual, emotional, critical, optimistic, creative, and process perspectives, organizations can make more rational and global decisions regarding AI integration. Nonetheless, it is important to state that Six Thinking Hats also has some drawbacks. The process may take a lot of time and effort to research each view, and some of the stakeholders may not be well acquainted with or enthusiastic about employing the framework. Also, the method can help develop various ideas, but it might not be sufficient to address the technical and operational aspects of AI technology implementation (Gupta & Bodhankar, 2023). To overcome these limitations, organizations might want to integrate the Six Thinking Hats approach with other decision-making methods that offer information on technical, strategic, and operational factors related to AI implementation.

3.8. OODA Loop

OODA Loop stands for Observe, Orient, Decide, and Act and it is a decision-making cycle intended by the US Air Force Colonel John Boyd in the 1980s. The name is actually an acronym of the four steps it comprises; namely, Observe, Orient, Decide, and Act which focuses on the cyclic process that enables people and companies to make decisions and respond to new conditions quickly (Rabaey, 2015). Invented to fit the military and battle environment, the OODA Loop has been applied to different decision-making domains, including the business and tech ones. Therefore, especially when it comes to AI technology adoption, the OODA Loop can be considered as a rather effective and dynamic decision-making model in the context of the constantly developing technology environment (Johnson, 2023). Thus, the cyclical nature of the OODA Loop enables organizations to constantly evaluate and adapt the AI strategies as it provides an opportunity to be prepared for any new opportunities or threats.

- **Observe:** The first of them is the accumulation and analysis of information about the current conditions and the state of the particular environment in which the use of artificial intelligence technology is planned (Vettorello, Eisenbart, & Ranscombe, 2019). These consist of tracking technology, markets, and regulations as well as the dynamics of competition. For instance, an organization may notice new AI technologies, customers' trends and changes in requirements, and other alterations. Through such factors, organizations can get acquainted with possible opportunities and threats related to the use of AI.
- **Orient:** In the orientation stage, organizations make sense of the information collected in the observation stage and evaluate the information regarding the use of AI technology. This relates to the way in which the observed factors fit into the organization's strategic plan, strengths, and limitations (Maccuish, 2012). For instance, an organisation may investigate how emerging AI technologies align with organisational structures, assess the integration of AI under updated regulations as well as compare competitive benefits of various AI platforms. In the case of AI, orientation is crucial for defining the organization's goals and possibilities for its intelligent solutions.
- **Decide:** The decision making phase entails choosing the right strategy out of the available ones depending on the observation and orientation phase. This entails decisions on which particular AI technologies to deploy, how to implement them and goals to set in AI integration (Vettorello et al., 2019). For instance, an organization may opt to acquire a specific AI system that gives the company an advantage or select a gradual AI deployment strategy to deal with risk. It should also be supported by the assessment of the organization's needs, as well as the potential benefits that can be obtained based on the choice of AI options.

- **Act:** The last one is the operation stage that means that the selected course of action will be put into practice and the AI adoption strategy will be commenced. This entails the use of AI technologies, incorporation of AI in the business operations and the evaluation of the AI systems (Johnson, 2023). For instance, an organization may decide to implement an AI for customer service, familiarize the workers with its application, and monitor the efficiency indicators to establish its impact. The action phase also encompassing of making adjustment where necessary due to some circumstances that may be experienced when implementing the AI strategy such that it meets the organizational objectives.
- **Strengths and Limitations:** The OODA Loop has several advantages in the case of AI technology implementation making it possible for organizations to effectively adapt to changes in the technology environment due to its cyclical and repetitive characteristics. Through the process of monitoring, allocating attention, selecting goals, and taking action, organisations can make decisions based on the conditions in the environment and adjust their strategies on AI (Węgrzyn, 2022). However, the model has to have a constant inflow of information and decisions need to be made swiftly, which may be problematic in conditions that are more intricate and dynamic. Moreover, the practical application of the OODA Loop also presupposes the constant and timely acquisition of relevant information, as well as its correct analysis and decision-making based on its results (In et al.). Nevertheless, when it comes to the OODA Loop in relation to AI technology adoption, there are technical and operational factors that have to be taken into consideration by organizations which are not part of this cycle. To avoid such limitations, it is possible for an organization to integrate the OODA Loop with other decision-making tools that offer further information on strategic, technical, and operational matters concerning AI implementation. For instance, using OODA Loop in conjunction with SWOT or PESTLE analysis can provide a broader perspective of internal and external conditions that affect it AI strategies. Being said that, feedback mechanisms and performance metrics are another advisable feature that can contribute to the improvement of AI solutions' strategies and the improvement of the decision-making process (Duan et al., 2019). Figure 8 illustrates how the OODA (Observe, Orient, Decide, Act) Loop can be applied to AI adoption and strategic decision-making.

Figure 8. OODA loop

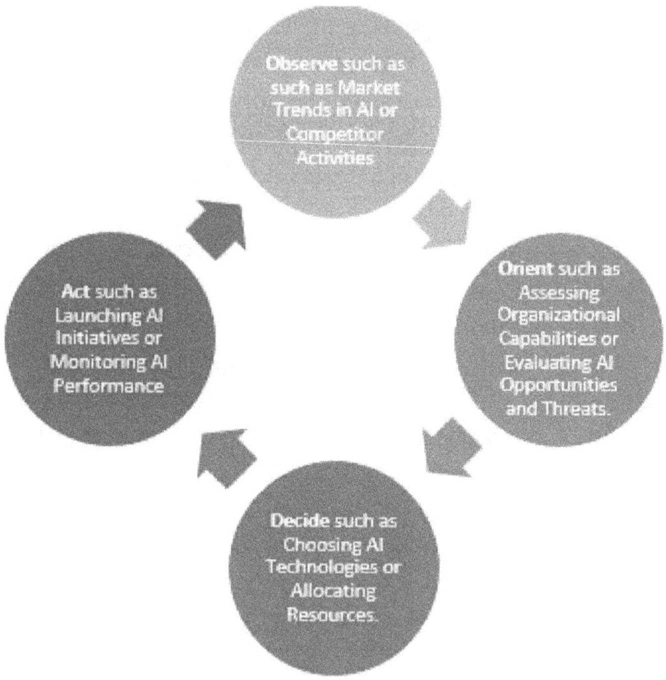

4. COMPARATIVE ANALYSIS

When comparing decision-making models that can be used to approach the implementation of AI technology, one comes to realize that each of the models has its own strengths and weaknesses and is, therefore, most appropriate for specific circumstances. Despite the fact that these models are targeted at providing support to strategic decisions, theyare very different in terms of the focus, the approach, and the suitability, which gives the decision-makers a set of tools required to address the challenges of AI integration. When comparing decision-making models concerning the adoption of AI technology both have their strengths and weaknesses.

SWOT and PESTLE analysis are very similar in terms of their objective of considering the outside environment within which an organization needs to operate, though they are not as comprehensive as each other. Since SWOT analysis covers both strengths and weaknesses of the organization as well as the opportunities and threats of the environment, it is an all-encompassing tool for achieving a general assessment of the organizational environment. In contrast, PESTLE goes further into the external macro environment focussing on the political, economic, social, technical, legal and environmental factors. This makes PESTLE especially useful for organizations that require an understanding of the external environment that may affect the organization's operations, such as changes in the regulatory environment or advancements in technology that may affect the integration of AI.

RBV and Core Competencies are similar in that both are internally focused, but they are not the same because RBV insists that the right resources be accumulated in the initial stage. In RBV, the range of value is wider and focuses on all organizational resources, material and non-material, which is explained by the fact that these assets can become a competitive advantage if AI technologies are integrated. In contrast, Core Competencies focuses on the strategic capabilities that set the organization apart from its competitors, thus informing decisions about how AI can improve the firm's key activities. For organizations that already have efficient internal mechanisms developed, these models are rather helpful for using AI as a strategic tool.

Porter's Five Forces and Ansoff Matrix are both tools designed to support market-oriented decisions, although the first one provides different visions of competition and the second one of growth. Porter's Five Forces is particularly used to analyse the competition within a particular industry, and thus is valuable for identifying how the implementation of AI might affect or be affected by competition in an industry. The Ansoff Matrix, on the other hand, helps organizations to link AI plans with growth aims, for instance, the creation of new products or penetration into new markets. It is particularly helpful to firms seeking to understand which of their current products or business segments AI could help grow or expand into new areas.

In the case of organizations functioning in environments with high uncertainty, constantly facing new challenges and needing to make quick decisions, Six Thinking Hats and OODA Loop are quite versatile and can be used in cycles. Six Thinking Hats promotes total decision-making since it encompasses different perspectives; it is useful when various opinions have to be taken into account in the AI adoption plans. OODA Loop can be effective in the conditions where the AI environment is constantly changing, and fast response is required since this model implies observation, orientation, decision-making, and action.

Finally, the appropriateness of each of the aforementioned models for adopting AI technology varies depending on the organization's environment and development goals. That way decision makers will be in a position to have a clear understanding of the strengths and weaknesses of each model and in this way be in a position to choose the best model that suits their situation. Thus, the models mentioned above can be most effective for many organizations when combined, as they cover internal and external aspects, the identification of strategic development directions, and adaptability to modern advances in AI technologies. This integrated approach helps to make the right decision on the use of AI, align it to the organization's strategic goals, and achieve sustainable competitive advantages.

5. BUSINESS CASES IN THE CONTEXT OF AI TECHNOLOGY ADOPTION AND DECISION MODELS

To contextualize how decision-making models are applicable in the adoption of AI technology, the following cases highlights how organisations are using such models to cater the complexities of AI integration.

a) OpenAI's Adoption of Generative AI Models (Feuerriegel, Hartmann, Janiesch, & Zschech, 2024):

An analysis of Open AI's development and deployment of the GPT series, especially GPT-3 and the recently unveiled GPT-4, provides a clear evidence of the application of Core Competencies and Resource-Based View (RBV). OpenAI was able to use its strengths in NLP and deep learning to build generative AI systems that are at the frontier of the technological advancements. The decision to focus on large-scale, versatile language models was based on the company's core competence in artificial intelligence and its strategic assets: data and compute. This case therefore underscores the importance of these decision models in aiding AI development strategies that reflect on organizational strengths.

b) Google's Application of Machine Learning in Search Algorithms (Singh, 2021):

The Google's refinement of its search algorithms through a machine learning system, more so with the advent of BERT (Bidirectional Encoder Representations from Transformers), exemplifies the use Porter's Five Forces and SWOT analysis. The internal and external factors led Google to incorporate the advanced ML techniques, including the competition influence and the need to protect its market position. The observation of this case helps to underpin the relevance of these models in the technology adoption decisions and, in particular, to identify how Google managed to contain the threats that emerged competitors in the AI-driven search space.

c) Tesla's Use of Deep Learning for Autonomous Driving (Muhammad, Ullah, Lloret, Del Ser, & de Albuquerque, 2020):

The application of Ansoff Matrix is evident from the way Tesla is introducing autonomous driving capabilities using the deep learning models. The integration of AI in their cars showcases that how they have begun moving into a new product category, autonomous driving, that is in line with their growth strategy. The application of AI technology in the company's business strategy as a way of market penetration and product development proves the effectiveness of Ansoff Matrix where the firm is focused on innovation and market expansion of autonomous vehicles.

d) IBM Watson Health's Shift in AI Strategy (Petiwala, Shukla, & Vyas, 2021):

The shift in focus of IBM Watson Health from general AI solutions for the healthcare sector to specific AI-based analytical tools for cancer care and genomic data proof the value of PESTLE and SWOT analysis. The execution was because decisions about the scope of coverage were based on external factors like change in legislation, emerging markets and technologies and internal factors that included the organisation's strengths and weaknesses. This, however, depicts how these decision models could be used to manage the approaches to AI adoption in light of changing external environment and internal strengths.

e) Microsoft's Investment in AI through Azure AI Services (Liu, 2022):

Microsoft's large-scale effort in increasing the Azure AI portfolio and providing generative AI and deep learning for enterprises corresponds to the OODA Loop and Six Thinking Hats. The heaviest investment in AI, therefore, was made in an incremental manner with close attention to the market needs and customers' feedback. When it comes to the application of AI to its cloud services, the Microsoft has also taken into consideration the distinctive views about the advantages and disadvantages of utilizing AI, which complies with the OODA Loop and Six Thinking Hats. This showcases how these models can assist organizations to be more adaptive to market changes in emerging AI markets.

The aforementioned cases reveal that the historically grounded and tested decision-making models are still valid and capable of being applied for the selection of the state-of-the-art modern AI technologies like generative AI, machine learning, and deep learning. When applied, these models help organizations to understand how AI can be integrated and how the choices made in this process correspond to overall organizational strategies and market trends.

6. REGULATORY PERSPECTIVE AND FUTURE OUTLOOK

The integration of artificial intelligence technologies including generative AI, machine learning, and deep learning in organizations is becoming more regulated due to the constantly changing regulatory environment (Ooi et al., 2023). Intensive efforts are being made by governments and various regulatory authorities across the globe to come up with frameworks that would address both the ethical, legal as well as the social considerations of AI (Saxena et al., 2021, 2023). These regulations are designed to provide better control and regulation of AI to avoid its misuse, especially in aspects such as data protection, biases in algorithms, and self-automated decisions (Yaghmai, 2021). For organizations, this implies that the decision-making frameworks relevant for AI adoption have to factor in the current and future regulatory framework. PESTLE analysis is particularly appropriate here because it can help an organisation determine the political/ legal environment and how it may affect the integration of AI (Grassi & Vallati, 2021). Noncompliance with these regulations can result in legal consequences, legal fines and lawsuits, and loss of reputation. Thus, choosing and applying AI technologies, decision-makers should take into consideration existing regulations and predict changes in legislation.

It is however evident that the future of adoption of AI technology would be full of both opportunities and challenges. Over time, AI will improve and become almost innate within the functioning of business and so, to keep up with the advances, organizations will have to adapt their decision-making frameworks to keep pace with technological advancements. The increased complexity of AI systems is probable to prompt the emergence of new decision-making approaches or the modification of the current ones to fit the intricacies of AI implementation. Nonetheless, as AI is integrated into more processes, the legal requirements for using AI systems will be more stringent. Ultimately, the organizations will face the necessity of dealing with advance regulations that are more specific and detailed regarding the AI ethics, data utilization, and security issues. The capacity of being adaptive to these changes will be very crucial, underscoring the importance of models like the OODA Loop that we take into consideration while making decisions.

7. LIMITATIONS AND IMPLICATIONS

Despite such models being a useful guide to AI technology adoption, they are not without their drawbacks. Some of these models were conceived before digital technology with the possibility of not wholly capturing the intricacies and speed of change in AI. For example, the models such as SWOT or Ansoff Matrix may oversimplify the complexity of AI technologies thereby failing to consider the interconnectedness of AI components or the ethical issues that are connected with the deployment of AI. Furthermore, some models may not be flexible enough in order to adapt to the rapidly changing developments in the field of AI. For instance, Porter's Five Forces analyse the competitive environment but may not fully capture the dynamics and disruptions that can be created by AI-driven innovations shifting the markets quickly. Furthermore, the use of these models needs expertise in both AI technologies and strategic management, which in many organizations might not be readily available since they may not have a specialized department in AI.

Notwithstanding these limitations, the use of decision making models in the adoption of AI technology has implication that affects organisations. On a strategic level, these models can assist organisations to place their AI systems within the overall organisational and business goals and objectives in order to ensure that AI investments are utilised to enhance competitive advantage and performance more generally. However, the imperatives of these models point to the fact that organizations need to reinvent their decision- making strategies and mechanisms periodically. At this regulatory level, organisations must not only be compliant with the existing regulations but also be proactive in the cases of the future changes. This will entail incorporating the concept of regulatory foresight into decision-making frameworks so as to ensure that adoption strategies for AI are compliant and sustainable. Finally, as AI technologies will advance and become increasingly business-critical, the need for cross-functional cooperation will rise as well. Decision-making around AI adoption will need to involve not just business leaders, but also experts in AI, ethics, law, and data science. Such an approach will guarantee that AI technologies will be integrated in key areas in manners that are both strategically beneficial, sustainable and compliant with regulatory standards.

8. CONCLUSION

The chapter explores the appropriateness and feasibility of the conventional decision making models in the context of the AI technology, especially in the context of generative AI, machine learning, deep learning. It is observed that which all models provide valuable information on decision-making and problem-solving during AI implementation, their applicability depends on the nature of the problems that may arise during such processes. The comparative analysis reveals that there is no one-size-fits-all approach in dealing with AI technology integration due to the external and internal factors that need to be addressed, as well as the strategic and operational goals of the organization that need to be met. Additionally, the chapter highlights that there may be a need to synchronize several models to achieve the organisation's objectives. The integration and the comparison of models is an attempt to help decision-makers to develop better and more sustainable AI adoption strategies that are coupled with organizational objectives and can adapt to the changing technological environment and regulations. Moreover, this chapter also points out that every new field requires modification of the existing models to fit the new avenues of development and conditions of the business world. Managers must be adaptive and constantly evaluating and modifying their plans to guarantee that AI solutions are implemented correctly and can also become a sustainable source of competitive advantage and legal requirements. With such issues in mind, it is evident that as AI technologies evolve, there will be a growing necessity for sound, adaptable, and contextually suitable decision support frameworks. In this regard, this chapter has outlined how traditional models can be operationalized and adapted to address the requirements of the AI environment, and has given foundational knowledge that leaders and key decision makers can use to successfully manage and coordinate the numerous challenges that the AI technology presents.

REFERENCES

Aithal, P., & Kumar, P. (2017). Ideal analysis for decision making in critical situations through six thinking hats method. [IJAEML]. *International Journal of Applied Engineering and Management Letters*, *1*(2), 1–9. DOI: 10.47992/IJAEML.2581.7000.0007

Allal-Chérif, O., Simón-Moya, V., & Ballester, A. C. C. (2021). Intelligent purchasing: How artificial intelligence can redefine the purchasing function. *Journal of Business Research*, *124*, 69–76. DOI: 10.1016/j.jbusres.2020.11.050

Anastasiu, L., Gavriş, O., & Maier, D. (2020). Is human capital ready for change? A strategic approach adapting Porter's five forces to human resources. *Sustainability (Basel)*, *12*(6), 2300. DOI: 10.3390/su12062300

Assensoh-Kodua, A. (2019). The resource-based view: A tool of key competency for competitive advantage. *Problems and Perspectives in Management*, *17*(3), 143–152. DOI: 10.21511/ppm.17(3).2019.12

Bag, S., Gupta, S., Kumar, A., & Sivarajah, U. (2021). An integrated artificial intelligence framework for knowledge creation and B2B marketing rational decision making for improving firm performance. *Industrial Marketing Management*, *92*, 178–189. DOI: 10.1016/j.indmarman.2020.12.001

Benbya, H., Davenport, T. H., & Pachidi, S. (2020). Artificial intelligence in organizations: Current state and future opportunities. *MIS Quarterly Executive*, *19*(4).

Borges, A. F., Laurindo, F. J., Spínola, M. M., Gonçalves, R. F., & Mattos, C. A. (2021). The strategic use of artificial intelligence in the digital era: Systematic literature review and future research directions. *International Journal of Information Management*, *57*, 102225. DOI: 10.1016/j.ijinfomgt.2020.102225

Chintalapati, S. (2020). BankBuddy. ai—Business Expansion and Marketing Dilemma: A Case Study to Discuss the Ansoff Growth Matrix Concepts Combined with Business Expansion Strategies for Expanding into Emerging Markets. *Emerging Economies Cases Journal*, *2*(1), 44–53. DOI: 10.1177/2516604220929994

Chowdhury, S., Dey, P., Joel-Edgar, S., Bhattacharya, S., Rodriguez-Espindola, O., Abadie, A., & Truong, L. (2023). Unlocking the value of artificial intelligence in human resource management through AI capability framework. *Human Resource Management Review*, *33*(1), 100899. DOI: 10.1016/j.hrmr.2022.100899

Cioffi, R., Travaglioni, M., Piscitelli, G., Petrillo, A., & De Felice, F. (2020). Artificial intelligence and machine learning applications in smart production: Progress, trends, and directions. *Sustainability (Basel)*, *12*(2), 492. DOI: 10.3390/su12020492

Clarissia, S. M. S. (2020). A study on Ansoff Matrix Technique: As a growth strategy and an adaptive learning technique adopted in the leading brand of products. *BIMS Journal of Management, 18.*

Danemo, J. (2018). How is AI influencing industry competition?: An exploration of online retailing using Porter's Five Forces Framework.

Dawes, J. (2018). The Ansoff matrix: A legendary tool, but with two logical problems. *But with Two Logical Problems (February 27, 2018).*

de Villiers, R. (2022). *Creative Thinking, Problem Solving and Ideation Tools The Handbook of Creativity & Innovation in Business: A Comprehensive Toolkit of Theory and Practice for Developing Creative Thinking Skills*. Springer.

Do, H., Budhwar, P., Shipton, H., Nguyen, H.-D., & Nguyen, B. (2022). Building organizational resilience, innovation through resource-based management initiatives, organizational learning and environmental dynamism. *Journal of Business Research, 141*, 808–821. DOI: 10.1016/j.jbusres.2021.11.090

Du, S., & Xie, C. (2021). Paradoxes of artificial intelligence in consumer markets: Ethical challenges and opportunities. *Journal of Business Research, 129*, 961–974. DOI: 10.1016/j.jbusres.2020.08.024

Duan, Y., Edwards, J. S., & Dwivedi, Y. K. (2019). Artificial intelligence for decision making in the era of Big Data–evolution, challenges and research agenda. *International Journal of Information Management, 48*, 63–71. DOI: 10.1016/j.ijinfomgt.2019.01.021

Dwivedi, Y. K., Hughes, L., Ismagilova, E., Aarts, G., Coombs, C., Crick, T., & Eirug, A. (2021). Artificial Intelligence (AI): Multidisciplinary perspectives on emerging challenges, opportunities, and agenda for research, practice and policy. *International Journal of Information Management, 57*, 101994. DOI: 10.1016/j.ijinfomgt.2019.08.002

Eierle, B., Hartlieb, S., Hay, D. C., Niemi, L., & Ojala, H. (2022). External factors and the pricing of audit services: A systematic review of the archival literature using a PESTLE analysis. *Auditing, 41*(3), 95–119. DOI: 10.2308/AJPT-2019-510

Enginoğlu, D., & Arikan, C. L. (2016). A literature review on core competencies. [IJM]. *International Journal of Management, 7*(3), 120–127.

Eriksen, B., & Mikkelsen, J. (2013). *Competitive advantage and the concept of core competence Towards a competence theory of the firm*. Routledge.

Ferreira, J. J., Fernandes, C. I., & Ferreira, F. A. (2022). What makes organizations unique? Looking inside the box. *Journal of Business Research, 139*, 664–674. DOI: 10.1016/j.jbusres.2021.10.017

Feuerriegel, S., Hartmann, J., Janiesch, C., & Zschech, P. (2024). Generative ai. *Business & Information Systems Engineering, 66*(1), 111–126. DOI: 10.1007/s12599-023-00834-7

Fountaine, T., McCarthy, B., & Saleh, T. (2019). Building the AI-powered organization. *Harvard Business Review, 97*(4), 62–73.

Fuertes, G., Alfaro, M., Vargas, M., Gutierrez, S., Ternero, R., & Sabattin, J. (2020). Conceptual framework for the strategic management: A literature review—descriptive. *Journal of Engineering, 2020*(1), 6253013. DOI: 10.1155/2020/6253013

Gerard, H., & Bruijl, T. (2019). The relevance of Porter's five forces in today's innovative and changing business environment: *SSRN*.

Gianiodis, P. T., Markman, G. D., & Panagopoulos, A. (2019). Factor market rivalry and interindustry competitive dynamics. *MDE. Managerial and Decision Economics, 40*(4), 446–459. DOI: 10.1002/mde.3014

Göçmen, Ö., & Coşkun, H. (2019). The effects of the six thinking hats and speed on creativity in brainstorming. *Thinking Skills and Creativity*, *31*, 284–295. DOI: 10.1016/j.tsc.2019.02.006

Grassi, A., & Vallati, M. (2021). An Exploratory Study on the Use of Artificial Intelligence to Initiate Legal Understanding for Business Development. *FLAP*, *8*(4), 1065–1082.

Greif, L., Kimmig, A., El Bobbou, S., Jurisch, P., & Ovtcharova, J. (2024). Strategic view on the current role of AI in advancing environmental sustainability: A SWOT analysis. *Discover Artificial Intelligence*, *4*(1), 45. DOI: 10.1007/s44163-024-00146-z

Gupta, R., & Bodhankar, A. (2023). Impact of Six Thinking Hats Techniques on the Legitimate Decision-making Skills of Managers. *Russian Law Journal*, *11*(5S), 449–456.

Hagendorff, T., & Wezel, K. (2020). 15 challenges for AI: Or what AI (currently) can't do. *AI & Society*, *35*(2), 355–365. DOI: 10.1007/s00146-019-00886-y

Henry, A. (2021). *Understanding strategic management*. Oxford University Press. DOI: 10.1093/hebz/9780198859833.001.0001

Horowitz, M. C., Allen, G. C., Kania, E. B., & Scharre, P. (2022). *Strategic competition in an era of artificial intelligence*: Center for a New American Security.

Ibeh, C. V., Asuzu, O. F., Olorunsogo, T., Elufioye, O. A., Nduubuisi, N. L., & Daraojimba, A. I. (2024). Business analytics and decision science: A review of techniques in strategic business decision making. *World Journal of Advanced Research and Reviews*, *21*(2), 1761–1769. DOI: 10.30574/wjarr.2024.21.2.0247

In, D. M. T. S. A., Andersson, B., Johansson, B., Carlsson, S., Barry, C., Lang, M., . . . Schneider, C. Improving Digital Decision Making Through Situational Awareness.

Isabelle, D., Horak, K., McKinnon, S., & Palumbo, C. (2020). Is Porter's Five Forces Framework Still Relevant? A study of the capital/labour intensity continuum via mining and IT industries. *Technology Innovation Management Review*, *10*(6), 28–41. DOI: 10.22215/timreview/1366

Jarrahi, M. H. (2018). Artificial intelligence and the future of work: Human-AI symbiosis in organizational decision making. *Business Horizons*, *61*(4), 577–586. DOI: 10.1016/j.bushor.2018.03.007

Johnson, J. (2023). Automating the OODA loop in the age of intelligent machines: Reaffirming the role of humans in command-and-control decision-making in the digital age. *Defence Studies*, *23*(1), 43–67. DOI: 10.1080/14702436.2022.2102486

Kabue, L. W., & Kilika, J. M. (2016). Firm resources, core competencies and sustainable competitive advantage: An integrative theoretical framework. *Journal of management and strategy, 7*(1), 98-108.

Kaggwa, S., Eleogu, T. F., Okonkwo, F., Farayola, O. A., Uwaoma, P. U., & Akinoso, A. (2024). AI in decision making: Transforming business strategies. *International Journal of Innovation and Scientific Research*, *10*(12), 423–444. DOI: 10.51244/IJRSI.2023.1012032

Kalota, F. (2024). A Primer on Generative Artificial Intelligence. *Education Sciences*, *14*(2), 172. DOI: 10.3390/educsci14020172

Kawshala, H. (2017). Theorizing the concept of core competencies: An integrative model beyond identification. *International Journal of Scientific and Research Publications*, *7*(2), 253–256.

Khan, U. U., Ali, Y., Petrillo, A., & De Felice, F. (2023). Macro-environmental factors and their impact on startups from the perspective of developing countries. *International Journal of Sustainable Engineering*, *16*(1), 166–183. DOI: 10.1080/19397038.2023.2238754

Krakowski, S., Luger, J., & Raisch, S. (2023). Artificial intelligence and the changing sources of competitive advantage. *Strategic Management Journal*, *44*(6), 1425–1452. DOI: 10.1002/smj.3387

Kurniawan, D., Iswahyudin, M. D., & Suciati, T. R. (2020). SWOT analysis and ansoff matrix in creative food industry business development: A study on creative food business "Komala". *Open Access Indonesia Journal of Social Sciences*, *3*(2), 128–136.

Li, J., Li, M., Wang, X., & Thatcher, J. B. (2021). Strategic Directions for AI: The Role of CIOs and Boards of Directors. *Management Information Systems Quarterly*, *45*(3), 3. DOI: 10.25300/MISQ/2021/16523

Liu, B. (2022). *Artificial Intelligence and Machine Learning Capabilities and Application Programming Interfaces at Amazon, Google, and Microsoft*. Massachusetts Institute of Technology.

Lubis, N. W. (2022). Resource based view (RBV) in improving company strategic capacity. *Research Horizon*, *2*(6), 587–596. DOI: 10.54518/rh.2.6.2022.587-596

Maccuish, D. (2012). Orientation: Key to the OODA loop–the culture factor. [JoDRM]. *Journal of Defense Resources Management*, *3*(2), 67–74.

Mannuru, N. R., Shahriar, S., Teel, Z. A., Wang, T., Lund, B. D., Tijani, S., & Galley, J. (2023). Artificial intelligence in developing countries: The impact of generative artificial intelligence (AI) technologies for development. *Information Development*, •••, 02666669231200628. DOI: 10.1177/02666669231200628

Mikalef, P., Fjørtoft, S. O., & Torvatn, H. Y. (2019). *Developing an artificial intelligence capability: A theoretical framework for business value.* Paper presented at the Business Information Systems Workshops: BIS 2019 International Workshops, Seville, Spain, June 26–28, 2019, Revised Papers 22. DOI: 10.1007/978-3-030-36691-9_34

Min, C., Liangwen, L., & Yue, X.-G. (2018). New Thoughts on Porter's" Five Forces Model" from the Perspective of Innovation. *IETI Transactions on Social Sciences and Humanities*, *1*, 105–113.

Muhammad, K., Ullah, A., Lloret, J., Del Ser, J., & de Albuquerque, V. H. C. (2020). Deep learning for safe autonomous driving: Current challenges and future directions. *IEEE Transactions on Intelligent Transportation Systems*, *22*(7), 4316–4336. DOI: 10.1109/TITS.2020.3032227

Nikmah, F., Rahmawati, R., & Sukma, E. A. (2021). Resource-based view: Implementation in Indonesia SMEs to achieve competitive advantage. *European Journal of Research and Reflection in Management Sciences Vol*, *9*(1).

Nishant, R., Kennedy, M., & Corbett, J. (2020). Artificial intelligence for sustainability: Challenges, opportunities, and a research agenda. *International Journal of Information Management*, *53*, 102104. DOI: 10.1016/j.ijinfomgt.2020.102104

Ooi, K.-B., Tan, G. W.-H., Al-Emran, M., Al-Sharafi, M. A., Capatina, A., Chakraborty, A., & Lee, V.-H. (2023). The potential of generative artificial intelligence across disciplines: Perspectives and future directions. *Journal of Computer Information Systems*, •••, 1–32.

Palazzo, M., & Micozzi, A. (2024). *The SWOT analysis: An evolving decision-making model Rethinking Decision-Making Strategies and Tools: Emerging Research and Opportunities*. Emerald Publishing Limited.

Palomares, I., Martínez-Cámara, E., Montes, R., García-Moral, P., Chiachio, M., Chiachio, J., & Fernández, B. (2021). A panoramic view and swot analysis of artificial intelligence for achieving the sustainable development goals by 2030: Progress and prospects. *Applied Intelligence*, *51*(9), 6497–6527. DOI: 10.1007/s10489-021-02264-y PMID: 34764606

Paschen, U., Pitt, C., & Kietzmann, J. (2020). Artificial intelligence: Building blocks and an innovation typology. *Business Horizons*, *63*(2), 147–155. DOI: 10.1016/j.bushor.2019.10.004

Patra, A. K., & Dash, R. (2023). Strategic Optimization of Human Resource System in the Corporation to Conquer the Global Challenges in Business. *Journal of the Management Training Institute, SAIL, Ranchi AN ISO 9001–2015 Institute, 58.*

Pereira, L., Pinto, M., da Costa, R. L., Dias, Á., & Gonçalves, R. (2021). The new SWOT for a sustainable world. *Journal of Open Innovation*, *7*(1), 18. DOI: 10.3390/joitmc7010018

Petiwala, F. F., Shukla, V. K., & Vyas, S. (2021). *IBM watson: redefining artificial intelligence through cognitive computing*. Paper presented at the Proceedings of International Conference on Machine Intelligence and Data Science Applications: MIDAS 2020. DOI: 10.1007/978-981-33-4087-9_15

Pietronudo, M. C., Croidieu, G., & Schiavone, F. (2022). A solution looking for problems? A systematic literature review of the rationalizing influence of artificial intelligence on decision-making in innovation management. *Technological Forecasting and Social Change*, *182*, 121828. DOI: 10.1016/j.techfore.2022.121828

Ployhart, R. E. (2021). Resources for what? Understanding performance in the resource-based view and strategic human capital resource literatures. *Journal of Management*, *47*(7), 1771–1786. DOI: 10.1177/01492063211003137

Provost, F., & Fawcett, T. (2013). Data science and its relationship to big data and data-driven decision making. *Big Data*, *1*(1), 51–59. DOI: 10.1089/big.2013.1508 PMID: 27447038

Przegalinska, A., & Jemielniak, D. (2023). *Strategizing AI in business and education: Emerging technologies and business strategy*. Cambridge University Press. DOI: 10.1017/9781009243520

Pumplun, L., Tauchert, C., & Heidt, M. (2019). A new organizational chassis for artificial intelligence-exploring organizational readiness factors.

Puyt, R., Lie, F. B., & de Graaf, F. (2017). Contagious ideas and cognitive artefacts: the SWOT Analysis evolution in business. *BAM2017Conference Proceedings*, 2-19.

Rabaey, M. (2015). Complex Adaptive Systems Thinking Approach to IT Investment.

Radonjić, A., Duarte, H., & Pereira, N. (2022). Artificial intelligence and HRM: HR managers' perspective on decisiveness and challenges. *European Management Journal.*

Raisch, S., & Krakowski, S. (2021). Artificial intelligence and management: The automation–augmentation paradox. *Academy of Management Review, 46*(1), 192–210. DOI: 10.5465/amr.2018.0072

Rastogi, N., & Trivedi, M. (2016). PESTLE technique–a tool to identify external risks in construction projects. [IRJET]. *International Research Journal of Engineering and Technology, 3*(1), 384–388.

Raydugin, Y. G. (2024). *RISK-BASED PROJECT DECISIONS IN SITUATIONS OF HIGH COMPLEXITY AND DEEP UNCERTAINTY*: Springer.

Saxena, D., Lamest, M., & Bansal, V. (2021). Responsible machine learning for ethical artificial intelligence in business and industry. In *Handbook of Research on Applied Data Science and Artificial Intelligence in Business and Industry* (pp. 639–653). IGI global. DOI: 10.4018/978-1-7998-6985-6.ch030

Saxena, D., Wall, P. J., & Lewis, D. (2023, September). Artificial Intelligence (AI) Ethics: A Critical Realist Emancipatory Approach. In *2023 IEEE International Symposium on Technology and Society (ISTAS)* (pp. 1-5). IEEE. DOI: 10.1109/ISTAS57930.2023.10305995

Sheikh, S. (2020). *Understanding the role of artificial intelligence and its future social impact.* IGI Global.

Shrestha, Y. R., Ben-Menahem, S. M., & Von Krogh, G. (2019). Organizational decision-making structures in the age of artificial intelligence. *California Management Review, 61*(4), 66–83. DOI: 10.1177/0008125619862257

Singh, S. (2021). BERT Algorithm used in Google Search. *Mathematical Statistician and Engineering Applications, 70*(2), 1641–1650. DOI: 10.17762/msea.v70i2.2454

Tariq, M. U., Poulin, M., & Abonamah, A. A. (2021). Achieving operational excellence through artificial intelligence: Driving forces and barriers. *Frontiers in Psychology, 12*, 686624. DOI: 10.3389/fpsyg.2021.686624 PMID: 34305744

Trunk, A., Birkel, H., & Hartmann, E. (2020). On the current state of combining human and artificial intelligence for strategic organizational decision making. *Business Research, 13*(3), 875–919. DOI: 10.1007/s40685-020-00133-x

Tsatsoula, E. (2018). Application of Ansoff's Matrix-Methodology: Marketing Growth Strategies For Products.

Turan, U., Fidan, Y., & Yıldıran, C. (2019). Critical thinking as a qualified decision making tool. *Tarih Kültür ve Sanat Arastirmalari Dergisi, 8*(4), 1–18. DOI: 10.7596/taksad.v8i4.2316

Vettorello, M., Eisenbart, B., & Ranscombe, C. (2019). *Toward better design-related decision making: A proposal of an advanced ooda loop.* Paper presented at the Proceedings of the Design Society: International Conference on Engineering Design. DOI: 10.1017/dsi.2019.245

Węgrzyn, D. T. (2022). *The adaptation of the OODA loop to the decision-making systems processing Big Data in the area of morality.* Paper presented at the Proceedings of the 26th International Database Engineered Applications Symposium. DOI: 10.1145/3548785.3548806

Yaghmai, R. (2021). A Critical Examination of How Artificial Intelligence Should Be Regulated in the United Kingdom. *BLR*, 59.

Yewei, Y., & Pereira, P. R. (2022). Sources of Sustained Competitive Advantage from the Perspective of Strategic Entrepreneurship-An Empirical Study on Manufacturing Enterprises in China.

Zohuri, B., & Rahmani, F. M. (2023). Artificial intelligence driven resiliency with machine learning and deep learning components. *Japan Journal of Research, 1*(1). Advance online publication. DOI: 10.33425/2690-8077.1002

Zugay, B., & Zakaria, R. (2023). *Ansoff matrix*. SAGE Publications, Inc. DOI: 10.4135/9781071924136

ADDITIONAL READING

do Vale Martins, R., Alturas, B., & Alexandre, I. (2021, June). Perspective for the use of adoption theories in artificial intelligence. In *2021 16th Iberian conference on information systems and technologies (CISTI)* (pp. 1-4). IEEE. DOI: 10.23919/CISTI52073.2021.9476340

Duan, Y., Edwards, J. S., & Dwivedi, Y. K. (2019). Artificial intelligence for decision making in the era of Big Data–evolution, challenges and research agenda. *International Journal of Information Management, 48*, 63–71. DOI: 10.1016/j.ijinfomgt.2019.01.021

FakhrHosseini, S., Chan, K., Lee, C., Jeon, M., Son, H., Rudnik, J., & Coughlin, J. (2024). User adoption of intelligent environments: A review of technology adoption models, challenges, and prospects. *International Journal of Human-Computer Interaction, 40*(4), 986–998. DOI: 10.1080/10447318.2022.2118851

Mogaji, E., Viglia, G., Srivastava, P., & Dwivedi, Y. K. (2024). Is it the end of the technology acceptance model in the era of generative artificial intelligence? *International Journal of Contemporary Hospitality Management, 36*(10), 3324–3339. DOI: 10.1108/IJCHM-08-2023-1271

Radhakrishnan, J., & Chattopadhyay, M. (2020). Determinants and barriers of artificial intelligence adoption–A literature review. In *Re-imagining Diffusion and Adoption of Information Technology and Systems: A Continuing Conversation: IFIP WG 8.6 International Conference on Transfer and Diffusion of IT, TDIT 2020, Tiruchirappalli, India, December 18–19, 2020, Proceedings, Part I* (pp. 89-99). Springer International Publishing. DOI: 10.1007/978-3-030-64849-7_9

Sitthipon, T., Kaewpuang, P., Jaipong, P., Sriboonruang, P., Siripipattanakul, S., & Auttawechasakoon, P. (2022). Artificial Intelligence (AI) Adoption in the Medical Education during the Digital Era: A Review Article. *Review of Advanced Multidispliniary Science. Engineering & Innovation, 1*(2), 1–7.

KEY TERMS AND DEFINITIONS

Artificial Intelligence (AI): Artificial Intelligence refers to the development of computer systems that can perform tasks typically requiring human intelligence. These tasks include learning, problem-solving, perception, and understanding natural language. AI enables machines to simulate human thinking and decision-making processes.

Decision Models: Decision Models are structured approaches or frameworks used to make decisions. They help in analyzing various options and outcomes to choose the best course of action. These models are often used in business and strategy to guide choices based on logic, data, and specific criteria.

Deep Learning: Deep Learning is a subset of Machine Learning that uses neural networks with many layers (hence "deep") to analyze and learn from vast amounts of data. It's particularly effective for tasks like image and speech recognition, where it can automatically discover patterns and make decisions with minimal human intervention.

Generative AI: Generative AI is a type of artificial intelligence that can create new content, such as text, images, music, or even software code, based on the data it has been trained on. It uses models like GPT (Generative Pre-trained Transformer) to generate human-like outputs, often used in creative fields and for automating content production.

Machine Learning: Machine Learning is a branch of AI focused on building systems that can learn from data and improve their performance over time without being explicitly programmed. It involves algorithms that analyze data, identify patterns, and make decisions with minimal human input, becoming more accurate as they are exposed to more data.

Strategic Decision: A Strategic Decision is a long-term choice made by an organization or individual that significantly impacts the overall direction and success. These decisions involve high stakes, complex considerations, and alignment with broader goals, often requiring careful analysis, foresight, and planning.

Chapter 6
Advancing Software Security:
A Comprehensive Framework for Vulnerability Assessment

Usharani Bhimavarapu
https://orcid.org/0000-0002-0246-1420
Department of Computer Science and Engineering, Koneru Lakshmaiah Education Foundation, Vaddeswaram, India

ABSTRACT

Threats in Software Development have become a critical concern in today's fast-evolving technological landscape. As software systems grow in complexity and importance, they become increasingly vulnerable to a wide range of security risks, including both internal and external threats. These threats can compromise the confidentiality, integrity, and availability of software, leading to significant financial losses, reputational damage, and legal consequences. Addressing these vulnerabilities early in the Software Development Life Cycle (SDLC) is essential to minimize potential threats. This paper explores the importance of implementing effective Risk-Based Vulnerability Management (RBVM) within software development processes. It highlights the challenges of identifying, assessing, and mitigating software security vulnerabilities through a risk-centric approach.

INTRODUCTION

Threats in software development are a critical concern for organizations, as they directly impact the security, integrity, and functionality of the software products being created. These threats can arise from various sources, including external attackers, malicious insiders, software flaws, and vulnerabilities introduced during the development process. External threats, such as hackers or cybercriminals, may exploit weaknesses in the software to gain unauthorized access, steal sensitive data, or cause system disruptions. Malicious insiders, including disgruntled employees or contractors, can also pose significant risks by intentionally introducing vulnerabilities or bypassing security measures for personal gain.

In addition to these human-driven threats, software development itself can be a source of risk due to inherent weaknesses in the development process. For instance, flaws in coding practices, insufficient input validation, and the use of insecure libraries or outdated dependencies can leave software susceptible to attacks like SQL injection, cross-site scripting (XSS), and buffer overflows. These vulnerabilities

DOI: 10.4018/979-8-3693-8407-7.ch006

are often difficult to detect early in the development cycle, especially if security is not prioritized or integrated into the Software Development Life Cycle (SDLC).

Another major threat in software development is related to inadequate or improper testing. Insufficient testing or failure to consider edge cases can lead to undetected bugs that may later be exploited. Furthermore, the fast-paced nature of modern software development, driven by agile methodologies and continuous delivery models, can sometimes result in rushed releases without thorough security evaluations. This rapid pace, coupled with the complexity of integrating various third-party components and services, increases the likelihood of introducing vulnerabilities that may not be discovered until after deployment.

Lastly, the rise of cloud computing and distributed systems introduces additional security challenges. Software applications are often deployed across multiple environments, including on-premises data centers, cloud services, and hybrid platforms, making it difficult to maintain consistent security policies and manage risks effectively. Misconfigurations in these complex environments, such as improperly set permissions or unpatched systems, can expose the application to significant vulnerabilities.

Addressing these threats requires a proactive and integrated approach, where security is considered at every stage of development, from planning and design to deployment and maintenance. By incorporating secure coding practices, conducting regular security assessments, and using tools like automated vulnerability scanners, organizations can better mitigate the risks associated with software development and ensure the creation of secure, resilient software systems.

The following studies focus on various methods for vulnerability detection and management, each offering unique approaches and facing specific limitations.Bayesian Attack Graphs (Batory et al., 2005) introduce a probabilistic model for visualizing and quantifying attack paths, but their effectiveness relies heavily on accurate data for probability assessments and becomes computationally expensive as the system grows. Fuzzy Logic-based Models (Belkina et al., 2012) use fuzzy logic for vulnerability prioritization, yet they struggle with imprecise data and subjective expert inputs, leading to potential inaccuracies. CVE-based Analysis (Benavides et al., 2015), which relies on the CVE database to identify vulnerabilities, is limited by only addressing known vulnerabilities, thus unable to predict emerging threats or zero-day attacks. The Threat-Focused Vulnerability Assessment (TFVA) model (Brailsford et al., 2011) maps vulnerabilities to potential threats but risks oversimplifying complex interactions between vulnerabilities and threats, requiring constant updates to remain relevant. Attacker-Behavior Modeling (ABM) (Chakraborty et al., 2017) simulates potential attack behaviors based on an adversary's goals but assumes certain behaviors that may not apply to highly skilled or adaptive attackers.

Deep Learning-based Vulnerability Detection (Cho et al., 2019) uses machine learning to detect vulnerabilities in large codebases, though it depends on large, labeled datasets that may not always be available or representative. Automated Keyword Extraction (Elbaz et al., 2021) leverages keyword extraction techniques to detect vulnerabilities in software documentation but may miss context-specific threats or generate false positives. The C/C++ Code Vulnerability Dataset (Fan et al., 2018) offers a comprehensive dataset for vulnerability detection, though it is limited to C/C++ and may not apply to other programming languages. Program Dependence Graphs (Ferrante et al., 1987) help model dependencies in programs to identify security weaknesses but may be computationally intensive and fail to capture all possible vulnerabilities. Automated Analysis Frameworks (Galindo et al., 2019) provide tools for automatic feature model analysis, yet they struggle to accurately capture the complexities of different software configurations and their impact on security.

Vulnerability Detection via Deep Learning (Gao et al., 2020) focuses on firmware vulnerability detection but faces challenges due to its reliance on large datasets. Passive Vulnerability Detection (Gawron et al., 2021) involves monitoring systems without requiring code changes, though it may suffer from false positives or performance degradation. Security Evaluations through Variability Modeling (Kenner et al., 2013) aids security evaluations in varied contexts but may not keep up with dynamic environments. Deep Learning Framework for Vulnerability Detection (Li et al., 2019) uses deep learning models for vulnerability detection but struggles to detect zero-day vulnerabilities. Patch-Based Vulnerability Matching (Liu et al., 2020) matches patches to vulnerabilities, but may not be effective for systems with inconsistent patching patterns.

Metasploit for Exploit Development (Maynor et al., 2014) is a tool for penetration testing but is limited to known vulnerabilities, requiring deep system knowledge. Vulnerability Management with ChatGPT (McClanahan et al., 2024) integrates AI tools like ChatGPT but faces challenges ensuring AI-generated results are accurate and actionable. CPE Matching for Vulnerability Detection (McClanahan & Li, 2018) relies on vendor matching but suffers from inaccuracies in string-based matching, potentially leading to false positives. Service Identification Based on CPE (Na et al., 2017) uses CPE to identify services but may miss newer or obscure services. Abstract Syntax Trees for Vulnerability Detection (Noonan et al., 2015) helps identify vulnerabilities in code, but may not handle obfuscation well.

Graph Convolutional Networks for Vulnerability Detection (Schlichtkrull et al., 2018) applies graph convolutional networks to relational data for vulnerability detection but is computationally costly for large codebases. Deep Learning for Vulnerability Matching (Tovarnak et al., 2020) uses machine learning for vulnerability matching but requires large training datasets, which may not always be available. Feature Models for Vulnerability Management (Varela-Vaca et al., 2018) enhance vulnerability management through feature models but struggle to capture all security configurations. Automated Security Testing (Varela-Vaca et al., 2021) automates security testing but may miss subtle flaws that require manual inspection. Cybersecurity Policy Compliance (Varela-Vaca et al., 2020) uses software product lines for policy compliance verification but may not account for non-standard configurations or edge cases.

Graph-Based Vulnerability Detection (Wang et al., 2021) uses graph learning to detect vulnerabilities but can be resource-intensive, making it less feasible for real-time applications. Enhanced Graph Representation Learning (Wen et al., 2020) simplifies graph learning for vulnerability detection, but risks oversimplifying complex systems. A Comprehensive Survey on Graph Neural Networks (Wu et al., 2020) discusses the use of GNNs for vulnerability detection but faces challenges with interpretability and scalability. Patch-Based Vulnerability Detection (Xu et al., 2020) focuses on detecting vulnerabilities in binary programs but may not apply to all binary formats. Vulnerability Detection with Code Property Graphs (Yamaguchi et al., 2018) uses code property graphs for vulnerability detection but may struggle with large or obfuscated codebases.

ComFormer for Code Comment Generation (Yang et al., 2022) employs transformer-based models for generating code comments to aid vulnerability detection but relies on the quality of training data and may not generate relevant comments for all code types. Vulnerability Detection Using Function Fingerprints (Zhao et al., 2019) detects vulnerabilities with function fingerprints but may not adapt well to non-standard or transformed code. Context Triggered Piecewise Hashing for Identifying Identical Files (Kornblum, 2006) uses hashing techniques to identify almost identical files but may struggle with obfuscated or dynamic files. Vulnerability Detection with Slice Property Graphs (Zheng et al., 2021) uses slice property graphs for detection but faces challenges with real-time detection in dynamic systems. Finally, Graph Neural Networks for Vulnerability Detection (Zhou et al., 2020) employs GNNs but is computationally demanding, with difficulties in scalability, while Comprehensive Vulnerability Identification via GNNs (Zhou et al., 2022) offers a thorough approach, although it requires substantial data and resources.

The proposed Risk-Based Vulnerability Management (RBVM) model overcomes several limitations associated with existing software security models. One major limitation is the reliance on static analysis or predefined vulnerability databases, which can miss emerging threats or fail to offer real-time insights. RBVM addresses this by incorporating dynamic risk-based assessment and integrating threat intelligence feeds (Baptiste & Jamal, 2019), enabling continuous monitoring and real-time detection of both known and unknown vulnerabilities (Patel et al., 2016). Additionally, RBVM improves prioritization, unlike many traditional models that treat all vulnerabilities as equal. With its risk-scoring system, RBVM allows vulnerabilities to be prioritized based on their potential impact, helping organizations focus on the most critical threats first (Feng et al., 2018).

Another limitation of traditional models is their complexity in integration, often requiring manual configuration and not aligning with existing security systems. RBVM overcomes this by being designed for integration flexibility. It seamlessly connects with systems like Security Information and Event Management (SIEM), patch management tools, and vulnerability scanners, thus simplifying the security management process (García & Lopez, 2017). Furthermore, many existing models still involve a lot of manual processes, which can lead to delays and errors. RBVM automates key processes such as vulnerability scanning and remediation workflows, significantly reducing the time and human effort involved (Zhou et al., 2017).

Traditional models also tend to lack contextualization, treating vulnerabilities in isolation rather than considering an organization's specific risk profile. RBVM introduces context-sensitive analysis, incorporating factors like asset criticality and business impact to generate more accurate risk assessments and prioritize vulnerabilities that directly affect the business (Adams & McNamara, 2015). Additionally, scaling vulnerability management efforts in large, complex environments can be a challenge. RBVM utilizes a microservice-oriented architecture, offering a scalable and modular approach to security management, which ensures that the platform can adapt to the growing needs of an organization (Allen et al., 2012).

By addressing these limitations, RBVM enhances vulnerability management, helping organizations focus on high-risk vulnerabilities, streamline workflows, and maintain robust security even in complex environments.

MATERIAL AND METHODOLOGY

The methodology overview focuses on integrating Risk-Based Vulnerability Management (RBVM) into the Software Development Life Cycle (SDLC) to enhance software security. It begins with identifying critical assets and mapping the IT infrastructure to align security goals with business objectives. RBVM tools are then selected and deployed across the environment, with integration into vulnerability scanners, SIEM systems, and patch management tools. Vulnerabilities are assessed, prioritized based on risk, and integrated into remediation workflows. Continuous monitoring and optimization ensure ongoing effectiveness. The process concludes with regular reporting and metrics to track progress and improvements in the organization's security posture.

Material

The study employed a comprehensive information-gathering approach that included dedicated surveys, focus groups, and active consultation with the company. Specifically, a survey and focus group were conducted with employees from the company to gain valuable insights. A total of 25 key employees were carefully selected as participants, representing a diverse range of roles within the Software Development Life Cycle (SDLC) of the core software products developed by the company. These roles included software developers, testers, analysts, and project managers, ensuring a broad spectrum of perspectives.

To further mitigate potential bias, we ensured that multiple participants from each role were included in the study. This approach provided a well-rounded and balanced view of the SDLC practices and challenges faced by the company. The survey and focus group were designed to capture the participants' experiences, challenges, and feedback, forming the foundation for a detailed understanding of the company's software development processes.

As previously mentioned, the primary methods for gathering information in this study were the survey and focus group discussions, which allowed for a combination of quantitative data and qualitative insights. This methodology ensured a robust and comprehensive analysis.

Nessus

Nessus is a robust platform that provides cutting-edge solutions for software security monitoring and optimization. It is widely recognized for its advanced capabilities in vulnerability assessment and source code analysis. Nessus specializes in static and textual source code analysis, which involves examining the software codebase without executing the program. This approach allows developers and security teams to identify vulnerabilities, misconfigurations, and potential security flaws early in the development cycle. By analyzing the code's structure, syntax, and dependencies, Nessus offers detailed insights into potential risks, such as insecure coding practices, outdated libraries, and compliance violations.

One of the key strengths of Nessus is its ability to perform comprehensive scans across diverse environments, including on-premises, cloud, and hybrid infrastructures. The platform supports a wide range of programming languages and frameworks, ensuring its relevance across different software development ecosystems. Additionally, Nessus provides actionable recommendations and remediation steps for identified issues, enabling teams to prioritize and address vulnerabilities efficiently.

Its intuitive user interface, customizable scan templates, and integration with CI/CD pipelines make it an invaluable tool for modern software development and security practices. By leveraging Nessus, organizations can ensure their applications are not only optimized for performance but also adhere to the highest security standards, safeguarding them against evolving cyber threats.

Risk-Based Vulnerability Management (RBVM)

Risk-Based Vulnerability Management (RBVM) is a proactive approach to identifying, assessing, and mitigating vulnerabilities in an organization's IT environment based on the risks they pose to critical assets. Configuring and tuning RBVM models or mechanisms involves several critical steps to ensure they are effectively aligned with an organization's unique risk profile and security objectives.

The configuration process begins with defining the organization's risk tolerance and establishing a framework for prioritizing vulnerabilities. This typically involves assigning a risk score to each vulnerability by factoring in its severity, exploitability, potential impact, and the criticality of the affected asset. Tools used for RBVM are often integrated with asset management systems, enabling organizations to identify and classify their assets according to their business value. Configurations are then tuned to ensure that the RBVM system focuses on the most critical vulnerabilities affecting the most sensitive assets.

Mechanisms within the RBVM platform are fine-tuned to incorporate data from various sources, such as threat intelligence feeds, vulnerability scanning tools, and penetration testing results. This enables the platform to assess the likelihood of exploitation based on real-world threat activity. Advanced RBVM systems may also leverage machine learning algorithms to predict potential vulnerabilities and prioritize remediation tasks dynamically. To further refine the mechanisms, organizations can configure rules that align with compliance standards, such as PCI DSS, HIPAA, or ISO 27001, ensuring that regulatory requirements are met.

Continuous monitoring and feedback loops are integral to tuning RBVM mechanisms. Organizations need to regularly evaluate the performance of their RBVM systems by reviewing metrics such as remediation timelines, reductions in exploit attempts, and improvements in overall security posture. Regular updates to vulnerability databases and risk models ensure that the mechanisms stay relevant in the face of evolving threats. Fine-tuning may also involve adjusting scan schedules, thresholds for alerts, and remediation workflows to strike a balance between operational efficiency and security effectiveness.

By carefully configuring and continuously tuning their RBVM systems, organizations can prioritize their resources effectively, address the most significant threats, and maintain a robust security posture while minimizing operational disruptions. This tailored approach ensures that RBVM mechanisms remain both relevant and impactful in a dynamic threat landscape.

The implementation and deployment of Risk-Based Vulnerability Management (RBVM) is a structured process aimed at integrating RBVM into an organization's existing security framework. This ensures that vulnerabilities are identified, assessed, and remediated based on the risks they pose to the organization's critical assets. The process begins with planning and requirement analysis, where the organization's risk appetite, business objectives, and compliance requirements are thoroughly understood. During this phase, teams identify critical assets, map out the IT infrastructure, and establish a risk assessment framework, ensuring alignment with existing cybersecurity strategies and tools like Security Information and Event Management (SIEM) systems, asset management databases, and threat intelligence platforms.

Next, organizations select an RBVM platform that suits their specific needs. This involves evaluating various tools that support advanced features such as machine learning for vulnerability prediction, integration with threat intelligence feeds, and customizable risk scoring. The selected platform should integrate seamlessly with the organization's current security architecture and support automation to reduce manual intervention. Once the platform is chosen, the deployment phase begins, which includes asset discovery, where all assets—such as servers, endpoints, cloud instances, and applications—are identified and classified. Integration with vulnerability scanners, SIEM systems, and patch management tools is then carried out, followed by configuring the system to match the organization's specific requirements, including scanning schedules, risk level thresholds, and custom risk-scoring algorithms.

Once the system is deployed, it begins scanning the environment for vulnerabilities, which are then prioritized based on their risk scores. These scores are determined by factors like exploitability, potential impact on business functions, and threat intelligence from external sources. The RBVM platform generates actionable reports that allow security teams to focus remediation efforts on the most critical vulnerabilities first. The remediation process is integrated with existing workflows, such as patch management systems and incident response teams, to ensure efficient and timely resolution. Automation helps speed up the process by deploying patches or implementing compensating controls.

Training is an essential component of the deployment process, ensuring that employees involved in vulnerability management understand how to use the RBVM platform effectively. This includes interpreting risk scores, configuring custom policies, and utilizing reporting features. Post-deployment, the RBVM system is continuously monitored to ensure its effectiveness. Regular updates are applied to the platform to incorporate the latest vulnerability data and threat intelligence. Feedback loops are established to refine risk models, improving the accuracy of prioritization. Periodic audits are also conducted to ensure compliance with security policies and regulations.

Finally, RBVM platforms provide detailed reports and dashboards that track remediation progress, risk reduction, and overall improvements in the organization's security posture. These reports are customizable to meet the needs of different stakeholders, such as technical teams and executive management. By successfully implementing and deploying RBVM, organizations can adopt a proactive, risk-focused approach to vulnerability management, ensuring that security resources are concentrated on addressing the most significant threats. This reduces the attack surface and enhances the organization's resilience against evolving cyber risks.

Security Assessment

The proposed methodology for security assessment involves a comprehensive approach to identifying, evaluating, and mitigating software vulnerabilities. The process begins with asset inventory and classification, where all software components, including third-party libraries and dependencies, are identified and classified based on their criticality, business impact, and sensitivity. This step ensures that resources are allocated effectively during the assessment. Next, threat modeling and risk identification are conducted to understand potential attack vectors and pinpoint high-risk areas within the software. By using established risk assessment frameworks like CVSS, the team can prioritize vulnerabilities based on their severity and potential impact. Vulnerability detection is carried out using a combination of Static Application Security Testing (SAST) for analyzing source code and Dynamic Application Security Testing (DAST) to simulate runtime attacks. Additionally, Software Composition Analysis (SCA) is utilized to examine third-party libraries for known vulnerabilities. These methods are complemented by regular penetration testing, both manual and automated, to uncover complex issues that automated tools may miss. Throughout the process, real-time threat intelligence is integrated to stay up-to-date with emerging vulnerabilities and attack trends. The findings are continuously assessed and addressed, ensuring a proactive approach to security and minimizing the risk of exploitation in the deployed application.

Vulnerability Prediction

Vulnerability prediction is a critical component of proactive security management, aimed at identifying and addressing potential vulnerabilities before they can be exploited. This process typically involves the use of advanced techniques such as machine learning, statistical models, and historical data analysis to predict where vulnerabilities are likely to occur in software. By analyzing patterns in code, development practices, and historical vulnerabilities, prediction models can highlight areas of the software that are prone to security issues.

A key aspect of vulnerability prediction is the use of static analysis tools, which examine the source code without executing it, to detect potential security flaws like buffer overflows, SQL injection risks, or insecure data handling practices. Dynamic analysis, on the other hand, is used to simulate real-world attacks on running applications, which helps in predicting how the software behaves in live environments and identifying runtime vulnerabilities such as improper session handling or authentication flaws.

In more advanced approaches, machine learning models can be trained on historical vulnerability data to predict which code modules or development practices are most likely to lead to security issues. These models can take into account various factors such as the complexity of the code, developer experience, frequency of code changes, and the presence of known security weaknesses in the software. Over time, these models become more accurate and efficient in predicting vulnerabilities, enabling development teams to focus their security efforts on the highest-risk areas.

By incorporating vulnerability prediction early in the software development lifecycle (SDLC), organizations can mitigate security risks before they manifest, reducing the cost and impact of later-stage remediation efforts. Additionally, these predictive models can be integrated into continuous integration/ continuous deployment (CI/CD) pipelines to provide real-time vulnerability assessments during development, further enhancing security.

Security Monitoring Platforms With Microservice-Oriented

Security monitoring platforms that utilize a microservice-oriented architecture Risk-Based Vulnerability Management (RBVM) security monitoring platforms that utilize a microservice-oriented architecture (MOA) offer a highly scalable, flexible, and modular approach to managing software vulnerabilities across an organization's IT environment. In this architecture, individual services are designed to handle specific tasks, such as vulnerability scanning, risk assessment, threat intelligence integration, and reporting, which can be independently deployed, updated, and scaled as needed. Each microservice focuses on a specific functionality, allowing for a more efficient and targeted approach to security monitoring.

For instance, a microservice could be dedicated to scanning applications for vulnerabilities, another to analyze the risk posed by each vulnerability, and a third to generate actionable reports or notifications for the security team. The microservices communicate with each other via lightweight APIs, enabling smooth data exchange and reducing the dependencies typically associated with monolithic systems. This design makes it easier to integrate various tools, such as vulnerability scanners, asset management systems, Security Information and Event Management (SIEM) platforms, and patch management solutions, into the RBVM platform.

The use of microservices also enhances the RBVM platform's resilience, as failures in one service do not necessarily affect the operation of others. Furthermore, scaling up the platform becomes more straightforward, as additional microservices can be added to handle increased workloads or new security requirements. This allows for real-time, dynamic adjustment of resources, ensuring the platform remains agile and responsive to emerging threats.

Additionally, with microservices, the RBVM platform can adopt continuous integration and continuous delivery (CI/CD) practices, ensuring that new features, patches, and updates can be deployed rapidly without disrupting the overall system. This approach significantly improves the platform's ability to adapt to new vulnerabilities and evolving security challenges while maintaining a streamlined and efficient monitoring process. Ultimately, by leveraging microservice-oriented architecture, organizations can build a robust, flexible, and scalable RBVM security monitoring platform that effectively manages vulnerabilities and minimizes security risks across the enterprise.

EXPERIMENTAL RESULTS

The experimental results presented in this study were obtained using a system configured with Windows 11. The system setup included a machine with an Intel Core i7 processor, 16GB of RAM, and an SSD for storage to ensure efficient data processing and minimize latency. Windows 11 was chosen due to its enhanced security features, improved support for hardware acceleration, and its ability to optimize performance for resource-intensive applications. The platform also benefits from a range of tools and utilities that support modern software development practices, such as enhanced support for virtualization, seamless integration with cloud-based platforms, and robust performance monitoring features (Microsoft, 2021). The system configuration was specifically selected to balance high computational capability with the need for stability and flexibility in running a variety of security tools and models for vulnerability management.

Table 1 outlines the performance of security assurance measures across various metrics, comparing targeted standards with achieved results and identifying their status and associated remarks. Vulnerability Scan Coverage achieved 98% against a target of 100%, earning a "Warning" status due to unscanned non-critical systems. Patch Management fell short of its weekly update target, with patches applied monthly, resulting in a "Caution" status attributed to resource delays. Conversely, Incident Response Time exceeded expectations, with a 20-minute response time against a 30-minute target, marked as "Compliant." User Access Control compliance reached 95% of accounts with appropriate access levels, short of the 100% target, leading to a "Caution" status due to some accounts with excessive privileges. Data Encryption met its 100% target, ensuring all sensitive data is encrypted and achieving "Compliant" status. However, Penetration Testing was conducted semi-annually instead of quarterly, resulting in a "Caution" status due to resource constraints. Security Awareness Training reached 90% employee participation, falling short of the 100% goal and marked as "Caution" for missed training by some employees. Backup and Recovery exceeded expectations with a 3-hour restoration time against a 4-hour target, achieving "Compliant" status. Lastly, Multi-factor Authentication (MFA) had a low adoption rate of 80% compared to the 100% target, earning a "Warning" status due to insufficient implementation in critical systems.

Table 1. Security assurance

Security Assurance Metric	Description	Target/Standard	Achieved Result	Status
Vulnerability Scan Coverage	Percentage of systems scanned for vulnerabilities	100% coverage	98%	Warning
Patch Management	Frequency of patch updates applied to systems	Weekly updates	Monthly updates	Caution
Incident Response Time	Time taken to respond to a security incident	30 minutes	20 minutes	Compliant
User Access Control	Percentage of accounts with appropriate access level	100% compliance	95%	Caution
Data Encryption	Percentage of sensitive data encrypted	100% encryption	100%	Compliant
Penetration Testing	Frequency of penetration tests conducted	Quarterly tests	Semi-annual tests	Caution
Security Awareness Training	Percentage of employees trained on security policies	100% participation	90%	Caution
Backup and Recovery	Time taken to restore from backups in case of disaster	4 hours	3 hours	Compliant
Multi-factor Authentication (MFA)	Percentage of users with MFA enabled	100% MFA	80%	Warning

Table 2 evaluates security management metrics, comparing achieved results against set targets, and provides insights into their status and remarks. Risk Assessment Coverage fell short of the 100% target, achieving only 85% coverage, earning a "Warning" due to the exclusion of some legacy systems. Security Policy Compliance reached 92%, slightly below the target, leading to a "Caution" status caused by incomplete adherence among some employees. Threat Intelligence Integration was at 75% instead of full integration, also marked as "Warning" due to outdated feeds in some systems. Access Control Management achieved 90% against a target of 100%, resulting in a "Caution" status due to delays in reviewing certain user roles. Incident Management Response exceeded expectations, resolving incidents in 18 hours against the 24-hour target, earning a "Compliant" status. However, Security Audits were conducted semi-annually instead of quarterly, resulting in a "Caution" status, attributed to resource limitations. Vulnerability Remediation exceeded the 72-hour target, taking 96 hours to address critical vulnerabilities, resulting in a "Warning" due to prioritization challenges. Similarly, Employee Security Training participation fell short at 80%, earning a "Caution" due to some employees missing mandatory sessions. Disaster Recovery Plan Testing was performed annually instead of bi-annually, earning a "Warning" due to resource constraints. Positive outcomes include the Security Incident Frequency, with only 3 incidents reported per quarter against a target of fewer than 5, earning a "Compliant" status. However, Security Awareness Campaigns fell short of the annual target of 3, with only 2 conducted, marked as "Caution" due to resource challenges.

Table 2. Security management

Security Management Metric	Description	Target/Standard	Achieved Result	Status
Risk Assessment Coverage	Percentage of systems assessed for security risks	100% coverage	85%	Warning
Security Policy Compliance	Percentage of employees adhering to security policies	100% compliance	92%	Caution
Threat Intelligence Integration	Percentage of security systems integrated with threat intelligence feeds	100% integration	75%	Warning
Access Control Management	Percentage of accounts reviewed for correct access rights	100% review	90%	Caution
Incident Management Response	Average time to resolve security incidents	24 hours	18 hours	Compliant
Security Audits	Frequency of internal security audits	Quarterly	Semi-annual	Caution
Vulnerability Remediation	Time taken to remediate critical vulnerabilities	72 hours	96 hours	Warning
Employee Security Training	Percentage of employees trained on security practices	100% participation	80%	Caution
Disaster Recovery Plan Testing	Frequency of disaster recovery plan tests	Bi-annual	Annual	Warning
Security Incident Frequency	Number of security incidents reported per quarter	Below 5 incidents	3 incidents	Compliant
Security Awareness Campaigns	Number of awareness campaigns conducted annually	At least 3 campaigns/year	2 campaigns	Caution

Table 3 evaluates the effectiveness of risk mitigation measures, highlighting the gaps between targets and achieved results, along with their implications. Risk Identification Coverage achieved 90% mitigation of identified risks, falling short of the 100% target and earning a "Caution" status due to incomplete mitigation of low-priority risks. The Residual Risk Level remains at a medium level instead of the target low level, marked as "Warning" because some risks continue to pose threats. The Mitigation Action Completion Rate reached 85%, below the 100% target, resulting in a "Warning" due to delayed or incomplete actions. Similarly, Risk Impact Reduction achieved only a 60% reduction against the 75% target, earning a "Caution" status as the impact reduction was less than anticipated. Compliance with Mitigation Timeframes was delayed by 10%, marked as "Warning" due to resource constraints. On a positive note, Resource Allocation for Mitigation achieved 95% utilization, earning a "Compliant" status as resources were largely used as planned. Monitoring and Review Frequency also met the quarterly target, maintaining a "Compliant" status with consistent reviews conducted on schedule. Conversely, the Risk Acceptance Rate exceeded the target, with 8% of risks accepted without mitigation instead of the acceptable 5%, leading to a "Caution" status due to cost or time constraints. Vulnerability Patch Timeliness took 96 hours instead of the 72-hour target, earning a "Warning" status as delays in patching vulnerabilities persisted. User Awareness on Risk Mitigation reached only 80% participation, falling short of the 100% target, marked as "Caution" due to incomplete attendance at awareness campaigns. Lastly, Third-Party Risk Mitigation achieved 90% compliance with vendor mitigation plans, below the 100% target, and received a "Warning" due to gaps in certain vendor practices. These findings emphasize the need for improved mitigation timelines, impact reduction strategies, and employee and vendor engagement in risk mitigation efforts.

Table 3. Risk mitigation

Risk Mitigation Metric	Description	Target/Standard	Achieved Result	Status
Risk Identification Coverage	Percentage of identified risks mitigated	100% identified risks mitigated	90%	Caution
Residual Risk Level	Remaining risk after mitigation actions	Low residual risk	Medium residual risk	Warning
Mitigation Action Completion Rate	Percentage of planned mitigation actions completed	100% completion	85%	Warning
Risk Impact Reduction	Reduction in potential impact after mitigation	75% reduction in impact	60% reduction	Caution
Mitigation Timeframe Compliance	Time taken to mitigate risks compared to planned timeline	On-time mitigation	10% delay	Warning
Resource Allocation for Mitigation	Percentage of allocated resources utilized for mitigation	100% resource utilization	95%	Compliant
Monitoring and Review Frequency	Frequency of monitoring and reviewing mitigation effectiveness	Quarterly reviews	Quarterly reviews	Compliant
Risk Acceptance Rate	Percentage of risks accepted without mitigation	Below 5% risk acceptance	8%	Caution
Vulnerability Patch Timeliness	Time taken to apply patches for identified vulnerabilities	72 hours after identification	96 hours	Warning
User Awareness on Risk Mitigation	Percentage of employees aware of risk mitigation measures	100% awareness	80%	Caution
Third-Party Risk Mitigation	Percentage of third-party vendors with risk mitigation plans	100% compliance	90%	Warning

Table 4 examines the performance of various threat mitigation measures, comparing their achieved results against targets, and highlighting areas of concern. Threat Detection Coverage reached 95% against a target of 100%, earning a "Caution" status due to monitoring system gaps that allowed some threats to go undetected. Conversely, the Response Time to Threats exceeded expectations, with an average of 45 minutes compared to the 1-hour target, earning a "Compliant" status. The False Positive Rate was commendably low at 3%, below the 5% threshold, also marked as "Compliant." However, Threat Impact Reduction achieved only a 70% reduction against the target of 80%, resulting in a "Caution" status as impact reduction was lower than anticipated. The Mitigation Action Completion Rate reached 90%, short of the 100% target, earning a "Warning" due to delays caused by resource constraints. Critical Threat Coverage mitigated 85% of critical threats instead of the full 100%, earning a "Warning" as some critical threats were not addressed. Similarly, Threat Intelligence Integration reached only 80%, leading to a "Caution" status due to delays in integrating some threat feeds. Patch Management Timeliness exceeded the 72-hour target, taking 96 hours to apply patches, earning a "Warning" status for delayed remediation of vulnerabilities. User Training on Threat Awareness achieved 85% participation, short of the 100% target, and marked as "Caution" because some employees missed the training. Third-Party Threat Mitigation showed 95% compliance among vendors, earning a "Caution" status due to incomplete mitigation by a few vendors. Monitoring and Review Frequency fell behind its monthly review target, with quarterly reviews conducted instead, earning a "Warning" due to missed monthly evaluations. Similarly, Disaster Recovery Plan Updates were conducted bi-annually instead of annually, marked as "Caution" due to updates missed in one cycle.

Table 4. Threat mitigation

Threat Mitigation Metric	Description	Target/Standard	Achieved Result	Status
Threat Detection Coverage	Percentage of threats detected through monitoring systems	100% threat detection	95%	Caution
Response Time to Threats	Average time taken to respond to a detected threat	1 hour response time	45 minutes	Compliant
False Positive Rate	Percentage of false positives detected by security systems	Below 5% false positives	3%	Compliant
Threat Impact Reduction	Reduction in the impact of a threat after mitigation	80% reduction in impact	70%	Caution
Mitigation Action Completion Rate	Percentage of planned threat mitigation actions completed	100% action completion	90%	Warning
Critical Threat Coverage	Percentage of critical threats mitigated	100% coverage	85%	Warning
Threat Intelligence Integration	Percentage of threat intelligence integrated into security systems	100% integration	80%	Caution
Patch Management Timeliness	Time taken to apply security patches for known threats	72 hours after identification	96 hours	Warning
User Training on Threat Awareness	Percentage of employees trained on threat mitigation practices	100% employee training	85%	Caution
Third-Party Threat Mitigation	Percentage of third-party vendors with active threat mitigation measures	100% vendor compliance	95%	Caution
Monitoring and Review Frequency	Frequency of monitoring and reviewing threat mitigation effectiveness	Monthly reviews	Quarterly reviews	Warning
Disaster Recovery Plan Updates	Frequency of updates to the disaster recovery plan based on new threats	Annual updates	Bi-annual updates	Caution

Table 5 compares the performance of various threat mitigation models across several key metrics. Risk-Based Vulnerability Management (RBVM) outperforms all other models in several areas, including Threat Detection Coverage (95%), with high performance across most metrics. Models 1 through 10 show varying results, with Model 1: Traditional CVE-based Model achieving the lowest Threat Detection Coverage (85%) and Model 6: Cloud-based Threat Detection performing slightly lower at 87%. In terms of Response Time to Threats, RBVM has the fastest response time of 45 minutes, while Model 5: Machine Learning-based Model and Model 6: Cloud-based Threat Detection have slower response times, with times of 70 and 80 minutes, respectively. Patch Management Timeliness also varies significantly, with RBVM at 96 hours, while Model 10: Hybrid Threat Mitigation Model leads in this category at 90 hours. Other models, such as Model 5 and Model 6, experience much longer patching times, around 130 to 140 hours. Risk Impact Reduction sees RBVM at 70%, and while Model 10 (Hybrid Threat Mitigation) performs best at 75%, many models fall short, such as Model 6 (Cloud-based Threat Detection) at just 50%. False Positive Rate is lowest in RBVM at 3%, while Model 5 (Machine Learning-based Model) has the highest at 7%. Critical Threat Mitigation is highest in RBVM (85%) and lowest in Model 10 (65%). In terms of User Awareness Integration, Model 4 (Behavior-based IDS) achieves the highest result (85%), while Model 6 (Cloud-based Threat Detection) lags behind at 65%. Third-Party Risk Mitigation is notably high in RBVM at 90%, compared to the relatively lower figures in other models, such as Model 5 (82%) and Model 6 (90%). Scalability is highest in RBVM, Model 1, and Model 4, which are all rated as High, whereas Model 6 (Cloud-based Threat Detection) is the lowest at Low. The overall Threat Mitigation

Efficiency is highest in Model 10 (Hybrid Threat Mitigation Model) at 82%, with RBVM following at 80%, and other models such as Model 6 (Cloud-based Threat Detection) at 65% performing much lower.

Table 5. Threat mitigation performance comparison

Performance Measure	**Risk-Based Vulnerability Management (RBVM)**	**Traditional CVE-based Model**	**Signature-based IDS**	**Heuristic-based IDS**	**Behavior-based IDS**	**Machine Learning-based Model**	**Cloud-based Threat Detection**	**Zero Trust Architecture**	**Threat Intelligence-driven Model**	**Automated Patch Management System**
Threat Detection Coverage	95%	85%	92%	88%	91%	87%	90%	93%	89%	94%
Response Time to Threats	45 minutes	60 minutes	50 minutes	65 minutes	70 minutes	80 minutes	75 minutes	55 minutes	50 minutes	65 minutes
Patch Management Timeliness	96 hours	120 hours	110 hours	100 hours	130 hours	140 hours	125 hours	115 hours	105 hours	90 hours
Risk Impact Reduction	70%	60%	65%	58%	62%	50%	55%	65%	63%	75%
False Positive Rate	3%	5%	4%	6%	7%	8%	6%	4%	5%	2%
Critical Threat Mitigation	85%	75%	80%	72%	78%	68%	74%	82%	79%	65%
User Awareness Integration	80%	70%	75%	85%	77%	65%	72%	80%	79%	74%
Third-Party Risk Mitigation	90%	85%	88%	80%	82%	90%	85%	87%	83%	86%
Scalability of Model	High	Medium	High	Medium	High	Low	Medium	High	Low	High
Overall Threat Mitigation Efficiency	80%	70%	75%	72%	76%	65%	74%	78%	74%	82%

CONCLUSION

In conclusion, addressing threats in software development is vital for ensuring the security and reliability of modern software systems. Through the implementation of Risk-Based Vulnerability Management (RBVM), organizations can adopt a proactive and systematic approach to identify, assess, and remediate vulnerabilities in their software. By integrating RBVM into the SDLC, vulnerabilities can be prioritized based on their potential impact on critical assets, allowing organizations to allocate resources effectively. This not only reduces the attack surface but also enhances overall security posture by ensuring that the most significant risks are addressed promptly. The findings suggest that adopting RBVM methodologies, coupled with effective training, awareness, and continuous monitoring, can significantly improve the resilience of software systems against evolving threats. Moving forward, further research into refining vulnerability prediction models and risk-scoring algorithms can help to optimize RBVM strategies, providing even more accurate and efficient management of vulnerabilities in software development.

REFERENCES

Batory, D., Benavides, D., & Ruiz-Cortes, A. (2006). Automated Analysis of Feature Models. *Communications of the ACM*, *49*(12), 45–47. DOI: 10.1145/1183236.1183264

Belkina, A. C., Ciccolella, C. O., Anno, R., Halpert, R., Spidlen, J., & Snyder-Cappione, J. E. (2019). Automated Optimized Parameters for T-Distributed Stochastic Neighbor Embedding Improve Visualization and Analysis of Large Datasets. *Nature Communications*, *10*(1), 5415. DOI: 10.1038/s41467-019-13055-y PMID: 31780669

Benavides, D., Trinidad, P., Ruiz-Cortés, A., & Segura, S. (2013). FaMa. In Capilla, R., Bosch, J., & Kang, K.-C. (Eds.), *Systems and Software Variability Management: Concepts, Tools and Experiences* (pp. 163–171). Springer. DOI: 10.1007/978-3-642-36583-6_11

Brailsford, S. C., Potts, C. N., & Smith, B. M. (1999). Constraint Satisfaction Problems: Algorithms and Applications. *European Journal of Operational Research*, *119*(3), 557–581. DOI: 10.1016/S0377-2217(98)00364-6

Chakraborty, S., Krishna, R., Ding, Y., & Ray, B. (2022). Deep Learning Based Vulnerability Detection: Are We There Yet? *IEEE Transactions on Software Engineering*, *48*(9), 3280–3296. DOI: 10.1109/TSE.2021.3087402

Cho, K., Van Merriënboer, B., Gulcehre, C., Bahdanau, D., Bougares, F., Schwenk, H., & Bengio, Y. (2014). Learning phrase representations using RNN encoder-decoder for statistical machine translation. arXiv preprint arXiv:1406.1078.

Elbaz, C., Rilling, L., & Morin, C. (2020, April). Automated Keyword Extraction from" One-day" Vulnerabilities at Disclosure. In NOMS 2020-2020 IEEE/IFIP Network Operations and Management Symposium (pp. 1-9). IEEE.

Fan, J., Li, Y., Wang, S., & Nguyen, T. N. (2020, June). AC/C++ code vulnerability dataset with code changes and CVE summaries. In *Proceedings of the 17th international conference on mining software repositories* (pp. 508-512).

Ferrante, J., Ottenstein, K. J., & Warren, J. D. (1987). The Program Dependence Graph and Its Use in Optimization. *ACM Transactions on Programming Languages and Systems*, *9*(3), 319–349. DOI: 10.1145/24039.24041

Galindo, J. A., & Benavides, D. (2020, October). A Python framework for the automated analysis of feature models: A first step to integrate community efforts. In *Proceedings of the 24th acm international systems and software product line conference-volume b* (pp. 52-55).

Galindo, J. A., Benavides, D., Trinidad, P., Gutiérrez-Fernández, A.-M., & Ruiz-Cortés, A. (2019). Automated Analysis of Feature Models: Quo Vadis? *Computing*, *101*(5), 387–433. DOI: 10.1007/s00607-018-0646-1

Gao, Z., Zhang, C., Liu, H., Sun, W., Tang, Z., Jiang, L., & Xie, Y. (2024). Faster and Better: Detecting Vulnerabilities in Linux-Based IoT Firmware with Optimized Reaching Definition Analysis. In *Proceedings of the 2024 Network and Distributed System Security Symposium*, San Diego, CA, USA (Vol. 26).

Gawron, M., Cheng, F., & Meinel, C. (2017, April). PVD: Passive vulnerability detection. In 2017 8th International Conference on Information and Communication Systems (ICICS) (pp. 322-327). IEEE.

Kenner, A., Dassow, S., Lausberger, C., Krüger, J., & Leich, T. (2020, February). Using variability modeling to support security evaluations: virtualizing the right attack scenarios. In *Proceedings of the 14th International Working Conference on Variability Modelling of Software-Intensive Systems* (pp. 1-9).

Li, Z., Zou, D., Xu, S., Jin, H., Zhu, Y., & Chen, Z. (2022). SySeVR: A Framework for Using Deep Learning to Detect Software Vulnerabilities. *IEEE Transactions on Dependable and Secure Computing*, *19*(4), 2244–2258. DOI: 10.1109/TDSC.2021.3051525

Li, Z., Zou, D., Xu, S., Ou, X., Jin, H., Wang, S., . . . Zhong, Y. (2018). Vuldeepecker: A deep learning-based system for vulnerability detection. arXiv preprint arXiv:1801.01681.

Liu, B., Shi, L., Cai, Z., & Li, M. (2012, November). Software vulnerability discovery techniques: A survey. In 2012 fourth international conference on multimedia information networking and security (pp. 152-156). IEEE.

Maynor, D. (2007). In Maynor, D., & Mookhey, K. K. (Eds.), *Metasploit Toolkit for Penetration Testing, Exploit Development, and Vulnerability Research* (pp. vii–ix). Syngress.

McClanahan, K., Elder, S., Uwibambe, M. L., Liu, Y., Heng, R., & Li, Q. (2024, February). When ChatGPT meets vulnerability management: the good, the bad, and the ugly. In *2024 International Conference on Computing, Networking and Communications (ICNC)* (pp. 664-670). IEEE.

McClanahan, K., & Li, Q. (2024, February). Towards Automatically Matching Security Advisories to CPEs: String Similarity-Based Vendor Matching. In *2024 International Conference on Computing, Networking and Communications (ICNC)* (pp. 233-238). IEEE.

Na, S., Kim, T., & Kim, H. (2018). Service Identification of Internet-Connected Devices Based on Common Platform Enumeration. *Journal of Information Processing Systems*, *14*, 740–750.

Noonan, R. E. (1985). An Algorithm for Generating Abstract Syntax Trees. *Computer Languages*, *10*(3-4), 225–236. DOI: 10.1016/0096-0551(85)90018-9

Schlichtkrull, M., Kipf, T. N., Bloem, P., Van Den Berg, R., Titov, I., & Welling, M. (2018). Modeling relational data with graph convolutional networks. In The semantic web: 15th international conference, ESWC 2018, Heraklion, Crete, Greece, June 3–7, 2018, proceedings 15 (pp. 593-607). Springer International Publishing.

Tovarňák, D., Sadlek, L., & Čeleda, P. (2021, May). Graph-based cpe matching for identification of vulnerable asset configurations. In *2021 IFIP/IEEE International Symposium on Integrated Network Management (IM)* (pp. 986-991). IEEE.

Varela-Vaca, Á. J., Borrego, D., Gómez-López, M. T., Gasca, R. M., & Márquez, A. G. (2023). Feature Models to Boost the Vulnerability Management Process. *Journal of Systems and Software*, *195*, 111541. DOI: 10.1016/j.jss.2022.111541

Varela-Vaca, Á. J., Gasca, R. M., Carmona-Fombella, J. A., & Gómez-López, M. T. (2020, October). AMADEUS: towards the AutoMAteD secUrity teSting. In *Proceedings of the 24th ACM Conference on Systems and Software Product Line: Volume A-Volume A* (pp. 1-12).

Varela-Vaca, Á. J., Gasca, R. M., Ceballos, R., Gómez-López, M. T., & Torres, P. B. (2019). CyberSPL: A Framework for the Verification of Cybersecurity Policy Compliance of System Configurations Using Software Product Lines. *Applied Sciences (Basel, Switzerland)*, *9*(24), 5364. DOI: 10.3390/app9245364

Wang, H., Ye, G., Tang, Z., Tan, S. H., Huang, S., Fang, D., Feng, Y., Bian, L., & Wang, Z. (2021). Combining Graph-Based Learning with Automated Data Collection for Code Vulnerability Detection. *IEEE Transactions on Information Forensics and Security*, *16*, 1943–1958. DOI: 10.1109/TIFS.2020.3044773

Wen, X. C., Chen, Y., Gao, C., Zhang, H., Zhang, J. M., & Liao, Q. (2023, May). Vulnerability detection with graph simplification and enhanced graph representation learning. In 2023 IEEE/ACM 45th International Conference on Software Engineering (ICSE) (pp. 2275-2286). IEEE.

Wu, Z., Pan, S., Chen, F., Long, G., Zhang, C., & Yu, P. S. (2019). A Comprehensive Survey on Graph Neural Networks. *IEEE Transactions on Neural Networks and Learning Systems*, *32*(1), 4–24. DOI: 10.1109/TNNLS.2020.2978386 PMID: 32217482

Xu, Y., Xu, Z., Chen, B., Song, F., Liu, Y., & Liu, T. (2020, July). Patch based vulnerability matching for binary programs. In *Proceedings of the 29th ACM SIGSOFT International Symposium on Software Testing and Analysis* (pp. 376-387).

Yamaguchi, F., Golde, N., Arp, D., & Rieck, K. (2014, May). Modeling and discovering vulnerabilities with code property graphs. In 2014 IEEE symposium on security and privacy (pp. 590-604). IEEE.

Yang, G., Chen, X., Cao, J., Xu, S., Cui, Z., Yu, C., & Liu, K. (2021, August). Comformer: Code comment generation via transformer and fusion method-based hybrid code representation. In 2021 8th International Conference on Dependable Systems and Their Applications (DSA) (pp. 30-41). IEEE.

Zhao, Q., Huang, C., & Dai, L. (2006). VULDEFF: Vulnerability Detection Method Based on Function Fingerprints and Code Differences. *Knowl.-Based Syst.* 2023, *260*, 110139. Kornblum, J. Identifying Almost Identical Files Using Context Triggered Piecewise Hashing. *Digital Investigation*, *3*, 91–97.

Zheng, W., Jiang, Y., & Su, X. (2021, October). Vu1SPG: Vulnerability detection based on slice property graph representation learning. In 2021 IEEE 32nd International Symposium on Software Reliability Engineering (ISSRE) (pp. 457-467). IEEE.

Zhou, J., Cui, G., Hu, S., Zhang, Z., Yang, C., Liu, Z., Wang, L., Li, C., & Sun, M. (2020). Graph Neural Networks: A Review of Methods and Applications. *AI Open*, *1*, 57–81. DOI: 10.1016/j.aiopen.2021.01.001

Zhou, Y., Liu, S., Siow, J., Du, X., & Liu, Y. (2019). Devign: Effective vulnerability identification by learning comprehensive program semantics via graph neural networks. *Advances in Neural Information Processing Systems*, •••, 32.

Chapter 7
Harnessing AI for Seamless Customer Support and Optimized Knowledge Management

Usharani Bhimavarapu
https://orcid.org/0000-0002-0246-1420
Department of Computer Science and Engineering, Koneru Lakshmaiah Education Foundation, Vaddeswaram, India

ABSTRACT

AI Software and Applications in Knowledge Management and Customer Support have emerged as transformative tools in modern business environments. By leveraging advanced machine learning algorithms, and deep learning techniques, AI-powered systems can significantly enhance both the management of organizational knowledge and the efficiency of customer support services. These AI applications assist in automating knowledge-sharing processes, improving decision-making, and providing real-time support to customers. In the realm of customer support, AI-driven chatbots and virtual assistants offer 24/7 assistance, streamline customer interactions, and reduce operational costs. In knowledge management, AI systems help organizations manage vast amounts of information, enabling better access to critical data and insights. This paper explores the integration of AI in knowledge management and customer support, examining how these technologies can improve service quality, drive innovation, and create more personalized experiences for customers.

INTRODUCTION

AI software and applications have become integral to modern knowledge management systems, transforming how organizations store, access, and utilize information. By leveraging machine learning, natural language processing (NLP), and deep learning, AI enables the automation and enhancement of knowledge management processes, making them more efficient and effective. One of the primary roles of AI in knowledge management is in information retrieval. AI-powered systems can analyze vast amounts of unstructured data, such as documents, emails, and social media content, and extract relevant

DOI: 10.4018/979-8-3693-8407-7.ch007

insights, making it easier for employees to find critical information when needed. These systems use advanced search algorithms that understand context and intent, improving the relevance and accuracy of search results.

Another key application of AI in knowledge management is knowledge discovery. AI tools can identify patterns and trends across datasets, uncovering hidden knowledge and providing actionable insights that human workers may overlook. For example, AI systems can analyze historical data to predict future trends, helping businesses make proactive decisions. Personalization is another area where AI excels, as it can tailor content and recommendations to individual users based on their past behavior, preferences, and role within the organization. This ensures that employees receive the most relevant information, fostering a more efficient and productive work environment.

AI also plays a significant role in collaboration and knowledge sharing. Virtual assistants and chatbots integrated with knowledge management platforms can help employees collaborate in real time by offering instant access to shared knowledge, facilitating communication, and assisting in problem-solving. These AI-driven tools can even automate routine tasks, allowing employees to focus on higher-level activities that require critical thinking and creativity. Furthermore, content management is enhanced through AI by automating the organization and classification of documents, reducing the time spent on manual tasks and ensuring information is easily accessible and up-to-date.

AI software and applications in knowledge management not only streamline the storage and retrieval of information but also enhance decision-making, improve collaboration, and support innovation within organizations. By harnessing the power of AI, businesses can better manage their knowledge assets, improve productivity, and remain competitive in an increasingly data-driven world.

AI in customer support has revolutionized how businesses interact with customers, offering personalized, efficient, and scalable solutions to meet evolving consumer demands. One of the most widely adopted AI-driven technologies in customer support is chatbots. These intelligent systems use Natural Language Processing (NLP) to understand and respond to customer inquiries in real-time, providing instant support 24/7. Chatbots can handle a wide range of queries, from basic FAQs to more complex issues, ensuring customers receive timely assistance without the need for human intervention. They can be integrated into websites, mobile apps, and social media platforms, offering seamless support across various communication channels.

Virtual assistants powered by AI take customer support to the next level by offering a more sophisticated level of interaction. These systems can guide customers through troubleshooting processes, recommend products, and even process transactions, all while learning from each interaction to improve future responses. Sentiment analysis, another key AI application, enables customer support systems to assess the emotional tone of customer interactions. This allows the system to tailor responses accordingly, providing empathetic or urgent support when needed and improving the overall customer experience.

AI can also optimize ticketing systems by automatically categorizing and prioritizing customer queries based on urgency, which helps human agents address the most pressing issues first. Predictive analytics further enhances AI in customer support by analyzing historical data to anticipate customer needs and proactively offering solutions or reminders. For example, AI might detect patterns in customer behavior, such as a frequent need for a product return, and suggest relevant solutions before the customer even asks.

Another significant benefit of AI in customer support is cost efficiency. By automating routine tasks, AI frees up human agents to focus on more complex or high-priority issues, reducing operational costs while maintaining a high level of service quality. Over time, AI systems can be trained to understand an increasing variety of customer concerns and provide more accurate, context-aware responses, continually enhancing their ability to support users effectively.

Ultimately, AI in customer support enhances service speed, consistency, and personalization, ensuring that businesses can deliver high-quality, efficient, and customer-centric experiences. As these technologies continue to evolve, their ability to handle complex inquiries, understand context, and predict customer needs will further solidify their role in transforming customer service operations.

Customer Relationship Management (CRM) systems rely on various models and techniques to help businesses manage interactions with current and potential customers. These models range from traditional frameworks to more sophisticated data-driven approaches, each with its strengths and limitations. The AIDA Model (Attention, Interest, Desire, Action) focuses on guiding customers through a sales funnel. However, its limitation lies in its linear approach, which doesn't account for the complex, non-linear paths many customers take today (Kotler et al., 2015).RFM Model (Recency, Frequency, Monetary) is based on transaction history to categorize customers. Its limitation is the inability to account for customer behavior beyond transactional data, such as sentiment or social engagement (Stone, 2020).The Customer Lifecycle Model tracks customer stages from awareness to loyalty. It can be limiting due to its simplistic view of customer relationships and inability to account for the cyclical nature of modern customer journeys (Peppers & Rogers, 2016).The 80/20 Rule (Pareto Principle) Focuses on the idea that 80% of a company's profits come from 20% of its customers. Its limitation is that it doesn't consider customers who are emerging or have potential to become high-value but are not yet profitable (Vilfredo, 1896). CLV (Customer Lifetime Value) Model helps predict the total revenue a customer will generate over their relationship with a brand. However, its limitation is that it often relies on historical data that may not account for changing customer behaviors (Gupta & Zeithaml, 2006).The Five A's Model (Aware, Appeal, Ask, Act, Advocate) Focuses on customer behavior during the purchasing journey. Its limitation is that it oversimplifies customer decision-making, failing to capture the complexity of emotions, social influences, and other factors (Kotler & Keller, 2012).The Service-Profit Chain Model Focuses on the connection between employee satisfaction, service quality, and customer loyalty. The limitation is that it does not address external factors like competition or market changes which can also affect customer loyalty (Heskett et al., 1994).The Customer Value Model calculates value based on perceived benefits and costs. Its limitation is that it doesn't incorporate long-term factors like customer emotional attachment or brand loyalty (Anderson et al., 1994).Kano Model classifies customer preferences into basic, performance, and excitement factors. However, its limitation is that it assumes a fixed set of needs, which may change over time or due to external influences (Kano et al., 1984).The Net Promoter Score (NPS) measures customer loyalty by asking how likely customers are to recommend a brand. A limitation of NPS is that it doesn't capture the full spectrum of customer sentiments and behaviors (Reichheld, 2003).The 4Ps (Product, Price, Place, Promotion) model often used in CRM to manage customer satisfaction. Its limitation is that it focuses more on the product than on the customer relationship or experience (McCarthy, 1960). Customer Segmentation Models group customers based on shared characteristics (demographics, behavior, etc.). The limitation is that segmentation often uses broad categories, potentially overlooking niche customer needs or behaviors (Smith, 1956).The Loyalty Model Focuses on building repeat business by rewarding customer loyalty. However, its limitation is that it assumes loyalty is driven only by rewards, ignoring other factors like customer experience or brand perception (Oliver, 1999).The AIDAS Model (Attention, Interest, Desire, Action, Satisfaction) Extends the AIDA model by adding satisfaction as a key factor. Its limitation is that it doesn't fully address customer retention post-purchase, focusing only on the initial sales cycle (Strong, 1925).The Customer Journey Mapping Model Tracks every touchpoint in the customer experience. While detailed, it can be limiting due to its complexity, making it difficult to implement and maintain in large, dynamic organizations (Sharma, 2018).CRM as a Data Warehouse Model emphasizes centralizing all customer data in one place for easier analysis and management. The limitation is that data integration can be complex, time-consuming, and prone to errors, especially with disparate data sources (Chen et al., 2012).Behavioral Targeting Model uses customer actions (e.g., clicks, searches) to personalize CRM strategies. Its limitation is that it may over-rely on behavioral data, ignoring other important factors like context, intent, and emotional factors (Tucker, 2014).The Customer Satisfaction Model Focuses on measuring and improving satisfaction as a core component of CRM. A key limitation is that satisfaction does not always correlate with customer loyalty or lifetime value (Fornell et al., 1996).The CRM Dashboard Model Provides real-time data visualization to track customer interactions and business KPIs. Its limitation is that dashboards often oversimplify customer data and don't always provide deep insights into underlying issues (Chaudhuri & Holbrook, 2001).The Predictive Analytics Model Uses statistical techniques to forecast future customer behaviors. However, its limitation is that predictions may be inaccurate if based on incomplete or biased data (Bose, 2009). The Omni-Channel Model Aims to provide a seamless experience across all customer touchpoints. Its limitation is the complexity of integrating multiple channels, especially in organizations with legacy systems or siloed data (Verhoef et al., 2015).The Personalized Marketing Model Uses customer data to tailor marketing efforts. Its limitation is that it can be perceived as intrusive or over-personalized if not done carefully, leading to privacy concerns or customer disengagement (Tam & Ho, 2005).The Customer Retention Model Focuses on keeping existing customers rather than acquiring new ones. Its limitation is that it can lead businesses to neglect the acquisition of new customers or fail to adapt to changing market conditions (Reichheld & Sasser, 1990).The Customer Acquisition Cost (CAC) Model Helps businesses understand the cost of acquiring a new customer. Its limitation is that it may not account for the long-term value a customer brings or changes in customer behavior post-acquisition (Sharma & Sheth, 2010).The Lead Scoring Model Uses algorithms to rank prospects based on their likelihood to convert. A limitation is that it can overlook qualitative factors like customer intent, emotions, or preferences, which might be just as important as quantitative data (Dixon et al., 2010).

The proposed segmentation and prediction models are designed to address the limitations of traditional CRM models by incorporating advanced techniques such as machine learning, deep learning, and dynamic customer profiling. For instance, traditional models like the RFM model often fail to capture evolving customer behaviors beyond transaction history. In contrast, the proposed segmentation model leverages real-time data from multiple sources, such as social media interactions, customer feedback, and browsing history, to create more nuanced and dynamic customer segments. This allows businesses to better understand changing customer needs and preferences over time.

Additionally, while traditional models like CLV rely heavily on historical data to predict customer value, the proposed prediction model utilizes machine learning algorithms, such as decision trees or neural networks, to predict future customer behaviors by considering a wider range of variables, including sentiment analysis, seasonal trends, and external market factors. This helps overcome the limitations of static models that may not fully account for the complexity of customer interactions and external influences.

Moreover, models like the 80/20 rule, which focus on past transactional data, can miss emerging high-value customers. The new segmentation models incorporate predictive analytics to identify potential high-value customers early in the customer journey, based on real-time interactions and behavioral patterns, thus overcoming the limitations of static historical data analysis.

The proposed models also address the limitations of linear models like the AIDA model by using machine learning techniques to account for the non-linear and personalized customer journeys that are common in today's complex, multi-channel environments. Furthermore, with the integration of AI-driven tools, businesses can continuously refine and update customer segments and predictions, providing a more agile and responsive approach to CRM.

These advanced models offer a more comprehensive, adaptive, and forward-looking approach to CRM, overcoming the limitations of traditional models by incorporating real-time data, predictive analytics, and dynamic customer segmentation. This ensures more personalized and effective customer relationship strategies, improving customer satisfaction, loyalty, and ultimately, business performance.

MATERIALS AND METHODOLOGY

The methodology for this study involves a mixed-methods approach, combining both qualitative and quantitative data collection techniques. Surveys and interviews are conducted with industry professionals to gather insights into the integration of AI in knowledge management and customer support. Data is analyzed through thematic analysis for qualitative responses and statistical methods for quantitative data. AI applications in customer support, such as chatbots and virtual assistants, are assessed for their impact on efficiency and customer experience. A case study approach is used to explore real-world implementations of AI technologies. The results are used to identify trends, challenges, and best practices in the field.

Material

To expand data collection for the analysis, efforts can be directed towards increasing the sample size and diversifying the range of industries included in the study. A broader scope can be achieved by incorporating more firms within the retail sector across various regions in India, thereby capturing regional variations and enhancing representativeness. Additionally, the inclusion of more micro, small, and medium enterprises (MSMEs) from industries related to or complementing retail, such as logistics, technology providers, and manufacturing, can offer valuable insights into sectoral interdependencies.

Expanding the diversity of industries can further enrich the study. Firms from sectors like food, security, and tourism, which were initially included, can be supplemented with other industries that play a significant role in shaping retail dynamics. A stratified sampling technique can be adopted to ensure the inclusion of firms with specific characteristics relevant to the research objectives. Moreover, focusing on regional variations by selecting enterprises from different geographic areas in India will help identify unique trends and challenges faced by firms operating in distinct market environments.

By adopting these measures, the data collection process can yield a more comprehensive dataset, allowing for a deeper understanding of the factors influencing the firms in the context of the research.

Customer Segmentation

Customer segmentation using Fuzzy C-Means (FCM) is a powerful data-driven technique that groups customers into segments based on similarities in their attributes while allowing overlap between clusters. Unlike traditional clustering methods like K-Means, which assign each customer to a single cluster, FCM assigns membership probabilities to multiple clusters, reflecting the inherent ambiguity and overlap in customer behaviors. This makes it particularly effective in capturing the nuances of real-world data where customers often exhibit characteristics of more than one segment.

The FCM algorithm operates by iteratively optimizing the placement of cluster centers and assigning membership values to data points. Each customer is represented as a data point in a multidimensional space, where dimensions correspond to attributes such as demographics, purchasing behavior, or psychographics. During the process, the algorithm minimizes an objective function, balancing the distance between customers and cluster centers while considering the fuzziness parameter, which controls the degree of overlap between clusters.

This approach has significant advantages for customer segmentation. By identifying overlapping segments, businesses can design more flexible strategies, such as creating hybrid marketing campaigns targeting customers who belong to multiple segments. For instance, a customer who exhibits traits of both a "budget-conscious" and "tech-savvy" segment can receive personalized offers that address both interests. Additionally, FCM provides richer insights into customer profiles, helping organizations identify trends and relationships that may not be evident with hard clustering methods.

Security and Privacy in CRM

Security and privacy in Customer Relationship Management (CRM) systems are paramount due to the sensitive nature of the data they manage, including personal, financial, and transactional information. To protect this data from unauthorized access and breaches, robust security protocols and privacy measures are essential. One of the primary methods for securing data is through encryption protocols. Transport Layer Security (TLS) protocols are widely used to encrypt data during transmission, ensuring that any communication between the CRM system and its users is securely protected from eavesdropping. These protocols encrypt data in transit, making it difficult for attackers to intercept or manipulate sensitive information during online exchanges.

In addition to encryption, authentication and authorization protocols are critical for controlling access to CRM data. OAuth 2.0 is one of the most common protocols used for secure, token-based authentication. It allows third-party applications to access the CRM system without exposing user credentials, ensuring that only authorized users can interact with sensitive data. OAuth 2.0 facilitates secure login and access to data based on predefined permissions, thus maintaining privacy and reducing the risk of unauthorized access. Furthermore, Multi-Factor Authentication (MFA) adds an extra layer of security, requiring users to provide additional verification beyond a password, such as a fingerprint or one-time passcode.

To protect data integrity and ensure proper access control, the CRM system implemented role-based access control (RBAC). This ensures that users can only access data that is relevant to their role, further minimizing the risk of exposing sensitive information to unauthorized personnel. Regular security audits and compliance with General Data Protection Regulation (GDPR) for maintaining privacy and ensuring that the CRM system adheres to data protection laws. By incorporating these protocols and security measures, organizations can protect their CRM systems from breaches, ensuring the confidentiality and privacy of customer data while building trust with their user base.

Churn Prediction

In churn prediction using Convolutional Neural Networks (CNN), customer data is transformed and passed through the network to predict the likelihood of churn. The process begins with input data preparation, where customer features such as demographics, transaction history, interaction logs, and service usage patterns are collected. This structured data is preprocessed to handle missing values, normalize numerical features, and encode categorical variables. The preprocessed data is then reshaped into a grid-like format, suitable for CNN input. For instance, in tabular data, each customer is represented as a 2D matrix where rows correspond to time steps or feature groups, and columns represent feature values.

Once the input data is ready, it is passed into the CNN. The first layer typically involves convolutional operations, where filters (or kernels) slide over the input grid to extract patterns, such as trends in customer behavior over time. These filters automatically learn spatial or temporal relationships between features, enabling the model to identify patterns indicative of churn, such as declining usage or irregular interaction frequency. The convolutional layer outputs feature maps that highlight these patterns, which are then passed through an activation function (e.g., ReLU) to introduce non-linearity and help the model learn complex relationships.

The feature maps are subsequently processed by pooling layers, which downsample the data to reduce its dimensionality while retaining key information. Pooling helps in summarizing patterns and improving computational efficiency, ensuring the network focuses on the most relevant features. Several convolutional and pooling layers can be stacked to progressively capture higher-level representations of the data.

The extracted features from the final pooling layer are flattened into a 1D vector and passed into fully connected layers. These layers act as classifiers, combining the extracted features to predict the likelihood of churn. Dropout layers may be added during this stage to prevent overfitting by randomly disabling neurons during training. Finally, the output layer, often with a sigmoid activation function, produces a probability score indicating the likelihood of a customer churning.

Throughout this process, backpropagation and optimization algorithms like Adam or SGD adjust the weights of the network based on the error between the predicted and actual churn labels. This iterative training process ensures that the CNN learns to generalize patterns effectively, enabling accurate churn prediction. By capturing complex, non-linear relationships in customer data, CNN-based churn prediction offers a robust and scalable approach for proactive customer retention strategies.

EXPERIMENTAL RESULTS

The experimental setup for evaluating the proposed segmentation and prediction models was conducted using a system configured with Windows 10. The system was equipped with an Intel Core i7 processor, 16 GB of RAM, and a 512 GB SSD to ensure smooth execution of data-intensive tasks, including real-time customer data processing and machine learning model training. The environment also included Python 3.8 and relevant machine learning libraries, such as TensorFlow, Keras, and scikit-learn, to facilitate the development and deployment of the segmentation and prediction models. Additionally, the system was configured with appropriate data storage solutions to handle large datasets and ensure efficient data access during model training and evaluation. This setup provided a robust foundation for conducting the experiments and evaluating the performance of the proposed models under various conditions.

Table 1 compares various clustering and machine learning models based on key characteristics such as model type, cluster membership, performance, computation time, and flexibility. Fuzzy C-Means (FCM) is a soft clustering model that allows multiple cluster membership. It delivers high performance with a computation time of approximately 30-60 minutes and is considered highly flexible due to its ability to assign data points to multiple clusters with varying degrees of membership. K-Means, a hard clustering model, assigns each data point to a single cluster. It has moderate performance and is relatively fast, requiring only 5-10 minutes for computation. However, it has low flexibility as it only accommodates rigid, non-overlapping clusters. Hierarchical Clustering, which is agglomerative, allows for multiple cluster memberships. It has moderate performance and a computation time of 1-3 hours. It is also moderately flexible, as it creates a hierarchy of clusters that can be adjusted to various levels of granularity. DBSCAN is a density-based model, providing multiple cluster memberships and high performance with a computation time of 15-30 minutes. It offers moderate flexibility, as it can identify clusters of arbitrary shape but is sensitive to parameter settings. The Gaussian Mixture Model (GMM) is a probabilistic model that allows multiple cluster memberships. It provides high performance with a computation time ranging from 30 to 90 minutes. GMM is highly flexible, as it assumes clusters are Gaussian-distributed and can adapt to different data distributions. Self-Organizing Maps (SOM), a neural network model, also supports multiple cluster memberships. It achieves high performance, with computation times between 1-2 hours, and is highly flexible due to its ability to visualize and cluster high-dimensional data in a low-dimensional map. K-Medoids is a hard clustering technique similar to K-Means, but it uses actual data points as cluster centers. It provides moderate performance and takes around 30-60 minutes to compute, with moderate flexibility. Latent Dirichlet Allocation (LDA), a topic modeling method, has low performance and requires 1-2 hours of computation. It has low flexibility, as it assumes a fixed number of topics and assigns each document to one or more topics based on a probabilistic model. Agglomerative K-Means, a hybrid of hard and soft clustering, allows for mixed cluster memberships. It has high performance and a computation time of 1-2 hours, with high flexibility due to its ability to combine the advantages of K-Means and hierarchical clustering. CART (Classification and Regression Trees), a decision tree model, assigns each data point to a single cluster and has moderate performance. Its computation time is relatively fast at 10-30 minutes, but its flexibility is low, as it is limited to tree-based structures and binary splits. Neural Networks (ANN) are highly powerful neural network models that provide multiple cluster memberships with very high performance. They require a significant computation time of 2-5 hours but are very flexible, capable of handling complex, non-linear relationships in data. Random Forest, an ensemble learning model, supports multiple cluster memberships and has high performance. It requires a computation time of 30-60 minutes and provides moderate flexibility due to its ensemble approach that can handle different types of data but is still tree-based. Overall, the models vary in terms of their computation time and flexibility. Soft clustering models like Fuzzy C-Means and probabilistic models like GMM tend to offer more flexibility, while hard clustering models like K-Means and decision trees like CART offer faster but less flexible solutions. More complex models, such as Neural Networks and Self-Organizing Maps, tend to perform better at the cost of longer computation times.

Table 1. Customer segmentation

Model	Type	Cluster Membership	Performance (e.g., Accuracy)	Computation Time	Flexibility
Fuzzy C-Means (FCM)	Soft Clustering	Multiple	High	~30-60 minutes	High
K-Means	Hard Clustering	Single	Moderate	~5-10 minutes	Low
Hierarchical Clustering	Agglomerative	Multiple	Moderate	~1-3 hours	Moderate
DBSCAN	Density-Based	Multiple	High	~15-30 minutes	Moderate
Gaussian Mixture Model (GMM)	Probabilistic	Multiple	High	~30-90 minutes	High
Self-Organizing Maps (SOM)	Neural Network	Multiple	High	~1-2 hours	High
K-Medoids	Hard Clustering	Single	Moderate	~30-60 minutes	Moderate
Latent Dirichlet Allocation (LDA)	Topic Modeling	Single	Low	~1-2 hours	Low
Agglomerative K-Means	Hybrid (Hard & Soft)	Mixed	High	~1-2 hours	High
CART (Classification and Regression Trees)	Decision Tree	Single	Moderate	~10-30 minutes	Low
Neural Networks (ANN)	Neural Network	Multiple	Very High	~2-5 hours	Very High
Random Forest	Ensemble Learning	Multiple	High	~30-60 minutes	Moderate

Table 2 presents a comparison of various churn prediction models across several performance metrics, including Accuracy, Precision, Recall, F1-Score, Computation Time, and Flexibility. The models vary significantly in terms of computational requirements and their ability to predict customer churn. Convolution Neural Networks (CNN), a deep learning model, achieves the highest accuracy (0.92), with precision (0.91), recall (0.90), and F1-score (0.90) also being impressive. However, its computation time is relatively high, ranging from 2-5 hours, and it offers very high flexibility, making it suitable for complex, non-linear churn prediction tasks. Logistic Regression, a statistical method, provides a moderate accuracy (0.83) and performs relatively well in terms of precision (0.80) but is less effective in terms of recall (0.75). It has the lowest computation time (~1-5 minutes) and is characterized by low flexibility, which limits its use for more complicated churn prediction scenarios. Decision Trees (CART), a machine learning model, achieves moderate performance with an accuracy (0.85) and F1-score (0.81). With a computation time of about 5-15 minutes, it is low in flexibility, as it tends to overfit when faced with highly complex data. Random Forest, an ensemble learning model, offers high performance with accuracy (0.90), precision (0.89), and recall (0.86), along with an F1-score (0.87). The computation time of 30-60 minutes is moderate, and its flexibility is moderate, making it a strong candidate for churn prediction tasks requiring a balance of speed and accuracy. Support Vector Machine (SVM), another machine learning model, achieves moderate to high performance with accuracy (0.88) and F1-score (0.82). It requires 10-30 minutes for computation and offers moderate flexibility for churn prediction tasks, though it may struggle with very large datasets. Naive Bayes, a probabilistic model, performs with moderate accuracy (0.82) and lower recall values (0.72). It is among the fastest models in terms of computation time (5-10 minutes) but has low flexibility due to its reliance on simplistic assumptions like feature independence. Gradient Boosting Machine (GBM), an ensemble learning method, achieves high performance, with accuracy (0.91), precision (0.90), and recall (0.88). With a computation time of 1-2 hours, it provides high flexibility, making it effective for complex churn prediction tasks. K-Nearest Neighbors (KNN), an instance-based model, performs moderately with accuracy (0.84) and precision (0.82). The computation time is between 10-20 minutes, and it has moderate flexibility, making it suitable for datasets where the relationship between data points is important but not overly complex. Artificial Neural Networks (ANN), another deep learning model, provides high performance with an accuracy (0.89) and precision (0.87). The computation time of 1-2 hours is moderate, and it offers high flexibility, allowing it to model complex churn behaviors. XGBoost, an ensemble learning method, achieves high accuracy (0.92) and high performance in terms of precision (0.91) and recall (0.89), along with an F1-score (0.90). It has a computation time of 30-60 minutes and offers high flexibility, making it one of the most effective models for churn prediction. LightGBM, another ensemble learning model, provides moderate to high performance, with accuracy (0.90) and F1-score (0.87). With a computation time of 20-40 minutes, it offers high flexibility and is particularly suitable for large-scale datasets with complex features. Deep Neural Networks (DNN), a deep learning model, delivers high performance with an accuracy (0.90), precision (0.88), and recall (0.85), along with an F1-score (0.86). It requires a computation time of 3-6 hours and offers very high flexibility, making it well-suited for complex churn prediction tasks.

Table 2. Churn prediction performance comparison

Model	Type	Accuracy	Precision	Recall	F1-Score	Computation Time	Flexibility
Convolution Neural Networks (CNN)	Deep Learning (ANN)	0.92	0.91	0.90	0.90	~2-5 hours	Very High
Logistic Regression	Statistical	0.83	0.80	0.75	0.77	~1-5 minutes	Low
Decision Trees (CART)	Machine Learning	0.85	0.83	0.80	0.81	~5-15 minutes	Low
Random Forest	Ensemble Learning	0.90	0.89	0.86	0.87	~30-60 minutes	Moderate
Support Vector Machine (SVM)	Machine Learning	0.88	0.85	0.80	0.82	~10-30 minutes	Moderate
Naive Bayes	Probabilistic Model	0.82	0.80	0.72	0.75	~5-10 minutes	Low
Gradient Boosting Machine (GBM)	Ensemble Learning	0.91	0.90	0.88	0.89	~1-2 hours	High
K-Nearest Neighbors (KNN)	Instance-Based	0.84	0.82	0.78	0.80	~10-20 minutes	Moderate
Artificial Neural Networks (ANN)	Deep Learning	0.89	0.87	0.84	0.85	~1-2 hours	High
XGBoost	Ensemble Learning	0.92	0.91	0.89	0.90	~30-60 minutes	High
LightGBM	Ensemble Learning	0.90	0.89	0.85	0.87	~20-40 minutes	High
Deep Neural Networks (DNN)	Deep Learning	0.90	0.88	0.85	0.86	~3-6 hours	Very High

Table 3 presents a performance comparison of various CRM automation models based on accuracy, implementation time, and cost efficiency. The models vary significantly in their performance outcomes, speed of implementation, and overall cost-effectiveness. AI-powered Chatbots, categorized under AI &

Automation, achieve an impressive accuracy of 92% with a fast implementation time of 1-2 weeks and are highly cost-efficient. This makes them highly suitable for automating customer interactions and support services. Automated Email Campaigns, a form of marketing automation, offer a moderate accuracy (85%), with a moderate implementation time of 2-4 weeks. While not as cost-effective as AI-driven solutions, they provide moderate cost efficiency, making them useful for targeted marketing strategies. Robotic Process Automation (RPA), a process automation model, delivers a moderate accuracy (80%) and has a moderate implementation time of 3-6 weeks. Despite the longer setup time, RPA is considered highly cost-efficient, making it suitable for automating repetitive and rule-based processes. CRM Software with Workflow Automation, part of CRM & workflow management, provides high accuracy (90%) and a moderate implementation time of 2-4 weeks. It is also highly cost-efficient, making it a great option for businesses looking to streamline customer management processes. Voice Assistants (IVR systems), a voice automation model powered by AI, offers 90% accuracy with a fast implementation time of 1-2 weeks. It provides moderate cost efficiency, suitable for businesses integrating voice interfaces for customer interaction. Predictive Analytics for Sales, a data science automation approach, achieves 88% accuracy, but requires a longer implementation time of 4-8 weeks. Despite the lengthy setup, it is considered highly cost-efficient due to its ability to forecast sales trends and customer behaviors accurately. Automated Customer Feedback Systems, another AI & automation model, provides 85% accuracy and a moderate implementation time of 2-4 weeks. It is moderately cost-efficient, ideal for businesses seeking to automate the collection and analysis of customer feedback. Social Media Automation, a form of marketing automation, has a moderate accuracy (80%) with a moderate implementation time of 2-3 weeks. It is highly cost-efficient, helping businesses automate social media management and interactions. Task and Appointment Scheduling Automation, categorized under CRM automation, excels with a high accuracy (95%) and fast implementation time of 1-2 weeks. It is also highly cost-efficient, making it ideal for automating scheduling tasks in CRM systems.Automated Data Entry and Updating, part of data automation, leads with the highest accuracy (98%) and a fast implementation time of 1-2 weeks, along with high cost efficiency, making it highly beneficial for businesses aiming to reduce manual data handling.

Table 3. Automation in CRM performance comparison

CRM Automation Model	Type	Accuracy	Implementation Time	Cost Efficiency
AI-powered Chatbots	AI & Automation	92%	Fast (1-2 weeks)	High
Automated Email Campaigns	Marketing Automation	85%	Moderate (2-4 weeks)	Moderate
Robotic Process Automation (RPA)	Process Automation	80%	Moderate (3-6 weeks)	High
CRM Software with Workflow Automation	CRM & Workflow Management	90%	Moderate (2-4 weeks)	High
Voice Assistants (IVR systems)	AI & Voice Automation	90%	Fast (1-2 weeks)	Moderate
Predictive Analytics for Sales	Data Science Automation	88%	Long (4-8 weeks)	High
Automated Customer Feedback Systems	AI & Automation	85%	Moderate (2-4 weeks)	Moderate
Social Media Automation	Marketing Automation	80%	Moderate (2-3 weeks)	High
Task and Appointment Scheduling Automation	CRM Automation	95%	Fast (1-2 weeks)	High
Automated Data Entry and Updating	Data Automation	98%	Fast (1-2 weeks)	High

Table 4 compares various customer engagement models based on metrics such as engagement rate, response time, customer satisfaction, scalability, and implementation time. The models display varying strengths in different aspects, catering to diverse business needs. AI-powered chatbots, which fall under AI & Automation, lead with an engagement rate of 85% and instant response times, contributing to high customer satisfaction. This model also offers very high scalability and fast implementation (1-2 weeks), making it ideal for businesses looking for scalable, real-time customer service solutions. On the other hand, automated email campaigns, categorized under marketing automation, show a moderate engagement rate of 75%, but still offer fast response times (1-2 minutes) and moderate customer satisfaction. This model also provides high scalability and requires a moderate implementation time of 2-4 weeks, making it suitable for businesses that need effective email marketing solutions. Social media automation, also part of marketing automation, has an engagement rate of 80% and provides fast response times (1-2 minutes), with moderate customer satisfaction and high scalability, making it effective for managing interactions across social media platforms in a timely manner. However, the moderate implementation time of 2-3 weeks may be a consideration for businesses seeking quicker solutions. Push notifications, part of engagement automation, stand out for their instant response times, moderate engagement rate of 70%, and very high scalability, making them ideal for businesses that need to send timely alerts to a large audience. While their customer satisfaction is moderate, their fast implementation time (1-2 weeks) makes them an attractive option for quick deployment. Live chat, categorized under customer support, provides a very high engagement rate of 90%, instant response times, and very high customer satisfaction. Although scalability is high, the moderate implementation time (2-4 weeks) makes it a practical solution for businesses looking to offer real-time support with a reasonable setup time. Gamification, part of engagement & loyalty, achieves a moderate engagement rate of 78%, with fast response times (1-3 minutes) and high customer satisfaction. Its moderate scalability and moderate implementation time (3-5 weeks) make it ideal for businesses aiming to boost customer loyalty and engagement through interactive, game-like experiences. Voice assistants (IVR), part of AI & Voice Automation, achieve an engagement rate of 80% with instant response times and high customer satisfaction. They also offer high scalability and fast implementation (1-2 weeks), making them suitable for businesses that want to automate voice-based customer interactions quickly. Predictive engagement, categorized under data science automation, has an engagement rate of 88%, but requires moderate response times of 5-10 minutes. With high customer satisfaction and high scalability, it is beneficial for businesses that want to anticipate customer needs, though its long implementation time (4-8 weeks) might make it less suitable for quick solutions. Lastly, survey automation, part of feedback automation, provides a moderate engagement rate of 65%, fast response times (1-2 minutes), and moderate customer satisfaction, with high scalability. Its moderate implementation time (2-4 weeks) makes it a good choice for businesses that wish to collect customer feedback efficiently. Automated customer feedback systems, another AI & Automation model, offer an engagement rate of 80%, fast response times, and high customer satisfaction, along with high scalability. This model's moderate implementation time (2-4 weeks) ensures a balance between deployment speed and effective functionality. Overall, AI-powered chatbots, voice assistants, and live chat offer the best combination of high engagement, instant response time, and high scalability, while predictive engagement and survey automation provide high scalability and strong customer satisfaction, albeit with longer implementation times. The comparison reveals that businesses can choose a model based on their specific needs—whether they prioritize speed, scalability, or customer satisfaction.

Table 4. Customer engagement performance comparison

Customer Engagement Model	Type	Engagement Rate	Response Time	Customer Satisfaction	Scalability	Implementation Time
AI-powered Chatbots	AI & Automation	85%	Instant	High	Very High	Fast (1-2 weeks)
Automated Email Campaigns	Marketing Automation	75%	Fast (1-2 minutes)	Moderate	High	Moderate (2-4 weeks)
Social Media Automation	Marketing Automation	80%	Fast (1-2 minutes)	Moderate	High	Moderate (2-3 weeks)
Push Notifications	Engagement Automation	70%	Instant	Moderate	Very High	Fast (1-2 weeks)
Live Chat	Customer Support	90%	Instant	Very High	High	Moderate (2-4 weeks)
Gamification	Engagement & Loyalty	78%	Fast (1-3 minutes)	High	Moderate	Moderate (3-5 weeks)
Voice Assistants (IVR)	AI & Voice Automation	80%	Instant	High	High	Fast (1-2 weeks)
Predictive Engagement	Data Science Automation	88%	Moderate (5-10 minutes)	High	High	Long (4-8 weeks)
Survey Automation	Feedback Automation	65%	Fast (1-2 minutes)	Moderate	High	Moderate (2-4 weeks)
Automated Customer Feedback Systems	AI & Automation	80%	Fast (1-2 minutes)	High	High	Moderate (2-4 weeks)

CONCLUSION

The integration of AI software and applications into knowledge management and customer support has demonstrated significant potential in enhancing organizational efficiency and customer satisfaction. By automating routine tasks and improving data access and decision-making, AI systems help businesses stay competitive and responsive to customer needs. AI-driven customer support tools, such as chatbots, reduce wait times and provide consistent, personalized service, while AI in knowledge management facilitates better collaboration and knowledge sharing across organizations. However, successful implementation requires careful attention to data security, privacy concerns, and continuous training to adapt to evolving customer expectations. As AI technologies continue to advance, their role in transforming knowledge management and customer support will only expand, offering even more opportunities for businesses to innovate and optimize their operations.

REFERENCES

Anderson, E. W., Fornell, C., & Lehmann, D. R. (1994). Customer satisfaction, market share, and profitability: Findings from Sweden. *Journal of Marketing, 58*(3), 53–66. DOI: 10.1177/002224299405800304

Bose, R. (2009). Advanced analytics: Opportunities and challenges. *Industrial Management & Data Systems, 109*(2), 155–173. DOI: 10.1108/02635570910930073

Chaudhuri, A., & Holbrook, M. B. (2001). The chain of effects from brand trust and brand affect to brand performance: The role of brand loyalty. *Journal of Marketing, 65*(2), 81–93. DOI: 10.1509/jmkg.65.2.81.18255

Chen, J. V., Yen, D. C., & Paquette, S. (2012). The influence of customer relationship management (CRM) systems on customer retention and acquisition. *International Journal of Information Management, 32*(6), 478–486.

Dixon, M., Freeman, K., & Toman, N. (2010). Stop trying to delight your customers. *Harvard Business Review, 88*(7-8), 116–122.

Fornell, C., Johnson, M. D., Anderson, E. W., Cha, J., & Bryant, B. E. (1996). The American customer satisfaction index: Nature, purpose, and findings. *Journal of Marketing, 60*(4), 7–18. DOI: 10.1177/002224299606000403

Gupta, S., & Zeithaml, V. A. (2006). Customer metrics and their impact on financial performance. *Marketing Science, 25*(6), 22–37. DOI: 10.1287/mksc.1060.0221

Heskett, J. L., Sasser, W. E., & Schlesinger, L. A. (1994). *The Service-Profit Chain: How Leading Companies Link Profit and Growth to Loyalty, Satisfaction, and Value*. Free Press.

Kano, N., Seraku, N., Takahashi, F., & Tsuji, S. (1984). Attractive quality and must-be quality. *Journal of the Japanese Society for Quality Control, 14*(2), 39–48.

Kotler, P., Armstrong, G., Saunders, J., & Wong, V. (2015). *Principles of Marketing* (7th ed.). Pearson Education.

Kotler, P., & Keller, K. L. (2012). *Marketing Management* (14th ed.). Pearson Education.

McCarthy, E. J. (1960). *Basic Marketing: A Managerial Approach* (2nd ed.). Irwin.

Oliver, R. L. (1999). Whence consumer loyalty? *Journal of Marketing, 63*(4_suppl1), 33–44. DOI: 10.1177/00222429990634s105

Peppers, D., & Rogers, M. (2016). *Managing Customer Relationships: A Strategic Framework*. Wiley. DOI: 10.1002/9781119239833

Reichheld, F. F. (2003). The One Number You Need to Grow. *Harvard Business Review, 81*(12), 46–55. PMID: 14712543

Reichheld, F. F., & Sasser, W. E. (1990). Zero defections: Quality comes to services. *Harvard Business Review, 68*(5), 105–111. PMID: 10107082

Sharma, A. (2018). *Customer Journey Mapping for Improved Experience*. Wiley.

Sharma, A., & Sheth, J. N. (2010). *The Customer Value Proposition in Business Markets*. Springer.

Smith, W. R. (1956). Product differentiation and market segmentation as alternative marketing strategies. *Journal of Marketing*, *21*(1), 3–8. DOI: 10.1177/002224295602100102

Strong, E. K. (1925). *The psychology of selling and advertising*. The Macmillan Company.

Tam, K. Y., & Ho, S. Y. (2005). Web personalization as a portfolio of marketing strategies. *Decision Support Systems*, *39*(1), 43–57.

Tucker, C. E. (2014). The economics of advertising and privacy. *Journal of Economic Literature*, *52*(4), 1–40.

Verhoef, P. C., Kannan, P. K., & Inman, J. J. (2015). From multi-channel retailing to omni-channel retailing. *Journal of Retailing*, *93*(2), 174–181. DOI: 10.1016/j.jretai.2015.02.005

Vilfredo, P. (1896). *Cours d'économie politique*. Librairie Rousseau.

Chapter 8
Leveraging Data Analytics for Promoting Environmentally Sustainable and Socially Resilient Cities Infrastructure

S. Heena
Birla Institute of Technology and Science, Pilani, India

Monika Sharma
B K Birla Institute of Engineering & Technology, Pilani, India

Shashank Gupta
Birla Institute of Technology and Science, Pilani, India

ABSTRACT

In this paper, we survey the existing literature on the integration of sustainability and smart applications. We focus on providing insights on the use of state-of-the-art Machine Learning mechanisms in context of the sustainable smart systems. A thorough discussion of various Deep Learning algorithms and frameworks which provide embedded intelligence for sustainable smart applications such as smart home, smart city, healthcare, industry, transportation, agriculture, etc. has been discussed. We then shed light on various Big Data Analytics techniques for mining the useful things along with potential of leveraging advanced deep learning techniques and why it is considered a favourable approach to accomplish analytics in sustainable systems. In the end, we discuss set of challenges and potential future directions for research that could serve as a foundation to encourage research and analytical discussions to promote the development of sustainable and smart systems.

1. INTRODUCTION

The sustainability of cities is considered as a desired outcome of smart systems proposal that actively leverages evolving technologies for its accomplishment (Yigitcanlar et. al.,2019). The upsurge of IoT has accompanied prosperity to a multitude of sustainable applications on several infrastructures namely

DOI: 10.4018/979-8-3693-8407-7.ch008

sensor networks, smart phones (Cai et. al., 2019), cognitive smart systems (Chen et. al.,2018), unmanned aerial vehicles (UAV) (Hu et. al.,2018) (Hu et. al., 2019) and many more. The process of designing sustainable smart applications generally emulate a work-flow model comprising of 5 components, problem formulation, data collection, data analysis, visualization and assessment (Nagarajan et. al., 2021) (Haseeb et. al., 2021). The latest advancement in DL has empowered researchers and analysts to train robust and powerful models that enables various sustainable applications, for example, edge computing (8), energy management (Wang et. al.,2018) and network caching (He et. al., 2018). In the past several years, various sustainable smart applications come to light in several vertical domains, namely smart city (Shorfuzzaman et. al., 2021), smart home, health, education, transportation, agriculture and many more and these domains have supported as a tool for tackling sustainability challenges (Ashraf et. al., 2021). The key component of many of such applications is an intellectual method based on learning for forecasting, e.g., classification, clustering & regression; data extraction and data analysis (Shafiq et. al., 2020). DL has been vigorously utilized in several smart sustainable systems even though a lot of ML mechanisms are present (Majumdar et. al., 2021). The combination of DL in sustainable smart system have been found among the top 3 tech trends in 2016 (Gartner et. al., 2016) declared at Garter Symposium. The reason behind such exhaustive trend of DL indicates that the conventional ML mechanisms fail to handle the surfacing analysis requirements of sustainable smart systems. Figure 1 illustrates a DL-based smart system. Sustainable smart applications require diverse up-to-date data analytics techniques and AI mechanisms as per the IoT data management and generation. The rapidly growing attraction towards smart systems and sustainability requires the contributors to understand its meaning, architecture, capabilities and associated issues (Chen et. al., 2021). IoT produces enormous amount of data and is vital for big data analytics. The estimated impact of knowledge automation on various businesses is shown in Figure 2. This estimated impact indicates the increased attraction towards the importance of IoT Big Data and the consequences of machine learning and deep learning on society. To get a more clear understanding of big data analytics in sustainable smart systems and how it is unlike from big data, we require to investigate some of the characteristics of IoT data. The following are the characteristics possessed by the data generated by sustainable smart systems (Zhou et. al.,2021).

Figure 1. A DL-based IoT system

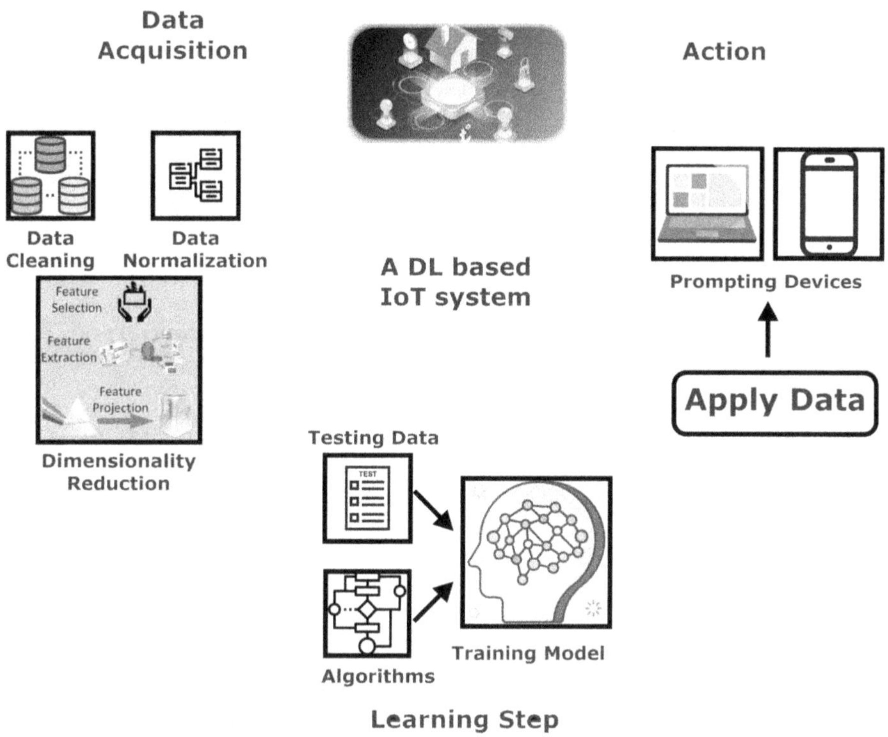

- Large-scale Data: Many of smart sustainable applications such as smart home, smart city, healthcare, government etc. uses distributed data gathering infrastructures and produces enormous data constantly.
- Heterogeneity: Several sustainable data gathering architectures collect diverse info leading to data heterogeneity.
- Space & Time correlation: Sensors are usually linked to a particular location and therefore possess a time and space mapping for every data point in the sustainable smart applications.

The integration of sustainable smart systems and big data could help in assisting the communication between several devices in a smart city and smart home (Khan et. al.,2013). Application domains, for example, smart grids, smart traffic, intelligent infrastructures, etc. can be beneficial from the earlier mentioned architectures. Several researches on big data concentrates on its management, particularly on analytics (Russom et. al.,2011) (Abu et. al.,2021). The advocates view smart systems as a potential for a sustainable urban planning, delivering technological propositions to urban challenges (LaValle et. al., 2010). Sustainable smart systems are not simple and comprised of unified infrastructures. The present 5G sustainable models are facing serious problems in dealing with the privacy and security of users (Kolias et. al.,2017). The application of existing security protection techniques, for example, authentication and access control, encryption, application and n/w security is quite difficult and incompetent for huge networks with various linked gadgets, with every subpart of the model with intrinsic weaknesses. 'Mirai' is one of the infamous botnets which has become the reason of DDos attacks in sustainable smart networks (Chen et. al.,2021). The present security mechanisms need to be strengthened to suit the sustainable smart applications. But the security techniques implemented for a particular security issue is rapidly overcame by various new kinds of attacks. Furthermore, recognizing what techniques are best for safeguarding these sustainable smart models for longer use is a problem due to the diversity of these applications. An emerging interest in integrating DL 5G sustainable systems for handling security attacks has recently been observed. Hence, the development of efficacious security mechanisms for sustainable smart systems poses a big research opportunity.

Figure 2. Economic impact of knowledge automation on various occupations by 2025

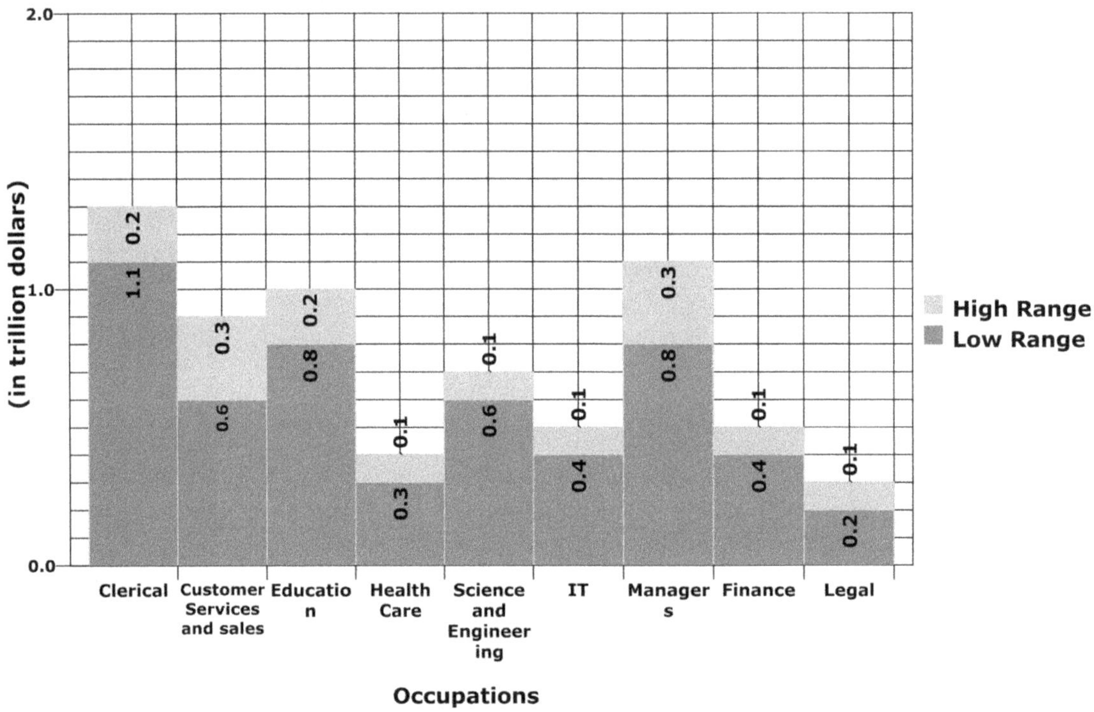

As per the best of our knowledge, this paper firstly extensively surveys the relationship between sustainable smart applications and deep learning & the implementation of DL techniques in these applications. A few studies (Adi et al., 2020) are present in the literature focusing on ML techniques utilized in IoT systems.

1.1 Key Contributions

This survey is dedicated to the researchers who are working in the field of IoT and big data analytics and developers who desire to design sustainable smart systems using the advanced ML and DL techniques. The various contributions in this paper could be outlined as below:

- Provided a comprehensive background of several state-of-the-art ML approaches and their categories in context of the sustainable smart applications equipped with technologies such as ZigBee, Wi-Fi, RFID, etc.
- Discussed the state-of-the-art advanced DL techniques and architectures along with several available DL frameworks and optimizing algorithms in context of sustainable smart systems and provided a comparison of the related work present in the literature.
- Discussed a vast variety of sustainable smart applications ranging from smart home, smart city to retail, agriculture that utilizes DL in their implementation and provided a comparison of several DL architectures with respect to 5G application domain for sustainable systems.
- Reviewed the relationship between DL, sustainable smart systems and Big Data Analytics and discussed some of the important data mining approaches that leverages big data along with the challenges faced by the presented approaches in sustainable smart cities.
- Outlined the several security attacks and problems encountered by sustainable smart applications in 5G environment and highlighted various ML and DL approaches to address those problems.

The entire paper is divided into 7 sections as illustrated in Figure 3. The section 2 highlights various state-of-the-art ML approaches along with their sub-categories. Section 3 presents several advanced DL approaches. It discusses and provides a comparison of abilities of famous frameworks for DL models implementation. This section also includes a discussion of various optimizing algorithms specifically w.r.t. sustainable smart applications. Section 4 reviews in detail various sustainable applications, for example smart home, smart city, transportation, healthcare, industry etc., that have leveraged DL approaches in their infrastructures. A variety of potential classification algorithms for sustainable smart systems have been reviewed in Section 5. Section 6 investigates the relationship between sustainable smart systems and big data and reviews the role of DL in Big Data for sustainable smart applications. The security attacks and challenges faced by sustainable smart systems have been outlined in Section 7 along with the possible ML and DL approaches of dealing with them.

Figure 3. Structure of the paper

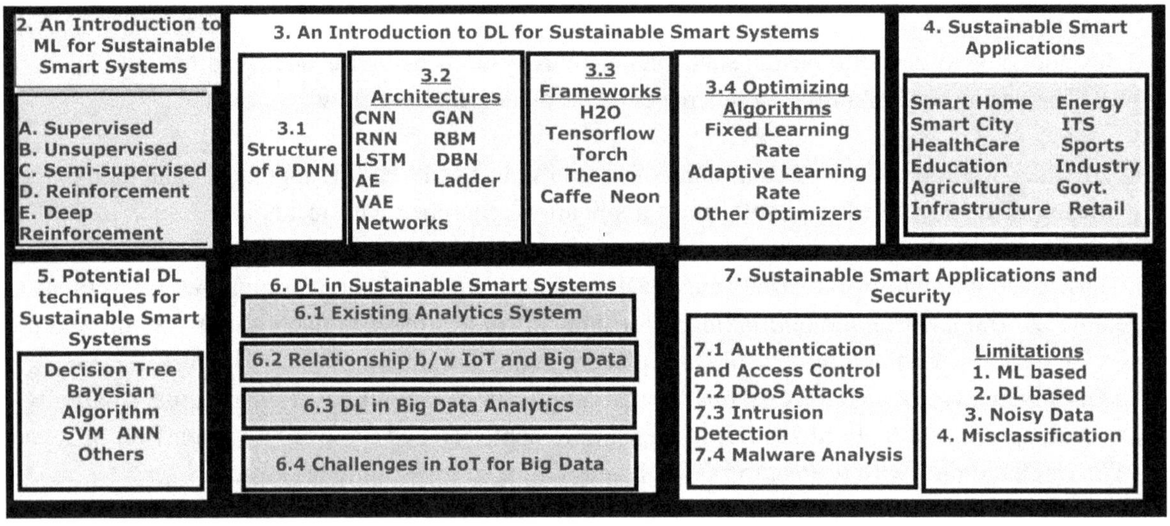

2. AN INTRODUCTION TO MACHINE LEARNING TECHNIQUES FOR SUSTAINABLE SMART SYSTEMS

Machine Learning describes intelligent strategies for optimising performance standards without any explicit instructions by learning from patterns in the data or prior experience(s). The machine learning techniques could be further grouped into four diverse techniques: supervised, semi-supervised, unsupervised, and reinforcement learning algorithms as illustrated in Figure 4. This section briefly explains the various categories of ML techniques.

Supervised Learning: These are employed when certain goals are identified to achieve from a given input dataset. The input data in these algorithms undergo the labelling process following which this data is used for training the network. The objective of such algorithms is to recognize a mapping function from an input instance to the output instance and determining different classes for the prediction of input instances to one of those classes.

Unsupervised Learning: The unsupervised learning algorithms are generally used when no mapping between the input and output is provided. The model tries to explore similarity and patterns among unlabelled data for the classification of input data into distinct groups without any need of labelled data. Clustering and Dimensionality Reduction are the two sub-categories of unsupervised learning algorithms. Examples of the unsupervised learning problems include customer segmentation, targeted marketing, compression, etc.

Semi-Supervised Learning: In the previously described algorithms, either all of the observations in the dataset have no labels or all of the observations have labels. Semi- supervised learning lies somewhere in the middle of supervised and unsupervised learning algorithms. In many realistic cases, labelling the input data is quite expensive as it needs manual expertise for it. Therefore, semi-supervised algorithms are considered best for the model construction when labels are not present in most of the examples.

Figure 4. Classification of ML algorithms

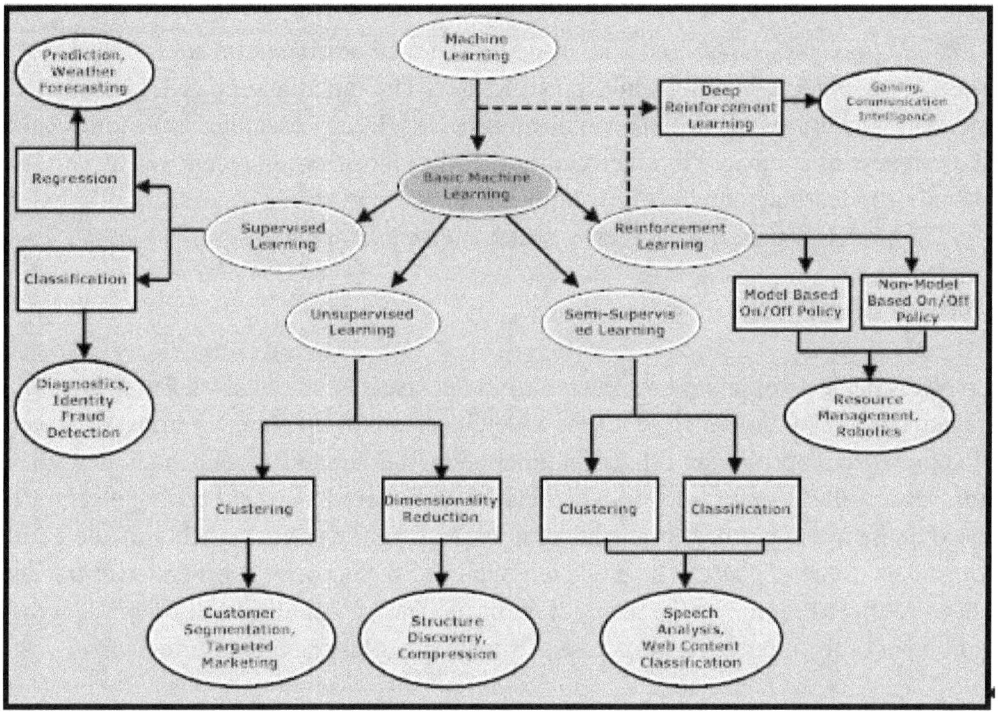

Reinforcement Learning (RL): These are the class of algorithms that enables an agent to learn by trial and error using feedback received from the model. The goal of algorithm is to maximize the reward by taking a sequence of decisions in a particular situation. These algorithms are known to be influenced from human and animal learning practices. All these characteristics make this type of learning algorithms an appealing technique in robotics applications where the system learns to perform specific actions without being explicit programmed. (Q Chen et. al.,2019).

Deep Reinforcement Learning (DRL): DRL integrates the decision-making capability of RL with the perception of DL. This technique uses RL for the determination of the best decision from unstructured data. DL assists RL by using action values approximation to calculate the reward associated with an action in the associated step. Even though DL possess the capability to learn from hidden and complex patterns in the data, it is highly vulnerable to classification errors. In this case, RL doesn't require feature creation and has the ability to learn from the environment, which aids DL in effective classification (Eugene et al., 2018).

3. AN INTRODUCTION TO DEEP LEARNING TECHNIQUES FOR SUSTAINABLE SMART SYSTEMS

Deep Learning involves supervised and unsupervised methods based on several layers of Artificial NNs to learn hierarchic presentations in deep structures. The functioning of DL is modelled after the signal processing techniques of the human brain and neurons. Deep Learning architectures have received increased awareness as compared to other traditional ML algorithms in recent years. This section discusses several deep learning architectures, frameworks and optimizing algorithms. Table I represents the various DL Models and their examples of sustainable smart applications

3.1 Structure of a DNN

A deep NN is made up of an i/p layer, various hidden layers & an o/p layer. Every layer of the DNN contains a number of neurons which performs a weighted sum of i/p obtained from the preceding layer (except first layer), and operates an activation function on the sum to generate the output. In each layer, the neurons (except the output layer) have associated with them a bias and a weight vector that needs be optimised in the training process. The neurons in the input layer are usually provided with random weights during the training phase. The predicted output of the network is generated at the last layer. A loss function is utilized to compute the accuracy of the model by computing the difference of the expected values and output of the model. The structure of a neuron is illustrated in Figure 5.

3.2 Architectures

DL models could be, in general, sub-grouped into 3 models: discriminative models, generative models, and hybrid models. Discriminative models are equipped with SL techniques, on the other hand, generative models provide unsupervised solutions, though this is not a strict distinction. The hybrid models are incorporated with the advantages of both generative and discriminative models within them. This section provides a quick overview of several common DL models. Figure 6 shows various Deep Learning models.

Figure 5. Structure of DNN

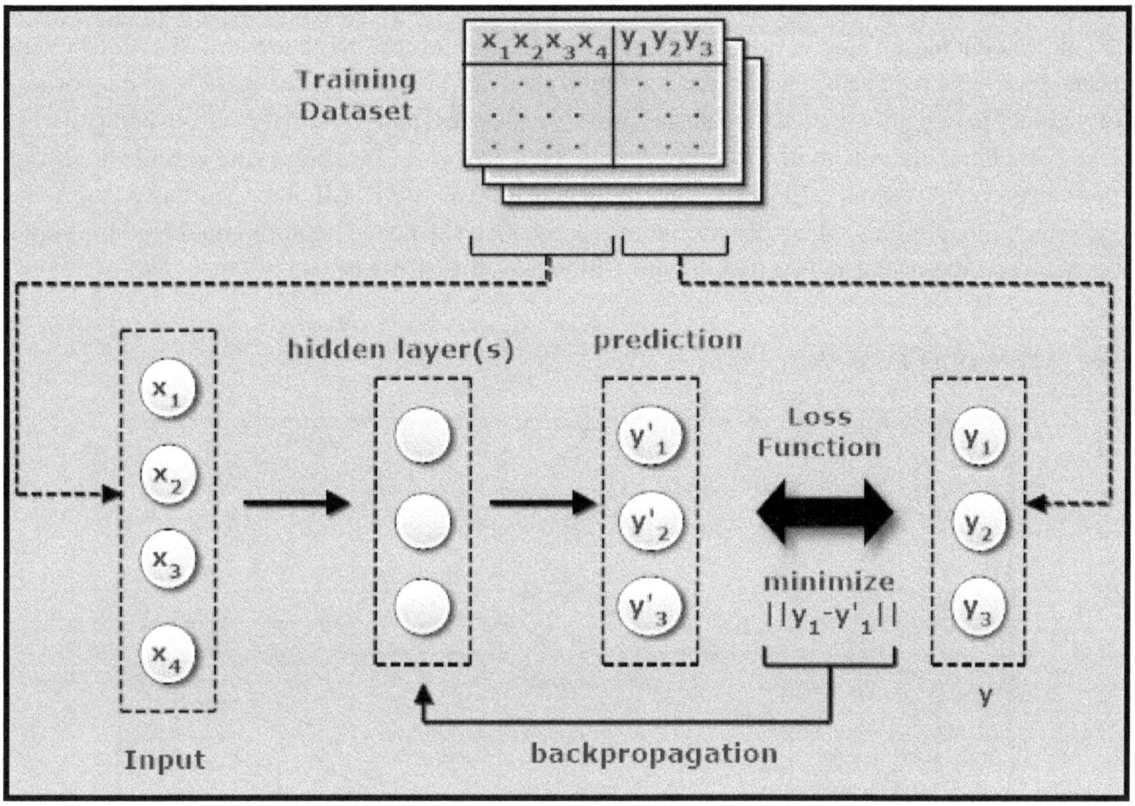

Convolutional Neural Networks (CNNs): A CNN takes two-dimensional data (such as an speech signal, video or image) as input and retrieves high-level characteristics from that data by passing it from a no. of hidden layers. Hidden layers in this type of model is made up of linked layer and fully connected layers. The learnable attributes embodies in convolution layer known as filters with the shape same as the input and smaller in dimension. The input volume is traversed by the filter of convolutional layer during the training phase for calculating the product of the i/p volume and filter and yielding a filter feature map. The pooling layers, that run on feature maps, are another component of a CNN. These are used to reduce the number of attributes, limit the spatial dimension of the representation, and processing times while also decreasing the risk of overfitting. (Mahdavinejad et. al.,2018)

Recurrent Neural Networks (RNNs): The prediction is based on prior knowledge in a myriad number of applications, so we must examine input sequences in addition to the classification of samples. Therefore, the current sample and the earlier observed sample are fed as input to an RNN. To put it another way, an RNN's output at time (t-1) influences its o/p at time (t). A feedback loop is present in each neuron, which uses the output from the current step as an i/p to the following step. It could be shown as if every neuron in an recurrent NN consists of internal memory for storing the details of the calculations from the earlier i/p. Backpropagation Through Time (BPTT) (Mohammadi et. al., 2018), a backpropagation algorithm's extension, is used to train the n/w. The BPTT technique is based on a method known as unfolding the RNN, which results in a feed-forward n/w over the duration of time (Zhang et. al.,2018) (Zhang et. al.,2018).

Long Short Term Memory (LSTM): LSTMs are based on the principle of gates for the units, with each gate calculating a value in the range (0,1). The neurons of an LSTM are also known as memory cells and each has a read gate, a write gate and forget gate, and along with a feedback loop for storing the information. These gates are used to manage memory cell access and restrain them from being disrupted by irrelevant i/p. A neuron could write the data to itself whenever the forget gate is set to 1. It forgets its previous content whenever the forget gate is switched off with a 0. All other neurons connected to a neuron can write to it only when the write gate is active. All the linked neurons could read the contents of the neuron if the read gate is active. Figure 7 illustrates this structure.

Figure 6. Categories DLModels

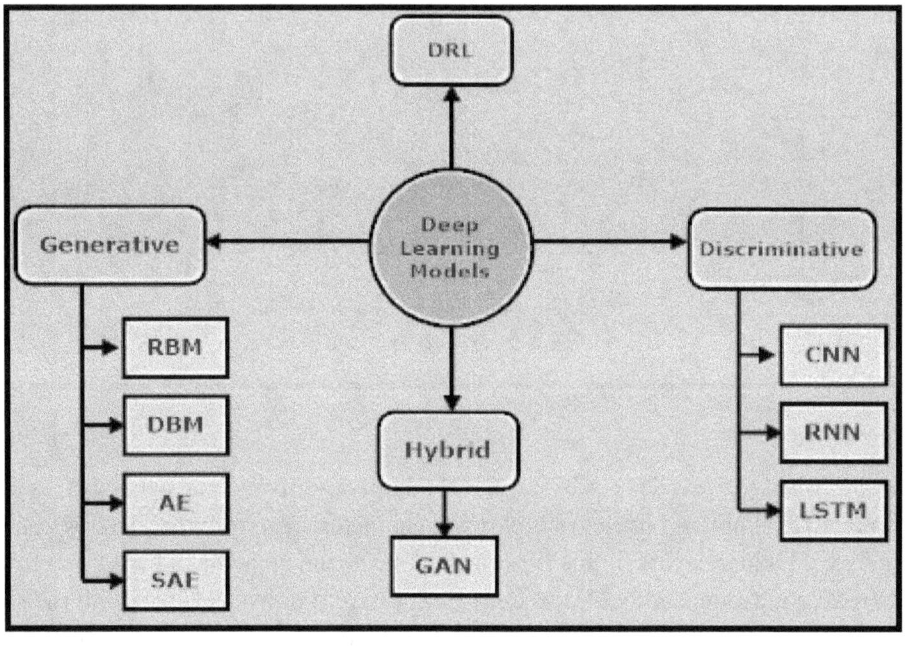

Autoencoders (AEs): Autoencoders comprises of an i/p layer and an o/p layer linked by several hidden layers. The no. of i/p and o/p layers in an autoencoder are same. The goal of such n/w is to regenerate the input by converting i/p to output in the straightforward possible manner, with the least amount of deviation from the input possible. Such neural networks are widely used to solve unsupervised and transfer learning problems (Baldi et.al., 2012). Figure 8 shows the structure of an autoencoder.

Figure 7. Structure of an LSTM cell

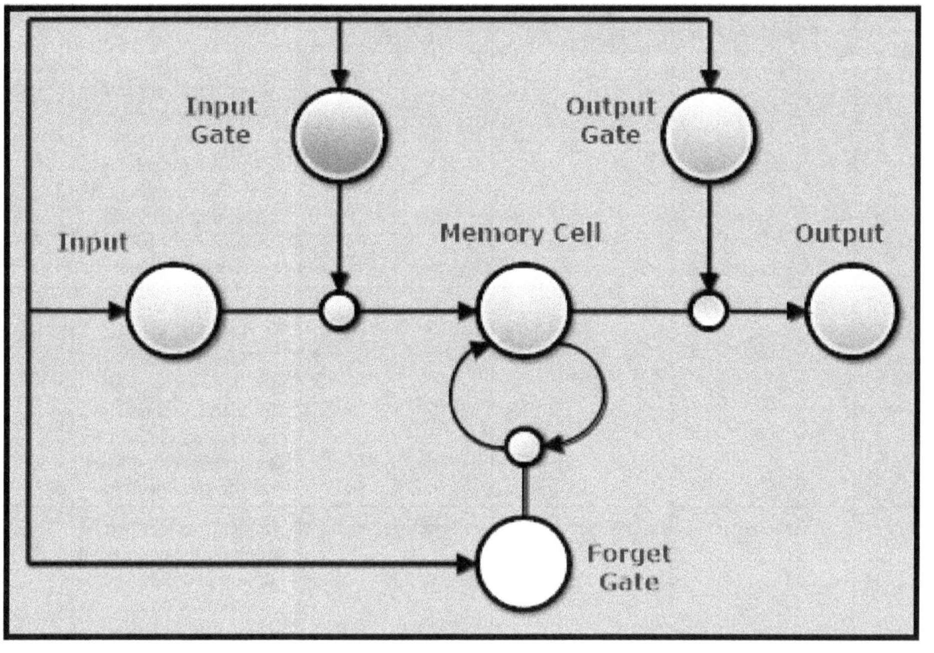

Table 1. Summary of various DL models and examples of sustainable smart applications

Model	Class	Learning Model	Input Data Type	Features	Examples of IoT Applications
AE (Autoencoders)	Generative	Unsupervised	Heterogeneous	Reconstructs the input data by transforming it into output without altering the input much. Utilized for solving unsupervised and transfer learning problems. Suitable for handling unlabelled data.	Emotion recognition Machinery fault diagnosis
RNN (Recurrent Neural Networks)	Discriminative	Supervised	Serial, time-series	Employs BPTT (Backpropagation Through Time) for training the network. Hidden layers provide the memory element for the storing computations of the previous layer.	Behaviour detection Movement pattern identification
RBM (Restricted Boltzmann Machine)	Generative	Unsupervised, Supervised	Heterogeneous	Implements a bi-partite graph for the connection between visible and hidden units. Good fit for dealing with feature extraction, dimensionality reduction and classification tasks.	Indoor localization Traffic Congestion Prediction Energy consumption prediction Posture Analysis
DBN (Deep Belief Network)	Generative	Unsupervised, Supervised	Heterogeneous	Utilized for the extraction of hierarchical representation of data and the reconstruction of the input data. Introduction of a classifier layer such as softmax enables it for prediction tasks.	Security threat Fault detection identification Emotional feature extraction
LSTM (Long Short Term Memory)	Discriminative	Supervised	Serial, long time independent data, time-series	Each neuron consists of a read gate, write gate and a forget gate. The gates control the memory cell access, inhibit the deviations by irrelevant i/p.	Human activity recognition Mobility Prediction Disaster prediction Educational performance prediction in online programs
CNN (Convolutional Neural Networks)	Discriminative	Supervised	2-Dimensional (images, audio, etc.)	Performs well compared to DNNs by supporting translation-equivariance computation. Each neuron in CNN is linked to a small set of the i/p resulting in fewer parameters and reduced training time.	Plant disease recognition Traffic sign recognition Flood or landslide prediction
Model	**Class**	**Learning Model**	**Input Data Type**	**Features**	**Examples of IoT Applications**

continued on following page

Table 1. Continued

Model	Class	Learning Model	Input Data Type	Features	Examples of IoT Applications
VAE (Variational Autoencoders)	Generative	Semi-supervised	Heterogeneous	Comprises of two networks- one for the generation data and the other for carrying out the inference approximation. Suitable for diverse and unlabelled data.	Failure detection Intrusion detection
GAN (Generative Adversarial Networks)	Hybrid	Semi-supervised	Heterogeneous	Consists of generative network- for generating new data and discriminative network- for discriminating fake data from the sample data. The goal is to generate new data that deceives the discriminator.	Image to text conversion Localization and wayfinding
Ladder Net	Hybrid	Semi-supervised	Heterogeneous	Comprises of two parts- Encoders (supervised part of the n/w) and decoders (unsupervised part of the n/w). Data reconstruction from the corrupted data at each layer makes it a good fit for noisy data.	Face Recognition Authentication Image classification Hand-written digits classification Vision-based IoT Analytics

Variational Autoencoders (VAEs): Variational AEs are among the most famous unsupervised frameworks with a fast backpropagation training process for designing complex generative models (Doresch et. al., 2016). It comprises of an encoder, for generating samples, & a decoder, for decoding the samples, with attributes φ(phi) and θ(theta), respectively. There exists a vector of latent variables, y, for each data point m. The encoder uses a fixed form distribution t(y|m) to estimate the posterior distribution pθ(y|m). Figure 9 shows the structure of a VAE n/w. This model has also been used for semi-supervised learning (Kingma et. al.,2016).

Generative Adversarial Networks (GANs): GANs are made up of 2 NNs: a generative n/w and a discriminative n/w, which produce high-quality as well as synthetic samples. The generative n/w generates data using distribution learnt from the sample data. The task of the discriminator network is to distinguish between sample data and false i/p data (data generated by the generator). Other n/w is optimised to generate i/p data such that discriminator cannot differentiate training data from the fake data. The goal function in GANs utilizes the concept of minimax games, where one n/w strives to maximise the value and the other tries to minimise it.

Restricted Boltzmann Machine (RBMs): An RBM is a two-layered generative stochastic artificial NN comprising of 2 layers: a visible layer with well-known i/p and a hidden layer with latent variables. The key difference between the RBMs and Boltzmann machines lies in the connection between the hidden and visible entities. The hidden layer and visible entities in RBM are linked to each other by a bipartite graph The aim of RBM training is to optimise the probability product of all the entities in the visible layer. This type of model is employed in the problems involving dimensionality reduction, classification, regression, and collaborative filtering.

Figure 8. Structure of an autoencoder

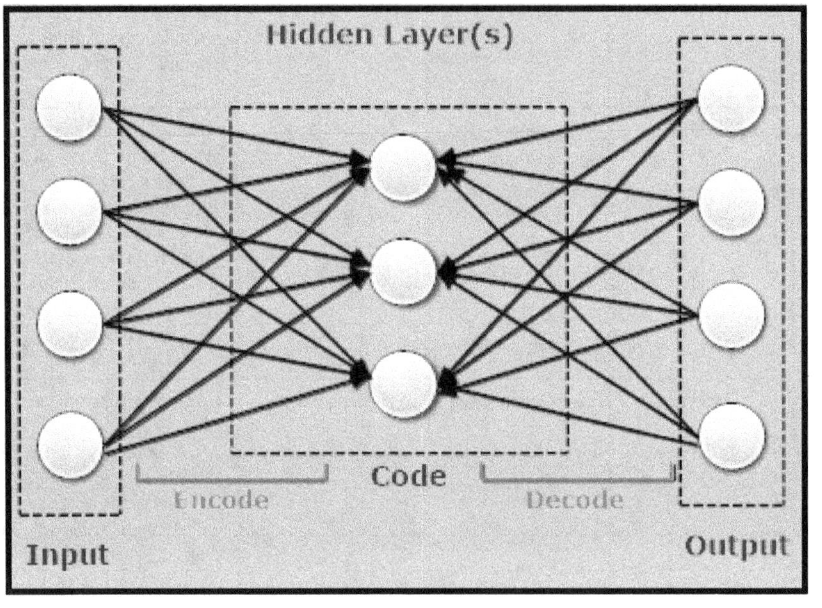

Figure 9. Structure of a variational autoencoder

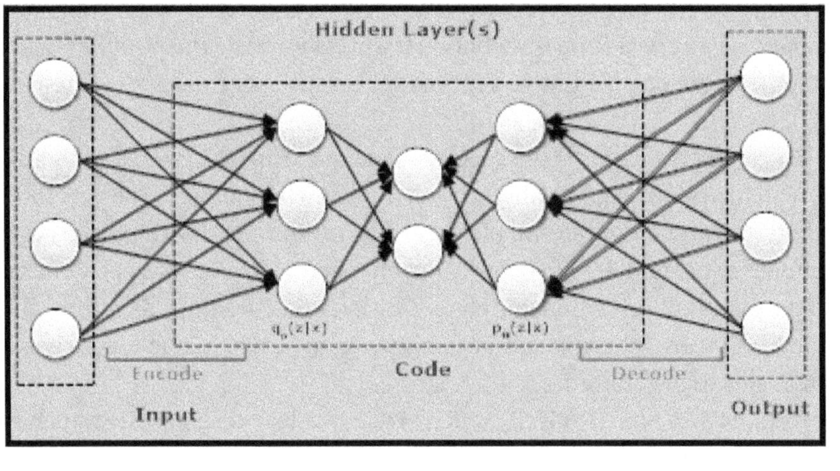

Deep Belief Network (DBNs): DBN are a special kind of generative network. They possess the ability to recreate their input data and retrieve hierarchical representations of the training dataset. Each layer n in DBN is interpreted as an RBM trained atop of (n-1)th trained layer which makes it an efficient as well as a fast algorithm in DL (Bengio et. al.,2009). The model can be deployed for prediction tasks by introducing a classifier layer like softmax.

Ladder Networks: A ladder network is made up of 2 encoders and a decoder. The encoders is the supervised component of the n/w, while the decoder is responsible for unsupervised learning. One of the encoder performs normal calculations, and called as a clean encoder whereas the other one, also known as corrupted encoder, introduces Gaussian noise to every layer of the network. The decoder could rebuild the representations at all the layers using a denoising function and the corresponding corrupted data. Each layer's denoising cost is calculated by finding the difference between rebuilt and clean data. The aim of the training process is to compute the total cost of the supervised and unsupervised networks to the lowest possible value (Rasmus et. al.,2015).

3.3 Deep Learning Frameworks for Sustainable Smart Systems

The introduction of various deep learning frameworks in past few years has aided the fast development of interest in using DL models in various domains. Depending upon the supported optimization techniques and comfort of deployment & development of deep learning models, each framework has its own pros and cons (Bahrampour et. al.,2015). Many of the frameworks described in this section have been extensively used in research to train Deep Neural Networks efficiently. Figure 10 gives a quick overview of various deep learning frameworks.

H2O: H2O is a ML framework with interface support for Python, R, Java, Scala, JSON, and JavaScript/CoffeeScript (Arora et. al., 2015). H2O is implemented using a feed-forward NNs, a DL technique, which could be trained using Support Vector Machines with backpropagation, in addition to various ML algorithms. H2O's Autoencoder is a multi-layer DNN structures, in which the whole network learns together rather than layer by layer. Classification, generalised linear models, clustering, ensembles, optimization techniques, data preprocessing, and DNNs are among the various algorithms supported in H2O as of July 2016.

Figure 10. DL frameworks

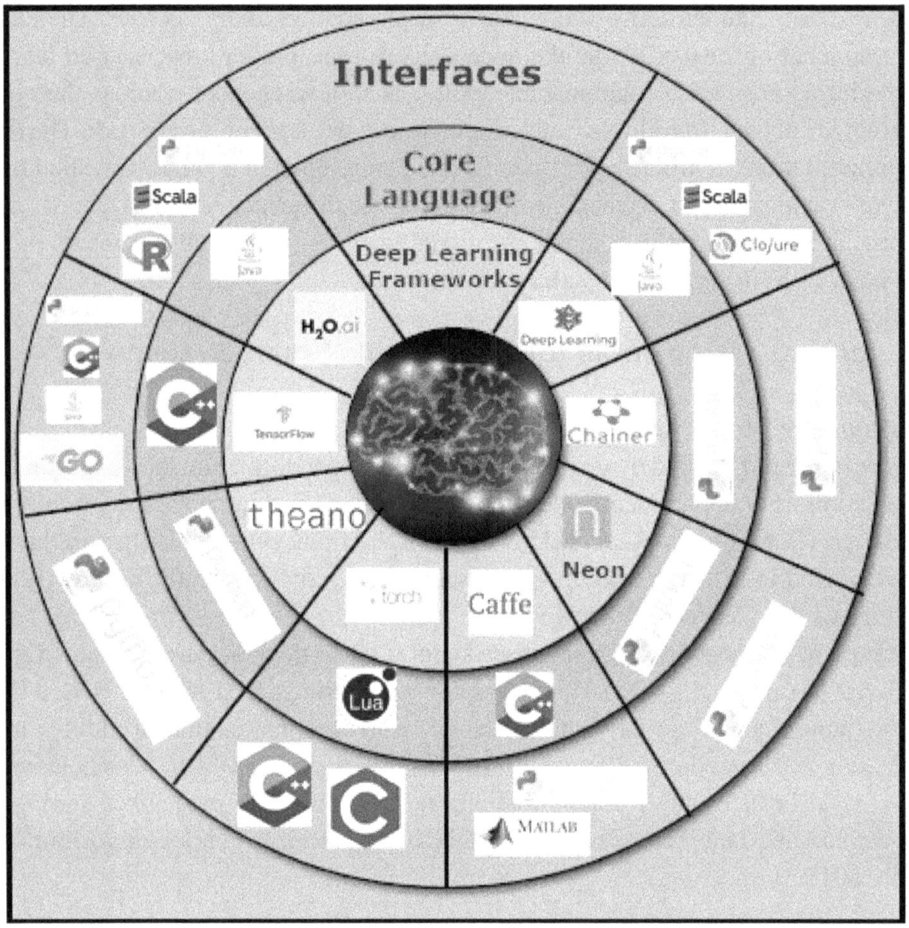

Tensorflow: Tensorflow (Abadi et. al., 2016) is an open-source library for ML technique that use a variety of Deep Neural Networks. TensorBoard, a package used for visualizing NN models and analyzing the learning and parameter updatation process of the network, is also available to developers. TensorFlow was created by the Google Brain team and later released as open source in November 2015 under the Apache 2.0 licence. Tensorflow provides support for techniques such as reinforcement learning techniques, deep learning algorithms and many more. In TensorFlow, computations are done using a data flow graph implementation, where batches of data are processed by a tensors consists of batches of data processed by mechanisms using graphs. Various DL toolboxes, such as Luminoth7, Keras6 and TensorLayer, have been launched to provide higher-level programming interfaces based on TensorFlow. (Steen et. al.,2016).

Torch: It is an open-source ML framework that includes a various of deep learning techniques for rapid advancement of DL models (Collobert et. al.,2011). It is built using Lua language and is designed to be quick and lightweight when training Deep Learning algorithms. It also provides support for ML algorithms and models for scientific computations. (Mocanu et. al.,2016). The neural networks in Py-

Torch is simple and the library's popularity is rising rapidly. It also includes a large number of pre-trained models that are simple to reuse and integrate.

Theano: Theano is a Python based library for effectively defining, optimising, and evaluating numerical calculations of multi-dimensional data (Amato et. al., 2017). It supports CPU and GPU modes, allowing developers to customise programmes to their specific machines. Theano, on the other hand, is harder to learn, and compiling a NN with it takes a considerable time. As TensorFlow implements its core idea and characteristics, its popularity is quickly dwindling.

Caffe: Caffe (Lee et. al.,2016) is a DL framework designed with speed, & modularity in mind. It makes use of Matlab's rapid convolutional network machine-vision library, ported to C and C++. It can be used to carry out image analysis with CNN and regional image analysis with RNN. Cafe is among the most widely used platforms for research studies and deployment mainly because to its performance and processing speed.

Neon: Neon3, a Python-based framework for modern deep NN like Visual Geometry Group (VGG) (Krizhevsky et al.,2012), AlexNet (Parkhi et. al.,2015), and GoogleNet (Sutskever et.al.,2013), is an open-source framework based on DL with high performance. On both CPUs and GPUs, it facilitates the development of several widely used models, such as AEs, RNNs, CNNs, and LSTMs. The list is growing as they use Deep Learning models to implement generative adversarial networks for semi-supervised learning. This framework also allows for easy switching of hardware platform back-ends.

3.4 Optimizing Algorithms for Sustainable Smart Systems

The objective functions in DL are typically difficult because they entail additions of extraordinarily huge no.s of data-wise likelihood functions. These functions frequently demonstrate large non-convexity with numerous local minima, saddle points, and critical points as the depth of the network rises. Traditional SGD algorithms are not fast in terms of convergence in such cases. Many techniques advances the conventional support vector machines to stabilise the optimization process and overcome this problem, permitting neural network models to learn quicker for mobile applications. Table II lists different optimization algorithms.

Table 2. Summary of optimizing algorithms for sustainable smart systems

Optimizing Algorithm	Description	Advantages	Disadvantages
Nesterov's momentum	Maintains the last gradient update for the following update by introducing momentum	The algorithm learns faster and is stable. It can escape local minima.	Learning rate needs to be decided.
SGD	Divides the dataset into mini-batches, calculates the gradient of each of the mini-batch one by one and updates the parameters	The algorithm is easier to implement.	The algorithm has a slower convergence speed and is unstable. The algorithm may get stuck in local minima.
Adagrad	Distinct learning rates are applied to different parameters	The algorithm adjusts the learning rate for each parameter and handles the sparse gradients well.	Global learning rate needs to be decided, gradients are hypersensitive to the regularizer.

continued on following page

Table 2. Continued

Optimizing Algorithm	Description	Advantages	Disadvantages
Adadelta	A self-adaptive learning rate is applied for improving Adagrad	The algorithms needs to adjust fewer parameters compared to other algorithms, has a faster convergence speed as well as no dependence on a global learning rate.	It might get stuck at late training in local minima.
RMSprop	Similar to Gradient Descent with momentum, uses root mean square as the constraint of the learning rate	The algorithm adjusts the learning rate for the attributes. Moreover, the learning rate does not decrease at late learning.	The algorithm needs a global learning rate and can't deal with sparse gradients.
Adam	Exponentially decaying average of previous gradients is stored by employing a momentum mechanism	The algorithm adjusts the learning rate for each parameter, is capable of dealing with sparse gradients and non-stationary problems and is efficient in terms of memory.	The algorithm might become unstable while training.
Nadam	Nesterov accelerated gradients are incorporated into Adam	The algorithm performs well in training phase of RNN.	—
Learn to optimize	RNN is used for representing the optimization problem as a learning problem	The algorithm doesn't need to design learning by hand.	The learning in the optimizer requires an additional RNN.
Quantized training	Gradients are quamtized to {-1,0,1} for training purpose.	The algorithm is memory efficient and can be used for distributed training.	The algorithm may lose training accuracy.
Stable gradient descent	The training and validation gradients are compared by employing a differential private mechanism. The mechanism also enables the reuse of samples and keeping them fresh.	The algorithm has faster speed of convergence compared to SGD. It is more stable compared to other algorithms and less prone to overfitting.	The algorithm only works for convex functions.

*Fixed Learning Rate SGD Algorithms:(*Sutskever et al., 2013) Sutskever propose a Nesterov's momentum version of the SGD optimizer, which applies the current velocity followed by the computation of gradients. When optimising convex functions, their approach shows a higher convergence rate. Another method is Adagrad, which applies adaptive learning to model attributes based on how often they are updated. This is well suited to dealing with sparse data and defeats support vector machines in terms of robustness. Adadelta is an improvement on the classical Adagrad algorithm that allows it to converge quicker while avoiding the use of a global learning rate. G. Hinton developed RMSprop, a popular SGD-based procedure. RMSprop splits the learning rate by an exponential smoothing of the mean of gradients and it doesn't need the learning rate to be initialized for every training iteration.

Adaptive Learning Rate SGD Algorithms: Kingma and Ba proposed Adam, an adaptive learning rate optimizer that integrates momentum through the gradient's first-order moment. The algorithm converges rapidly and is highly robust to model systems, making it the first choice when deciding which algorithm to use.

Other Optimizers: According to Andrychowicz et al., the optimization process could even be dynamically learned. They present gradient descent as a training problem, illustrating that neural network training can generalise well. Wen et al. suggests a distributed-systems-specific training algorithm. In the training processing, they approximates float gradient values to (1,0,+1), which ideally requires twenty times lesser gradient communications between network nodes. Szegedy et al. demonstrated a gradient approximation procedure that allows the goal function to converge with chances equal to 1 to optima, with a two percent loss of accuracy on average on GoogleLeNet training in their experiments. For comparing training and validation gradients, as well as reusing and keeping specimen anew, Zhou et al. use a differential private technique. Overfitting during training can be drastically decrease this way.

4. SUSTAINABLE SMART APPLICATIONS

DL approaches have shown remarkable success in the domain of image and speech recognition, fault detection and signal processing. There does not exist a single NN that excels in every field. There are some approaches that are known to work better than others in some domains. One such example is the case of Autoencoders that are known to perform best in fault detection applications whereas CNNs are known for their performance in vision-based tasks. The goal, therefore, boils down to finding the right set of NNs that can provide impressive results with minimal effort (Eykholt et.al.,2018). Figure 11 illustrates some of the most popular IoT applications.

4.1 Smart Homes

The idea refers to making a home smart in a variety of ways such as automating reoccurring tasks, providing convenience, increasing safety and security, and utilising AI to boost the productiveness in a time efficient way. The definition of smart homes includes a wide variety of IoT-based technologies that can help boost a home's energy efficiency, its occupants' comfort, and standards of living. As shown in Table III, a slew of systems have been designed in past few years using DL approaches in a variety of smart home applications.

Figure 11. Various sustainable smart applications

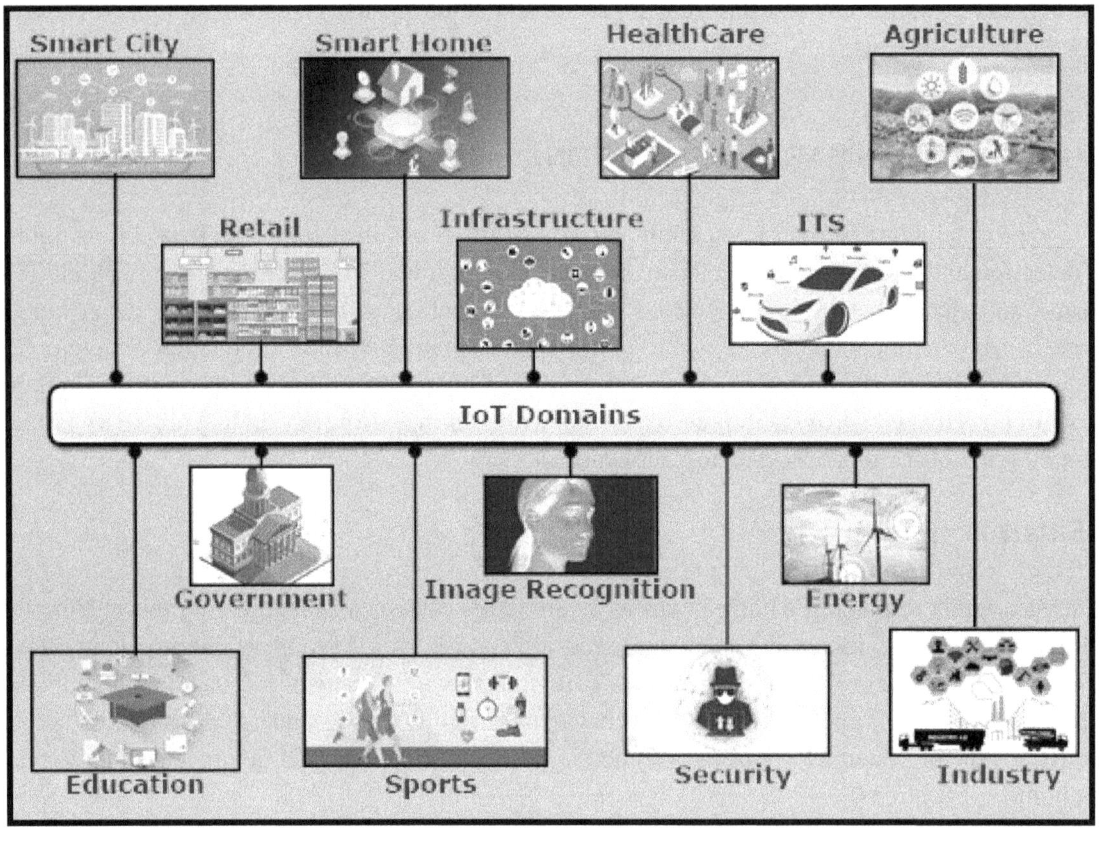

Indoor Localization: Indoor localization allows a variety of smart home services, including elder tracking, wireless intruder detection, and baby monitoring, but it is plagued by propagation issues such as multi-path effect, fading, and delay distortion. Traditional positioning schemes such as Bayesian model, SVM, K nearest neighbours (KNN), and compressive sensing, are built on techniques that are ineffective when dealing with large amounts of data. Deep neural networks were used to achieve this aim. Gu et al. suggested a SDELM algorithm. The complete use of unlabelled data helps this method achieve optimal localization efficiency while also reducing calibration effort. Based on the findings that APs obtain dissimilar data at different locations. Wang et al. created a solution with no requirement of devices. A total of 9 APs are used for gathering data about locations followed by processing of raw data using a wavelet using a wavelet filter. semi-supervised Deep Extreme Learning Machine algorithm (SDELM).

Intelligent Control: Home applications possess internet connectivity and offer intelligent solutions. WSNs and PLCs (Power Line Communications) are used to build a smart control network. A one coordinator WSN is built into a PLC transceiver which is installed in all the quarters to reduce the effect of interference on the control n/w as well as excessive energy energy consumption. WSN coordinator is in charge of sending environmental data to management units from WSNs through PLCs. Deep Learning methods are also widely used in automated virtual assistants like Siri, Cortana, Google Assistant and

Alexa. These products, built on a dialogue system, will serve as the smart home assitants and controllers of the upcoming generations.

Table 3. Summary of sustainable smart home applications

Domain	Category	Model	Learning Model	Model	Category of Learning Model	Comments
Smart Home	Indoor Localization	Wi-fi based localization	Semi-supervised	DNN	Generative	SDELM (Semi-supervised deep learning machine) alleviates the the calibration effort and attains satisfactory performance on localization.
		Bluetooth low energy signal strength based localization	Semi-supervised	DRL	Discriminative	Leverages labelled and unlabelled data for low energy signal strength localization
		CSI-based fingerprinting for indoor localization	Unsupervised Supervised	RBM	Generative Model	The data collected from Wi-Fi Channel Information(CSI) is utilized in a 4-layer RBMs for obtaining locations. The approach is device-oriented and requires people having cell phones connected to APs.
		Device free wireless localization and activity recognition	Unsupervised Supervised	RBM	Generative Model	Classifies the locations depending upon the features retrieved from raw CSI data using random forest approach.
	Home Robotics	Autonomous navigation	Supervised	CNN	Discriminative	A learning algorithm used for spotting objects from videos & images captured using RGB depth camera.
		Hand-eye coordination for robotic grasping	Supervised	CNN	Discriminative	Uses CNN for improving the hand-eye coordination for handling the objects using monocular camera images independent of the robot pose.

Home Robotics: Home robots possess the ability of accomplishing a range of jobs in in domestic settings using sensors, actuators, and databases. Localization, human-robot interaction, navigation, map creation, object recognition, and object handling are some of the main functionalities that should be included in home service robots presents a modern method for autonomous navigation that uses ML and pattern recognition techniques, for example, CNNs in recognizing characteristics or features in videos or photographs. To enhance and test Human-Robot Interaction, several possible matching artefacts found by the robot using DL n/w object detectors are viewed on a display mounted on the supported robot.

4.2 Smart City

Smart city encompasses different fields such as transit, education, and management. All of these fields result in Big Data, when combined with ML, yields high-quality performance. Waste management is one among the most critical applications of smart city management programmes. Such a system involves activities such as garbage classification and monitoring the quantity of garbage generated by a town at any given time. Using deep CNNs, as discussed in, is an easy and direct method for solving this problem. Li et al. leveraged a logistic regression model for the final forecasts and a stacked AE for attribute retrieval to construct a DL system for the prediction of air quality. Using smart cameras and deep CNNs, Amato et designed a decentralised method to distinguish filled and vacant parking spaces in parking lots.

Energy

IoT big data emerges from the bi-directional coordination between the smart grid and the energy users. Local energy demand trends are of concern to energy producers, who want to forecast the necessities and choose reasonable options depending on real-time analysis. Two RBMs are used to predict energy demand in residential houses for short time intervals. A Conditional and a Factored Conditional RBM are used in the model. Predicting the electricity from wind, solar, or various other forms of renewable sources of energy is a hot research area on the smart grid side. For example, analyse the efficiency of many DL models, including AEs, DBNs, and MLP, as well as LSTMs, in forecasting the solar capacity of twenty one solar plants.

4.3 Intelligent Transportation Systems (ITS)

ITS data is a major outlet that is gaining more and more popularity these days. ITS promotes the development of strategies for identifying and understanding traffic signals. Such processes are needed for applications including driver assistance systems, mobile maps and autonomous driving to provide reliable services. Table IV provides a summary of smart transportation applications.

Traffic Flow Prediction: The traffic flow prediction is a key issue in transportation modelling and ITS architecture, that relies majorly on real-time and past traffic data obtained from a variety of sensors nowadays. Classic machine learning techniques, such as SVM, demands long time as well as a consume enormous power to effectively use such huge heterogeneous data. DL has recently drawn attention from industry and researchers because of its potential to derive inherent features from data and manipulate large amounts of traffic data. Many studies have centred on using deep learning to forecast traffic and crowd movement.

Table 4. Summary of sustainable smart transportation applications

Domain	Category	Model	Learning Model	Model	Category of Learning Model	Comments
Smart Transportation	Traffic Prediction	Traffic flow prediction	Unsupervised Supervised	DBN	Generative	It comprises of two parts – unsupervised learning part at the bottom for extracting features from the traffic data and supervised learning part at the top for multitask learning.
		Traffic flow prediction	Unsupervised	SAE	Generative	Utilizes historical data for feature extraction and prediction using these features.
		Short-term traffic prediction	Supervised	LSTM	Discriminative	-
		Crowd Flow prediction	Supervised	CNN	Discriminative	-
	Traffic Monitoring	Real-time object detection		RPN Faster R-CNN YOLO SSD		Leverages CNNs & multi-scale strategy for improving the speed and accuracy.
		Object Tracking	Supervised	CNN	Discriminative	
		Object Tracking	Supervised	RNN	Discriminative	
		Road Accident detection		SDAE		Leverages the spatio-temporal volumes of raw pixel intensity for learning feature representation instead of traditional hand-crafted features.
	Autonomous Driving	Real-time object detection	Supervised	CNN	Discriminative	The system focuses on small, fast, energy efficient and accurate models.
		End-to-end learning for object detection	Supervised	CNN	Discriminative	The unprocessed pixels coming from a front-facing camera are used to map to the steering instructions.
		Learning driving from video datasets	Supervised	FCN-LSTM	Discriminative	Large scale crowd sourced vehicular data is used for training the end-to-end n/w to forecast multi-modal continuous as well as discrete driving behaviour.

Traffic Monitoring: The development of automatic traffic monitoring systems, that performs a vital task of minimising the burden of human operators as well as informing drivers about unsafe conditions, is among the most appealing research areas of smart transportation. Item identification, facial recognition object and tracking are three ways DL is used in traffic video analysis. RPN (region proposal n/w) which forwards convolutional characteristics of full image to the detection n/w, allowing for near-costless region proposals. Frame object recognition is recognised as regression issue to separate bounding boxes and assign type probabilities.

Autonomous Driving: The automation of cities relies heavily on autonomous driving. For vision-based autonomous driving technologies, there are two main paradigms: mediated sensing techniques and behaviour reflex techniques. Architectures that use mediated vision methods calculates a high-dimensional depiction of the world, such as lanes, road signals, traffic lights, buses, pedestrians, and so on. The method involves the training of an end-to-end FCN-LSTM n/w to forecast multi-modal continuous and discrete driving activities.

4.4 Healthcare and Wellbeing

Individuals and societies have benefited from the use of IoT and DL to provide healthcare and well-being solutions. For example, designing technologies focused on smartphone applications to reliably monitor food diets is a line of research that can aid in the control of an individual's health and well-being. Deep learning methods could be the key to turning large amounts of biomedical data into better human health. Table V lists several popular deep learning-based smart healthcare applications.

Health Monitoring: Sensor-enabled smartphones and wearables are now commonly used to allow a range of mobile APPs for health tracking. Hammerla et al.,2016 use CNNs and LSTMs to interpret activity data and integrate the findings to improve the estimation of freezing gaits in Parkinson's patients. Zhu et al., 2015 use a CNN model to estimate energy consumption using data from heart rate sensors and triaxial accelerometers. Hannun et al., 2019 uses a thirty-four layered CNN for mapping a set of ECG specimens to a set of rhythm groups. In electrocardiograms, the system surpasses the output of certified cardiologists in identifying a broad variety of spectrum of cardiac arrhythmias.

Disease Analysis: Image recognition and interpretation is a vital subject in the domain of healthcare. DL has been extensively employed in disease image processing, following its popularity in computer vision. In automated segment cartilage and osteoarthritis risk estimation, CNNs are utilized to estimate a hierarchic characterization of knee MRI scans.

Table 5. Summary of sustainable smart healthcare applications

Domain	Category	Model	Learning Model	Model	Category of Learning Model	Comments
Smart Healthcare	Health Monitoring	Human Activity Recognition	Supervised Supervised	CNN LSTM	Discriminative Discriminative	Operates and examine the data gathered from wearable sensors (accelerometer, gyroscope, etc.) and FRID tags
		Human Action Monitoring	Supervised Supervised	3D CNN LSTM	Discriminative Discriminative	Captures discriminative long-range spatial temporal features by dumping 3D CNN entries as an input to the LTSM Architecture.
		Energy Expenditure estimation	Supervised	CNN	Discriminative	Data aggregated from sensors such as triaxial accelerometer and heart rate sensors is given as input to CNN for detecting principal features.
		Arrhythmia Detection and classification	Supervised	CNN	Discriminative	A single-lead ECG signal is fed to a 34 layer deep neural network for classifying 10 arrythmias as well as sinus rhythm.
	Disease Analysis	Knee cartilage Segmentation	Supervised	CNN	Discriminative	CNN takes in MRI scans of low-field knee for segmenting cartilage and predicting the likelihood of osteoarthritis.
		Detection of diabetic detinopathy in retinal fundus images.	Supervised	CNN	Discriminative	High Sensitivity and specificity.
		Smart Personal Health advisor	Supervised	CNN	Discriminative	A small personal health advisor for assistance and physiological and psychological advice pertaining to health related matters.

Agriculture

A stable population and a balanced world necessitate the production of healthy crops and the implementation of effective plant-growing methods. The use of DNNs to detect disease in plants has proved to be a feasible approach. Sladojevic et al., 2014 published a study on plant disease identification method that can distinguish diseased leaves from stable ones in 13 groups with a 96 percent accuracy using CNNs. Furthermore, for automatic harvesting, fruit identification and deciding whether the fruit is raw or ripe is important.

4.5 Education

From kindergarten through higher education, DL and IoT help in improving the quality of educational programmes. Learners' data can be collected using mobile devices, and deep computational tools can be used to forecast and analyse learners' success and achievements. In this field, AR(Augmented Reality) technologies integrated with mobile and wearables gadgets may be used to inspire pupils, make lessons and studies fascinating, and make educational learning methods more effective.

Industry

Cyber-physical systems (CPS) and IoT are key components in advancing industry in the direction of smart manufacturing in the industrial field. In such implementations, having high-accuracy intelligent systems is important, as it directly contributes to improved assembly/product line performance and competitiveness, as well as lower maintenance and operating costs. As a result, DL has the potential to make a significant contribution to this area. In the smart industry age, humongous data generated in manufacturing can be analysed to provide manipulators and computers with capabilities comparable to humans. This section focuses primarily on the application of DL in a few particular industrial applications, as outlined in Table VI.

Manufacture Inspection: Various visual inspection methods have been proposed to identify representative features with specialist expertise in order to identify product defects in large-scale manufacturing. Many of these approaches are focused on advanced machine learning techniques suggests a DL-based classification model for applying a consistent examination method. The fog computing environment has been adapted to a CNN-based framework, which greatly increases its computing performance.

Fault Assessment: A smart factory must track machinery conditions, detect potential failures, discover main source of failures, and integrate this knowledge into manufacturing control and production in order to enforce smart manufacturing. It proposes a continuous sparse auto-encoder (CSAE) that extracts nonlinear features from input data by incorporating a stochastic Gaussian unit to an activation function. A two-layer neural network model based on sparse filtering is explored for learning characteristics or attributes from the signals produced from mechanical vibrations.

Table 6. Summary of sustainable smart industry applications

Domain	Category	Model	Learning Model	Model	Category of Learning Model	Comments
Smart Industry	Machinery Fault Diagnosis	Fault Diagnosis and Identification	Supervised	Wavelet-based CNN	Discriminative	The wavelet transform is utilized to convert 1-D vibration signal into a 2-D signal which is served as input to the CNN.
		Transformer Fault Diagnosis	Supervised	CSAE	Discriminative	The non-linear features of the input data is extracted by introducing a Gaussian stochastic component in an activation function
	Manufacture Inspection	Robust Inspection System	Supervised	CNN	Discriminative	The computation load to the fog nodes is alleviated using fog computing to deal with big data in real time.
		Surface Integration Inspection	Supervised	CNN	Discriminative	Proposed method beats the traditional manpower inspection system in performance, time and cost.

4.6 Government

Governments can benefit immensely from the improved and insightful connectivity that the integration of IoT and DL can offer. For example, policymakers must be able to recognise and forecast natural hazards (landslides, hurricanes, forest fires, and so on) as well as control the atmosphere in order to take effective steps. Liu et. al., 2016 suggested an approach using optical remote sensing images to model geological landslides using a deep AEs network and Softmax classifiers. A CNN architecture is used in another research by Liu et al., 2016 to detect severe climate phenomena like tropical cyclones, air floods, and weather fronts. Furthermore, damage monitoring in city infrastructures such as bridges, water pipes, and so on is a domain where DL and IoT can help governments.

4.7 Sport and Entertainment

Sports analytics has progressed quickly in recent years, and it now plays a vital role in achieving a competitive edge for a team or player. In this area, analytics and predictions can be used to monitor player actions, results, and score capture, among other things. A DL system for building an intelligent basketball arena was suggested. This system employs a Support Vector Machine to pick the right camera for broadcasting in real-time from a pool of cameras positioned across the field. This device was found to have a 94.59 percent accuracy score.

4.8 Retail

Online shopping has skyrocketed as a result of the explosion of smart devices. Visual search methods have recently been used to retrieve product pictures. CNNs are used in this visual scan of the clothing & apparel industry, to identify articles in online stores equivalent or close to those featured in a movie or on the street. The image characteristics, as well as the most recently projected directional characteristics, are given into an RNN to produce the o/p direction and posture.

4.9 Smart IoT Infrastructure

Sensors, actuators, media, and a multitude of other gadgets populate IoT ecosystems, producing vast volumes of n/w traffic data and M2M. As a result, the tracking, and alignment of the devices is subjected to big data analytics using sophisticated ML algorithms in order to detect obstructions, optimise efficiency, and ensure service standards. Conditional VAE and deep AEs were used for network intrusion detection, respectively. The use of crowd-funded wireless network data such as signal strength as part of these activities will assist in the creation of trustworthy solutions. For example, as shown by the OpenSignal smartphone application, big data could be exploited to generate accurate coverage maps for cellular n/w in order to increase network efficiency.

5. POTENTIAL DEEP LEARNING CLASSIFICATION TECHNIQUES FOR SUSTAINABLE SMART SYSTEMS

The aim of classification methods is to group objects into a finite number of classes. The method takes in two datasets (labelled and unlabelled) as input, the labelled set of data is utilized in training the model and the unlabelled set is utilized to assess output of the outcomes. Decision trees, SVM, NNs, DL, rule-based induction and Bayesian networks are some of the most commonly used classification techniques, as shown in Table VII.

Decision Tree Algorithm: This algorithm is a popular predictive machine learning modelling technique that creates a model from the real values of parameters in the data. Both regression and classification problems can benefit from decision trees. The leaves of a tree structure depicts labels of various categories, while the branches depict the parameters driving those labels. Regression trees are decision trees in which the target variable takes continuous values. Because of their speed and accuracy, decision trees are frequently used in machine learning algorithms. Regression tree, ID3, Classification and C4.5/5.0 are some of the most common decision tree algorithms.

Table 7. Summary of various deep learning algorithms for sustainable IoT systems

Algorithm	Description	Application/Suitability	Complexity
Naïve Bayes	It is a probabilistic classification method with the naïve assumptions of conditional and positional independence b/w each pair of attributes.	It is mostly employed for solving text classification, face recognition, intrusion detection and anomaly detection problems. Used for the classification of features into two(binary) or more (multi) classes. The independence assumptions helps the classifier to perform better with less training data compared to other models.	O(nP)
K-Nearest Neighbour	A technique for used for regression and classification machine learning problems. It works by calculating the similarity of new data points with the nearest K-neighbours and placing the new data point into category of the most similar neighbour.	It is a lazy learning technique as it doesn't involve a separate training process and utilizes all training data while classification. The algorithm requires only two parameters- K for deciding the number of nearest datapoints for similarity calculation and a similarity calculation function (e.g. Euclidean or Manhattan). Large datasets involve high computational costs and memory storage leading to slower prediction and degradation of the performance of the algorithm. Uses lies in the arena of image recognition, speech recognition video recognition etc.	O(nP)
Random forest and Decision Tree	A supervised learning that tries to create an uncorrelated forest of decision trees using the data features. The decision trees are then merged to get accurate and stable prediction of the target variable. The approaches are generally used in classification and regression problems.	It can handle large datasets with high dimensionality and therefore it is considered as a dimensionality reduction method. The algorithm handles the bias-variance trade-off well and average out the results across multiple trees	$O((n^2)P)$ $O((n^2)Pn_{trees})$ where P=no. of features n_{trees}=no. of trees n=no. of training samples
Support Vector Machines (SVM)	A supervised learning algorithm utilized for solving regression and classification problems. The goal of this method is to obtain a hyperplane in N-dimensional space for uniquely classifying the samples where N represents the no. of attributes.	The algorithm works well for binary &multi-class classification problems. It does not perform well for noisy data because of overlapping of classes. The algorithm is not suitable for working with large datasets as the required training time increases. The method finds its uses in face recognition, text classification, protein fold detection etc.	$O(n^2P+n^3)$
Algorithm	**Description**	**Application/Suitability**	**Complexity**

continued on following page

Table 7. Continued

Algorithm	Description	Application/Suitability	Complexity
Neural Networks (NN)	The algorithm involves recognizing the relationship b/w the features of I/P training data and its O/P by passing the data through layers of interconnected nodes until the network's inability to correctly classifying the output minimizes.	The algorithm is highly susceptible to overfitting and therefore requires the fine-tuning of the hyperparameters. It can identify the complex non-linear relationships b/w the variables & thus find all feasible exchanges b/w the predictor attributes. A variety of NNs that have been presented are RNNs, CNNs, MLP(Mult-Layer Perceptron) etc.	$O((Pnl_1)+(nl_1)(nl_2)+\ldots)$ where n=no. of training samples P=no. of features nl_i=no. of neurons at layer l in a NN.
Deep Learning	A Feed-Forward NN comprising of various hidden layers such that these operate on the input received from the (n-1)th layer and forwards the results of the computations to the nth layer. The nodes within each layer are connected to the nodes of the following layer but doesn't have any connection within its layer.	The algorithm's performance can be improved by supplying enough data for proper feature extraction and learning. It has the ability to identify meaningful features from unstructured data such as image, text, etc. obtained from various real-life problems. The main benefit of this technique over others is its potential to perform feature engineering by itself without explicitly told to do so and thereby improving model accuracy.	For Multi-Layer Perceptron(MLP) & other neural n/w, it takes $O(2^n)$ to converge to optimum solution & O(#epochs × #samples × #features × #neurons) for approximate solution.

Bayesian Algorithms: For classification and regression problems, Bayesian methods employ Bayes' theorem Naive Bayes (NB), Bayesian belief network, and Gaussian naive Bayes, are the most common Bayesian algorithms. NB classifier techniques were used with positive outcomes for human activity recognition. The NB technique identifies human actions that most closely match the sensor readings that were recorded.

Support Vector Machine (SVM): SVM is one of the most extensively utilized classification and regression algorithms for various problems involving statistical learning, such as text classification, face & object recognition, handwriting analysis, and spam detection. The goal of the method is to discover a hyperplane in N-dimensional space which could be used to distinguish between samples, where N represents the no. of attributes.

Artificial Neural Network Algorithms (ANNs): Biological neural networks influenced the creation of ANN models. ANNs are often used for classification and regression problems. Hopfield Network, Perceptron, Radial Basis Function Network, and Back-Propagation, are some of the most commonly used ANN algorithms (RBFN). ANNs have a variety of benefits, including the ability to discover dynamic non-linear relations b/w predictor & response variables and the capability to discover each conceivable relation b/w predictor variables. They also require less mathematical preparation.

Deep Learning Algorithm: Deep learning algorithms use a deep structure (various layers with many linear or non-linear conversions) to reflect an advanced version of ANNs. DL claims that it will substitute manual attribute selection with effective semi-supervised or unsupervised attribute learning and hierarchic attribute retrieval techniques. Some of the extensively used DL techniques are CNN, DBM, DBN, RNN, and Stacked Auto-Encoders. DL has proven to be effective in a variety of applications involving Big Data Analytics, including NLP, stock exchange investing, medical diagnosis, n/w surveillance, and image recognition. Table VIII lists various algorithms and IoT use-cases.

6. DL IN SUSTAINABLE SYSTEMS

Big data analytics refers to the methods of scanning a database, mining, and examine data in order to boost the efficiency of an application. Big data analytics necessitates software and tools to be capable of converting vast amounts of organised, semi-structured and unstructured data into readable form & metadata configuration for analysis purposes. The techniques in these applications employed for analysis should recognise trends, patterns, and correlations in the data across a wide range of time horizons. As a result of the complexity of the data and the scalability of the elementary techniques that enable those operations, big data analytics is a major problem for various applications.

6.1 Existing Analytics Systems

Various analytic categories are utilized based on the specifications and demands of IoT applications. The analytic categories are briefly explained in this section under real-time analytics, off-line analytics, and memory-level analytics categories.

Real-time analytics: Data obtained from sensors is commonly used for real-time analytics. In this case, data is continuously changing, necessitating the use of fast data analytics tools to achieve an analytical outcome in a limited amount of time. As a result, two architectures for real-time analysis have been proposed: parallel processing clusters of standard relational databases and memory-based computing platforms. Real-time analytics architectures include Greenplum and Hana.

Table 8. Various deep learning algorithms and their sustainable use cases

Algorithms	IoT Applications	Optimizing Factor	Type of Data
Classification	Smart Traffic	Traffic Prediction, Maximize Data Compression	Massive Data, Real-time data collected from vehicular sensors such as accelerometer, gyroscope, etc.
Clustering	Smart Traffic Smart Health	Traffic Prediction, Maximize Data Compression	Data captured by wearable devices such as glucometers, heartbeat monitors, blood pressure monitors etc. Real-time data gathered from vehicular sensors, e.g. accelerometer, gyroscope, etc.
SVR	Smart Weather Prediction	Forecasting	Stream data coming from humidity sensors, temperature sensors, wind speed monitors etc.
Linear Regression	Economics, Market Analysis Energy Usage	Real-Time Prediction, Alleviate amount of data	Historical Data, Real-time stock data
SVM	All use cases	Data Classification, Real-Time Prediction	User data, cookies, denoising data, click stream data from websites, image data etc.
KNN	Smart Citizen	Travelling pattern of passengers, Efficiency of learned metric	Stream Data generated from real-time location tracking,
Naïve Bayes	Smart Agriculture Smart citizen	Food Safety, Travelling pattern of passengers, Estimate the number of passengers	Data collected from soil moisture detectors, gas sensors, etc. Real-time location data
Algorithms	**IoT Applications**	**Optimizing Factor**	**Type of Data**

continued on following page

Table 8. Continued

Algorithms	IoT Applications	Optimizing Factor	Type of Data
K-Means	Smart city Smart Home, Smart Citizen, Controlling Air and Traffic	Outlier Identification, Passengers Travel Trends, Fraud Detection	Stream Data, Historical Data, Massive Data
Feed Forward Neural Network	Smart Health	Forecast the State of Elements, Alleviating Energy Expenditure	Data captured by wearable devices such as glucometers, heartbeat monitors, blood pressure monitors etc.
PCA	Public Place Surveillance	Bug Identification	Image captured using CCTVs
Canonical Relation Analysis	Public Places Surveillance	Bug Identification	Image captured using CCTVs

Off-line analytics: Whenever a fast response isn't required, off-line analytics is generally used. To minimise the cost of data format migration, many Internet businesses use Hadoop-based off-line analytics architecture. This form of analysis boosts the quality of data acquired. SCRIBE, Kafka, TimeTunnel, and Chukwa are examples of off-line analytics architectures that can address data collection demands.

Memory-level analytics: Where the size of the data is less than the memory of a cluster, memory-level analytics is used. Cluster memory has hit the terabyte (TB) stage these days. Therefore, to increase analytical performance, many internal database technologies are needed. Real-time processing can be done with memory-level analytics. MongoDB is one such example of this architecture.

6.2 Relationship Between Sustainable Smart IoT Systems and Big Data Analytics

Big data analytics is gaining popularity as a vital IoT scheme for improved decision-problems. The analysis of data around "connected things" is among the most crucial aspect of IoT. In IoT, big data analytics necessitates extracting a vast volume of data and caching it in a variety of storage systems. The opportunity to exchange knowledge across platforms and establish a shared operating picture to allow creative applications is given by the connection of actuating and sensing devices by a unified architecture. The management of IoT data can be understood into 3 steps as displayed in Figure 12. The first and foremost step is to manage data origins, wherein connected sensors uses applications to communicate with each another. This intercommunication of devices, smart traffic lights, smart home gadgets and CCTV cameras, for example, generates a vast volume of data in various forms. This information could be saved on the cloud in low-cost commodity storage. The generated data is referred to as "large data" in the second phase because of their volume, variety & velocity. This large volumes of data is then stored in shared distributed fault-tolerant databases in big data files. The final stage employs analysis tools, for example, Splunk, Spark, Skytree and MapReduce, to assess the large processed IoT datasets. Starting with training results, the four stages of analytics progress to analysis tools, requests, and reports.

Figure 12. Sustainable smart systems and big data analytics

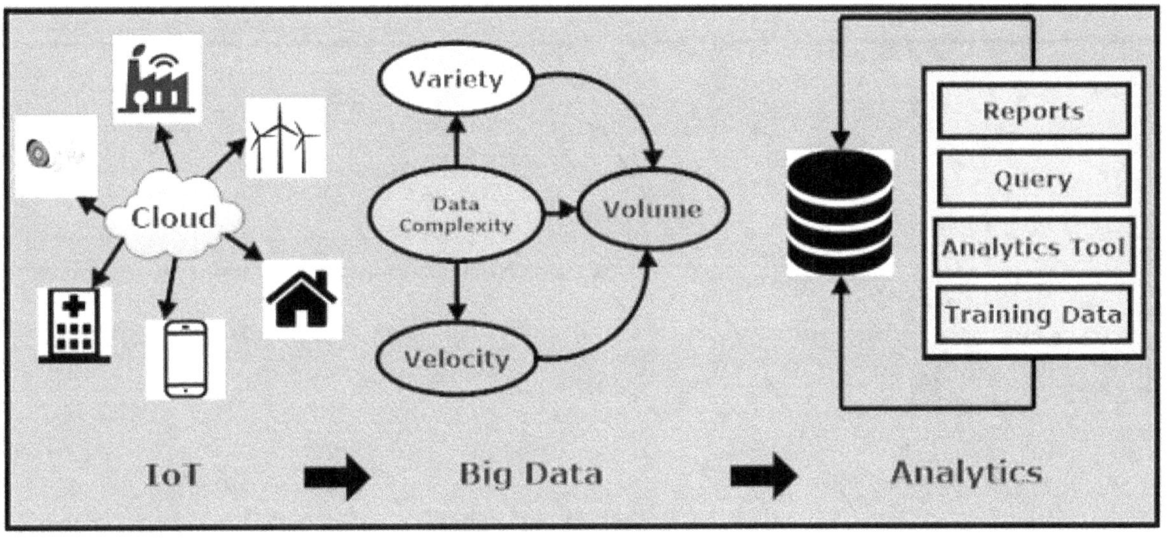

6.3 Deep Learning in Big Data Analytics

The aim of the Big Data Analytics is to retrieve the vital knowledge that leverages in forecasting, detecting latest patterns, discovering unseen details, and eventually in decision-making. The progression of big data changes the demands for analysis. The demand of optimal techniques is in each and every area of big data administration, for example storage, capturing, preprocessing, & analytics. Big data analytics needs alike or speedy processing than the traditional analytics systems along with reduced price for high-velocity, highvariety and high-volume data. Data mining enacts a major part in big data analytics, and majority of the mechanisms are designed using data mining techniques based on the application requirements. In this regard, we discuss various mechanisms which could be applied in many big data applications. Few of the analytics mechanisms are powerful for analytics in IoT applications. Diversified and voluminous sample sets helps in achieving more insights in big data. But it isn't true all the time as more data might contain additional abnormalities or ambiguities . We describe various big data analytics techniques such as association rule mining, classification, prediction analytics and clustering. Figure 13 illustrates the flow from IoT data generation to DL techniques addressing the knowledge abstraction.

Classification: It is a supervised learning technique that leverages preliminary information as sample set to categorize data into classes. A predetermined class is allotted to a data point, and hence, the aim of forecasting a category for a data point is accomplished. Discovering unseen patterns adds additional challenges for big data. Naïve, semi-naïve Bayes, Bayes multi-nets and selective naïve, are the various types of classification. The analysis of data patterns and cronstructing classes are carried out with SVM, that is another classification technique for big data analytics. Likewise, K-NN is imparts efficient methods for discovering unseen trends from data sets, in a wat that extracted data points are indistinguishable to the defined class.

Figure 13. Sustainable smart IoT system data generation and DL techniques to address their knowledge abstraction

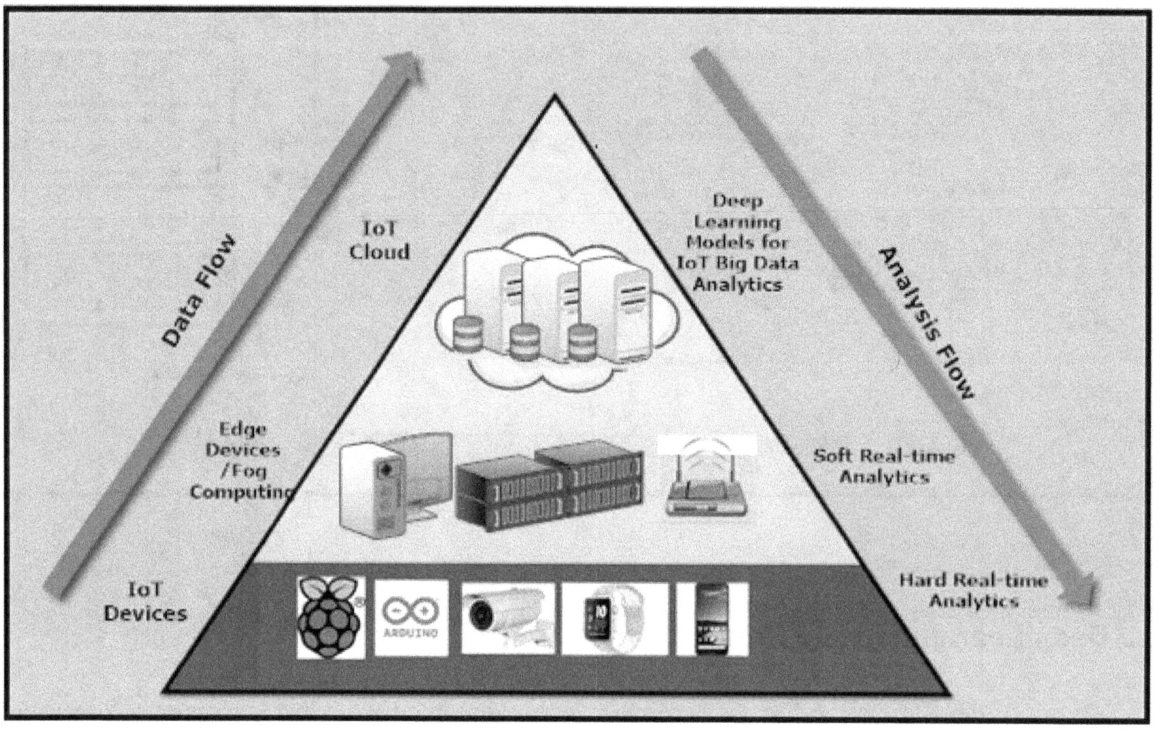

Clustering: As opposed to classification, clustering utilizes an unsupervised learning mechanism and generates classes for provided data based on distinguishing useful characteristics. The familiar techniques utilized for clustering are partitioning and hierarchical clustering. The hierarchical clustering technique merges tiny clusters of sample points to build a hierarchical tree & construct agglomerative clusters. The reverse process generates divisive clusters by splitting a large cluster into smaller meaningful clusters.

Association Rule Mining: Association rule mining concentrates on discovering and producing inferences based on the presence of numeric & nonnumeric data. Data processing is applied in 2 ways in association rules. The first method involves the processing of sequential data using the techniques based on the previous knowledge, for example, MSPS and LAPINSPAM, to recognize associations. The second noteworthy data processing mechanism is temporal sequence analysis, that utilizes techniques to examine the patterns present in a event in continuous data.

Predictive Analytics: Predictive analytics leverages historic data, that is also referred to as training set, to identify the outcome as patterns or trends in the data. Fuzzy logic and SVM techniques are employed to recognize relationships b/w dependent and independent attributes and to derive regression curves for forecasting, e.g. for natural calamity. Moreover, data presentation is a vital need in big data analytics.

Time Series Analysis: This method lowers the high dimensionality linked with big data and provides characterization for better decision making. Research accompanying time series presentation involves ARMA, wavelet functions, and bitmaps. Time series analysis is employed in disaster prediction, social network analysis, e-governance and speech recognition.

6.4 Challenges in DL for Big Data Analytics for Sustainable Smart Systems

Scarcity of massive IoT Datasets: The scarcity of massive real-world datasets for sustainable smart systems applications is a major roadblock in implementing DL models for IoT, as more data is needed for DL to achieve higher accuracy. Furthermore, having more data stops the models from being overfitting. This scarcity is preventing the deployment and adoption of DL-based IoT analytics. Figure 14 displays typical datasets appropriate for DL for researchers focusing on machine learning applications in the IoT.

Figure 14. Common datasets for deep learning in IoT

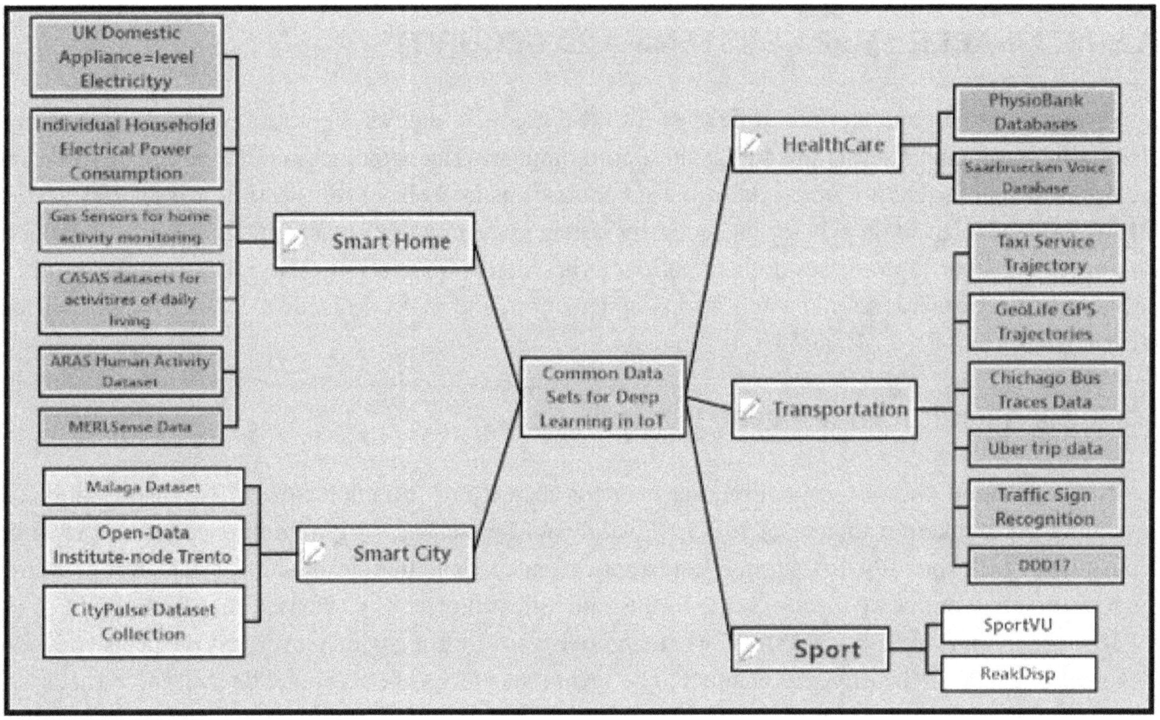

Preprocessing: Another problem for IoT implementations is translating raw data into a format that can be fed into DL models. To produce good results, most DL approaches need some kind of preprocessing. Preprocessing is more difficult in IoT implementations because the system must cope with data from many channels, all of which might have varying forms and implementations, along with displaying missing data.

Secure and Privacy Preserving DL: Sustainable Smart Systems' data can be transmitted across the Internet for analytics and thus be observed around the globe, therefore, maintaining data protection and privacy is a major concern in many sustainable smart applications. Malicious attacks, such as data Incorrect Data Injection or adversarial sample inputs, may also be used against DL training models. In this case, DL models must have a mechanism for detecting irregular or invalid data.

Deep Learning for IoT Devices: The specifications of managing DNNs in resource-constrained devices present a new challenge for IoT system designers when designing DL on IoT devices. These specifications are likely to increase as the scale of datasets grows every day, and new techniques emerge to be part of DL in IoT solutions.

Deep Learning Limitations: DL models, despite their promising performance in a variety of applications, have a range of pitfalls. Another drawback is that DL models are primarily focused on classification, whereas various applications of IoT (for example, energy load prediction and temp. prediction) require regression in their analytical core. Some works have attempted to enhance DNNs with regression, combination of SVR and DBN. However, further research is needed to clarify certain facets of DL regression.

7. SUSTAINABLE SMART SYSTEMS AND SECURITY

Sustainable smart applications utilizes various technologies such as Bluetooth, Wi-fi, Z-wave as their underlying communication architectures. These communication technologies associates with them various security drawbacks that are inherited in these applications as well. In this section, we discuss various ML techniques focused on privacy and security issues in sustainable smart applications and networks. This section primarily discusses authentication, attack detection and mitigation, Distributed Denial of Service (DDoS) attacks, anomaly and intrusion detection, and malware analysis. Table IX lists various security issues and used ML and DL techniques.

7.1 Authentication and Access Control

It is considered one of the vital requirement for security in IoT applications. The users should be authenticated to take advantages of IoT applications and/or services without any need to worry about security attacks. Generally, IoT services and applications depend upon exchange of data across various devices. In this section, we discuss some of the authentication techniques based on ML and DL.

ML-based Approaches: A physical layer technique was proposed which leverages the properties such as signal strength of the physical channel. The technique is based on using ML and game theory for isolating spoofers. Nagarajan et al., 2021 suggested an ANN-based authentication technique in IoT n/ws. Authentication based on PUF (Physically Unclonable Function) could be efficacious in IoT applications in which the physical characteristics of the transmitting/communicating device are used for analysis.

DL-based Approaches: Some researcher deploys a three-layered DNN to study behavioural and physiological features utilized in authentication. DNN retrieves the kind of activity (moving or stationary) in the first layers, then the characteristics are learnt in the 2nd layer, and high-level characteristics in the 3rd layer depending on which, users are authenticated. Gu et al., 2015 suggested a recurrent NN based authentication technique that utilizes voice instructions in smart home IoT systems. This technique achieved an accuracy of more than 90% and was found to perform better than ML techniques.

7.2 Attack Detection and Mitigation

The conventional attack identification and removal techniques depend on cryptographic techniques and faces accuracy loss, leading to wrong results. Accordingly, algorithms namely Support Vector Machines, Deep Learning, K-NN, unsupervised learning and autoencoders have been applied. Some of the mechanisms used for attack detection and mitigation are discussed below.

ML-basedApproaches: A semi-SL attack recognition technique that uses Fuzzy C-Means mechanisms and Extreme ML (ESFCM). This mechanism was used because of its ability of handling labelled data and thereby increasing the rate of detection of attacks. Also they analysed various Machine Learning techniques for detecting attack in smart grid and discovered that in small n/ws, K-Nearest Neighbour produces better results and in large n/ws, Support Vector Machines works good in achieving high attack detection accuracy.

DL-based Approaches: Diro et. al. 2018 suggested a Deep- Learning based technique by utilizing fog computing. The mechanism considers various attributes from the learning technique and computes the result of the learning mechanism for the provided input. The motive behind leveraging the fog architecture was the resource restraints and the nature of IoT application. They also suggested a distributed attack identification technique using DL in IoT. They utilized fog computing technique (that is the one among the recommended technique used in IoT applications) to apply Deep Learning techniques for attack detection. The suggested three-layered stacked AE attains 99.2% accuracy.

7.3 DoS and Distributed DoS (DDoS) Attacks

Conventional DDoS detection & mitigation techniques in IoT devices are implemented on the entry points, the gatewaysand routers of IoT n/w using intrusion detection as well as mitigation techniques. No single mechanism can be applied to all IoT applications for the detection & mitigation of DDos attacks. In this section, we discuss some of the DL and ML based approaches for DDos attacks detection and mitigation.

ML-based Approaches: Ye et al., 2018 suggested a Support Vector Machine-based detection technique in SDN operated IoT n/w. The mechanism is known to attain an accuracy 95.24%. that could be pushed further by supplying more data. Tan et al., 2013 uses MCA (Multivariate Correlation Analysis) which detects attacks based on the outcomes of the data flow between the processing, server side and decision making. The traffic produces features which are operated on by MCA. The accuracy attained by the mechanism is above 99%.

Table 9. Security problems in IoT and applied ML techniques

Security Issue	ML techniques	Comparison of ML techniques
Authentication and access control	DL and LSTM ANNs RNNs Q-learning and Dyna-Q DNN	Despite the availability of data, Deep learning algorithms performs better than mainstream ML because of its ability to perform feature engineering on its own without explicitly told to do so. RNN provides a system accuracy of 90% and leaves behind other ML/DL techniques in terms of efficiency, accuracy and complexity.
Attack detection and mitigation	SVM DL Unsupervised learning, stacked AE Extreme Learning Machine (ELM)-based semi-supervised Fuzzy C-Means (ESFCM) KNN SVM	SVM works well in larger networks whereas K-NN works well in smaller networks for attack detection accuracy. ESFCM is a semi-supervised fuzzy C-Means technique that handles the labelled data problems and gives good performance at a faster detection rate. However, DL models outperforms ML algorithms in terms of detection accuracy. Autoencoder based detection mechanism uses normal traffic to build the detection model and updates itself automatically as the time goes.
Distributed DOS attack	KNN SVM Random Forest and Decision Tree NN Multivariate Correlation Analysis (MCA) Q learning	MCA (Multivariate Correlation Analysis) is based on the principle of anomaly-identification in attack detection and gives an overall accuracy of 99%. SVMs performs well on small datasets having data comprising of huge no. of features. This technique is recognised for its generalization capability. ANNs gives as large as 99.4% accuracy in a limited set for DDoS attacks in experimental evaluation. Random forests algorithms eliminate the need of feature selection by taking advantage of a huge no. of potential features. The variance-bias trade-off is not linear for these algorithms in the sense that variance decreases with the no. of trees in the forest while bias remains the same.
Anomaly/Intrusion detection	K-means clustering ANNs Novelty and Outlier Detection Decision Tree Naïve Bayes	K-Means algorithm does not require the explicit descriptions of various attacks classes by a system administrator and is generally used when there is a scarce of labelled data. Decision trees because of their high classification accuracy and easy implementation are easy-to-use in intrusion detection scenarios. The independence assumptions in Naïve Bayes makes it feasible to handle high dimensionality data by reducing into a single dimension. The algorithm has the potential to deal with continuous/categorical arbitrary no. of independent features. DL algorithms have clearly outperformed various traditional techniques such as fuzzy model, NNs, and Hidden Markov Model (HMM) in terms of handling large networks traffic data and complex classification problems. However, DL algorithms demand terabytes of data specific to a problem for the training phase.
Security Issue	**ML techniques**	**Comparison of ML techniques**
Malware analysis	RNN Random forest supervised classifier Deep eigen space learning and Deep Convolutional Networks SVM PCA CNN ANN Linear SVM SVM and PCA Deep Q networks	RNN methods perform with the detection accuracy of 98%. DL techniques are recommended over Traditional ML algorithms as ML algorithms do not work well with larger databases and have shallow architectures. Deep Q networks can achieve accuracy of 98.79% and mean error of 0.12% among MLP, LVQ, and Back Propagation Neural Network (BPNN). ANNs can achieve higher accuracy than CNNs but suffer from huge processing costs incurring from large networks. PCA works by reducing the complexity of n/w designed for malware analysis and achieves dimensionality reduction.

DL-based Approaches: Hodo et al., 2016 employed supervised ANNs to prevent these attacks in IoT. The ANN mechanism deployed by the researchers attained 99.4% accuracy on a limited sample set. Kulkarni et. al., 2009 utilized MLP (multi-layer perceptron) technique to identify attacks in sensor n/ws, mostly deployed in IoT applications.

7.4 Anomaly/Intrusion Detection

Various machine learning mechanisms are utilized to identify intrusions and anomalies in IoT n/w and their types. Intrusion detection mechanisms require special focus depending on the principal features of the IoT technology used. In this section, we will describe some of the mechanisms used for Anomaly detection and mitigation.

DL-based Approaches: There is a technique based on trust for discovering intrusions in IoT n/w. Contrary to the conventional techniques, the suggested trust-based mechanism considers the confidence level in an application in addition to the class and kind of traffic. DL is also exploited for IDS in assorted IoT networks. The researchers carried out experiments to discover the optimum hyperparamter to detect the false alarm & finding the rate of detection.

7.5 Malware Analysis

Malicious code injection is one of the most infamous attack arena in IoT and operates by taking advantage of the prevailing vulnerabilities in IoT applications. Interfering the IoT gadgets physically for s/w moderation or misconfiguration of attributes related to security could also allow attackers for malicious code injection. Some of the common types of malware are spyware, bot, trojan and ransomware. In this regard, many techniques are known to detect malware and some of them are briefly discussed below.

ML-based Approaches: Alam et. al., 2013 utilized random forest classification to identify android malware. The classification algorithm is used to check the accuracy of the detected malware specimens in android applications. They also suggested a mechanism based on Support Vector Machine for categorizing the malware in android-based applications. Even though SVM suffers from high classification time because of the elimination of useless attributes, yet it is recommended mainly due to accurate results and less complexity.

DL-based Approaches: Haddad et al., 2018 suggested a deep learning technique based on RNN for malware analysis in IoT. The researchers used various sample sets for training the model and testing with a new malware. In the testing phase, LSTM was found to give better results in comparison to the other classifiers with the accuracy of 98%. Meidan et al., 2018 leveraged deep AEs to identify Botnet attacks. The n/w behaviour was extricated to segregate the abnormal n/w behaviour using deep AEs.

7.6 Limitations of ML and DL Techniques in IoT Security

ML-based Limitations: Machine Learning techniques are employed to recognize certain trends, similarities and patterns in sample sets consisting of enormous examples and could forecast for the newly received data. We noticed that the primary shortfall of Machine Learning techniques is that these chiefly requires a training set for learning, and then the trained n/w is operated on the real-time data. This might not cover the entire gamut of attributes and characteristics of the data. Moreover, the sample set used to train a model present various new cyber attacks and security problems.

DL-based limitations: Inspite that the recent research in this area has demonstrated excellent performance, a few domains still require concentrated, optimized, as well as IoT-specific enhancements. The present analytical and theoretical principles are yet absent. It is noticeable that the integrated computational potential of Reinforcement Learning and Deep Learning attracts storage and computational overhead. And therefore, in spite of the performance, these mechanisms might not be suitable for the resource-restricted applications. Additionally, DL is also prone to over and mis-classification.

Noisy Data poses a problem for ML and DL techniques: Real-world data is predominantly degraded with noise which has negative impacts on the performance of the techniques employed for classification. Deep Learning algorithms possess greater classification abilities in comparison to the conventional Machine Learning techniques, yet, these techniques weakened by the noisy data.

Misclassification deteriorates the performance of Machine learning and Deep Learning Algorithms: It is caused because of the choice of features and parameters that are not appropriate for classification. It occurs when the chances of misclassification of a group, variable or a class are same. The damage of misclassification can result in detrimental effects in real case scenarios, for example, healthcare and businesses applications. So, to reduce the consequences of misclassification it is advised to gather enormous data for the rare classes. Additionally, distribution of training data must be carefully modified so as to have less impact the model's prediction and inference capabilities. For example, increasing the no. of diseased patients in training set will result in the model predicting the diseased more frequently.

8. CONCLUSION

In this paper, we explored the potential of emerging sustainability of smart systems. The study indicates that the cities need to be sustainable in order to become smart. It is evident that various sustainable smart systems could be catered with DL tools and techniques. DL architectures are robust enough to deal with large-scale data analytics issues associated with sustainable smart cties, buildings, house etc. DL proposes an advanced outlook to solve conventional problems and aid us in discovering new approaches in sustainable smart applications. The objective of our survey has been to explore the integration of sustainability in the development of smart systems leveraging communication technologies such as ZigBee, Wi-Fi, RFID, 5G etc and the necessity of urban turnaround for sustainability. The relationship of sustainable smart systems and Big Data was explored as well as Big Data Analytics mechanisms and tools for data mining were also discussed. Furthermore, security problems in context of sustainable smart applications exploiting 5G for communication were explored in detail in addition to the several future research opportunities in this domain. However, the design of a sustainable model using low assets and robust security mechanism with high accuracy is still an issue and an open research area for future developments.

REFERENCES

Abadi, M., Agarwal, A., Barham, P., Brevdo, E., Chen, Z., Citro, C., . . . Zheng, X. (2016). Tensorflow: Large-scale machine learning on heterogeneous distributed systems. *arXiv preprint arXiv:1603.04467*.

Abeshu, A., & Chilamkurti, N. (2018). Deep learning: The frontier for distributed attack detection in fog-to-things computing. *IEEE Communications Magazine*, *56*(2), 169–175.

Abu-Rayash, A., & Dincer, I. (2021). Development of integrated sustainability performance indicators for better management of smart cities. *Sustainable Cities and Society*, *67*, 102704.

Adi, E., Anwar, A., Baig, Z., & Zeadally, S. (2020). Machine learning and data analytics for the IoT. *Neural Computing & Applications*, *32*, 16205–16233.

Alam, M. S., & Vuong, S. T. (2013, August). Random forest classification for detecting android malware. In 2013 IEEE international conference on green computing and communications and IEEE Internet of Things and IEEE cyber, physical and social computing (pp. 663-669). IEEE.

Alsheikh, M. A., Lin, S., Niyato, D., & Tan, H. P. (2014). Machine learning in wireless sensor networks: Algorithms, strategies, and applications. *IEEE Communications Surveys and Tutorials*, *16*(4), 1996–2018.

Amato, G., Carrara, F., Falchi, F., Gennaro, C., Meghini, C., & Vairo, C. (2017). Deep learning for decentralized parking lot occupancy detection. *Expert Systems with Applications*, *72*, 327–334.

Andrychowicz, M., Denil, M., Gomez, S., Hoffman, M. W., Pfau, D., Schaul, T., & De Freitas, N. (2016). Learning to learn by gradient descent by gradient descent. *Advances in Neural Information Processing Systems*, •••, 29.

Arora, A., Candel, A., Lanford, J., LeDell, E., & Parmar, V. (2015). Deep learning with h2o. H2O. ai, Mountain View, 587.

Ashraf, J., Keshk, M., Moustafa, N., Abdel-Basset, M., Khurshid, H., Bakhshi, A. D., & Mostafa, R. R. (2021). IoTBoT-IDS: A novel statistical learning-enabled botnet detection framework for protecting networks of smart cities. *Sustainable Cities and Society*, *72*, 103041.

Bahrampour, S., Ramakrishnan, N., Schott, L., & Shah, M. (2015). Comparative study of deep learning software frameworks. arXiv preprint arXiv:1511.06435.

Baldi, P. (2012, June). Autoencoders, unsupervised learning, and deep architectures. In Proceedings of ICML workshop on unsupervised and transfer learning (pp. 37-49). JMLR Workshop and Conference Proceedings.

Bengio, Y. (2009). Learning Deep Architectures for AI.

Branch, J. W., Giannella, C., Szymanski, B., Wolff, R., & Kargupta, H. (2013). In-network outlier detection in wireless sensor networks. *Knowledge and Information Systems*, *34*, 23–54.

Cai, C., Hu, M., Cao, D., Ma, X., Li, Q., & Liu, J. (2019). Self-deployable indoor localization with acoustic-enabled IoT devices exploiting participatory sensing. *IEEE Internet of Things Journal*, *6*(3), 5297–5311.

Chen, D., Wawrzynski, P., & Lv, Z. (2021). Cyber security in smart cities: A review of deep learning-based applications and case studies. *Sustainable Cities and Society*, *66*, 102655.

Chen, M., Herrera, F., & Hwang, K. (2018). Cognitive computing: Architecture, technologies and intelligent applications. *IEEE Access : Practical Innovations, Open Solutions*, *6*, 19774–19783.

Chen, Y., & Zhang, D. (2021). Evaluation and driving factors of city sustainability in Northeast China: An analysis based on interaction among multiple indicators. *Sustainable Cities and Society*, *67*, 102721.

Collobert, R., Kavukcuoglu, K., & Farabet, C. (2011). Torch7: A matlab-like environment for machine learning. In BigLearn, NIPS workshop.

Diro, A. A., & Chilamkurti, N. (2018). Distributed attack detection scheme using deep learning approach for Internet of Things. *Future Generation Computer Systems*, *82*, 761–768.

Doersch, C. (2016). Tutorial on variational autoencoders. arXiv preprint arXiv:1606.05908.

Eykholt, K., Evtimov, I., Fernandes, E., Li, B., Rahmati, A., Xiao, C., & Song, D. (2018). Robust physical-world attacks on deep learning visual classification. In *Proceedings of the IEEE conference on computer vision and pattern recognition* (pp. 1625-1634).

Gartner, C. D. (2016). The gartner top 10 strategic technology trends for 2016. Gartner webinar.

Gu, Y., Chen, Y., Liu, J., & Jiang, X. (2015). Semi-supervised deep extreme learning machine for Wi-Fi based localization. *Neurocomputing*, *166*, 282–293.

Haddad Pajouh, H., Dehghantanha, A., Khayami, R., & Choo, K. K. R. (2018). A deep recurrent neural network based approach for internet of things malware threat hunting. *Future Generation Computer Systems*, *85*, 88–96.

Hammerla, N. Y., Halloran, S., & Plötz, T. (2016). Deep, convolutional, and recurrent models for human activity recognition using wearables. arXiv preprint arXiv:1604.08880.

Hannun, A. Y., Rajpurkar, P., Haghpanahi, M., Tison, G. H., Bourn, C., Turakhia, M. P., & Ng, A. Y. (2019). Cardiologist-level arrhythmia detection and classification in ambulatory electrocardiograms using a deep neural network. *Nature Medicine*, *25*(1), 65–69.

Haseeb, K., Din, I. U., Almogren, A., Ahmed, I., & Guizani, M. (2021). Intelligent and secure edge-enabled computing model for sustainable cities using green internet of things. *Sustainable Cities and Society*, *68*, 102779.

He, X., Wang, K., Huang, H., Miyazaki, T., Wang, Y., & Guo, S. (2018). Green resource allocation based on deep reinforcement learning in content-centric IoT. *IEEE Transactions on Emerging Topics in Computing*, *8*(3), 781–796.

Hermans, M., & Schrauwen, B. (2013). Training and analysing deep recurrent neural networks. *Advances in Neural Information Processing Systems*, •••, 26.

Hodo, E., Bellekens, X., Hamilton, A., Dubouilh, P. L., Iorkyase, E., Tachtatzis, C., & Atkinson, R. (2016, May). Threat analysis of IoT networks using artificial neural network intrusion detection system. In *2016 International Symposium on Networks, Computers and Communications (ISNCC)* (pp. 1-6). IEEE.

Hu, M., Liu, W., Lu, J., Fu, R., Peng, K., Ma, X., & Liu, J. (2019). On the joint design of routing and scheduling for vehicle-assisted multi-UAV inspection. *Future Generation Computer Systems*, *94*, 214–223.

Hu, M., Liu, W., Peng, K., Ma, X., Cheng, W., Liu, J., & Li, B. (2018). Joint routing and scheduling for vehicle-assisted multidrone surveillance. *IEEE Internet of Things Journal*, *6*(2), 1781–1790.

Khan, Z., Anjum, A., & Kiani, S. L. (2013, December). Cloud based big data analytics for smart future cities. In 2013 IEEE/ACM 6th International Conference on Utility and Cloud Computing (pp. 381-386). IEEE.

Kingma, D. P. (2014). Adam: A method for stochastic optimization. arXiv preprint arXiv:1412.6980.

Kingma, D. P., Mohamed, S., Jimenez Rezende, D., & Welling, M. (2014). Semi-supervised learning with deep generative models. *Advances in Neural Information Processing Systems*, ●●●, 27.

Kolias, C., Kambourakis, G., Stavrou, A., & Voas, J. (2017). DDoS in the IoT: Mirai and other botnets. *Computer*, *50*(7), 80–84.

Krizhevsky, A., Sutskever, I., & Hinton, G. E. (2012). Imagenet classification with deep convolutional neural networks. *Advances in Neural Information Processing Systems*, ●●●, 25.

Kulkarni, R. V., & Venayagamoorthy, G. K. (2009, June). Neural network based secure media access control protocol for wireless sensor networks. In 2009 international joint conference on neural networks (pp. 1680-1687). IEEE.

LaValle, S., Lesser, E., Shockley, R., Hopkins, M. S., & Kruschwitz, N. (2010). Big data, analytics and the path from insights to value. *MIT Sloan Management Review*.

Lee, J., Wang, J., Crandall, D., Šabanović, S., & Fox, G. (2017, April). Real-time, cloud-based object detection for unmanned aerial vehicles. In *2017 First IEEE International Conference on Robotic Computing (IRC)* (pp. 36-43). IEEE.

Li, H., Ota, K., & Dong, M. (2018). Learning IoT in edge: Deep learning for the Internet of Things with edge computing. *IEEE Network*, *32*(1), 96–101.

Li, X., Peng, L., Hu, Y., Shao, J., & Chi, T. (2016). Deep learning architecture for air quality predictions. *Environmental Science and Pollution Research International*, *23*, 22408–22417.

Liu, Y., & Wu, L. (2016). Geological disaster recognition on optical remote sensing images using deep learning. *Procedia Computer Science*, *91*, 566–575.

Majumdar, S., Subhani, M. M., Roullier, B., Anjum, A., & Zhu, R. (2021). Congestion prediction for smart sustainable cities using IoT and machine learning approaches. *Sustainable Cities and Society*, *64*, 102500.

Meidan, Y., Bohadana, M., Mathov, Y., Mirsky, Y., Shabtai, A., Breitenbacher, D., & Elovici, Y. (2018). N-baiot—Network-based detection of iot botnet attacks using deep autoencoders. *IEEE Pervasive Computing*, *17*(3), 12–22.

Mocanu, D. C., Mocanu, E., Nguyen, P. H., Gibescu, M., & Liotta, A. (2016, October). Big IoT data mining for real-time energy disaggregation in buildings. In *2016 IEEE International Conference on Systems, Man, and Cybernetics (SMC)* (pp. 003765-003769). IEEE.

Mohammadi, M., Al-Fuqaha, A., Guizani, M., & Oh, J. S. (2017). Semisupervised deep reinforcement learning in support of IoT and smart city services. *IEEE Internet of Things Journal*, *5*(2), 624–635.

Nagarajan, S. M., Deverajan, G. G., Chatterjee, P., Alnumay, W., & Ghosh, U. (2021). Effective task scheduling algorithm with deep learning for Internet of Health Things (IoHT) in sustainable smart cities. *Sustainable Cities and Society*, *71*, 102945.

Parkhi, O., Vedaldi, A., & Zisserman, A. (2015). Deep face recognition. In BMVC 2015-Proceedings of the British Machine Vision Conference 2015. British Machine Vision Association.

Pascanu, R. (2013). How to construct deep recurrent neural networks. arXiv preprint arXiv:1312.6026.

Qiu, J., Wu, Q., Ding, G., Xu, Y., & Feng, S. (2016). A survey of machine learning for big data processing. *EURASIP Journal on Advances in Signal Processing*, *2016*, 1–16.

Rasmus, A., Berglund, M., Honkala, M., Valpola, H., & Raiko, T. (2015). Semi-supervised learning with ladder networks. *Advances in Neural Information Processing Systems*, ●●●, 28.

Rathore, S., & Park, J. H. (2018). Semi-supervised learning based distributed attack detection framework for IoT. *Applied Soft Computing*, *72*, 79–89.

Russom, P. (2011). Big Data Analytic s. TDWI Best Practices report, TDWI Reserarch, 4th Quarter.

Shafiq, M., Tian, Z., Bashir, A. K., Jolfaei, A., & Yu, X. (2020). Data mining and machine learning methods for sustainable smart cities traffic classification: A survey. *Sustainable Cities and Society*, *60*, 102177.

Shorfuzzaman, M., Hossain, M. S., & Alhamid, M. F. (2021). Towards the sustainable development of smart cities through mass video surveillance: A response to the COVID-19 pandemic. *Sustainable Cities and Society*, *64*, 102582.

Sladojevic, S., Arsenovic, M., Anderla, A., Culibrk, D., & Stefanovic, D. (2016). Deep neural networks based recognition of plant diseases by leaf image classification. *Computational Intelligence and Neuroscience*, *2016*(1), 3289801.

Steen, K. A., Christiansen, P., Karstoft, H., & Jørgensen, R. N. (2016). Using deep learning to challenge safety standard for highly autonomous machines in agriculture. *Journal of Imaging*, *2*(1), 6.

Sutskever, I., Martens, J., Dahl, G., & Hinton, G. (2013, May). On the importance of initialization and momentum in deep learning. In *International conference on machine learning* (pp. 1139-1147). PMLR.

Tan, Z., Jamdagni, A., He, X., Nanda, P., & Liu, R. P. (2013). A system for denial-of-service attack detection based on multivariate correlation analysis. *IEEE Transactions on Parallel and Distributed Systems*, *25*(2), 447–456.

Wang, F., Fan, X., Wang, F., & Liu, J. (2018). Backup battery analysis and allocation against power outage for cellular base stations. *IEEE Transactions on Mobile Computing*, *18*(3), 520–533.

Wang, J., Zhang, X., Gao, Q., Yue, H., & Wang, H. (2016). Device-free wireless localization and activity recognition: A deep learning approach. *IEEE Transactions on Vehicular Technology*, *66*(7), 6258–6267.

Wen, W., Xu, C., Yan, F., Wu, C., Wang, Y., Chen, Y., & Li, H. (2017). Terngrad: Ternary gradients to reduce communication in distributed deep learning. *Advances in Neural Information Processing Systems*, •••, 30.

Werbos, P. J. (1990). Backpropagation through time: What it does and how to do it. *Proceedings of the IEEE*, *78*(10), 1550–1560.

Ye, J., Cheng, X., Zhu, J., Feng, L., & Song, L. (2018). A DDoS attack detection method based on SVM in software defined network. *Security and Communication Networks*, *2018*(1), 9804061.

Yigitcanlar, T., Kamruzzaman, M., Foth, M., Sabatini-Marques, J., Da Costa, E., & Ioppolo, G. (2019). Can cities become smart without being sustainable? A systematic review of the literature. *Sustainable Cities and Society*, *45*, 348–365.

Zhou, Y., Chen, S., & Banerjee, A. (2018). Stable Gradient Descent. In UAI (pp. 766-775).

Zhou, Y., Yi, P., Li, W., & Gong, C. (2021). Assessment of city sustainability from the perspective of multi-source data-driven. *Sustainable Cities and Society*, *70*, 102918.

Zhu, J., Pande, A., Mohapatra, P., & Han, J. J. (2015, October). Using deep learning for energy expenditure estimation with wearable sensors. In 2015 17th International Conference on E-health Networking, Application & Services (HealthCom) (pp. 501-506). IEEE.

Chapter 9

Innovative Approaches for Earthquake Estimation Using AI and ML Techniques

Sachin Upadhye
https://orcid.org/0000-0001-7255-1838
Department of Computer Science and Application, School of Computer Science and Engineering, Ramdeobaba University, India

Shanmugasundaram Senathipathi
https://orcid.org/0009-0001-5853-9522
Financial Services, Capgemini America Inc, New York, USA

Krishna Kumar Shreedharan
https://orcid.org/0009-0007-1038-7367
Capgemini America Inc., Chicago, USA

M. Veerapathran
https://orcid.org/0000-0002-5515-247X
Department of Civil Engineering, Dr. N.G.P. Institute of Technology, Coimbatore, India

Santosh Dubey
https://orcid.org/0009-0004-8516-0894
Department of Electronics and Communication Engineering, United College of Engineering and Research, Prayagraj, India

K. K. Baseer
https://orcid.org/0009-0003-1456-2709
Department of Computer Science and Engineering, GITAM School of Technology, GITAM University (Deemed), Bengaluru, India

ABSTRACT

Predictive techniques are increasingly crucial in earthquakes for early warning and risk mitigation due to the increasing frequency and impact of these natural disasters. Artificial Intelligence (AI) and Machine Learning (ML) are transforming earthquake estimation as they help analyze vast amounts of data, identify patterns, and improve the accuracy of the prediction. This chapter deals with new AI and ML approaches in estimating seismic activity that include deep learning models, neural networks, and support vector machines. These techniques, in contrast, make more precise predictions in terms of magnitude, location, and intensity using real-time data from seismic sensors, geological surveys, and historical records of earthquakes. AI-driven models help to provide faster computation and adaptability with insights that may not be possible with other methods. Data scarcity and model validation and uncertainty challenges are also discussed along with the future directions in AI-enhanced seismic forecasting.

DOI: 10.4018/979-8-3693-8407-7.ch009

INTRODUCTION

Earthquakes rank amongst the most destructive forces of nature, causing loss of human life, property, and economic disruption worldwide. Even till date, earthquakes remain to be one of the toughest challenges for scientists and engineers when it comes to their accuracy in prediction since they are governed by complex and dynamic geological processes. Traditional methods that involve the analysis of fault lines, seismic wave propagation, and historical records are giving some insights, though the limitations are quite evident in not being able to predict earthquakes with appropriate accuracy and timeliness (Xie, Ebad Sichani, et al., 2020). The unpredictability of the seismic events requires the development of advanced techniques that can handle large amounts of data and find hidden patterns to ensure accurate predictions that can limit the effects of earthquakes. In this regard, AI and ML have emerged as the revolutionary tools that transform how earthquakes are estimated and predicted.

The AI and ML techniques exploit computational models simulating human learning in the pursuit of identifying complex patterns in big data. These technologies have achieved unprecedented success in health care, finance, weather forecasting, and autonomous systems and are being applied for the first time to seismic estimation. The increasing availability of big data, advancements in AI algorithms, and the computational power open frontiers for seismic prediction that were previously unseen(Mousavi & Beroza, 2023). Unlike deterministic methods, AI and ML algorithms can use massive and heterogeneously distributed datasets from seismic sensors, geological surveys, and historical records to make data-driven predictions. These types of models excel at discovering very subtle correlations and anomalies within the data set, hence providing researchers an opportunity to get closer to accurate magnitude, location, and intensity estimates for an earthquake.

The principal reasons AI and ML are used in the estimation of earthquakes is real-time processing of numerous data sources of seismic networks, satellite imagery, and ground motion sensors. It will enable early warning systems, giving people several seconds to minutes of advance notice before an earthquake actually happens. Such early warning systems can significantly reduce the loss of life and economic losses through timely evacuation, closure of critical infrastructure, and triggering of emergency response measures(Bhatia et al., 2023). For instance, AI-based systems can clearly distinguish between small tremors and large earthquakes in real-time seismic wave patterns, providing more rapid and reliable warning in comparison to traditional methods.

These include widely used machine learning algorithms that are SVMs, Random Forest and Decision Trees for earthquake estimation because of the way these algorithms can classify data regarding outcome prediction. With all this information, one could potentially draw out a predictive model to determine earthquakes. Deep Learning techniques, which include Convolutional Neural Networks (CNNs) and Recurrent Neural Networks (RNNs), are gaining attention for their ability to process spatial and temporal data. CNNs capture spatial features in seismic data, and RNNs model the temporal evolution of seismic events, making them a suitable choice for predicting the occurrence and progression of an earthquake(Marano et al., 2024). Hybrid approaches, wherein multiple AI techniques are used to improve prediction accuracy, further enhance these models(Xie, Sichani, et al., 2020).

Data preprocessing is another crucial aspect of AI and ML in earthquake estimation. It deals with cleaning and preparing raw data for analysis. Seismic datasets are often noisy, incomplete, and heterogeneous, and extracting meaningful insights is not an easy task. Techniques such as feature extraction, normalization, and anomaly detection using AI-driven data preprocessing can filter noise and highlight relevant features. Additionally, the scarcity of data that often faces earthquake prediction is well addressed using techniques such as data augmentation and transfer learning. Such methods enhance the generalization capability of models and enable prediction with very few historical data(Mignan & Broccardo, 2020).

Several challenges and limitations remain that must be addressed in order to make AI and ML more effective in earthquake estimation. The quality and amount of data used for training AI models determine their accuracy. Since seismic sensors are not evenly spread out, especially in distant or underdeveloped regions, seismic data may be incomplete or biased. Moreover, AI models require proper validation so that they are reliable; false predictions may cause unnecessary panic or complacency. Another great challenge in the wide adoption of AI-based earthquake prediction systems is the computational challenges of requiring high-performance computing resources and real-time processing capabilities(Falcone et al., 2020).

Earthquake processes are dynamic and nonlinear in nature, making it complicated for AI and ML models to simulate the behavior. Earthquakes are a function of multiple factors including the movement of tectonic plates, fault interaction, and geological conditions. These are difficult to model precisely. Researchers are developing hybrid models that combine AI with traditional geophysical methods to exploit the strengths of both approaches. For example, integration of AI models with finite element analysis and geospatial simulations can provide more comprehensive and accurate predictions. Additionally, IoT technology and real-time data analytics can improve the performance of AI models by continuously monitoring seismic activity(Abdalzaher et al., 2023).

The future of earthquake estimation will be in the further development and refinement of AI and ML techniques. Big data analytics, cloud computing, and edge computing will improve the speed and efficiency of processing seismic data. Interdisciplinary collaboration between geophysicists, data scientists, and engineers will also drive the development of innovative solutions for earthquake prediction. AI and ML have the potential to make seismic forecasting a more proactive and data-driven discipline in the attempt to mitigate the impact of earthquakes on society(Ren et al., 2020).

Application of Artificial Intelligence and Machine Learning in earthquake estimation represents a great step forward in seismic prediction. It can analyze big and complex data, thereby finding patterns and correlations that traditional methods usually overlook. Indeed, the technologies offer faster computational, adaptability, and real-time information for earthquake forecasting and warnings. However, in spite of these challenges-data scarcity, model validation, and a general limitation in computing-further research and technological input have been making their strides into more accurate and robust predictions of earthquakes(Sun et al., 2022). As we continue to harness the power of AI and ML, this potential becomes increasingly achievable toward improving earthquake preparedness, reducing losses, and saving lives. The following chapter discusses the different AI and ML techniques used in earthquake estimation, their advantages, challenges, and future prospects, and how such innovative approaches transform the seismic forecasting field.

Objectives

This chapter aims to:

a) Discuss the role Artificial Intelligence and Machine Learning have played and will play in earthquake estimation
b) Identify the new AI and ML techniques, including deep learning, neural networks, and support vector machines, which could help improve seismic prediction

c) Examine integration of real-time data coming from seismic sensors, geological surveys, and historical records for the precise prediction of earthquakes
d) Discuss data scarcity, model validation, and uncertainty in earthquake prediction.
e) Compare the AI-based approach methods with a traditional method on prediction;

FUNDAMENTALS OF EARTHQUAKE PREDICTION

Earthquake prediction has remained one of the toughest and most critical areas of research in geoscience. There are different methods developed over time to estimate seismic events through geological, geophysical, and statistical approaches. It generally aims to know how, when, and at what location an earthquake might occur with enough precision so that its destructive force might be mitigated(Jiao & Alavi, 2020). Even though traditional approaches have been insightful enough in revealing the behavior of earthquakes, they inherently suffer from drawbacks in terms of accuracy, reliability, and scalability. Recent advancements in Artificial Intelligence (AI) and Machine Learning (ML) have opened new avenues for much more accurate and data-driven approaches in the estimation of earthquakes, thereby revolutionizing seismic prediction. This chapter goes deep into the roots of earthquake prediction, which cover traditional methods, the shortcomings of those methods, and the development of AI and ML technologies(Lu et al., 2022). The figure 1 depicts the general process of earthquake prediction.

Figure 1. General process of earthquake prediction

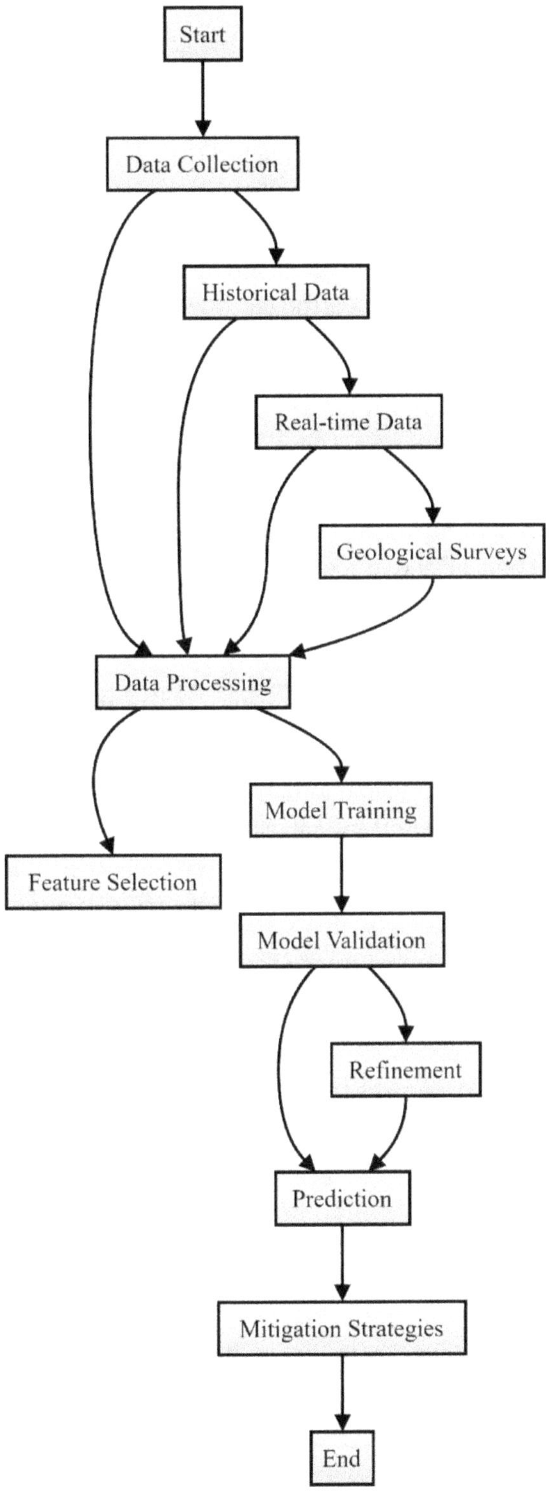

Traditional Methods of Earthquake Estimation

The conventional methods of estimating earthquakes are mainly based on analyzing historical seismic data, geological surveys, and observations of seismic activities. The three main approaches can be categorized as: statistical, geophysical, and empirical methods(Thai, 2022).

Historical data analysis: This involves the analysis of past earthquake occurrences to determine patterns, trends, and recurrence intervals. Probably the most important statistical model used to forecast the probability of future events based on historical data is the Gutenberg-Richter law, which gives the frequency-magnitude relationship of earthquakes. From the historical records, the researchers can find the probability of earthquakes in a specific region over a given time period.
Seismological Techniques: Seismology plays a central role in earthquake prediction by analyzing seismic waves generated by tectonic activities. Techniques such as seismic gap analysis identify regions where stress has accumulated along fault lines, increasing the likelihood of future earthquakes. Seismic sensors and accelerometers measure ground motion and fault activity, providing critical data for earthquake estimation.
Geological and Geophysical Surveys: The conventional approach primarily focuses on fault line mapping, the identification of active tectonic zones, and subsurface geological structures. For measurement of tectonic plate movements and the accumulation of stress along faults, geophysical techniques follow GPS-based ground deformation monitoring and satellite imagery. These surveys help predict those areas that are prone to seismic activity.

The researchers also looked at foreshocks. Foreshocks are small earthquakes that occur sometimes before large earthquakes. Scientists have examined anomalous phenomena, including changes in groundwater levels, behavior of animals, and releases of radon gas, as potential precursors to earthquakes. Although these traditional methods have added a lot to earthquake research, they often fail to predict the complex dynamic nature of seismic events because they rely on deterministic assumptions and historical trends.

Limitations of Conventional Techniques

Traditional methods: although conventional earthquake estimation techniques had been in use for so many years, they also have their weaknesses that reduce their practical effectiveness in coming up with accurate forecasts regarding earthquakes(Joshi et al., 2024).

Lack of real-time predictive capability: the traditional techniques like seismic gap analysis and history data modeling predict probabilistically over long timescales but could not predict earthquakes in real time. This limits their usages for early warning system where immediate and actionable information is required.
Data Scarcity and Bias: Earthquake prediction becomes accurate if more reliable and extensive seismic data are provided. Unfortunately, many parts of the Earth, especially remote or less developed regions, have a lacking seismic sensor network and historical records, which make predictions biased as well as reduce the reliability of the traditional models.

The **complexity of seismic processes** is that an earthquake occurs due to a highly dynamic and nonlinear nature of geological processes, such as movements in the crust, the interaction of faults, and the accumulation of stress. Such complicated processes cannot be modeled by traditional methods since they often base their work on simplified assumptions and deterministic models. It lacks the ability to identify hidden patterns in large datasets. There is too much seismic data that comes from the global sensor networks and satellite imagery to process with conventional statistical and geophysical techniques. Traditional approaches lack the necessary computational power and analytical tools for analyzing huge, heterogeneous datasets and hidden patterns that might improve the predictions.

Uncertainty and False Predictions: Many earthquake precursors, such as foreshocks or changes in the level of groundwater, are inconsistent and not reliable as a precursor for seismic activity. Ambivalence of such signals with no common predictive framework leads often to false alarms or missed predictions, which can demote public confidence in the method.

Given these limitations, there is a growing need for more advanced, adaptive, and data-driven approaches to earthquake prediction. This has paved the way for the integration of AI and ML techniques, which offer new possibilities for addressing the challenges of conventional methods.

Emergence of AI and ML Approaches

The field of Artificial Intelligence and Machine Learning has proven to be quite robust in the estimation of earthquakes, offering new solutions that overcome the flaws of conventional approaches. AI and ML techniques are developed with the view to analyze vast amounts of data, identify complex patterns, and then produce highly accurate predictions by learning through experience. Unlike the deterministic assumptions in conventional approaches, AI-based models are intrinsically adaptive, scalable, and capable of handling real-time data.

The key advantage of using AI and ML in earthquake prediction is the ability to analyze heterogeneous data from different sources, including seismic sensor networks, satellite imagery, GPS measurements, and historical records of earthquakes. This way, an AI model could identify very faint correlations and anomalies that indicate a possibility of an upcoming earthquake. For example, deep learning techniques, such as Convolutional Neural Networks (CNNs) and Recurrent Neural Networks (RNNs), have been used to analyze spatial and temporal patterns in seismic data with great success. Machine Learning algorithms, SVMs, Decision Trees, and Random Forests are increasingly used for earthquake event classification and earthquake magnitude and location prediction. These models can learn from history's data on earthquakes as well as fault movement and, therefore, can develop predictive frameworks adaptable to new data over time. Hybrid models combining two or more AI techniques can present improved accuracy and robustness in earthquake estimation.

AI and ML approaches are also well-suited for real-time earthquake prediction and early warning systems. AI models can detect seismic wave patterns by processing live data from seismic sensors and differentiate between minor tremors and significant earthquakes within seconds. This capability enables the development of reliable early warning systems that provide critical advance notice to reduce casualties and infrastructure damage. Additional techniques of data preprocessing through AI include feature extraction, noise filtering, and anomaly detection under the headings of challenges about quality and data scarcity. Data augmentation and transfer learning enable the AI to better generalize with limited historic data, thereby making these AI models worthwhile, particularly for regions having sparse records of seismicity.

With AI and ML, science has evolved earthquake prediction by overcoming traditional approaches with adaptable, data-driven, and real-time solutions. The new technologies will bring in a great potential toward better accuracy, efficiency, and reliability in seismic prediction and thus toward better preparedness, early warning, and risk mitigation. As AI and ML continue to advance, they will transform the integration with geophysical models and real-time data analytics to enhance the estimation of earthquakes and help safeguard communities from the destructive power of seismic events.

AI AND ML TECHNIQUES IN EARTHQUAKE ESTIMATION

It brings with it the revolutionary advent of Artificial Intelligence (AI) and Machine Learning (ML), which has remedied the shortcomings of earlier approaches in earthquake estimation. Earthquake prediction is generally influenced by complex, nonlinear processes ascertained by geological, geophysical, and environmental variables. AI and ML algorithms have emerged as transformative tools in seismic prediction, primarily due to their ability to process vast amounts of data, identify intricate patterns, and deliver predictive insights. These techniques employ the usage of historical data, real-time seismic signals, and multi-modal datasets to detect subtle correlations that might indicate impending seismic events. The subsequent section outlines a number of key AI and ML methods that are currently shaping the face of earthquake estimation and risk management, including machine learning algorithms, deep learning models, neural networks, and SVMs(AlAli & Anifowose, 2022; López-Castro et al., 2022). The figure 2 illustrates the utilization of AI and ML techniques in estimating earthquakes.

Figure 2. Application of AI and ML techniques in earthquake estimation

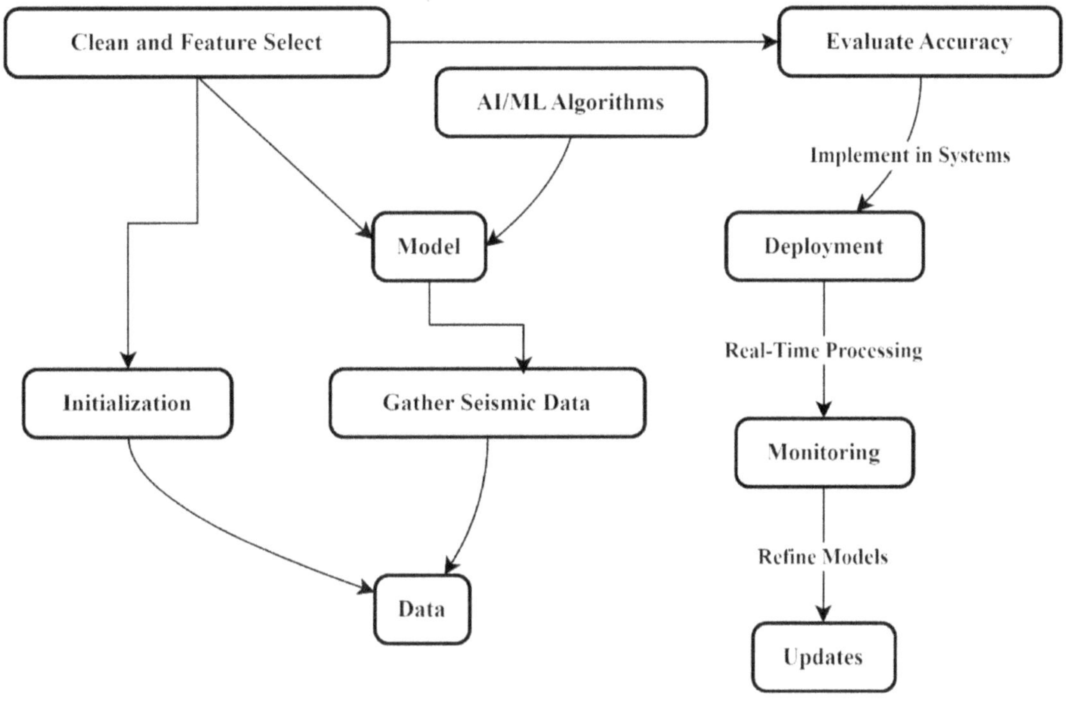

Machine Learning Algorithms

Machine learning algorithms are taking prominence in earthquake prediction. They can process big datasets and identify trends missed by traditional methods. Using machine learning algorithms, they can process the history of earthquakes, seismic waveforms, and fault zone measurements to predict magnitude, location, and probability(AlAli & Anifowose, 2022; Albahri et al., 2024).

Supervised Learning: Supervised learning algorithms train on labeled data sets containing historical records of earthquake activity. Algorithms like Decision Trees, Random Forests, and Support Vector Machines can be used in classifying seismic activity, and predictions regarding the outcomes, including the probability or magnitude of earthquakes, can be made with them. For example, a Random Forest model analyzes more than one decision path that gives robust predictions about fault line activity.

Unsupervised learning: These techniques apply k-means clustering and PCA in order to identify seismic patterns and group together similar regions in terms of their seismic behavior. They thereby help in identifying earthquake hotspots and risk-prone regions.

Reinforcement Learning: There have recently been research studies on reinforcement learning used for earthquake prediction and warning systems. Reinforcement learning models can optimize the detection strategy of earthquakes and can be updated in real time in order to refine the prediction.

These machine learning techniques can efficiently process complex datasets from seismic networks, satellite imagery, and GPS systems, thereby offering robust earthquake predictions.

Deep learning models

Deep learning has been identified to be particularly good at earthquake estimation because it can handle huge volumes of complex data. These models employ multi-layered artificial neural networks that learn more complex patterns within seismic data, making for better and more timely predictions(Albahri et al., 2024; Shafapourtehrany et al., 2023).

Convolutional Neural Networks (CNNs): CNNs are very efficient at processing spatial data like satellite imagery and seismic waveforms. Using the processing of 2D and 3D data, CNN can detect tectonic movement, faults zone activity, as well as seismic anomalies features. A CNN-based models are very applicable for classifications of Earthquake signals together with probable seismic event by a certain accuracy. One example about the real time application was using CNN models for detection of the presence of pre-earthquake phenomena signs with the aid of real time seismic data.
Recurrent Neural Networks (RNNs): RNNs are very specific for time-series data like seismic waveforms and historic records of earthquakes. RNNs, like Long Short-Term Memory (LSTM), a type of RNN, can model temporal dependencies in seismic signals to predict earthquake magnitudes and sequences. RNNs look into the development of seismic activity over time, making short-term predictions possible from recent trends.
Autoencoders: Another deep learning technique that is being used for anomaly detection in seismic data is autoencoders. Autoencoders compress and then reconstruct seismic signals, looking at the anomalies that could actually indicate the build-up of stresses or even activity within fault zones. It is highly efficient in pre-seismic signals identification.

Deep learning models can process multi-modal data, including real-time seismic signals, geological maps, and satellite imagery, to make reliable predictions. With adaptability to new data, identification of complex patterns makes deep learning invaluable in estimating earthquakes.

Neural Networks and Their Applications

Artificial neural networks, derived from the human brain, find wide applications in earthquake prediction by analyzing nonlinear as well as high-dimensional seismic data. Neural networks mainly consist of multiple layers of connected artificial neurons that process the input data and deliver some form of prediction. ANNs are very flexible, learning from historical data about earthquakes, thus making their predictions highly accurate. Feedforward neural networks are the most simplified types of ANN applied in earthquake estimation. These take in various seismic data, including faults' activities and measurements by ground deformation, to come up with the output estimates such as earthquake magnitude and probability(Abdalzaher et al., 2023).

MLP: An MLP was able to learn the classification of seismic signals and earthquake event prediction. It distinguishes between normal and preseismic activities in terms of input features, for instance, amplitude and frequency of seismic waves or ground acceleration.

Hybrid Neural Networks: Recently, hybrid models have been developed that combine ANNs with other machine learning techniques, such as SVMs or Random Forests, to enhance the accuracy of the predictions. Such models utilize the strengths of different algorithms to provide robust earthquake predictions.

Some of the applications of neural networks are in early warning systems, seismic hazard evaluation, and aftershock prediction within earthquake estimation. Neural networks can identify patterns that otherwise appear to be unnoticed by using vast volumes of seismic data.

Support Vector Machines

Support Vector Machines (SVMs) are popular machine learning algorithms in the area of seismics that can actually classify the seismic data into categories while it can classify complex and nonlinear relationships very well. Thus, making SVM effective for the study of earthquakes.

Classification of Seismic Signals: SVM is applied to classify the seismic signals into normal activity or foreshocks or precursors of significant earthquakes. By analyzing features such as wave amplitude, frequency, and duration, SVM models can distinguish harmless tremors from precursors of potentially significant earthquakes.

Magnitude and Location Prediction: The SVM regression models can be used to predict earthquake magnitude and location by making use of such input features as ground acceleration, tectonic stress, and fault movement data. In this model, it analyses the historical records of the past earthquakes and finds out the patterns in relation to a certain magnitude and areas.

Feature Selection and Dimensionality Reduction: SVMs can handle high-dimensional seismic data sets by selecting the appropriate features for earthquake prediction. This reduces the complexity and computational cost of predictive models with better accuracy.

SVMs have been applied in real-world applications of earthquake prediction systems and prove their feasibility in the real-time prediction of seismic anomalies and actual events. These models with real-time information from the seismic networks have helped researchers to come up with robust early warning systems that provide actionable information and mitigate the risks. AI and ML techniques such as machine learning algorithms, deep learning models, neural networks, and support vector machines have been revolutionizing earthquake estimation in light of the shortcomings associated with traditional approaches. It is capable of processing extensive complex data, finding slight patterns, and making real-time predictions. AI and ML will be used to research and develop early warning systems that are more reliable. These developments will improve seismic hazard assessments and help prepare communities for catastrophic events. The development of AI into geophysical models and its real-time sensor networks will soon be very important in limiting the disastrous impacts of earthquakes and ensuring the safety of communities all over the world.

DATA SOURCES AND PREPROCESSING

The success of AI and ML techniques in earthquake estimation is highly dependent on the quality, diversity, and volume of data. Seismic predictions are inherently challenging because earthquakes are highly complex and unpredictable. Hence, robust data collection, preprocessing, and management strategies must be in place to ensure accurate predictions and early warning systems. Different sources of data, such as seismic sensor networks, geological, and historical records, and remote sensing data, contribute valuable inputs for the training of predictive models(AlAli & Anifowose, 2022; López-Castro et al., 2022). Seismic data, however, may be noisy, inconsistent, or redundant in nature, thereby necessitating sophisticated preprocessing techniques including cleaning, feature selection, and noise handling. This chapter will discuss the critical sources of data and preprocessing strategies that can be adopted in developing a reliable AI and ML-based earthquake prediction system. The process of data sources and preprocessing in AI and ML techniques for earthquake estimation is illustrated in Figure 3.

Figure 3. Process of data sources and preprocessing in AI and ML techniques for earthquake estimation

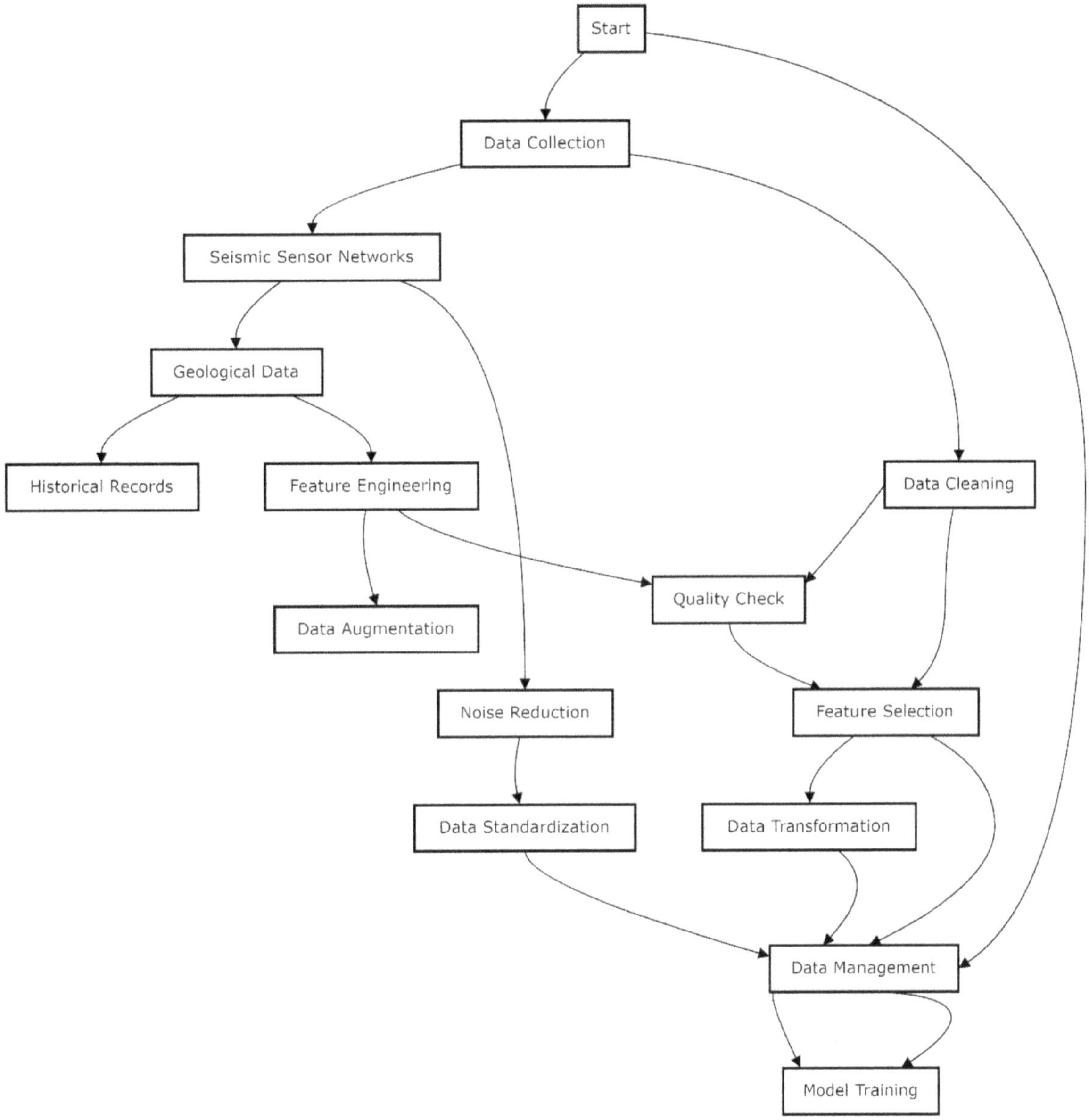

Seismic Sensor Networks

Majorly, seismic sensor networks mainly constitute real-time earthquake monitoring and data acquisition. Comprising interlinked seismic stations fitted with sensitive instruments including seismometers, accelerometers, and GPS sensors, measuring ground motion and vibrations together with tectonic activities(Abdalzaher et al., 2023).

Seismometers: This equipment records the ground movement caused by seismic waves, P, S, and surface waves. High-frequency data that seismometers collect prove useful in studying when an earthquake occurred, its magnitude, and how fast the earthquake traveled.
Accelerometers: Measure the level of ground shaking occurring in earthquakes. Such information is fundamental for instant assessment of the magnitude and assessing damage potential.

These comprise of the GPS Networks that watch how tectonic plates are moving and what deformation happens to the grounds. Monitoring of time change in movements helps identify some changes to determine when these stress-build up along with slip rate faults before generating seismic events. Seismic sensor networks will generate huge volumes of data in real time, which may be collected and transmitted to some central processing systems. More often than not, environmental vibrations, sensor errors, or human activity will interfere with the data, creating a need for preprocessing earthquake estimation.

Geological and Historical Data

Geological and historical data are the core of AI and ML-based earthquake prediction systems. Datasets of this nature offer long-term insight into seismic patterns, fault zone behavior, and recurrence intervals of earthquakes(Shafapourtehrany et al., 2023).

Geological data includes fault lines, plate tectonics, rock formations, and crustal stress. Geological maps, field surveys, and remote sensing imagery are also utilized to identify active fault zones and seismic hotspots. High-resolution images of ground deformation and fault activity, for example, can be attained from satellite data with SAR and LiDAR technology.

Historical earthquake datasets contain the information of the magnitude, location, depth, and date of occurrence of earthquakes. These records are important in training the machine learning models that could be used in tracing time-space trends. Among the data available are the standardized records of earthquakes provided by USGS (United States Geological Survey) earthquake catalog and the EMSC (European-Mediterranean Seismological Centre) database. Details regarding the stress field, heat flow, and subsurface structure, obtained by geophysical investigations that are seismic tomography, measurements through gravitational survey, and magnetotelluric measurements are essential to understand the ground activity's physical process. This will enable AI and ML models to see long-term trends as well as short-term anomalies while bringing geological as well as historical datasets and real-time seismic data together for more precise predictions of earthquakes.

Data Cleaning and Feature Selection

Data pre-processing is important, as predictive models should yield accuracy and efficiency. For seismic datasets, there seems to be a lot of noisy data, missing values, and irrelevant features that affect the output of the models. Preparing data for AI and ML algorithms is through data cleaning and feature selection.

Data cleaning: It is the elimination of inconsistencies, errors, and missing values in a data set. Some examples include: Noise removal by environmental conditions such as traffic, construction, or weather. Missing value imputation by the statistical method, mean imputation, interpolation, or KNN imputation. Removal of outliers as they might affect the prediction process.

Feature Selection: This is the process of determining the most relevant input variables for training the model. Key features in earthquake prediction are seismic wave characteristics (such as amplitude, frequency, and duration), ground motion measurements, GPS displacement, and geological parameters. Feature selection methods like PCA, RFE, and correlation analysis are used to reduce dimensionality and improve model efficiency.
Signal processing: Fourier Transform, wavelet analysis, and spectral analysis are the signal processing techniques that yield meaningful features of seismic waveforms and filter out the noise.

The use of effective data cleaning and feature selection improves the quality of input data and thus improves the performance of AI and ML models.

Handling Data Scarcity and Noise

One of the major challenges faced in earthquake prediction is that there is a scarcity of labeled seismic data, especially when monitoring infrastructure is limited in areas. Moreover, seismic data is noisy due to sensor inaccuracies or environmental disturbances and human activities. The handling of data scarcity and noise is important for creating reliable predictive models(Abdalzaher et al., 2023; Ren et al., 2020).

Data Augmentation: Synthetic data generation techniques are applied to generate synthetic data from existing datasets. Methods such as SMOTE (Synthetic Minority Over-sampling Technique) and noise injection help balance the dataset and improve model robustness. For example, synthetic seismic waveforms can be generated to train deep learning models in regions with limited earthquake records.
Transfer Learning: The whole concept of transfer learning focuses on using pre-trained models for abundant data regions and later adapting them to limited data regions. Transfer learning reduces the large volume of labeled data with respect to knowledge learned from the dataset.
Noise Reduction: To reduce noise in seismic data, signal processing techniques such as wavelet denoising, low-pass filtering, and adaptive noise cancellation are applied. These methods filter out irrelevant vibrations and improve the signal-to-noise ratio.
Combining Multiple Data Sources: Use of data from multiple sources can be helpful in compensating for data gaps and hence provides a better view of the seismic activity. Multi-modal fusion techniques in data enable a predictive model to learn from diverse datasets. It helps identify hidden correlations.

By addressing the issues of data scarcity and noise, AI and ML models become more resilient and accurate in predicting seismic events, even in regions where data availability is limited. Sources and preprocessing are two significant features of an AI and ML-based system for earthquake prediction. A base for these predictive models is seismic sensor networks, geological surveys, historical records, and satellite imagery; on the other hand, data cleaning, feature selection, and noise reduction assure the quality and reliability of data. When diverse data sources, scarcity of data, and robust preprocessing techniques are employed, researchers may construct accurate and reliable systems of earthquake estimation. Such approaches not only provide a means of improved predictability but also early warnings, thereby reducing risks and impacts from seismic disasters.

CASE STUDIES OF AI AND ML APPLICATIONS

The application of AI and ML in earthquake prediction has received much attention lately because it has the potential to improve accuracy, efficiency, and the capability of real-time forecasting. The case studies are demonstrated with how AI and ML were successfully implemented to predict the earthquake magnitude, location, and enhance early warning systems. Below are three key areas in which AI and ML have shown promising results: the prediction of earthquake magnitude and location, real-time earthquake early warning systems, and comparative analyses of different AI models(AlAli & Anifowose, 2022; Jia & Zhou, 2024; López-Castro et al., 2022).

Predicting the Magnitude and Location of Earthquakes

Precise prediction of the magnitude and location of seismic activities is one of the critical goals of the application of AI and ML in the prediction of earthquake events. Traditional methods primarily rely on limited historical records, but modern AI utilizes vast quantities of real-time data in seismic networks, geological surveys, and images from space satellites to enable much more accurate predictions than traditional techniques.

It can predict the magnitudes and locations of earthquakes in areas like Japan and California, by using sensor data combined with GPS measurements and geological features. Machine Learning algorithms such as Random Forest, SVM, and DNN are trained on comprehensive datasets, which include seismic activity, fault lines, and historical earthquake records. For example, one of the models constructed in California based on information from more than 100 stations of seismic recording stations estimated the probability of an earthquake occurrence in a certain territorial area within a specific period of time. It demonstrated better accuracy and speed to respond in real time against conventional methods.

Real-Time Earthquake Early Warning Systems

AI and ML have revolutionized the system of real-time EEW by giving faster warnings and more accurate predictions than the conventional systems. This is because conventional systems used only network data and post-event analysis, resulting in slow responses. AI empowers real-time systems to detect first waves of seismic activity within seconds and to issue early alerts to threatened communities.

For example, in Mexico and Taiwan, machine learning algorithms will predict the magnitude and potential effects of earthquakes based on real-time seismic data analyzed in those countries. There are thousands of sensors, accelerometers, and GPS networks that detect the slightest seismic activity, which these systems have recorded, sending out warnings to first responders, infrastructure, and the general public. Among the models used here are CNNs and LSTM networks. It can identify patterns in seismic data and determine the intensity of possible earthquakes. The alerts from AI-enhanced early warning systems have been reported to be given in fewer seconds after detecting seismic waves as compared to the conventional way; hence, the time to notify the public will take longer since most seismic activity that requires evacuation is detected almost in its initial stages.

A Comparative Analysis of AI Models

The different AI and ML models used have been compared in studies for finding which one gives the best output with respect to earthquake prediction. These studies have considered evaluating different models based on their performance with regard to accuracy, precision, recall, and computation efficiency. The comparative study of Random Forest, Support Vector Machines (SVM), and Deep Neural Networks (DNN) proves the use of DNN-based models in processing the data for big data with strong and numerous feature interactions. While generalization capability with models was strong, it also found that SVM performed as the best model for the data for the non-linear pattern observed in the data(Sundar et al., 2024; Sundaramoorthy et al., 2024).

Another comparative analysis looked into the use of ensemble learning techniques, such as Gradient Boosting Machines (GBMs) and Bagging, which combined multiple models to improve overall prediction accuracy. The results showed that ensemble-based methods outperformed individual models in terms of reducing error rates and enhancing the robustness of predictions. The approaches of transfer learning were considered in which models are pre-trained on large data sets for fine-tuning over local seismic data. It shows significant boosts in performance, especially in places with lesser historical data about earthquakes.

Hence, a comparative study of AI models gives insight into how diverse algorithms complement each other towards optimizing earthquake prediction. The deep learning, machine learning, and ensemble methods are such approaches in AI that advance the scope of seismic analysis towards innovative solutions for real-time and accurate estimation of an earthquake.

CHALLENGES AND LIMITATIONS

The integration of AI and ML techniques in earthquake prediction carries much promise but still exhibits a number of challenges and limitations. These include aspects of data availability and quality, model accuracy and validation, and computational challenges on the development and deployment side. Addressing these challenges could be critical for further enhancement of predictive capabilities and hence the broad adoption of AI-based earthquake estimation methods(Bhatia et al., 2023; Marano et al., 2024; Matin & Pradhan, 2022). The figure 4 highlights the challenges and limitations in AI and ML techniques for earthquake prediction.

Figure 4. Challenges and limitations in AI and ML techniques for earthquake prediction

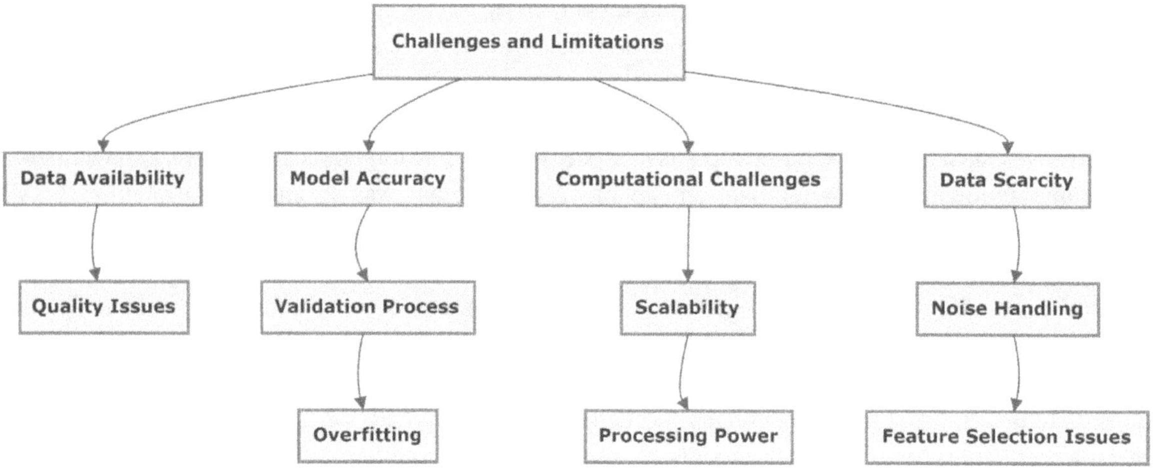

Data Availability and Quality Issues

Availability of good data is one of the biggest issues presented by AI and ML to predict earthquakes. Quality, reliable seismic data is used for training effective models; however, the data collection infrastructure remains primitive in many regions. Sparse or unevenly distributed seismic sensor networks have resulted in incomplete coverage of active fault zones and areas prone to seismic activity. In theory, historical earthquake records, if available, suffer from inconsistency, missing data, and errors in measurements which result in a lesser-good training dataset. External interference factors which may include environmental noises, malfunction of sensors, or even human interferences. These may affect the actual collection of real-time data. For example, there may be noise data contaminated with traffic or industry related to seismic activities and then this may mislead those predictive models hence end up providing wrong predictions or providing false positives in trying to forecast earthquakes. Underdeveloped or remote locations face their challenges in getting enough data for effective models.

The use of new data augmentation techniques, transfer learning, and multi-source data fusion help improve the quality of seismic datasets to overcome such problems and results.

Model Accuracy and Validation

High accuracy in AI and ML models is a very complex task as the inherent uncertainties associated with seismic events are very pronounced. Earthquakes are highly stochastic phenomena, heavily influenced by geological, environmental, and temporal factors that make it challenging to produce universally accurate models. Whereas models can learn from patterns in historical data and current real-time seismic data, predicting when and where an earthquake will occur is inherently probabilistic(AlAli & Anifowose, 2022; López-Castro et al., 2022).

Another key factor involved is model validation; with overfitting liable to occur if models happen to be trained over datasets very simple. Deep learning and complicated machine learning models need a lot of validation for good generalization of datasets. Traditional methods in validations include cross-validation as well as leave-one-out validations, which would never be helpful in capturing a very rare event of seismic, thus making predictions a bit biased. Besides, there is not large enough benchmark datasets, so comparison of model performances among the regions or methodologies would become quite challenging.

Real-world deployment also involves dealing with a trade-off between false positives and false negatives. A highly sensitive model would raise alarms too frequently, resulting in alert fatigue, while a conservative model may not report critical seismic events, hence putting public safety at risk. This is a challenge for scientists and engineers working in this domain to fine-tune and iteratively improve on these trade-offs. Curate AI predictions even in the face of limited data.

Computational Complexity

The training and deployment of the AI and ML models for the prediction of earthquakes are extremely computational and resource-intensive. This depends on the data to be manipulated-the large datasets, in general, and the real-time data streams of this study. Machine learning models and deep learning architectures such as Convolutional Neural Networks and Long Short-Term Memory networks require an enormous amount of computational capability and memory(Albahri et al., 2024; Jia & Zhou, 2024).

Large-scale seismic data needs to be processed with modern hardware infrastructure like HPC clusters or cloud-based infrastructures. In some geographical locations, this will actually slow down the model's training and degrade real-time inference. Models trained from high-resolution datasets incur the latency of high resolution whenever deployed in real-time applications hence making it challenging to fast update early warning systems. Energy consumption in training and inference can also be high. Since the amount of data to be processed is huge, along with the fact that iterative refinement of the model will be needed, enormous amounts of resources are required in order to ensure that the model keeps improving continuously. Research work is currently underway to optimize model architectures, apply pruning techniques on models, and enhance data preprocessing to cut down on the computational overhead.

Summarily, computational challenges are to be overcome by the development of innovative strategies such as parallel processing, optimization of AI models, and the application of edge computing that brings the predictions closer to the end-users. These will help in making AI-driven earthquake prediction systems work efficiently in diverse environments. AI and ML have shown significant advancements in earthquake prediction but several challenges and limitations are still present. Basic challenges include the availability of data, quality of data, and the existence of noisy or incomplete data. The accuracy of models demands verification and a suitable balancing between false positives with false negatives and requires tuning. Last but not the least are computational challenges for large data in processing; the same require a great amount of resources, such as high-performance hardware and algorithmically optimized. These challenges will be addressed through innovative data handling, model optimization, and computational advancements, which are critical to advancing the field of AI-driven earthquake estimation.

FUTURE DIRECTIONS AND INNOVATIONS

AI and ML in the domain of earthquake prediction is fast-changing and has much to do with technological advances and new discoveries in the nature of seismic phenomena. The research thus undertaken has now started coming out with new innovations and directions which hold good promise towards overcoming the challenges of today. These include the design of hybrid AI models, IoT and real-time analytics, as well as Big Data, as well as the employment of cloud computing. All of these areas are pivotal in improving the precision, efficiency, and scalability of systems used for earthquake prediction(Lu et al., 2022; Shafapourtehrany et al., 2023; Sun et al., 2022). Figure 5 highlights the future directions and innovations in AI and ML for earthquake prediction.

Figure 5. Future directions and innovations in AI and ML for earthquake prediction

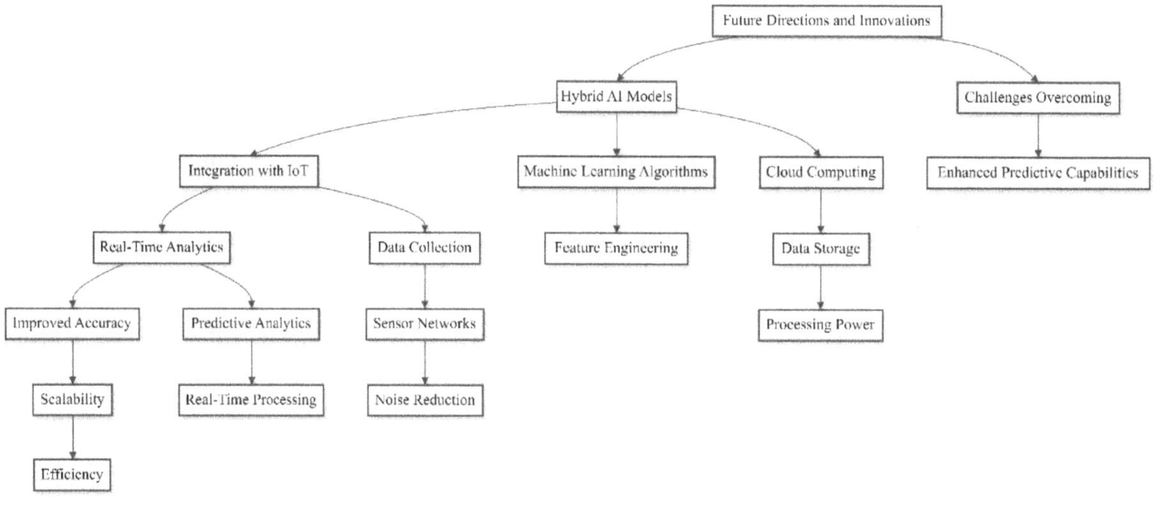

Hybrid AI Models to Enhance the Predictive Precision

Hybrid AI models are a significant innovation in earthquake prediction, integrating various techniques of machine learning so that their strengths could be harvested. The models will encompass algorithms like supervised, unsupervised, and reinforcement learning to develop an integrated framework of seismic event forecasting. For example, the approach that combines machine learning models like Random Forest and SVMs with deep learning models like CNNs or LSTM networks provides a more detailed understanding of seismic patterns(AlAli & Anifowose, 2022).

Hybrid AI models are particularly effective at intricate interlinks in multiple seismic variables that include geological data and records of seismic events that are happening over time with sensor real-time data: both spatial and temporal understandings aid them in accuracy through removal of most bias factors involved in single model application, hence generalization toward new regional and datasets. Additionally, hybrid models also update towards changing data; dynamic updation based on evolving data keeps the prediction related with any new seismic activity happening over time.

Integration of IoT and Real-Time Data Analytics

The Internet of Things is transforming the way seismic data is collected, processed, and analyzed in real-time. With more widespread use of IoT devices such as seismic sensors, accelerometers, and environmental monitoring systems, continuous and comprehensive collection of seismic data from different locations is now possible. The integration of IoT with real-time data analytics enables better precision in the detection of early warning signs of potential earthquakes. Real-time data streams gathered through IoT-enabled networks are processed using advanced AI and ML models, thus allowing for prompt detection of seismic events and even early warnings. Using cloud-based platforms for real-time data analysis, IoT-based earthquake prediction systems can issue immediate alerts to authorities and the public, thus dramatically reducing response times at critical times. Additionally, IoT networks can be used for edge computing, where analysis occurs at the source level, thereby minimizing latency and increasing system responsiveness(Abdalzaher et al., 2023).

This integration also supports collaboration across industries and disciplines. For instance, the integration of IoT networks with environmental monitoring can better understand the impact of human activities on seismic activity, offering an integrated approach to risk assessment and mitigation.

Role of Big Data and Cloud Computing

The massive explosion in seismic data has led to using Big Data analytics and cloud computing in order to process the massive amount of information generated by sensor networks and IoT devices. Traditional ways of storage and processing are not well-suited to handle such a volume and complexity of real-time data captured. Here, the scalable infrastructure given by cloud computing helps in efficiently processing and storing massive datasets(Agrawal et al., 2023; Satav et al., 2023).

Big Data analytics can take meaningful insights from seismic data and allow for a finer-grained and more accurate prediction. It benefits machine learning models in enhancing feature selection, noise reduction, and the capability to model complex relationships between variables. It facilitates collaborative research and sharing of models through cloud-based platforms, ensuring that all these advancements are available to a wider audience: researchers, emergency responders, and policymakers. Further, improvement in distributed computing frameworks like Apache Spark or Hadoop optimizes seismic data processing for real-time analytics, ensuring that models are always up to date and are ready to provide timely and accurate earthquake forecasts.

The future of AI and ML in earthquake prediction lies in continuous innovation and integration of advanced technologies. Hybrid AI models represent a strong approach toward the enhancement of accuracy through a combination of different learning techniques. The IoT and real-time data analytics increase the possibility of collecting and analyzing seismic data faster, and the use of cloud computing and Big Data leads to the scalability and collaboration of various datasets. In other words, these inventions are avenues to having better working systems in earthquake prediction as they are better prepared systems in disaster management strategies.

CONCLUSION

Artificial Intelligence and Machine Learning integration in the area of earthquake prediction provides tremendous potential to overcome deficiencies of traditional methods. Great strides have been made in seismic event understanding and forecasting using hybrid models, IoT, real-time data analytics, and cloud computing. Areas to be overcome include improving data quality, model accuracy, and computational constraints, which will require innovation and refinement.

Hybrid AI models bring a comprehensive approach through the integration of multiple algorithms in order to capture the complexity of seismic data. Integration with IoT facilitates real-time data collection, including early warning systems that prepare timely responses against earthquakes. In addition, Big Data and cloud computing process vast datasets and enhance predictability, but encourage inter-industrial collaboration.

The role of these innovations will continue to evolve as technology goes ahead, enabling more accurate, efficient, and scalable earthquake prediction systems. There is immense hope in the future for developing our understanding of seismic activities toward safer and more resilient communities.

REFERENCES

Abdalzaher, M. S., Elsayed, H. A., Fouda, M. M., & Salim, M. M. (2023). Employing machine learning and iot for earthquake early warning system in smart cities. *Energies*, *16*(1), 495. DOI: 10.3390/en16010495

Agrawal, A. V., Shashibhushan, G., Pradeep, S., Padhi, S., Sugumar, D., & Boopathi, S. (2023). Synergizing Artificial Intelligence, 5G, and Cloud Computing for Efficient Energy Conversion Using Agricultural Waste. In *Sustainable Science and Intelligent Technologies for Societal Development* (pp. 475–497). IGI Global.

AlAli, A., & Anifowose, F. (2022). Seismic velocity modeling in the digital transformation era: A review of the role of machine learning. *Journal of Petroleum Exploration and Production Technology*, *12*(1), 1–14. DOI: 10.1007/s13202-021-01304-0

Albahri, A., Khaleel, Y. L., Habeeb, M. A., Ismael, R. D., Hameed, Q. A., Deveci, M., Homod, R. Z., Albahri, O., Alamoodi, A., & Alzubaidi, L. (2024). A systematic review of trustworthy artificial intelligence applications in natural disasters. *Computers & Electrical Engineering*, *118*, 109409. DOI: 10.1016/j.compeleceng.2024.109409

Bhatia, M., Ahanger, T. A., & Manocha, A. (2023). Artificial intelligence based real-time earthquake prediction. *Engineering Applications of Artificial Intelligence*, *120*, 105856. DOI: 10.1016/j.engappai.2023.105856

Falcone, R., Lima, C., & Martinelli, E. (2020). Soft computing techniques in structural and earthquake engineering: A literature review. *Engineering Structures*, *207*, 110269. DOI: 10.1016/j.engstruct.2020.110269

Jia, K., & Zhou, S. (2024). Machine Learning Applications in Seismology. [). MDPI.]. *Applied Sciences (Basel, Switzerland)*, *14*(17), 7857. DOI: 10.3390/app14177857

Jiao, P., & Alavi, A. H. (2020). Artificial intelligence in seismology: Advent, performance and future trends. *Geoscience Frontiers*, *11*(3), 739–744. DOI: 10.1016/j.gsf.2019.10.004

Joshi, A., Raman, B., Mohan, C. K., & Cenkeramaddi, L. R. (2024). Application of a new machine learning model to improve earthquake ground motion predictions. *Natural Hazards*, *120*(1), 729–753. DOI: 10.1007/s11069-023-06230-4

López-Castro, B., Haro-Baez, A. G., Arcos-Aviles, D., Barreno-Riera, M., & Landázuri-Avilés, B. (2022). A systematic review of structural health monitoring systems to strengthen post-earthquake assessment procedures. *Sensors (Basel)*, *22*(23), 9206. DOI: 10.3390/s22239206 PMID: 36501906

Lu, X., Plevris, V., Tsiatas, G., & De Domenico, D. (2022). Artificial intelligence-powered methodologies and applications in earthquake and structural engineering. [). Frontiers Media SA.]. *Frontiers in Built Environment*, *8*, 876077. DOI: 10.3389/fbuil.2022.876077

Marano, G. C., Rosso, M. M., Aloisio, A., & Cirrincione, G. (2024). Generative adversarial networks review in earthquake-related engineering fields. *Bulletin of Earthquake Engineering*, *22*(7), 3511–3562. DOI: 10.1007/s10518-023-01645-7

Matin, S. S., & Pradhan, B. (2022). Challenges and limitations of earthquake-induced building damage mapping techniques using remote sensing images-A systematic review. *Geocarto International, 37*(21), 6186–6212. DOI: 10.1080/10106049.2021.1933213

Mignan, A., & Broccardo, M. (2020). Neural network applications in earthquake prediction (1994–2019): Meta-analytic and statistical insights on their limitations. *Seismological Research Letters, 91*(4), 2330–2342. DOI: 10.1785/0220200021

Mousavi, S. M., & Beroza, G. C. (2023). Machine learning in earthquake seismology. *Annual Review of Earth and Planetary Sciences, 51*(1), 105–129. DOI: 10.1146/annurev-earth-071822-100323

Ren, C. X., Hulbert, C., Johnson, P. A., & Rouet-Leduc, B. (2020). Machine learning and fault rupture: A review. *Advances in Geophysics, 61*, 57–107. DOI: 10.1016/bs.agph.2020.08.003

Satav, S. D., Lamani, D., Harsha, K., Kumar, N., Manikandan, S., & Sampath, B. (2023). Energy and Battery Management in the Era of Cloud Computing: Sustainable Wireless Systems and Networks. In *Sustainable Science and Intelligent Technologies for Societal Development* (pp. 141–166). IGI Global.

Shafapourtehrany, M., Batur, M., Shabani, F., Pradhan, B., Kalantar, B., & Özener, H. (2023). A comprehensive review of geospatial technology applications in earthquake preparedness, emergency management, and damage assessment. *Remote Sensing (Basel), 15*(7), 1939. DOI: 10.3390/rs15071939

Sun, Z., Sandoval, L., Crystal-Ornelas, R., Mousavi, S. M., Wang, J., Lin, C., Cristea, N., Tong, D., Carande, W. H., Ma, X., Rao, Y., Bednar, J. A., Tan, A., Wang, J., Purushotham, S., Gill, T. E., Chastang, J., Howard, D., Holt, B., & John, A. (2022). A review of earth artificial intelligence. *Computers & Geosciences, 159*, 105034. DOI: 10.1016/j.cageo.2022.105034

Sundar, R., Srikaanth, P. B., Naik, D. A., Murugan, V. P., Karumudi, M., & Boopathi, S. (2024). Achieving Balance Between Innovation and Security in the Cloud With Artificial Intelligence of Things: Semantic Web Control Models. In *Advances in Web Technologies and Engineering* (pp. 1–26). IGI Global. DOI: 10.4018/979-8-3693-1487-6.ch001

Sundaramoorthy, K., Singh, A., Sumathy, G., Maheshwari, A., Arunarani, A., & Boopathi, S. (2024). A Study on AI and Blockchain-Powered Smart Parking Models for Urban Mobility. In *Handbook of Research on AI and ML for Intelligent Machines and Systems* (pp. 223–250). IGI Global.

Thai, H. T. (2022, April). Machine learning for structural engineering: A state-of-the-art review. In *Structures* (Vol. 38, pp. 448–491). Elsevier.

Xie, Y., Ebad Sichani, M., Padgett, J. E., & DesRoches, R. (2020). The promise of implementing machine learning in earthquake engineering: A state-of-the-art review. *Earthquake Spectra, 36*(4), 1769–1801. DOI: 10.1177/8755293020919419

Xie, Y., Sichani, M. E., Padgett, J., & DesRoches, R. (2020). Machine learning applications in earthquake engineering: Literature review and case studies. *17th World Conference on Earthquake Engineering*.

Chapter 10
Enhancing the Efficiency of Industrial Automation Using Smart Programming in AI and IoT: A Study

Gautam Solaimalai
https://orcid.org/0009-0000-3045-3834
U.S. Bank, USA

ABSTRACT

This chapter analyzes the transformation that integration with AI and IoT can make possible in industrial automation. This chapter explains how smart programming techniques, including machine learning algorithms, predictive analytics, and edge computing, may optimize operational efficiency, minimize downtime, and improve decision-making processes. The case studies described here include real-time monitoring and adaptation of control systems and predictive maintenance powered by AI and IoT. It places much emphasis on communication among interlinked devices. The chapter highlights the role of big data as a factor in making things automatic, besides ways of surmounting problems of cybersecurity and scale. The book further outlines long-term effects on these technologies' impact in fostering sustainability and cost-effectiveness with improved productivity. This book is useful in guiding the industrialists in the direction of smart programming toward innovation and competitiveness in its industrial processes.

INTRODUCTION

The rapid advancement in technology has opened a new era in industrial automation where AI and IoT play a transformative role. In a scenario where industries are trying to improve efficiency, reduce operational costs, and become sustainable, the convergence of AI and IoT through smart programming emerges as the key enabler. This is an integration which facilitates smart decision-making, seamless connectivity, and real-time adaptability to modify the face of traditional industrial processes. Smart programming is, indeed, the base for the formation of this evolution and capability in developing

DOI: 10.4018/979-8-3693-8407-7.ch010

adaptive algorithms, predictive models, and workflows in efficient workflows for modern industrial environments(Su et al., 2023).

Industrial automation, on the other hand, has been a main pillar in productivity enhancement as it focused always on optimizing processes, thus reducing human intervention for repetitive tasks. However, the growing market demands, resource constraints, and increased need for precision in operations have highlighted the inadequacies of traditional automation systems. AI and IoT, with smart programming, help overcome these challenges by incorporating features like self-learning systems, predictive maintenance, and interconnected networks of devices. These technologies allow industries to transition from reactive to proactive and predictive operational models, thus enabling better asset utilization and decision-making(Bhambri & Rani, 2024).

The heart of this transformation is smart programming that allows algorithms to be developed for processing large volumes of data from IoT devices. For example, through machine learning models, one can identify patterns, predict equipment failures, and optimize production schedules. Powered by AI, predictive analytics turns data into actionable insights and reduces downtime and increases efficiency in operations. Edge computing further enhances this ecosystem by enabling localized data processing, ensuring real-time responsiveness, and reducing latency issues. These innovations not only streamline operations but also contribute to significant cost savings and enhanced resource allocation(Sarker, 2022).

The most impactful application of AI and IoT in industrial automation is predictive maintenance. Traditional methods of maintenance include scheduled or reactive repairs, which are characterized by the downtime resulting from it and higher costs. With AI algorithms and IoT sensors, predictive maintenance allows industries to monitor equipment health continuously and predict failures before they happen. This proactive approach reduces downtime, extends the lifespan of assets, and ensures continuous production. In a similar manner, smart factories enabled by IoT-connected devices and AI-powered systems show how intelligent automation can make a difference in manufacturing processes. These factories utilize real-time data for adaptive control to ensure optimal performance and quality assurance(Tyagi et al., 2020a).

However, with such high potential, there are also many challenges in the integration of AI and IoT with industrial automation. The chief challenge here is cybersecurity since a large amount of data, being sensitive, would be transferred between the devices. Thus, there exists a great risk of breaches of data and cyber attacks, and therefore strong security protocols and encrypted communication frameworks should be present. The challenge is that AI and IoT systems are highly scalable, which makes it a challenge for industries to strike a balance between the volume of data, smooth integration, and operational efficiency. Strategic planning, investment in secure infrastructure, and continuous technological advancements would help overcome these challenges(Nirmala et al., 2022).

Sustainability in industrial automation is very important today, considering the day-to-day environmental issues on every individual's mind. Energy efficiency through AI and IoT can be achieved by optimizing resource utilization and minimizing waste. For instance, an AI-driven energy management system analyzes consumption patterns and makes actionable suggestions to reduce energy usage. IoT sensors can scan emissions and find inefficiency points. These enable industries to come within environmental compliance while at the same time reducing carbon footprint, in line with the best global sustainability goals, opening a window of opportunity where industries can be positively impacting on the preservation of the environment while strengthening their operational efficiencies(Pan et al., 2021).

The future of industrial automation looks bright and promising, as AI and IoT adoption will continue to advance its innovation. The 5G technology trend, on the way, will make it even more connected and at faster data transmission speeds to achieve a more robust and scalable IoT ecosystem. The new horizon for autonomous systems powered by AI will revolutionize industrial operations through self-optimizing and self-healing processes. Industrialized digital twins are used for the simulation of real systems in real time for proper planning and decision-making(Chander et al., 2022).

This chapter focuses on multifaceted roles of AI and IoT in industrial automation. In this context, smart programming forms the driving force for change. The underlying technologies and practical application and emerging trends of such advancements will be analyzed so that a comprehensive understanding is drawn of how these changes transform industries. This includes challenges and opportunities associated with the transition that will offer actionable insights for industry professionals seeking to harness the power of AI and IoT(Jain & Chandrasekaran, 2020).

The integration of AI and IoT through smart programming is a paradigm shift in industrial automation, empowering industries to provide unprecedented levels of efficiency, adaptability, and innovation while addressing important concerns related to resources, sustainability, and demands in the marketplace. Its strategic adoption forges the next wave for the evolution of the industrial landscape, enabling it not only to serve the pursuit of operational excellence but also define the horizon for the automation of the future in ways unforeseen before(Babayigit & Abubaker, 2023; Chi et al., 2022). This chapter lays the foundation for discussing these transformative innovations, their practical uses, and their ability to mold a more efficient and sustainable industrial future.

Objectives

This chapter will describe an in-depth understanding of how the integration of AI and IoT with smart programming contributes to the improvement of industrial automation. It aims to prepare the reader with insights about emerging technologies, such as machine learning, predictive analytics, and edge computing, toward improved efficiency and reduced downtime. The chapter will also cover applications such as real-time monitoring, adaptive control, and predictive maintenance and also face issues such as cybersecurity and scalability. In addition, it identifies sustainable practices and future trends in industrial IoT and presents actionable strategies that industry professionals can use to achieve innovation, productivity, and competitive advantage in automated operations through smart programming.

TECHNOLOGIES IN AI AND IOT FOR AUTOMATION

It is through the synergy of AI and IoT that industrial automation has taken on new dimensions, including intelligent systems that can auto-optimise, make real-time decisions, and predict. The driving force behind this change are the technologies of machine learning and predictive analytics, edge computing, and big data with cloud integration. Such technologies are what support smart automation, thus providing industries with more efficiency, reduced downtime, and improved productivity(Tzafestas, 2018a). Figure 1 depicts the advancements in AI and IoT technologies for automation.

Figure 1. Technologies in AI and IoT for automation

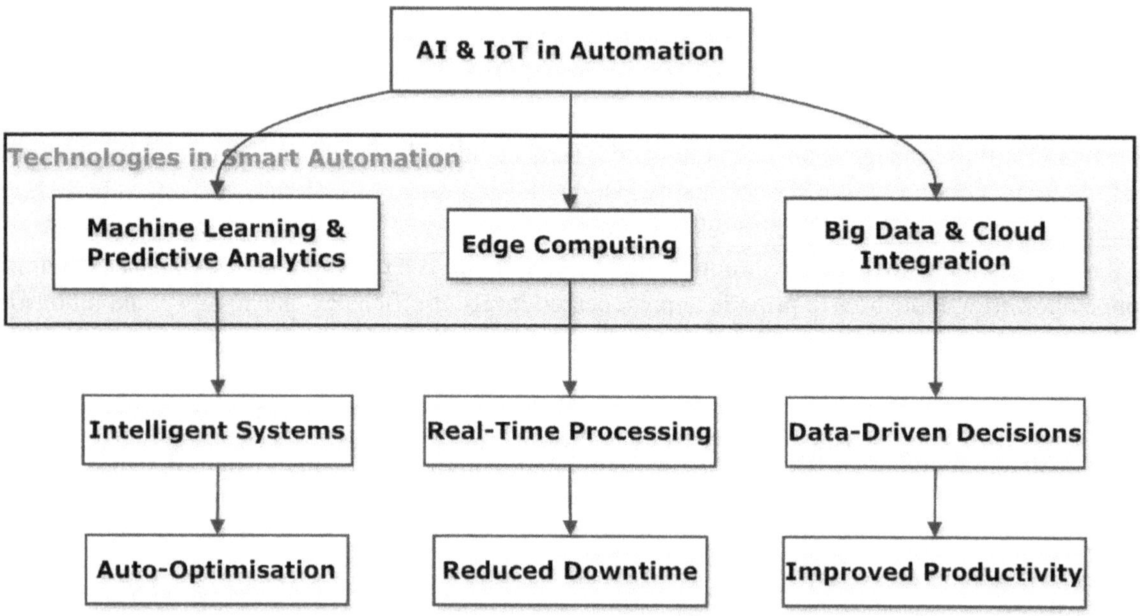

Machine Learning and Predictive Analytics

Machine learning (ML) is the heart of AI technology because it allows systems to learn from data, identify patterns, and make decisions without significant human involvement. ML algorithms, in industrial automation, are used for data analysis through IoT-connected devices that make predictive analytics possible. Predictive analytics differs from normal data analysis as it allows the determination of the problems or opportunities that are likely to happen beforehand. For example, in predictive maintenance, ML models analyze sensor data from industrial equipment to identify signs of wear or failure. This allows industries to schedule maintenance proactively to avoid costly downtime and increase the life of equipment(Kollu et al., 2022a).

ML also further optimizes the process by making decisions in real-time. For instance, in manufacturing, algorithms used in ML monitor production lines and find inefficiencies that require adjustments to improve throughput. The same capabilities can be extended to quality control where ML-powered vision systems detect defects in real-time, thus ensuring product quality and reducing waste. With predictive analytics integrated into industrial processes, organizations are provided with a competitive advantage that comes in terms of reduced costs, increased reliability, and quicker responses.

Edge Computing and Real-Time Processing

One such transformative technology in industrial automation involves edge computing, which challenges IoT ecosystems' latency and bandwidth constraints(Dubey et al., 2021a). Unlike traditional systems, where data is communicated with centralized servers for processing, edge computing processes data nearer to its source-at the edge of the network-with the decentralized approach ensuring a real-time response critical in applications requiring immediate decision-making. Industrial automation benefits from edge computing that aids in fast data processing and processing of IoT sensors and devices. For example, in an assembly line, irregularities are quickly recognized and corrected by the devices on the edge without hampering the workflows. Again, in robotics, with this capability, autonomous systems have a faster response time toward environmental changes, hence precise and safe. In cases where split-second decisions have become critical to operational efficiency- manufacturing, logistics, energy-this capability has value-added significance.

In addition, this reduces the dependency on constant connectivity to the cloud and gives a better reliability to systems. This is very ideal for remote or challenging sites, such as oil rigs or mining sites, as consistent internet access might be unfeasible. It promotes scalability, reduces operational cost, and improves the entire system performance by spreading computation tasks across edge devices.Big Data and Cloud Integration

Big Data and Cloud Integration

Big data technologies in collaboration with cloud computing will make the infrastructure needed to manage, analyze, and extract value out of this huge amount of data generated by IoT. Cloud integration provides a platform for scalable storage and processing and advanced analytics tools for extraction of actionable insights. This allows the organization to track their performance, trends, and improve on their operations using big data analytics in industrial automation. For instance, factories powered by IoT can track such KPIs as efficiency in production, energy usage, and reliability of equipment in use. Such enables an organization to establish hidden patterns and correlations, which can not be observed with routine procedures. These patterns enable making real data-informed decisions hence boost large-scale productivity(Islam, 2024a).

Cloud integration complements big data as it provides central access and enables collaboration. With the use of cloud platforms, companies from different locations can process real-time data, distribute insights, and agree upon actions. This has become a matter of urgency in global supply chain management because effective communication and information sharing are very essential. Additionally, cloud-based automation solutions allow industries to implement ML models at scale, which also further enhances operational efficiency. This adds to advanced AI applications, such as digital twins. A digital twin is an industrial representation of physical systems. It simulates and optimizes processes in a controlled environment. It provides very good insight into performance by integrating real-time data from IoT devices for predictive maintenance, risk assessment, and strategic planning.

Interplay of Such Technologies

All of machine learning, edge computing, big data, and cloud integration have combined to strengthen the powers of AI and IoT in industrial automation. For instance, real-time predictive maintenance at the edge is supported by ML models while cloud platforms are utilized for long-term trend computation. Similarly, data pre-filtering in edge computing supports big data analytics, which ensures only relevant information is processed at the edge(Pramanik et al., 2018a). These technologies further meet key challenges like energy efficiency and sustainability. It maximizes resource usage and reduces waste as well as carbon footprint. As a result, industrial automation harmonizes with the world's green objectives. For instance, the use of big data by AI-based energy management systems helps to discover inefficiencies and makes energy-saving recommendations for greener operation.

Machine learning and predictive analytics, edge computing, and big data along with cloud integration would, therefore be the fundamental technological enablers ushering in the revolution of industrial automation. They would empower industries to fully explore their potential in AI and IoT-aided innovation, efficiency, and sustainability. Over such technologies, organizations could realize not only overcoming operational difficulties but also paving the way toward a smarter, better interconnected industrial future.

PROGRAMMING IN AI AND IOT FOR AUTOMATION

The programming paradigms and frameworks form the backbone of AI and IoT-driven automation in seamless integration, intelligent decision-making, and dynamic adaptability. Advanced programming methodologies allow systems to process data, execute commands autonomously, and be responsive in real time. From the development of machine learning models to edge processing solutions, programming becomes the critical enabler of enhancing industrial efficiency. The process of programming in AI and IoT for automation is depicted in Figure 2.

Figure 2. Process of programming in AI and IoT for automation

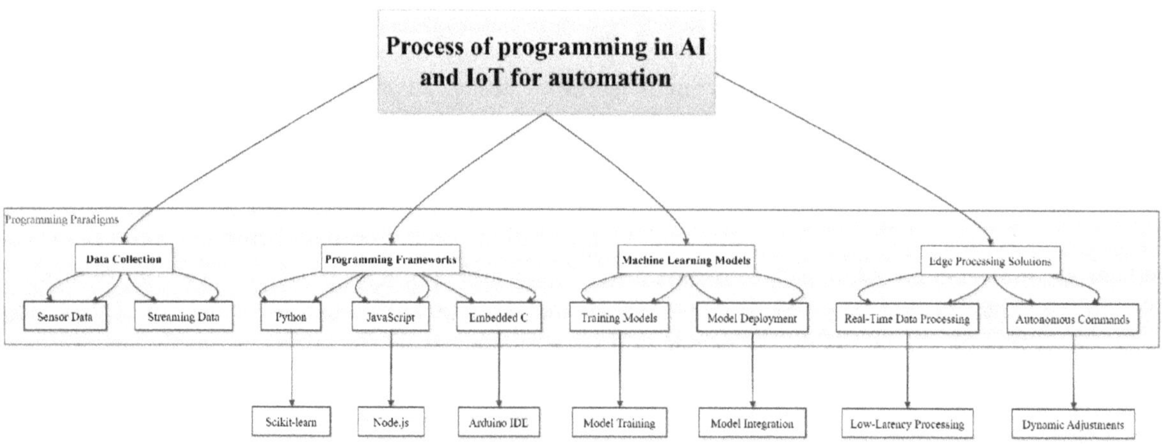

Machine Learning Programming: MLs rely on the programming languages of Python, R, and Java in developing models in order to analyze data and predict outcomes as well as auto-making decisions. For instance, the immense libraries of Python such as TensorFlow, PyTorch, and Scikit-learn make it easier to establish predictive and classification models available in industrial automation. One good example is that through the programming of ML, algorithms for predictive maintenance evaluate the sensor data in predicting failures within equipment. In addition, reinforcement learning algorithms, mostly developed in Python or MATLAB, make it possible for auto systems to improve workflows according to learning in their environments(Dubey et al., 2021b).

IoT Programming Frameworks: The frameworks and languages used in programming IoT systems must support device connectivity, communication protocols, and real-time processing. C, C++, and Python are some of the most widely used languages for writing firmware for IoT devices. These languages ensure efficient data exchange and low-power operation. Middleware platforms such as Node.js and MQTT enable seamless communication between IoT devices and cloud systems. For example, Node.js supports real-time event-driven applications that are crucial for monitoring and controlling industrial automation systems.

Embedded Systems Programming: Often, embedded systems are used that are programmed at the hardware level to control IoT devices. For efficiently developing resource-constrained applications, C, C++, and Assembly languages are used. With embedded programming, microcontrollers and sensors can be made to do certain tasks like data collection, environmental situation monitoring, or actuators control-all are essential for responsive and accurate automation.

Edge Computing Programming: Edge computing programming deals with decentralized processing closer to the sources of data, reducing latency. AWS IoT Greengrass and Microsoft Azure IoT Edge provide frameworks for developing applications for the edge. Python and Rust are widely used languages in the development of lightweight and high-performance edge applications. The programs can be used to create real-time analytics for, for example, industrial system anomaly detection without always being connected to the cloud(Islam, 2024b; Tzafestas, 2018b).

Cloud Integration and API Development: Connecting IoT systems with centralized data processing platforms involves cloud computing and APIs. RESTful APIs and SDKs such as AWS SDK, Azure SDK are used for secure transmission, storage, and analytics of data. Backend programming is done using Java, Python, or Ruby to ensure a seamless integration between IoT devices and cloud services, allowing the execution of advanced functionalities like big data processing and long-term analytics.

Programming for Interoperability and Standards: This can only be achieved if the programming frameworks comply with standards such as OPC UA, MQTT, and CoAP. For instance, OPC UA enables interoperable communication between devices from different manufacturers, while MQTT is the most widely used for lightweight data transfer in constrained environments. Libraries in programming languages like JavaScript and Python support libraries to simplify the implementation of such protocols.

AI Model Deployment and Optimization: During the implementation of AI models in the IoT ecosystem, programming must be done to optimize and make AI models resource-effective and compatible. There are two most popular frameworks that provide the optimization of AI models for deployment on edge devices or embedded systems. They are TensorFlow Lite and ONNX. These tools are used by programmers to compress and fine-tune the model so that it is functional within resource-constrained environments(Pramanik et al., 2018b).

Security Programming for Automation: With the increasing usage of connected devices, cyber security has emerged as the prime requirement in industrial automation. Secure coding practices include encryption protocols applied using TLS, SSL, boot security, and authentication protocols. The use of languages such as Python and Java has aided in developing secure protocols for communication; hardware programming at the level ensures maintaining integrity at the device.
Event Driven and Reactive Programming: It remains an essential application of industrial automation to respond in real time to events. Another fantastic example is the usage of frameworks like Node-RED. Developers can develop flows that react to events: from sensor alerts to system anomalies. Reactive programming is part of effective handling of asynchronous data streams, implemented with technologies such as RxJS or Akka.
Visualization and Dashboard Development: Thus, programming of data visualization and dashboards has to occur so that automation of AI and IoT turns accessible and actionable. Interactive dashboards are created by the developers using D3.js, Tableau SDKs, or Plotly with real-time insights into operations, thus enabling stakeholders to keep track of performance by seeing trends and making right decisions(Kollu et al., 2022b; Pramanik et al., 2018b).
Programming for Automation Testing and Deployment: Automation systems involve much testing for reliability as well as functionality. The frameworks involved are Selenium in the case of automation testing and Docker in terms of containerization. Both Python and Java are widely used for script writing, whereas tools involving deployment across industrial networks through Kubernetes manage that.

The driving force for innovative applications of AI and IoT in automation is programming. Intelligent systems can be designed by programming to perform predictive analytics, carry out real-time decision-making processes, and integrate devices seamlessly. These industries unlock the full potential of automation to achieve higher productivity with cost savings and smarter and more resilient operations by using diverse programming languages, frameworks, and paradigms.

APPLICATIONS OF SMART PROGRAMMING IN INDUSTRIAL AUTOMATION

The integration of smart programming into industrial automation is quite revolutionary since it has enabled real-time monitoring and reporting, predictive maintenance, and real energy management. Businesses are in turn optimizing efficiency, curtailing downtime, and offering far more sustainability through machine learning models and IoT connectivity alongside advanced algorithms. Listed here are some of the key applications of smart programming in industrial automation(Dey & Sen, 2020; Mamodiya et al., 2014). Figure 3 depicts advanced programming methodologies used in industrial automation.

Figure 3. Advanced programming methodologies in industrial automation

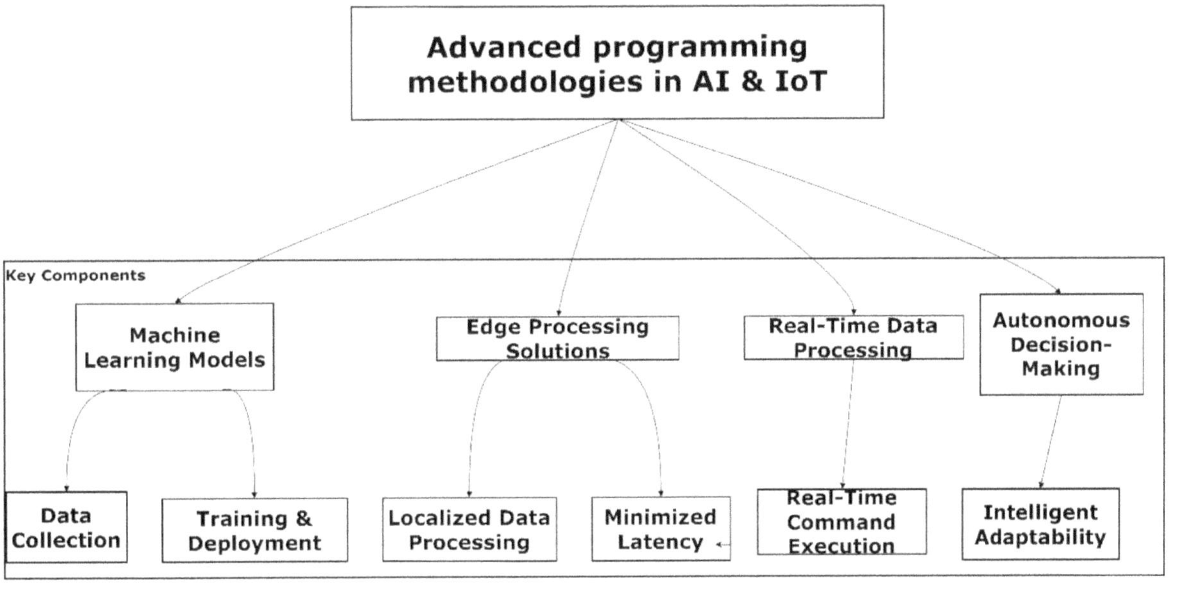

Real-Time Monitoring and Control

Smart programming enables real-time monitoring and control of industrial systems, thus ensuring that these operate smoothly and responsively. With IoT-connected sensors and devices, industries collect large amounts of data, which must be processed for actionable insights. Programming languages like Python, JavaScript, and C++ are used to create frameworks and applications that handle streams of data in real-time. For instance, in manufacturing environments, smart programming enables the monitoring of production lines in real-time. Such monitoring involves processing data based on sensor information on a machine to realize abnormalities such as overheats or strange vibrations. On detection, the system modifies the operation in order to avoid expensive breakdowns or inefficiencies. Lastly, predictive analytics, further powered by machine learning models, make this real-time control even more superior in terms of predicting possible malfunctions that may happen beforehand. Edge computing enhances the real-time control by processing information locally at the source that reduces latency and enables one to make decisions in the shortest time possible. Industries such as pharmaceuticals require that precision control be achieved with regard to product quality during batch production.

Predictive Maintenance Systems

Predictive maintenance has become a critical application of smart programming in industrial automation. Traditional methods included maintenance schedules based on fixed intervals or reactive repairs, with resulting inefficiencies and increased operational costs. Smart programming introduces predictive analytics, wherein machine learning models analyze historical and real-time data to anticipate when maintenance is required. It evaluates sensor data arriving at machines like motors, pumps, and conveyor belts in prediction of failure, evaluating sensors using algorithms built out on languages such as Python and R. In another context, an automated system will break down patterns of wear and abnormal vibrations into ideas it can suggest about potential intervention in maintenance(Samad & Kiliccote, 2012; Tyagi et al., 2020b).

Predictive maintenance systems analyze all the data that the IoT devices are constantly streaming. Through programming frameworks like TensorFlow or Apache Spark, a central server processes and transforms this data into actionable insight, thereby reducing downtime, minimizing costs to repair, and providing an extended life for the industrial equipment. Furthermore, with the deployment of smart algorithms, the maintenance activities are scheduled only when necessary, thus optimising labor resources and hence, improving the overall efficiency of operations. Predictive maintenance is used in various industries such as automotive, aerospace, and energy sectors, wherein the reliability of equipment determines the smoothness of operation.

Energy Management and Optimization

This is an area that has grown in interest for industrial automation with regard to sustainability and cost issues. Smart programming will allow an industry to monitor the real-time consumption of energy and develop strategies to reduce waste and increase efficiency. Smart programming optimizes the use of energy at all stages of production through IoT-enabled sensors and energy management systems. For example, temperature sensors in a heating system can provide real-time data to an AI-powered algorithm that adjusts the energy output to meet specific requirements while minimizing unnecessary consumption. Such energy management software is developed using programming languages such as Python and Java(Nitzan, 1976; Tommila et al., 2001). This system can process large datasets collected from smart meters, environmental sensors, and machinery. They analyze the usage patterns, detect anomalies, and provide insights for continuous improvement. Smart programming is designed to dynamically manage the loading, so that usage and consumption of energy may also be optimized according to need. In this process of optimization, industries ensure savings in terms of energy costs while maintaining efficiency without any performance compromise. In data centers, it becomes essential to ensure power efficiency combined with management of cooling and ventilation. In addition, using advanced machine learning algorithms, predictive models can predict future energy needs; hence, the industries can make proactive strategies in terms of managing resources. This further ensures environmental sustainability as the industries achieve regulatory compliance and standards on energy efficiency.

Smart programming is, now, a fundamental element in the automation of industries that will trigger changes in real-time monitoring, predictive maintenance, and energy management. These will enable industries to take hold of complex systems with more control, minimal time being down, optimal resource utilization, and better sustainability. With the continued evolution of technology, it is the role of smart programming to further grow into its aspects of supporting the development of intelligent, efficient, and robust industrial operations.

CHALLENGES AND SOLUTIONS

The integration of smart programming in industrial automation has changed the face of operations by allowing enhanced efficiency, real-time decision-making, and productivity. However, with such progress comes significant challenges that must be addressed to ensure the successful implementation of these solutions(Islam, 2024b; Yadav et al., 2024). Figure 4 presents the challenges and solutions of integrating smart programming in industrial automation. Below are the key challenges faced in industrial automation and corresponding solutions:

Figure 4. Challenges and solutions of integrating smart programming in industrial automation

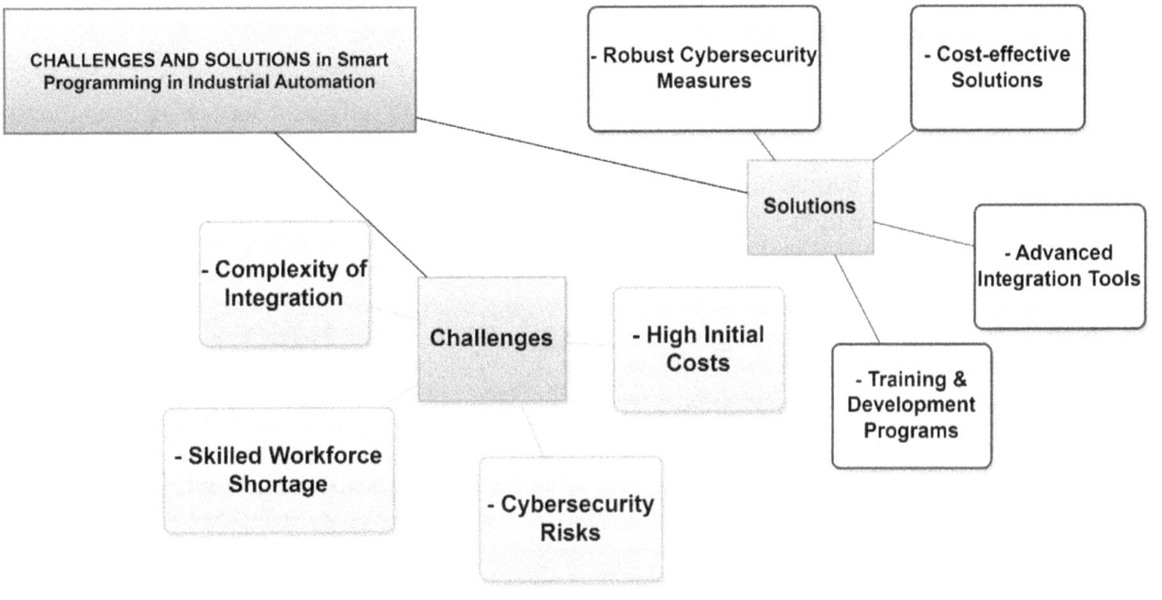

Cybersecurity Risks and Mitigation

Cybersecurity is the most important element in industrial automation. This is because the growing IoT device interconnectivity coupled with the use of cloud-based solutions leaves industrial systems open to cyberattacks such as data breaches, ransomware, and unauthorized access. Therefore, smart programming must have security protocols that would safeguard sensitive data and maintain system integrity.

Challenges:

a) Complexity in interconnected systems increases
b) Risk of unauthorized access and data manipulation increases
c) Edge computing and cloud storage risks

Solutions:
Implementation of Strong Encryption: Advanced encryption techniques must be implemented in smart programming for the security of data in transit and at rest. TLS, AES, and secure APIs can ensure the confidentiality and integrity of data.
Continuous Security Audits: Monitoring and security audits help identify vulnerabilities and eliminate threats in real-time. Regular updates to programming frameworks and software can mitigate emerging risks.
Zero Trust Security Model: The Zero Trust model is applied where devices and users are constantly authenticated irrespective of location that reduces the risk of unauthorised access.
Intrusion Detection Systems (IDS): Intrusion detection systems in the IoT environment assist in the identification of suspicious activities and mitigate potential breaches before they escalate.

Workforce Training and Adoption

Implementing smart programming in industrial automation will only be a success if it can boast a qualified workforce that manages, maintains, and exploits the use of sophisticated systems. After all, technology may progress, but the human component of industrial workforces faces several difficulties when adopting new automation technologies, mainly in integrating AI and IoT into industrial processes(Bhambri & Rani, 2024; Su et al., 2023).

Issues

a) Lack of adoption of new technology
b) Little understanding of AI and IoT capabilities
c) Training is always a necessity to keep up with new languages and frameworks

Solutions

a) Extensive Training Programmes: Employee training with specific courses in AI, machine learning, IoT, and the best practice for programming shall be given, so people will easily be migrated into automated systems.
b) Cross Disciplinary learning: The training program involving IT professionals, automation engineers, and business teams facilitates understanding that smart programming relates to other business goals
c) Hands on Workshops and Simulations: Practical hands-on trainings through the help of workshops and simulation environments for actual adaptation on the automation systems by workers.
d) Knowledge Sharing Platforms: Implementing knowledge-sharing platforms or forums within organizations allows the workforce to be updated on the latest trends and best practices in industrial automation.

It is relatively quite a challenge to introduce smart programming in industrial automation by having to deal with a series of layers on matters concerning cybersecurity, scalability, interoperability, and the workforce's ability to adapt. Through such means, by implementing the latest security practices, open standards, scalable architectures, and continuous training, businesses can overcome the identified challenges and maximize the value derived from intelligent automation systems. The changing technology landscape will also necessitate proactive and adaptive behavior in sustaining success in industrial automation.

CASE STUDIES AND INDUSTRY INSIGHTS

Smart factories have transformed the way various industries operate due to the Internet of Things (IIoT) and advanced smart programming. By incorporating IoT devices, sensors, and intelligent algorithms, manufacturers have been able to reach unprecedented levels of automation, efficiency, and data-driven decision-making. Here are some key insights and case studies illustrating successful implementation of IIoT in smart factories(Tzafestas, 2018a).

Smart Factories and IIoT Implementation

One of the most prominent instances of IIoT adoption is Bosch's smart factory in Germany. Bosch, as part of its production line, has implemented IIoT technologies that enable real-time monitoring and control of machinery and processes. Bosch has optimized efficiency in production, reduced wastage, and increased general output through intelligent sensors and smart programming. Machine learning algorithms combined with real-time data from IoT devices allow for predictive maintenance, thus minimizing downtime and increasing equipment lifetime(Nirmala et al., 2022; Sarker, 2022; Yadav et al., 2024).

General Electric (GE) is another excellent example in the case of its digital transformation in aviation manufacturing. Through IIoT, GE has streamlined operations within its facilities by monitoring engines, turbines, and other parts to perform predictive maintenance. GE achieves real-time detection of possible faults through smart programming, reducing costly repairs and making products reliable in the aviation sector. Such improvement in operational efficiency brings compliance with strict regulatory standards for aerospace manufacturing. In the automotive industry, Tesla's Gigafactory is one of the outstanding examples of the smooth inclusion of IIoT into production processes. With smart programming, Tesla maximizes energy efficiency, inventory control, and manufacturing processes. Tesla can thereby enhance the quality and performance of its electric vehicles and can respond promptly to market requirements by using IoT-enabled devices and advanced analytics.

Key Insights

1. Smarter factories use IoT and smart programming which helps in collecting data to be analyzed in real-time; they enable quick decision making with subsequent process adjustments. Sensor data with historical patterns predicts when failures will occur in the equipment, thus reducing down times and minimizing maintenance costs. Systems like Siemens and Johnson Controls implement such systems that will ensure smooth running lines of production and cost-minimization.
2. Smarts or manufacturing plants use IIoT in a big way as means to energise the processes that help ensure optimized resource use and carbon footprints reduction. Companies, such as Nestle have adopted IIoT solutions for optimizing energy usage by their manufacturing plants. This interoperability and scalability in IIoT are mainly benefits because of the seamless and convenient operation from devices made by different companies providing scalability and adaptive manufacturing ecosystems in various smart factory applications. Smart factories primarily benefit from such interoperability in

IIoT. Despite the many advantages, issues such as cybersecurity threats, interoperability problems, and workforce adaptation are still prevalent. Companies are working on strong security protocols, standardization of communication protocols, and continuous training to overcome these issues.

In a nutshell, the smart factory and its implementation with IIoT are remodelling industries by promising more productivity, cost effectiveness, and more customized products. In the age of intelligent programming and smart solutions, organizations have found an edge over competitors and are preparing the ground for a more connected, efficient, and sustainable future.

SUSTAINABILITY TRENDS

As industries keep evolving, the integration of sustainable practices with advanced automation technologies becomes increasingly important. Green automation, AI-driven efficiency improvements, and Industrial IoT are changing the industrial operation scenario. These innovations aim at reducing the environmental impact, enhancing resource optimization, and achieving long-term sustainability. The following are some of the important aspects of sustainability and future trends in smart automation(Chander et al., 2022; Tyagi et al., 2020b, 2020a). The figure 5 presents five key sustainability trends and solutions in the realm of smart automation.

Figure 5. Sustainability trends in smart automation

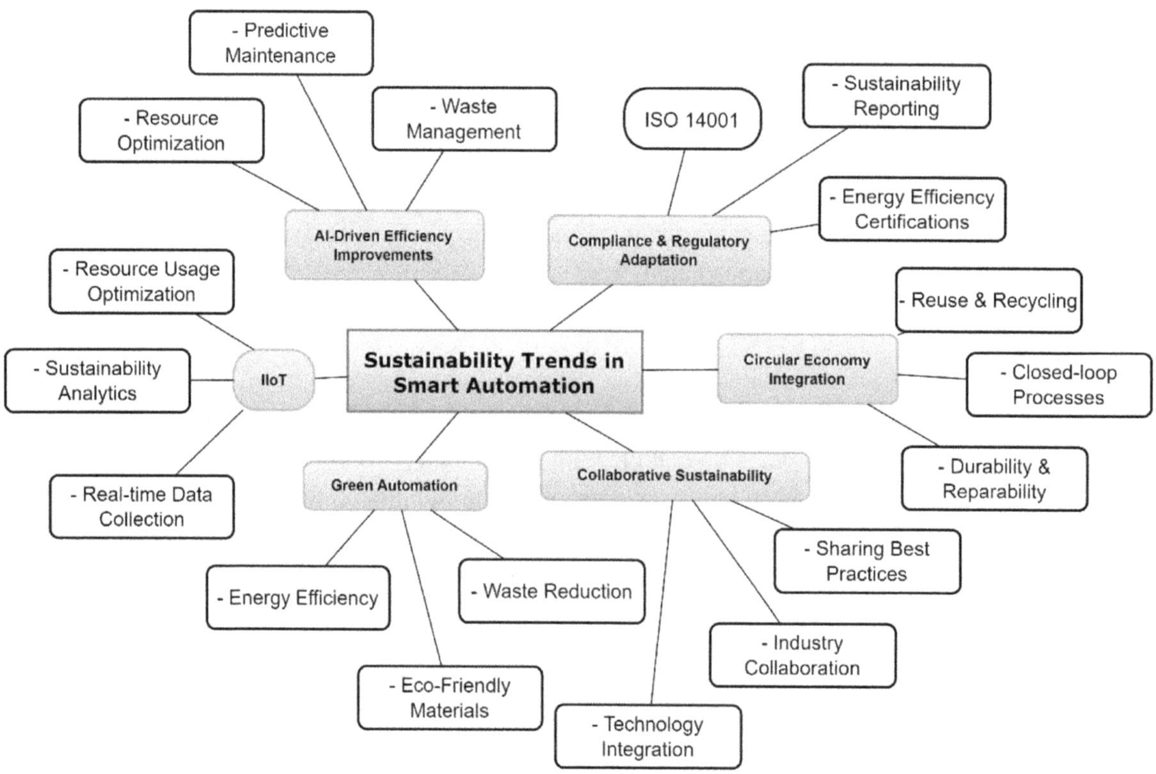

Green Automation Technologies

Green automation aims at the use of environmentally friendly technologies to optimize industrial processes while reducing waste, energy consumption, and carbon emissions. In this pursuit, industries strive to achieve sustainability goals, and green automation presents a crucial solution. Sustainable resources, energy-efficient devices, and smart programming are the core elements in the creation of more environmentally responsible manufacturing systems.

The technologies that feature in green automation include energy harvesting sensors, low power IoT devices, and integration of renewable energy. Bosch has a smart manufacturing facility, which includes green technologies, such as energy harvesting sensors, as well as solar powered equipment, to reduce its carbon footprint. General Electric also has IIoT systems monitoring and optimizing energy consumption throughout its operations, for more sustainable industrial production.

Additionally, AI-driven predictive analytics can contribute to significant sustainability. It does this by examining large datasets of IIoT devices with smart programming to identify patterns that cause inefficiencies and excessive use of resources. Manufacturers can then implement changes, for example, turning off machines during off-peak hours or improving the manufacturing process to minimize waste material.

AI-Driven Efficiency Improvements

Artificial Intelligence is playing a crucial role in the efficiency improvements of industrial automation. With machine learning models and predictive analytics, AI allows smarter decision-making, process optimization, and resource allocation. Real-time data, which AI algorithms analyze through IoT devices, provides business insights that reduce operational inefficiencies while fostering sustainability. For instance, in predictive maintenance systems by AI, it predicts failure time of equipment and the possible schedule for repair, therefore no unnecessary downtime and minimum wastes. It has worked excellently in the automotive industry where AI-powered systems for maintenance help companies keep resources managed while having minimum environmental impacts from such operations. Also, AI can optimize supply chain logistics and reduce excess inventory, so manufacturing operations become lean and sustainable. It can be made possible through the smart programming of AI and is the most holistic way towards sustainability-synthesis of operational efficiency with ecological responsibility(Dubey et al., 2021a; Tzafestas, 2018b).

Sustainability and emerging trends in smart automation represent a synergy of technology as well as ecological responsibility. The green automation technologies, artificial intelligence-driven efficiency improvements, and other IIoT advancements are working toward a greener future for industries. Through such innovations, not only does operational performance get optimised but the way to further industrialization as an ecology-friendly industrial world is achieved.

FUTURE OF INDUSTRIAL AUTOMATION

The future of industrial automation is increasingly being coupled with Artificial Intelligence (AI) and Internet of Things (IoT) technologies. With its advancement, smart programming laced with AI and IoT promises to revolutionize the way manufacturing and industrial processes will be conducted in the future(Bhambri & Rani, 2024; Islam, 2024a; Yadav et al., 2024). It is a development that will lead to more efficient, sustainable, and adaptable systems matching the fluid nature of today's industry. Some of the critical areas the development of industrial automation is going into are listed below.

Improving Decisions with AI-Based Insights

The most significant advancement through the use of AI-based insights in industrial automation is related to improved decision-making. The smart programming uses algorithms of AI to interpret humongous amounts of data, which are collected from the IoT comprising sensors, machines, and production systems. With such insight, predictive analytics enables the business to predict probable equipment failures, process inefficiencies, and supply chain disruption. It will further expand its capability to advanced machine learning models that will refine accuracy with every changing pattern in data. It will then result in the creation of autonomous and semi-autonomous systems that will learn, adapt, and optimize the process without human intervention. As such, there will be a continued improvement in productivity and resource management.

Edge Computing and Localized Processing

Consequently, reliance on edge computing increases as convergence of AI and IoT grows. Edge computing facilitates the processing of data nearer to the source or near the device and near devices instead of relying only on cloud-based solutions. It reduces latency and hence improves real-time processing, which is quite vital for most applications, for example, industrial automation in terms of real-time monitoring and control. The future smart programming will be merged with advanced edge computing solutions that would allow processing data at the source, faster and more reliable since the IoT devices will be placed in remote locations or areas where real-time responsiveness is essential for automation systems. Future developments will be based upon the scalability and modularity of industrial automation systems. Smart programming, combined with AI and IoT, will allow manufacturers to build flexible automation solutions that expand or adapt seamlessly to accommodate their changing production demands. Modular systems will make it simple to integrate new devices and systems and also ensure compatibility across different industrial processes. Moreover, standards and interoperability frameworks for APIs would be created so that heterogeneous systems interoperate smoothly without difficulty. It will enable the adoption of smart devices in such a manner that work efficiently at every point in production environment.

Sustainable Best Practices in Automation

Sustainability will be the key theme of industrial automation in the future. With AI and IoT, they would play an essential role in helping to optimize energy management, resource consumption, and reduction of waste. For intelligent programming, energy consumption, material usage, and emission rates would also be included in environmental parameters to enable production processes defined as greener. Through predictive analytics, these systems will enable industries to adopt circular economy practices in that the material will be reused or recycled. Moreover, the insights of AI will facilitate real-time energy optimization that will allow businesses to cut operational costs while meeting the highest sustainability requirements.

Workforce Integration and Training

As industrial automation technology advances, it will tend to focus on the training and adoption of smart programming in the workforce. There will be an emphasis on enhancing productivity and making better decision-making through AI-powered tool knowledge and IoT devices through employee training and adoption in future development. Companies will need to implement continuous learning that allows staff to adapt as automation systems grow more advanced. Complexity will be reduced and made easier to use as AI-based user interfaces and automation platforms increase accessibility of the smart system to various categories of users, and industries will be equipped to perform with higher efficiencies and effectiveness.

Security and Privacy Considerations

The future of industrial automation will face highly intricate cybersecurity problems. As a result of the increasing number of interconnected smart devices and IoT networks, data security and privacy will be the most sensitive areas. Smart programming is evolved with robust encryption, safe data transfer protocols, real-time threat detection mechanisms, to safeguard all the sensitive information. In short, smart programming in AI and IoT future industrial automation will rely on intelligent, sustainable, and adaptive systems as a future goal. It has the prospect of revolutionizing the operations of future businesses by maximizing efficiency, minimizing environmental impacts, and responding to the changed demand of industry today.

CONCLUSION AND STRATEGIC RECOMMENDATIONS

Smart programming, thus bringing together Artificial Intelligence with Internet of Things, represents an emerging paradigm in industrial automation-efficiency, adaptability, and innovation. This chapter has been an elaborate journey on how the cutting-edge technologies of machine learning, predictive analytics, and edge computing allow for decisions, predictive maintenance, and perfect, seamless communication between those things that are connected, such as reducing operational downtimes, improving productivity, and supporting cost-effective practice.

The applied uses shown above-the real-time monitoring and even adaptive control systems, show tremendous potential of AI and IoT in making the most complex processes in the industry automatically self-sufficient. Case studies as presented here only reinforce this measurable aspect by asset usage and energy management besides hard dollar cost savings. But then it is those critical challenges about cybersecurity threats, scalability and workforce skills gaps that call for strategic answers. Organizations need to focus on strong security protocols, scalable architectures, and training programs to fully leverage the power of these technologies.

Looking ahead, sustainability will become a prime focus area with AI-driven solutions opening the pathways for energy-efficient and environmentally friendly industrial practices. Future industrial IoT will be more intelligent, connected ecosystems that can autonomously optimize operations. The chapter concludes by emphasizing the strategic importance of embracing AI and IoT-driven automation in the quest for competitive advantage and long-term success. Industries can apply these technologies to not only improve their operational efficiency but also help advance the broader goals of sustainability and innovation sin the emerging global industrial landscape.

REFERENCES

Babayigit, B., & Abubaker, M. (2023). Industrial internet of things: A review of improvements over traditional scada systems for industrial automation. *IEEE Systems Journal*, *18*(1), 120–133. DOI: 10.1109/JSYST.2023.3270620

Bhambri, P., & Rani, S. (2024). Challenges, opportunities, and the future of industrial engineering with IoT and AI. *Integration of AI-Based Manufacturing and Industrial Engineering Systems with the Internet of Things*, 1–18.

Chander, B., Pal, S., De, D., & Buyya, R. (2022). Artificial intelligence-based internet of things for industry 5.0. *Artificial Intelligence-Based Internet of Things Systems*, 3–45.

Chi, H. R., Wu, C. K., Huang, N.-F., Tsang, K.-F., & Radwan, A. (2022). A survey of network automation for industrial internet-of-things toward industry 5.0. *IEEE Transactions on Industrial Informatics*, *19*(2), 2065–2077. DOI: 10.1109/TII.2022.3215231

Dey, C., & Sen, S. K. (2020). *Industrial automation technologies*. CRC Press. DOI: 10.1201/9780429299346

Dubey, A. K., Kumar, A., Kumar, S. R., Gayathri, N., & Das, P. (2021a). *AI and IoT-based intelligent automation in robotics*. John Wiley & Sons. DOI: 10.1002/9781119711230

Dubey, A. K., Kumar, A., Kumar, S. R., Gayathri, N., & Das, P. (2021b). *AI and IoT-based intelligent automation in robotics*. John Wiley & Sons. DOI: 10.1002/9781119711230

Islam, M. S. (2024a). AI and IoT in Automation and Security: A Vision for Next Generation Applications. *IUP Journal of Electrical and Electronics Engineering*, *17*(4), 7–32. DOI: 10.20944/preprints202408.0289.v1

Islam, M. S. (2024b). AI and IoT in Automation and Security: A Vision for Next Generation Applications. *IUP Journal of Electrical and Electronics Engineering*, *17*(4), 7–32. DOI: 10.20944/preprints202408.0289.v1

Jain, S., & Chandrasekaran, K. (2020). Industrial automation using internet of things. In *Security and privacy issues in sensor networks and IoT* (pp. 28–64). IGI Global Scientific Publishing. DOI: 10.4018/978-1-7998-0373-7.ch002

Kollu, P. K., Kumar, K., Kshirsagar, P. R., Islam, S., Naveed, Q. N., Hussain, M. R., & Sundramurthy, V. P. (2022a). Development of Advanced Artificial Intelligence and IoT Automation in the Crisis of COVID-19 Detection. *Journal of Healthcare Engineering*, *2022*(1), 1987917. DOI: 10.1155/2022/1987917 PMID: 35281536

Mamodiya, U., Sharma, P., & Sharma, P. (2014). Review in industrial automation. *IOSR Journal of Electrical and Electronics Engineering (IOSR-JEEE)*, *9*(3), 33–38.

Nirmala, P., Ramesh, S., Tamilselvi, M., Ramkumar, G., & Anitha, G. (2022). An artificial intelligence enabled smart industrial automation system based on internet of things assistance. *2022 International Conference on Advances in Computing, Communication and Applied Informatics (ACCAI)*, 1–6. DOI: 10.1109/ACCAI53970.2022.9752651

Nitzan. (1976). Programmable industrial automation. *IEEE Transactions on Computers, 100*(12), 1259–1270.

Pan, M., Su, W., & Wang, Y. (2021). Review of research on the curriculum for artificial intelligence and industrial automation based on edge computing. *2021 International Conference on Networking and Network Applications (NaNA)*, 222–226. DOI: 10.1109/NaNA53684.2021.00045

Pramanik, P. K. D., Pal, S., & Choudhury, P. (2018). Beyond automation: The cognitive IoT. artificial intelligence brings sense to the Internet of Things. *Cognitive Computing for Big Data Systems Over IoT: Frameworks, Tools and Applications*, 1–37.

Samad, T., & Kiliccote, S. (2012). Smart grid technologies and applications for the industrial sector. *Computers & Chemical Engineering*, *47*, 76–84. DOI: 10.1016/j.compchemeng.2012.07.006

Sarker, I. H. (2022). AI-based modeling: Techniques, applications and research issues towards automation, intelligent and smart systems. *SN Computer Science*, *3*(2), 158. DOI: 10.1007/s42979-022-01043-x PMID: 35194580

Su, W., Xu, G., He, Z., Machica, I. K., Quimno, V., Du, Y., & Kong, Y. (2023). Cloud-edge computing-based ICICOS framework for industrial automation and artificial intelligence: A survey. *Journal of Circuits, Systems, and Computers*, *32*(10), 2350168. DOI: 10.1142/S0218126623501682

Tommila, T., Ventä, O., & Koskinen, K. (2001). Next generation industrial automation–needs and opportunities. *Automation Technology Review*, *2001*, 34–41.

Tyagi, A. K., Fernandez, T. F., Mishra, S., & Kumari, S. (2020). Intelligent automation systems at the core of industry 4.0. *International Conference on Intelligent Systems Design and Applications*, 1–18.

Tzafestas, S. G. (2018). Synergy of IoT and AI in modern society: The robotics and automation case. *Robot. Autom. Eng. J*, *31*(5), 1–15. DOI: 10.19080/RAEJ.2018.03.555621

Yadav, N., Gupta, V., & Garg, A. (2024). Industrial Automation Through AI-Powered Intelligent Machines—Enabling Real-Time Decision-Making. In *Recent Trends in Artificial Intelligence Towards a Smart World: Applications in Industries and Sectors* (pp. 145–178). Springer.

Chapter 11
Practical Application of Quantum-Enhanced Machine Learning:
Prediction of Atomic Mass and Properties

S. Deepajothi
Department of Computing Technologies, SRM Institute of Science and Technology, Chennai, India

U. V. Anbazhagu
https://orcid.org/0000-0003-2310-530X
Department of Computing Technologies, SRM Institute of Science and Technology, Chennai, India

K. Priyadharshini
https://orcid.org/0009-0008-1426-7503
Department of Computing Technologies, SRM Institute of Science and Technology, Chennai, India

Sibi Amaran
Department of Computing Technologies, SRM Institute of Science and Technology, Chennai, India

G. Kalanandhini
Department of Electronics and Communication Engineering, Prince Shri Venkateshwara Padmavathy Engineering College, Chennai, India

S. Boopathi
https://orcid.org/0009-0008-5822-1056
Mechanical Engineering, Muthayammal Engineering College, Namakkal, India

ABSTRACT

This chapter discusses the application of techniques from quantum machine learning at unprecedented levels of accuracy that are used in predicting atomic mass and properties. These would mean it will explain advanced machine algorithms, tailored specifically for systems involving quantum, which lend deeper knowledge and better understanding of atomic nature such as electronic structure and chemical bonding. The integration of QML techniques results in a process of which it will be efficient to process large datasets of quantum, implying that meaningful insights may come out of complex quantum phenomena. Some focal areas are, for example, neural networks and their utilization in quantum support vector machines and generative models that can predict atomic properties. The chapter explores the practical applications of Quantum Machine Learning in scientific research, highlighting the transformative potential of AI in advancing quantum science.

DOI: 10.4018/979-8-3693-8407-7.ch011

INTRODUCTION

The rapid development of artificial intelligence and quantum computing opened up new frontiers for scientific research. One of the most promising intersections is Quantum Machine Learning (QML), an application of machine learning methodologies to quantum systems that is expected to enhance our ability to understand and predict the behavior of complex phenomena. It specifically refers to the fact that AI-driven quantum techniques are quite important for predicting atomic properties, like atomic mass, electronic structures, and chemical bonding. The next generation of these advancements has the potential to revolutionize fields like computational chemistry, materials science, and molecular biology to gain a deeper understanding of atomic behaviors and develop new materials with specific properties(Faber, 2019).

These are primarily based on the classical approach known classically to calculate atomic mass and properties, effective as these approaches have proven to be limited in precision and scope especially for big, complex data sets. Quantum systems, of course, have added even further to their own complexities by having high-dimensional features and requiring computational techniques suited to the goal of accuracy in describing quantum phenomena. This is where quantum machine learning steps in-to access quantum-enhanced algorithms for processing and analyzing the quantum data in ways previously impossible. With AI coupled with quantum computing, scientists are now able to predict atomic properties more accurately than ever before(Pinheiro et al., 2020a).

This strength at the core of quantum machine learning is to process and deal with data at quantum levels, comprising patterns that are complexly intertwined, very hard to decipher, or read by other forms of classical methods. It's exponentially larger in capacity since, through quantum states, they can represent the information contained in them in computers; hence, by these properties in machine learning models, they identify hidden structures and forecast outcomes and simulations for a quantum system. Some other examples of new quantum algorithms are quantum neural networks. They have developed this hybrid with the help of quantum circuits to enhance the learning properties and provide knowledge about the atomic structure(Sajjan et al., 2022).

QML possesses predicting attributes with the incorporation of numerous algorithms like Quantum Support Vector Machines (QSVM), Quantum Generative Adversarial Networks (QGAN), and Variational Quantum Circuits (VQC) among others. The technique allows for the processing of dense quantum datasets and large-scale high-dimensional predictions. The present work, thus has avenues for discovery into the atom-atom interaction properties as well as material behavior. This has proved useful in drug discovery, material design, and environmental science, where it is imperative to manipulate the atomic and molecular properties in an extremely precise manner(Naseri et al., 2023a).

In predicting atomic mass, QML provides a notable advantage that decreases the overheads computationally with increased accuracy. Conventional approaches have to waste much more computational resources for simulating atomic systems. This happens exponentially with greater complexity of the system. Quantum machine learning algorithms make use of quantum parallelism, which means faster computation and less time required to simulate. This will be able to predict atomic properties with higher accuracy and provide access to new chemical space that was inaccessible earlier, due to the computational limitation(Huang et al., 2020).

The application of QML in the prediction of atomic properties has addressed key challenges in terms of the demand for robust models that will generalize well over different quantum systems. Quantum data-trained models inherently suffer from noise and errors arising due to the quantum measurements themselves, as any quantum measurement inherently introduces it(Faber et al., 2018). Quantum error correction techniques and hybrid quantum-classical approaches are used to make the model more reliable for the accurate prediction of atomic masses and other properties. This opens new avenues in the prediction of atomic properties while increasing accuracy. Applications will grow to address increasingly complex problems in computational physics, chemistry, and more. Researchers continue to develop new methodologies combining quantum principles with machine learning, which leads to innovation in areas such as material science, nanotechnology, and advanced computing systems(Vedavyasa & Kumar, 2024).

Hence, quantum machine learning is the future for the understanding and prediction of atomic properties. Scientists working through the harnessing of might through quantum computing and cutting-edge techniques of machine learning are well-set to make headway into the accurate prediction of atomic masses or any similar related properties. This chapter discusses how these developments are shaping the future of quantum-based scientific research, highlighting the potential of AI-driven quantum methodologies to unlock new insights into the microscopic world of atoms and molecules(Christensen et al., 2020).

Objectives

The main purpose of the chapter is to explore the possibilities of applying Quantum Machine Learning for predicting atomic mass and properties, providing a comprehensive understanding on how QML exploits quantum computing in cooperation with machine learning techniques that handle complex, high-dimensional data from atomic systems. The chapter also aims to depict the opportunities and challenges associated with QML, with prospects for solving complex quantum problems. The chapter will be explored in detail to contribute to advancing scientific research and practical applications of quantum computing and machine learning.

BACKGROUND: QUANTUM COMPUTING

Quantum Computing: Quantum computing is a region of computing that utilizes principles of quantum mechanics to undertake computations at a scale far beyond that possible with or envisioned by any classical computer. In contrast to classical computers, where information is processed using bits (0s and 1s), quantum computers use quantum bits or qubits, which can represent 0 and 1 in the same state, known as superposition. This property makes quantum computers capable of parallel computation, solving very complex problems in a small fraction of the time needed by a classical system. Quantum mechanics is that branch of physics that deals with the behavior of matter and energy at extremely small scales, like subatomic particles: electrons, photons, and atoms(Karandashev & von Lilienfeld, 2022; Sajjan et al., 2021). It is completely different from classical physics since it deals with continuous variables and definite outcomes. Quantum mechanics, however, introduces probabilistic phenomena and the concept of wave-particle duality. This means that a particle can behave as a wave or a particle depending on how it is measured.

a) Superposition: An idea that qubits are capable of representing more than one state simultaneously, including any combination of 0 and 1. That enables quantum computers to calculate lots of things simultaneously.
b) Entanglement: When qubits are entangled, this interdependence leads to changes in the state of one affecting another, regardless of their location in relation to one another.

c) Quantum Tunneling: It is a phenomenon through which particles can pass over potential barriers, which are impossible for classical particles to penetrate. The effect is crucial for quantum computation in solving difficult optimization problems.Quantum States and Operations

Quantum operations are reversible. That means the inverse of a quantum operation can be applied to return to the starting state. Reversibility is crucial in quantum computation, as the qubits tend to decohere easily because of their interaction with the environment. These include quantum states, operations, and gates together as the basis for quantum algorithms designed to exploit quantum mechanics to solve problems in efficient ways(Faber et al., 2020). Quantum computing will most likely revolutionize such diverse areas as cryptography, optimization, drug discovery, and even artificial intelligence, to be pushed beyond the computationally possible.

QUANTUM MACHINE LEARNING TECHNIQUES IN ATOMIC MASS PREDICTION

Quantum machine learning, QML, has been exciting in addressing some of the most challenging scientific problems, among them the prediction of atomic mass and related properties. This allows researchers to include quantum computing and machine learning methodologies when addressing problems that cannot be treated classically by a system, especially those relating to the intricate quantum behavior of atomic systems(Christensen et al., 2020; García-Ramos et al., 2024; Heinen et al., 2020a). The prominent methods used include neural networks, quantum support vector machines, or QSVM, and generative models in developing QML frameworks that have been applied to predict atomic mass. The process of Quantum Machine Learning (QML) in predicting atomic mass is depicted in Figure 1.

Figure 1. Process of quantum machine learning (QML) in atomic mass prediction

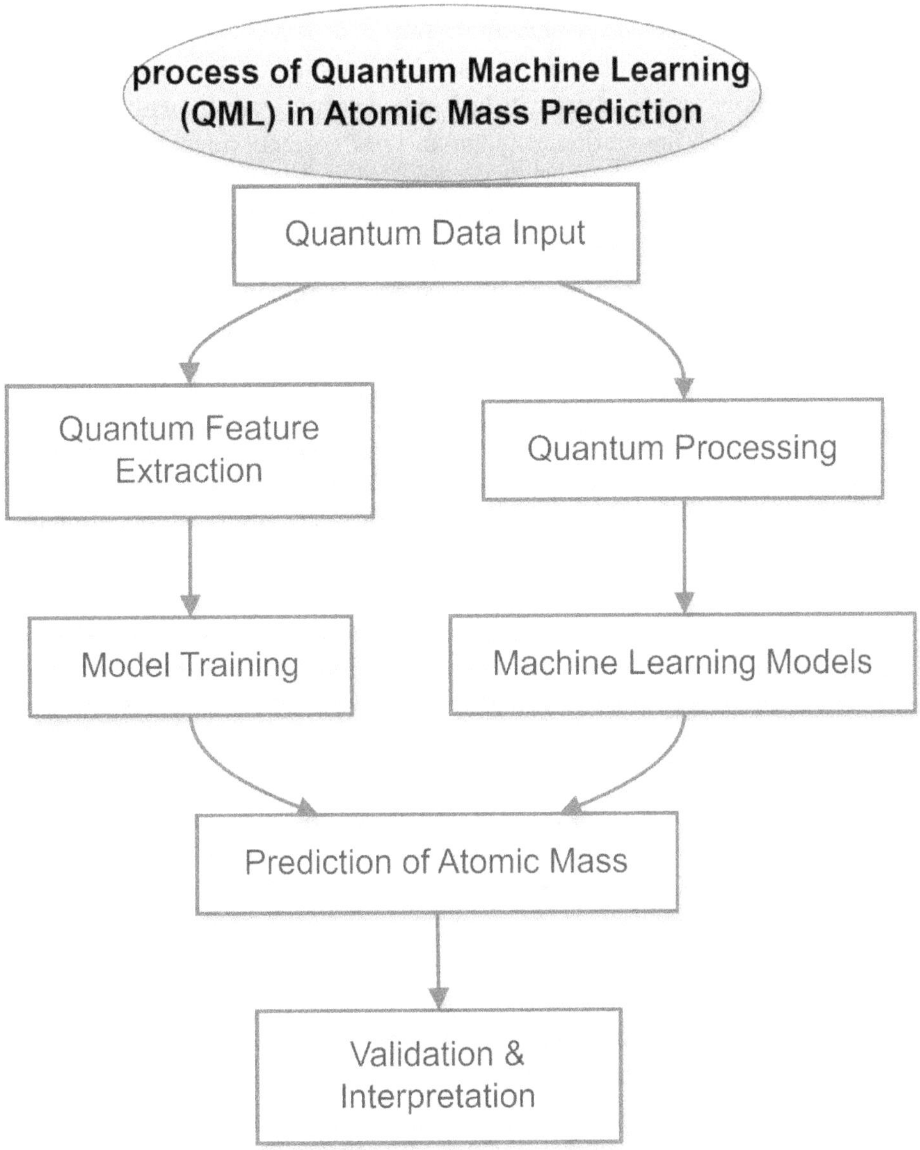

Neural Networks in Quantum Computing

In this sense, neural networks are an important building block of the classical world of machine learning; they found a natural extension in quantum computing through quantum neural networks or QNNs. In the context of QML, quantum neural networks use quantum circuits to process information. Circuits work essentially like the classical neural networks but operate on qubits instead of classical bits(Guan et al., 2021; Zhou et al., 2023a). QNNs have the key benefit of being able to work on high-dimensional quantum data by exploiting quantum parallelism in order to enhance processing efficiency. In atomic mass prediction, QNNs model the relation between atomic structures and their corresponding masses by capturing complex correlations between quantum states. The layers of quantum gates and operations are what extract the features that the quantum dataset needs to make accurate predictions about atomic properties. Furthermore, noisy quantum data can be handled very effectively with these networks as they are robust and reliable through integration of quantum error correction techniques(Devi et al., 2024). QNNs usually contain quantum circuits composed of parameterized gates where the trainable parameters change the quantum state in such a way that minimizes the errors in predictions. This means that the neural network learns adaptively what features of the quantum world are significant to atomic mass, and therefore, it makes this tool very versatile for high-precision scientific simulations.

Quantum Support Vector Machines

Another strong method that has also been utilized in QML, to predict atomic mass is QSVM. This is the counterpart of support vector machines with a quantum version. Traditional support vector machines are highly used in classical machine learning, particularly in applications whose problems fall into the classes of classification and regression. This method has extended the concept because it integrates quantum kernels capable of processing efficiently in a very high-dimensional quantum feature space. In atomic mass prediction, QSVMs use quantum kernels to efficiently handle complex quantum data and improve the accuracy of predictions. QSVMs map quantum data into a higher-dimensional Hilbert space to uncover intricate patterns and relationships between atomic structures and their properties. These machines operate by finding optimal hyperplanes that best separate different atomic states based on their mass-related properties, allowing for precise classification or regression tasks(Huang & Von Lilienfeld, 2021; Vedavyasa & Kumar, 2024).

The strength of QSVM is that it scales well with the size and complexity of the quantum data. Furthermore, QSVMs are noise robust. The errors are very common in quantum systems; therefore, noise robustness is a major factor. Quantum operations, such as rotations and measurements, also play a big role in the construction of quantum kernels to ensure the model for machine learning maintains high accuracy even with imperfect quantum data. Generative models are also widely used in quantum machine learning, such as the generation of quantum data and simulations for atomic mass prediction. For example, there is the QGANs, which combines the generative models with the adversarial networks in developing quantum systems with controlled properties.

Atomic Mass Prediction QGANs This means that QGANs are used to generate synthetic quantum data that represents realistic behavior of the atomic system. It produces artificial quantum states that correspond to atomic configurations and through these synthetic quantum states, scientists may predict the atomic mass in high precision. This will be a process of adversarial training that includes a discriminator that monitors the realism of the produced quantum state and a generator that repeatedly refines its output till it achieves highly faithful quantum data. QGANs facilitate the scientists to explore hitherto unknown atomic states, thus discovering new materials with favorable atomic properties. Besides this, the feasibility of other atomic configurations using QGANs can facilitate innovation in drug discovery and materials engineering as well as in molecular simulations.

Implementation and Challenges

It makes possible more holistic approaches towards atomic mass prediction through this integration of quantum machine learning techniques—the neural networks, QSVM, and generative models. These complement each other in the processing of the handling of the quantum data, providing features as facets and recognition toward simulation and generation capabilities(Faber et al., 2018; Huang & Von Lilienfeld, 2021). On the other hand, QML application within atomic mass prediction poses some level of challenge. The dominant problem in applying QML in atomic mass prediction will be managing noise and inherent error within the quantum system because quantum states decohere. The computing of quantum data must ensure to include decoherence. Besides, it is cumbersome to train and execute massive quantum models computationally within large datasets due to progressions needed within quantum hardware and optimization techniques.

Despite these challenges, quantum machine learning advances continue to open new avenues in scientific discovery and technological innovation. The iteration of refinements to quantum algorithms as well as more efficient design of quantum circuits moves them toward more accurate and scalable solutions for atomic mass prediction, which might be transformative in a range of applications for both the scientific and industrial sectors.

APPLICATION OF QML IN ATOMIC MASS PREDICTION

This is where the Quantum Machine Learning, or QML, application is very well recognized in predicting atomic masses due to its high ability in dealing with complex quantum data. Integrate quantum computing with the techniques of machine learning and get a solution to deal with issues associated with the high-dimensionality and noise as well as the complexity inherently associated with the atomic system. This chapter looks into the key steps involved in the QML for the prediction of atomic masses: Data Collection and Preparation and Model Development and Training(Sun, 2025; Zhou et al., 2023b). The application of Quantum Machine Learning (QML) in predicting atomic mass is depicted in Figure 2.

Figure 2. Application of quantum machine learning (QML) in atomic mass prediction

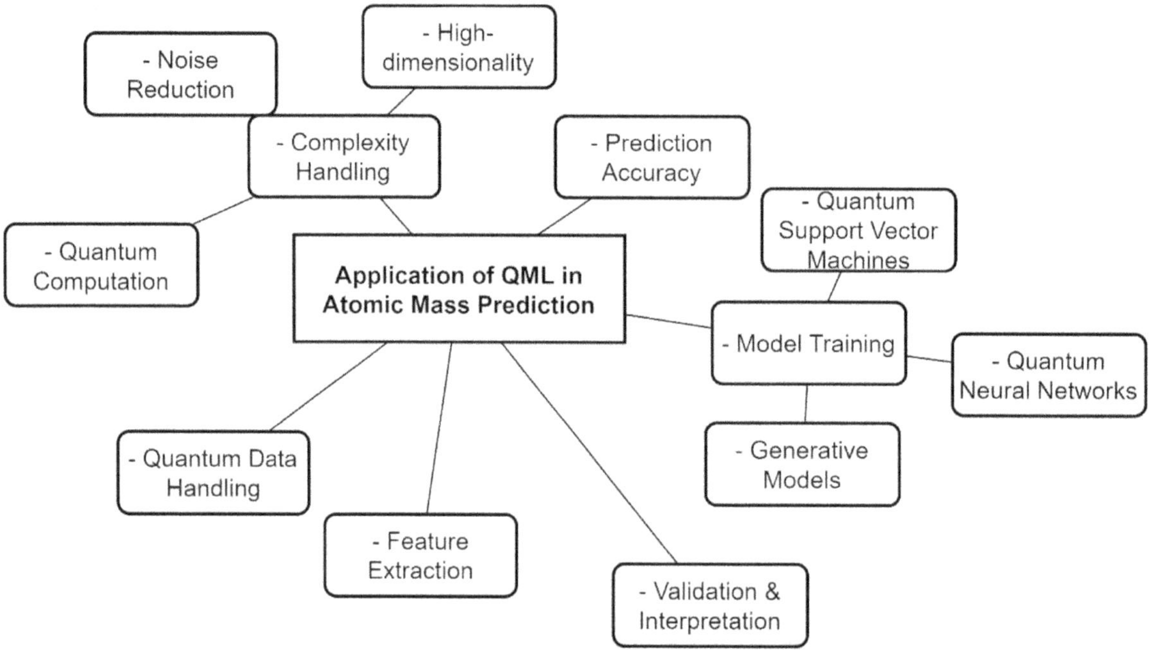

Data Collection and Preparation

The first step to be taken when applying QML for predicting atomic mass is the preparation and collection of data. Data sources in quantum systems can come from theoretical simulations, experimental measurements, or computational simulations(Dhanya et al., 2023; Rahamathunnisa et al., 2023).

Quantum Data Sources:

a) Theoretical Simulations: Usually performed with quantum chemistry methods like Density Functional Theory (DFT), Quantum Monte Carlo (QMC), and coupled-cluster approaches. These generate quantum states, electronic configurations, and molecular structures for different atomic and molecular systems.
b) Experimental Measurements: Experimental data in the form of spectroscopy, atomic scattering, or other quantum observables are required for the validation of predictions and accuracy in atomic mass estimation.
c) Computational Simulations: Quantum simulations provide datasets rich with quantum properties like orbital energies, electronic structures, and transition states, which are fed into machine learning models.

Data Preparation

Quantum data is often noisy, contains missing values, and inconsistencies. The process of preparing this data includes the following steps:

a) Data Cleaning: Removing errors, inconsistencies, and duplicate entries in quantum data.
b) Feature Engineering: Transformation of raw quantum data into meaningful features that reflect properties of the atoms relevant for mass prediction. This would include techniques such as extraction of molecular descriptors, interaction energies, and atomic charges.
c) Data Normalization and Scaling: Quantum systems have varying scales, including energies and distances. To ensure that the values used for training quantum machine learning models are uniform, data normalization becomes essential.

Dimensionality Reduction

Because quantum systems are intrinsically complex, quantum data of high dimensions is reduced using methods such as PCA or QPCA, for example. The thinking is to identify the most influential features that drive atomic mass and reduce the complexity of the training model.

Quantum Feature Engineering

It uses the encoding of quantum information into vectors that are classical, where the machine learning algorithm will then work. Techniques in encoding qubit states are amplitude encoding and binary encoding through the use of classical bits to bridge between quantum and classical machine learning.

Model Development and Training

Once the quantum data is collected and prepared, the next step is to develop and train QML models for atomic mass prediction. This stage includes designing quantum circuits, training quantum models, and fine-tuning the parameters to optimize prediction accuracy.

Quantum Neural Networks (QNNs): Quantum neural networks are used to model complex relationships between atomic properties and atomic mass. To achieve this, quantum neural networks start by designing a circuit that simulates the physics behind atomic systems. Quantum circuits encode quantum information within high-dimensional space, such that machine learning models perform regression tasks related to atomic mass.

a) ***Architecture:*** Quantum neural networks are built out of layers of quantum gates, parameterized circuits, and measurements. The operations within the layers, such as rotations, entanglement, and state manipulations, together lead to the prediction of atomic mass.
b) ***Training:*** Parameters of the quantum circuits (like angles of rotation gates in quantum circuits) are optimized using classical optimizers, such as gradient descent during training. Quantum backpropagation techniques are applied to calculate gradients, thereby enabling the model to modify its parameters.

QSVM, or Quantum Support Vector Machines

QSVMs are different from the traditional approach of model development because they transform quantum data into a higher-dimensional feature space using quantum kernels. The goal is to find an optimal hyperplane that separates different atomic states based on mass-related properties.

a) Kernel Design: Quantum Kernels, which are based on quantum operations like Pauli matrices and Hadamard gates, help in capturing complex patterns in quantum datasets. Such kernels are used to map atomic features into a space where classical SVMs can perform better.
b) Training: The QSVM model was trained with semi-definite programming techniques like SDP that maximizes the accuracy of predictions by finding the best possible hyperplane and balance the bias-variance tradeoff for atomic masses.

   Generative Models for Quantum Systems: One of the main roles that generative models like Quantum Generative Adversarial Networks (QGANs) play in atomic mass prediction involves the generation of realistic atomic structures and simulation of many quantum scenarios. The architecture of QGAN is basically two key components. These are the generator and discriminator, responsible for generating quantum states and judging the authenticity of synthetic data, respectively. When the training is done, the generator keeps improving as the discriminator's ability to differentiate between real and synthetic quantum data is minimized over time(Huang et al., 2020).

   Use in Atomic Mass Prediction: These models produce different sets of quantum states. This provides the opportunity for researchers to study new atomic configurations and predict atomic masses for unseen or complex atomic systems.

   Model Evaluation and Optimization: Finally, quantum models' performance is evaluated with respect to Mean Absolute Error (MAE), Root Mean Square Error (RMSE), and accuracy scores at the last phase of model development. The hyperparameter tuning technique for hyperparameter optimization, where either the depth of a quantum circuit or gate parameters can be adjusted, further improves the generalization capabilities and accuracy of models.

The application of quantum machine learning technique integrates unique quantum computing features, the latest state-of-art machine learning to make robust predictions on atomic masses. Techniques of QML, namely neural networks, support vector machines, and generative models allow for careful collection, preparation, and development of models when trying to sort out the intricacy of quantum systems that will be able to give precision accuracy predictions. The noise error, lack of scalability, limited hardware and further research into the quantum algorithms would, nevertheless continue to advance the field and make the scientific breakthrough for industrial applications.

EXPLORING ATOMIC PROPERTIES USING QML

Quantum Machine Learning is one of the promising ways that can be used to find atomic properties by utilizing quantum computing's ability to process data in complex and high dimensions. Advanced machine learning techniques when integrated with quantum computing could give researchers deeper insights about atomic behaviors, energy levels, electronic structures, and even chemical bonding(Zhou et al., 2023b). The subsequent section discusses two very important aspects of atomic property research: Energy Levels and Electronic Structure and Chemical Bonding Analysis. The process of atomic properties using QML is depicted in Figure 3.

Figure 3. Process of atomic properties using QML

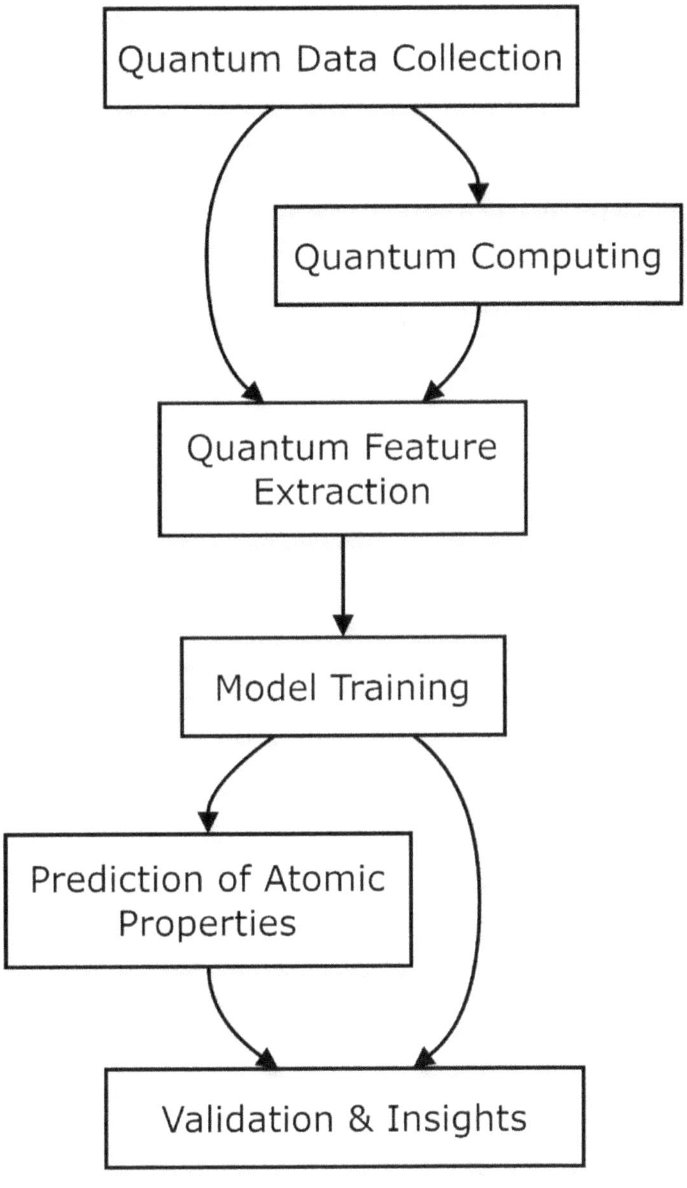

Energy Levels and Electronic Structure

Energy levels and electronic structures are the basic properties that control the behavior of atoms and molecules. QML techniques provide ways to model and predict quantum states with a detailed understanding of these properties(Sun, 2025).

Quantum Representation of Energy Levels: Quantum systems exhibit discrete energy levels, and quantum mechanical principles dictate that the electrons are in different orbitals or states. QML relies on quantum circuits and algorithms to simulate these energy levels with high accuracy. For example, QNNs can be used to map the relationship between electronic configurations and their corresponding energy levels. Once trained on quantum data, such networks can predict energy gaps, excitation energies, and ionization potentials with minimal error.

Quantum Feature Extraction in Electronic Structure: Electronic structures can be represented meaningfully by using quantum feature extraction techniques such as amplitude encoding and quantum state preparation. In these, qubits are used to encode information about the electron distributions, shapes of orbitals, and quantum correlations. Such representations will be required for understanding the interaction between electrons and the nucleus and also how they contribute to many atomic properties.

High-Dimensional Quantum States: The quantumness of data makes it possible to represent high-dimensional spaces when the classical approach is weak. Quantum algorithms are robust and can handle extreme complexity in electronic structures, thus paving the way for predicting those properties that are determined through intricate electron interactions. It is crucial for materials science, molecular simulations, and quantum chemistry, as energy levels play a significant role in these fields.

Quantum Simulations and Validation: Quantum computing allows the simulation of energy landscapes that cannot be feasibly explored by classical methods. Atomic property predictions are validated by comparison with experimental data and classical computational results, ensuring accuracy and reliability.

Chemical Bonding Analysis

Chemical bonding is one of the central aspects of atomic interactions, which affects reactivity, stability, and molecular structure. Quantum Machine Learning techniques offer a powerful framework for analyzing and predicting bonding properties using quantum-based models(Christensen et al., 2020; Faber et al., 2018, 2020).

Quantum Representation of Chemical Bonding: Chemical bonding is simply the interaction of electron clouds between atoms and leads to different kinds of bonds between atoms: covalent, ionic, metallic, and hydrogen. QML approaches concentrate on quantification of such interactions through circuits and generative models: QSVMs could differentiate bond types from each other or distinguish the quantum patterns that imply the existence of each type as useful tools in predicting a bond strength or bond lengths. Quantum computations calculate bond energies based on electron density maps and atomic interactions. Even generative adversarial networks, known as QGANs, generate realistic quantum states that represent many molecular configurations based on an understanding of how chemical bonds are made and broken. These capabilities are used in simulating reactions and predicting the energetic feasibility of chemical reactions at a quantum level.

Quantum Feature Engineering for Bonding Analysis: It has also appeared in quantum feature engineering as very basic in translating complex molecular structures into usable quantum data, which are translated using quantum encoding techniques of bond orders, valence electrons, and orbital overlap, gaining the researcher some insight on the properties of the bonds. Thus, these engineered features yield more accurate descriptions of atom interaction, making bonding analysis stronger in QML applications.

Predictive Power of Quantum Models: QML further boosts the predictive power of chemical bonding analysis, simulating the interactions at an atomic level, and their impact on the stability and molecular structure. In other words, this has proved critical for drug design, materials engineering, and synthesis.

IMPLEMENTATION PROCEDURE OF QML IN ATOMIC MASS PREDICTION

The steps for atomic mass prediction using QML are premised on the application of several steps, which consider applying quantum algorithms together with machine learning methods to analyze and predict atomic properties. Consequently, this brings together two features, namely, features that quantum computers have and features that classical machine learning methods . The procedure followed in using QML in atomic mass prediction is as follows(Zhou et al., 2023c). The flow-chart (Figure 4) depicts the implementation procedure of QML in Atomic Mass Prediction.

Figure 4. Flow-chart for implementation procedure of QML in atomic mass prediction

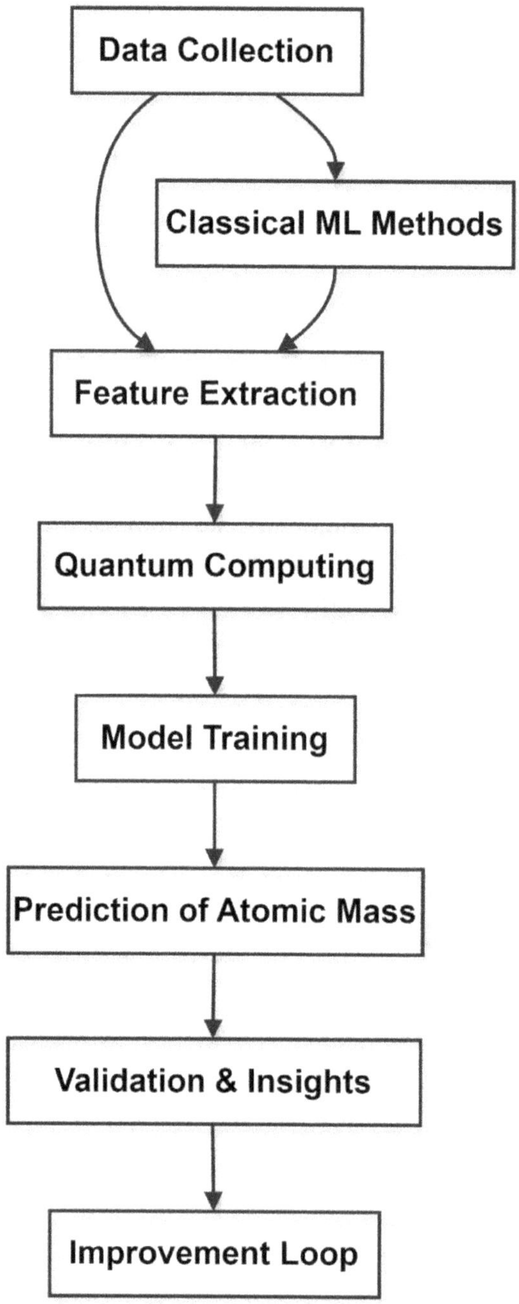

Data Collection and Preparation

The first step involved is the collection of quantum data that would be necessary in the implementation of QML in predicting atomic mass. Such sources may be derived from a theoretical simulation, experimental measurement, as well as computational chemistry models(Pinheiro et al., 2020b).

Sources of Quantum Data: Quantum mechanical simulations, such as DFT, QMC, or ab initio calculations, compute quantum states and electronic configurations to produce atomic properties. This can also be applied by experimenting data, which are primarily taken from spectroscopy or some form of quantum measurement for the verification of a prediction.

Pre-processing: The preparation involves all sorts of pre-processing as seen with feature extraction, reducing noises, and normalization processes on quantum data. These high-dimensional quantum states must therefore be encoded into any representations possible using amplitude, angle, or binary encodings to then become the representation, inputted into their machine learning models.

Quantum Feature Engineering

Feature engineering is an important part of QML implementation, especially when dealing with quantum data. This step involves extracting relevant features from quantum states to create inputs suitable for machine learning models(Heinen et al., 2020b).

Quantum Feature Extraction: Such interactions in quantum systems between the particles are highly complex; it is not very straightforward to directly model the same. These complex relationships can be easily grasped by machine learning models, where these quantum features help in understanding better relationships about atomic properties with respect to mass. For example, features might encode molecular orbitals, electron densities, or energy gaps for prediction. Quantum circuits convert quantum states into vectors that represent atomic properties. Quantum encoding, where qubits are used for discrete values, is a technique used to capture information about the structure and behavior of atoms and molecules. This allows complex quantum data to be represented more effectively.

Model Development Using Quantum Machine Learning Techniques

After quantum data preparation, the development and training of a quantum model for atomic mass prediction begins. This may include choosing the appropriate quantum algorithms and designing quantum circuits specifically for mass prediction tasks(Naseri et al., 2023b).

a) Quantum Neural Networks (QNNs): Quantum Neural Networks are used in modeling complex atomic interactions as the layers of quantum gates can mimic the quantum operations. QNNs can learn from the quantum data that predicts the atomic masses refining the input features based on the logic operations of entanglement and superposition.
b) Quantum Support Vector Machines: The application of quantum kernels in QSVM makes it possible to map the data in a high-dimensional quantum space where atomic properties are more likely to become linearly separable with respect to the desired classification and prediction of the right complex atomic masses.

c) Generative Models: QGANs applied to synthetic quantum states generation supports development of extended training datasets besides predictions of atomic masses for different systems. It helps the models create real quantum data, hence, enhancing their performance.

Training Quantum Models

Training quantum models is essentially the optimization of quantum circuits by means of classical techniques such as gradient descent or other optimization methods tailored to quantum operations. This optimizes model parameters to reduce prediction errors and maximize accuracy.

a) Quantum Backpropagation: Quantum backpropagation would require computing gradients of quantum circuits during training. It is applied to update the parameters of quantum gates in the circuit such that atomic masses are better predicted. Using quantum-specific gradient calculations, models converge quickly toward optimal solutions.
b) Hybrid Quantum-Classical Optimization: Hybrid approaches combine quantum and classical computations to enhance the accuracy and scalability of atomic mass predictions. This approach involves letting classical systems handle training data while complex computations are tackled by quantum circuits, minimizing errors from quantum noise and ensuring efficient learning.

Evaluation and Validation of Quantum Models

After training, the quantum models are evaluated in terms of predictive accuracy. This is done by comparing model predictions with experimental or theoretical benchmarks for reliability and performance assessment.

a) Performance Metrics: Such common performance metrics as Mean Absolute Error (MAE), Root Mean Square Error (RMSE), and scores of R^2 will be applied to evaluate whether quantum models are good atomic mass predictors. Such metric would provide some idea about whether the quantum model generalizes well to new data.
b) Testing and Cross-Validation: Quantum models are cross-validated to ensure that they are as robust as possible. This is especially the case if there is limited data available about quantum.

Scaling Quantum Models for Large Systems

One of the challenges in implementing QML for atomic mass prediction is the processing of large, complex quantum datasets. Scalability is an important aspect ensuring that quantum models can handle many interacting particles in a system.

a) Quantum Error Correction: To reduce quantum noise and error, error correction methods are included in the training process. This guarantees that models trained on noisy or incomplete quantum data make accurate predictions.

b) Distributed Quantum Computing: Distributed quantum computing frameworks can actually scale up quantum models such that multiple quantum processors work cooperatively to handle large data sets efficiently. This really improves the ability to deal with high-dimensional quantum information as well as the accuracy of the predictions for larger atomic systems.

Quantum Machine Learning involves a broad process of data collection to the development and evaluation of a model in predicting atomic mass. Researchers overcome the shortcomings of the classical approach through the use of quantum computing techniques, which include quantum neural networks, support vector machines, and generative models. Continual improvements in quantum hardware, error correction, and hybrid quantum-classical frameworks ensure that QML-based atomic mass prediction scales well with accuracy and efficiency, bringing new possibilities in quantum chemistry, material science, and molecular research.

CHALLENGES AND OPPORTUNITIES IN QML FOR QUANTUM SYSTEMS

Quantum Machine Learning or QML is the quickly developing field that focuses upon the specific properties of quantum computing to solve complex problems, but it has still suffered from various challenges that it requires to be addressed for implementing itself in quantum systems successfully. Among the critical challenges—computational complexity and accuracy besides interpretation of models—are of more value in developing QML(Huang & Von Lilienfeld, 2021; Sajjan et al., 2022; von Lilienfeld et al., 2020). Figure 5 presents the challenges and opportunities in Quantum Machine Learning (QML) for Quantum Systems.

Figure 5. Challenges and opportunities in QML for quantum systems

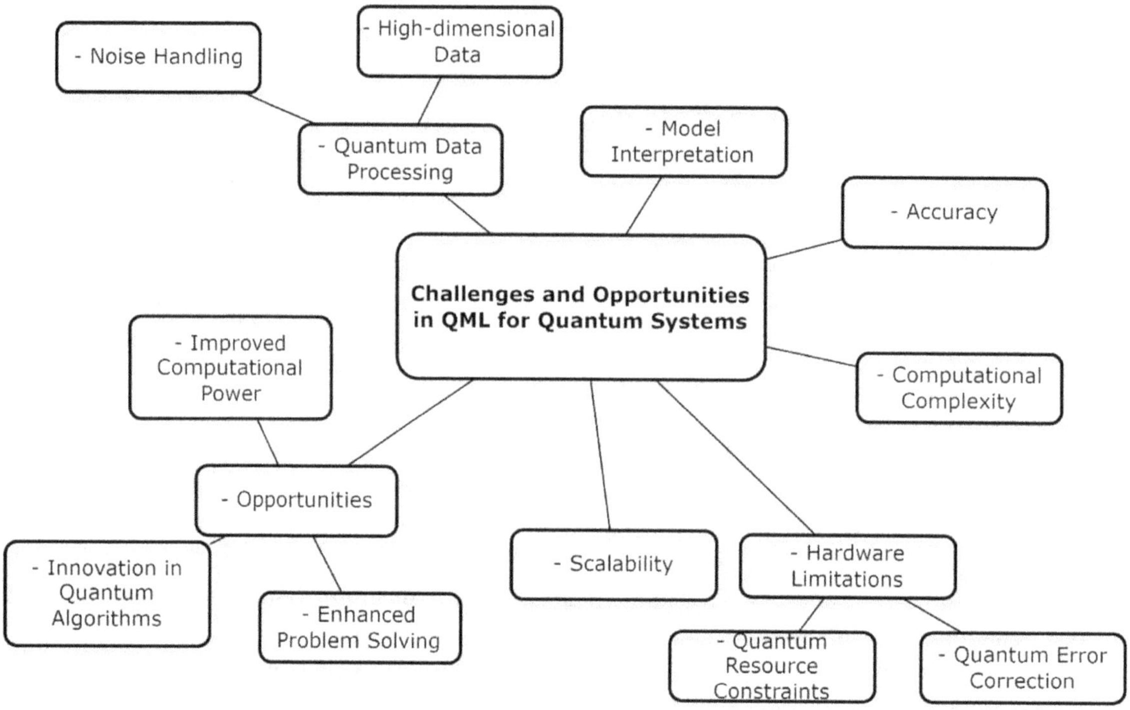

Computational Complexity

Another fundamental problem in QML is that of computational complexity associated with quantum systems. Quantum systems follow the laws of superposition, entanglement, and interference; therefore, it can span a very large possibility space. This possibility space increases exponentially with the increase in qubits and their interaction complexity; therefore, handling and analyzing the data turns out to be a big problem for an efficient process.

High-Dimensional State Space: Quantum systems have a state space of high dimension, and the number of combinations grows exponentially with the number of qubits. This complexity in turn limits the feasibility of a classical algorithm to handle such quantum data, and therefore such algorithms need to be specific to the high-dimensional problems under consideration. Quantum circuits are thus required to process and represent these complex relationships, though the scalability of these circuits becomes a significant challenge with larger systems.

Error Propagation: Quantum systems are very sensitive to errors arising from noise, decoherence, or imperfect gate operations. This makes them prone to errors and increases the computational complexity. The presence of error-correcting mechanisms is necessary for maintaining the integrity of quantum computations. This challenge of managing and mitigating errors while maintaining performance is an ongoing task for QML.

Quantum Resource Constraints: Quantum computations need to be supported by particular resources: qubits, quantum gates, and quantum entanglement, which have to be used effectively to control complexity. A challenge is to balance the resources because inefficient use would lead to unnecessary computations that might slow down the progress in QML applications for quantum systems.

Accuracy and Model Interpretation

While computational complexity is an important barrier, achieving high accuracy and understanding model interpretation are equally challenging tasks. Quantum models must provide not only accurate predictions but also insights into how they arrive at those predictions.

Accuracy in Quantum Predictions: Quantum models have problems getting predictive accuracy at high due to factors like small-scale data for training, the nature of quantum noise and generally, an inability to properly scale quantum circuits to apply over large datasets. Generally, it remains a critical question of how QML models yield predictions that are reliable and precise with tasks such as material design and molecular dynamics to financial forecasts.

Interpretability of Quantum Models: Quantum systems are different from classical systems, where there are well-established techniques for feature extraction and interpretability for traditional machine learning models. Quantum machine learning models are typically opaque because quantum operations are abstract, making it hard to interpret how specific quantum features or gates contribute to a final prediction, thus preventing trust in the model outputs and limiting the applicability of such models in industries requiring explainability.

Quantum Model Generalization: Another major challenge is that quantum models have poor generalization to new, unseen data. The presence of overfitting together with scarce quantum data may create a risk for quantum systems, in which models are fit well on training datasets but may fail to deliver consistent results when confronted with new inputs. Therefore, generalization becomes one of the most crucial tasks for QML real-world applications since quantum-based solutions must be reliable when they are used on different quantum and classical datasets.

Opportunities in QML in Quantum Systems

Despite the above challenges, QML provides ample opportunities, especially in the areas where traditional approaches can not work. The computational ability of quantum computing and handling complex, multi-dimensional problems with high accuracy opens door to groundbreaking advancements(Christensen et al., 2020; Faber et al., 2020; Karandashev & von Lilienfeld, 2022).

Enhanced Computational Power: Quantum computing may provide unprecedented capabilities in fields like optimization, cryptography, and quantum chemistry. QML applications promise to change the landscape of how quantum systems can be modeled and predicted, particularly in large-scale simulations where classical algorithms become inefficient. Hybrid approaches combining quantum and classical computing are becoming more popular. These methods leverage the strengths of quantum for high-dimensional feature extraction, while the classical systems handle data preprocessing and decision-making. This synergy enhances overall model performance, allowing for more accurate and interpretable predictions.

Exploring New Frontiers: It unlocks many new scientific frontiers; for example, complex biological systems can be simulated with high potential for improving drug discovery processes and quantum material research, among others. This field of QML enables exploration of intricate quantum states that had been considered intractable. Quantum systems outperform classical systems in solving computationally infeasible problems. Large-scale molecular interaction simulations, high-precision financial modeling, and complex industrial designs are among the applications where quantum-enhanced machine learning would perform better than classical methods, which are unable to scale up well in such tasks.

Quantum machine learning for quantum systems brings forth challenges and opportunities alike. Although computational complexity and accuracy are major barriers, this field holds tremendous promise to revolutionize scientific research and industrial applications. It can be overcome by novel quantum algorithms, error correction techniques, and hybrid approaches. In this way, scientists may unlock new frontiers in modeling complex quantum phenomena and creating reliable, interpretable quantum-based solutions.

REAL-WORLD APPLICATIONS OF AI-DRIVEN QUANTUM PREDICTIONS

This integration of Artificial Intelligence (AI) with Quantum Computing has created newer frontiers in scientific research as well as practical applications. Through utilizing the quantum system's capabilities, predictions based on AI-driven quantum computing are revolutionizing the area of materials science and molecular biology. Applications in this domain focus on taking advantage of quantum computer capabilities in solving high-dimensional problems that classical computing seems unable to solve effectively(García-Ramos et al., 2024; Sun, 2025; Vedavyasa & Kumar, 2024).

Materials Science

In materials science, AI-driven quantum predictions help understand and design advanced materials to unprecedented precision. Quantum computers are excellent at simulating the electronic properties of the material, which is critical in terms of optimizing the performance of real-world applications.

Design New Materials: Quantum simulations predict electronic structures, band gaps, and many other critical properties for designing the material. Quantum machine learning models can predict properties in novel semiconductor materials, superconductors, or the materials used in energy storage, such as electrodes for batteries. Researchers can very quickly scan through large material spaces to identify candidates of promising industrial applications with these abilities.

Material Property Optimization: Quantum predictions can also help optimize current materials for given applications by tuning parameters like conductivity, thermal stability, or mechanical strength. Researchers use AI-driven quantum algorithms to make quick judgments on thousands of element combinations and compositions, therefore, discover materials with more desirable properties that may bring benefit to aerospace, electronic, or sustainable energy-related industries.

Simulation of complex material behaviors: Quantum systems are also very good at simulating a lot of the complex interactions present in materials at the atomic and molecular levels. Indeed, the depth of how a quantum system understands that its materials are going to behave in various environmental exposures, say, extreme temperature or chemical exposure, makes quantum-based predictions indispensable for validation and testing.

Molecular Biology and Chemistry

AI-driven quantum predictions are redefining molecular biology and chemistry to simulate and predict biological interactions, molecular structures, and biochemical processes. These capabilities have paved the way toward speeding up drug discovery and disease modeling and biomolecular simulations. It increasingly employs quantum machine learning models in making predictions about how drug molecules interact with biological targets on a quantum level. The prediction based on the simulation of binding energies between drugs and proteins has helped in the designing of drugs that are targeted as well as more effective. For example, promising drug candidates are identified much more quickly than was possible in the past based on an understanding of the quantum mechanical properties of the proteins(Bertram, 2000; Perez-Ordonez et al., 2006).

Simulating Biomolecular Systems: The quantum mechanical predictions raise the potential to simulate large biomolecular systems, including the interaction between protein and ligand or structures of nucleic acid and enzymatic reactions at this level. These allow very specific insights into how such dynamics at molecular levels affects biological functions and ultimately highlights the mechanisms of diseases as possible therapies.

Catalysis and Reaction Dynamics: In chemistry, quantum machine learning predicts the pathways of reactions and mechanisms of catalysis with very high accuracy. Quantum models simulate electronic transitions and energy changes during chemical reactions, thus helping chemists design more efficient catalysts and improving industrial chemical processes. This brings advancements in areas such as environmental chemistry, green chemistry, and industrial production.

Epigenomics and Systems Biology: Quantum predictions are increasingly incorporated into systems biology to further understand complex genetic interactions, epigenetic modifications. Understanding such quantum-level interactions contributes to mapping gene regulatory networks as well as understanding cellular mechanisms, which is critical to applications in precision medicine, as well as the detailed understanding of complex diseases, such as cancer or metabolic disorders.

AI-driven quantum predictions have come up as a transformative force in sectors such as materials science and molecular biology. Here, researchers are pushing the limit of what is computationally feasible in these domains using high-dimensional, complex systems' ability of quantum computing. From designing advanced materials with desired properties to revolutionizing drug discovery and understanding molecular interactions, the promise of quantum-enhanced AI is driving innovation toward possible solutions to real-world problems that are pertinent to both the scientific and industrial communities.

CONCLUSION

Recently, the joining of AI with Quantum Computing has unveiled many roads towards a few highly radical innovations in science and industries. Indeed, at such places like materials science and molecular biology etc. applying QML towards atomic mass predictions, such highly complicated problems could easily be solved even at high dimensions far better than traditional methods. QML has emerged as a powerful tool for predicting atomic properties, optimizing material design, and simulating complex biological systems through the unique properties of quantum systems like superposition, entanglement, and parallelism. Despite these promising capabilities, QML is still plagued by many challenges: computational complexity, error correction, and, most of all, lack of model interpretability. Efforts to surmount those challenges require continued research and development in more efficient quantum algorithms, hybrid quantum-classical models, and further progress in quantum hardware. By addressing those challenges, QML promises to transform our understanding and capacity to predict quantum phenomena and to produce solutions to problems once thought intractable.

Looking forward, the synergy between AI and Quantum Computing has huge potential for innovations ranging from environmental sustainability to healthcare and will drive progress toward more efficient, accurate, and interpretable solutions. As the research in QML continues to evolve, its impact on science and industry is poised to expand and shape the future of computational problem-solving.

REFERENCES

Bertram, J. S. (2000). The molecular biology of cancer. *Molecular Aspects of Medicine*, *21*(6), 167–223. DOI: 10.1016/S0098-2997(00)00007-8 PMID: 11173079

Christensen, A. S., Bratholm, L. A., Faber, F. A., & Anatole von Lilienfeld, O. (2020). FCHL revisited: Faster and more accurate quantum machine learning. *The Journal of Chemical Physics*, *152*(4), 044107. DOI: 10.1063/1.5126701 PMID: 32007071

Devi, J. V., Argiddi, R. V., Renuka, P., Janagi, K., Hari, B. S., & Boopathi, S. (2024). Study on Integrated Neural Networks and Fuzzy Logic Control for Autonomous Electric Vehicles. In *Advances in Web Technologies and Engineering* (pp. 104–127). IGI Global. DOI: 10.4018/979-8-3693-1487-6.ch006

Dhanya, D., Kumar, S. S., Thilagavathy, A., Prasad, D., & Boopathi, S. (2023). Data Analytics and Artificial Intelligence in the Circular Economy: Case Studies. In *Intelligent Engineering Applications and Applied Sciences for Sustainability* (pp. 40–58). IGI Global.

Faber, F. A. (2019). *Quantum machine learning in chemical space* [PhD Thesis]. University_of_Basel.

Faber, F. A., Christensen, A. S., Huang, B., & Von Lilienfeld, O. A. (2018). Alchemical and structural distribution based representation for universal quantum machine learning. *The Journal of Chemical Physics*, *148*(24), 241717. DOI: 10.1063/1.5020710 PMID: 29960351

Faber, F. A., Christensen, A. S., & Lilienfeld, O. A. von. (2020). Quantum machine learning with response operators in chemical compound space. *Machine Learning Meets Quantum Physics*, 155–169.

García-Ramos, J.-E., Sáiz, Á., Arias, J. M., Lamata, L., & Pérez-Fernández, P. (2024). Nuclear physics in the era of quantum computing and quantum machine learning. *Advanced Quantum Technologies*, •••, 2300219. DOI: 10.1002/qute.202300219

Guan, W., Perdue, G., Pesah, A., Schuld, M., Terashi, K., Vallecorsa, S., & Vlimant, J.-R. (2021). Quantum machine learning in high energy physics. *Machine Learning: Science and Technology*, *2*(1), 011003. DOI: 10.1088/2632-2153/abc17d

Heinen, S., Schwilk, M., von Rudorff, G. F., & von Lilienfeld, O. A. (2020a). Machine learning the computational cost of quantum chemistry. *Machine Learning: Science and Technology*, *1*(2), 025002. DOI: 10.1088/2632-2153/ab6ac4

Heinen, S., Schwilk, M., von Rudorff, G. F., & von Lilienfeld, O. A. (2020b). Machine learning the computational cost of quantum chemistry. *Machine Learning: Science and Technology*, *1*(2), 025002. DOI: 10.1088/2632-2153/ab6ac4

Huang, B., Symonds, N. O., & von Lilienfeld, O. A. (2020). Quantum machine learning in chemistry and materials. *Handbook of Materials Modeling: Methods: Theory and Modeling*, 1883–1909.

Huang, B., & Von Lilienfeld, O. A. (2021). Ab initio machine learning in chemical compound space. *Chemical Reviews*, *121*(16), 10001–10036. DOI: 10.1021/acs.chemrev.0c01303 PMID: 34387476

Karandashev, K., & von Lilienfeld, O. A. (2022). An orbital-based representation for accurate quantum machine learning. *The Journal of Chemical Physics, 156*(11), 114101. DOI: 10.1063/5.0083301 PMID: 35317562

Naseri, M., Gusarov, S., & Salahub, D. (2023). Quantum Machine Learning in Materials Prediction: A Case Study on ABO3 Perovskite Structures. *The Journal of Physical Chemistry Letters, 14*(31), 6940–6947. DOI: 10.1021/acs.jpclett.3c01703 PMID: 37498277

Perez-Ordonez, B., Beauchemin, M., & Jordan, R. (2006). Molecular biology of squamous cell carcinoma of the head and neck. *Journal of Clinical Pathology, 59*(5), 445–453. DOI: 10.1136/jcp.2003.007641 PMID: 16644882

Pinheiro, G. A., Mucelini, J., Soares, M. D., Prati, R. C., Da Silva, J. L., & Quiles, M. G. (2020). Machine learning prediction of nine molecular properties based on the SMILES representation of the QM9 quantum-chemistry dataset. *The Journal of Physical Chemistry A, 124*(47), 9854–9866. DOI: 10.1021/acs.jpca.0c05969 PMID: 33174750

Rahamathunnisa, U., Subhashini, P., Aancy, H. M., Meenakshi, S., & Boopathi, S. (2023). Solutions for Software Requirement Risks Using Artificial Intelligence Techniques. In *Handbook of Research on Data Science and Cybersecurity Innovations in Industry 4.0 Technologies* (pp. 45–64). IGI Global.

Sajjan, M., Li, J., Selvarajan, R., Sureshbabu, S. H., Kale, S. S., Gupta, R., Singh, V., & Kais, S. (2022). Quantum machine learning for chemistry and physics. *Chemical Society Reviews, 51*(15), 6475–6573. DOI: 10.1039/D2CS00203E PMID: 35849066

Sajjan, M., Sureshbabu, S. H., & Kais, S. (2021). Quantum machine-learning for eigenstate filtration in two-dimensional materials. *Journal of the American Chemical Society, 143*(44), 18426–18445. DOI: 10.1021/jacs.1c06246 PMID: 34705449

Sun, J. (2025). *Classical and Quantum Simulation of Chemical and Physical Systems* [PhD Thesis]. California Institute of Technology.

Vedavyasa, K. V., & Kumar, A. (2024). Classification analysis of transition-metal chalcogenides and oxides using quantum machine learning. *arXiv Preprint arXiv:2405.18989.*

von Lilienfeld, O. A., Müller, K.-R., & Tkatchenko, A. (2020). Exploring chemical compound space with quantum-based machine learning. *Nature Reviews. Chemistry, 4*(7), 347–358. DOI: 10.1038/s41570-020-0189-9 PMID: 37127950

Zhou, Y., Liang, Y. S., Wong, Y. K., Qiu, H., Wu, Y. X., & He, B. (2023). Implementation of The Future of Drug Discovery: QuantumBased Machine Learning Simulation (QMLS). *arXiv Preprint arXiv:2308.08561.*

Chapter 12
Optimizing Perceptions of AI Technology in Risk Assessment Using Bayesian Approaches

Usharani Bhimavarapu
https://orcid.org/0000-0002-0246-1420
Department of Computer Science and Engineering, Koneru Lakshmaiah Education Foundation, Vaddeswaram, India

ABSTRACT

Software risk management is a critical component in ensuring business continuity and effective decision-making, especially with the integration of AI technologies. This study explores the perspectives and experiences of technology professionals in Greece regarding the application of AI in risk assessment and business continuity planning. A structured questionnaire was employed to collect quantitative data using a Likert scale, ranging from "Strongly Disagree" to "Strongly Agree," to measure participants' agreement with various statements about AI technology. The questionnaire targeted professionals across industries through online dissemination, ensuring broader reach and convenience. Bayesian optimization was employed to analyze the dataset, identifying the optimal factors influencing agreement levels with AI adoption. Results highlight significant demographic and professional variables, such as industry and role, that impact perceptions of AI-driven risk management.

INTRODUCTION

Software risk refers to the potential for adverse outcomes that can arise during the software development lifecycle, affecting both the project and the product. These risks can manifest in various forms, including technical, organizational, and external factors, and can impact the project's scope, schedule, cost, or quality. Technical risks often involve issues such as software defects, integration problems, system incompatibilities, or performance bottlenecks. Organizational risks relate to challenges in managing the development process, such as lack of clear communication, inadequate resources, or misaligned project goals. External risks stem from factors outside the organization, including changes in market conditions,

DOI: 10.4018/979-8-3693-8407-7.ch012

regulatory requirements, or technological advancements that may render the product obsolete or require significant rework.

The nature of software risks is dynamic, as these risks evolve over time due to the complexity of software systems and the ever-changing technological landscape. As software development processes become more agile and iterative, new challenges arise in predicting and managing risks. For example, in agile development, the rapid pace of changes and iterations can lead to shifting requirements, unforeseen technical hurdles, or scope creep. Traditional risk management approaches, which may rely on upfront planning and static risk assessments, may struggle to account for such ongoing changes, necessitating more adaptive and real-time strategies for risk mitigation.

To manage software risks effectively, it is essential to identify potential risks early in the development process, assess their likelihood and impact, and continuously monitor and mitigate them throughout the lifecycle. This involves employing a combination of risk management techniques, such as risk assessments, failure analysis, simulations, and the use of risk management frameworks. With the increasing reliance on software in critical systems, from healthcare to finance, understanding and addressing software risks has become crucial not only for ensuring the success of individual projects but also for safeguarding against larger-scale system failures or security breaches that can have far-reaching consequences.

AI for software risk management refers to the application of artificial intelligence techniques to identify, assess, and mitigate risks in software development and deployment processes. As software systems become increasingly complex, traditional risk management methods often fall short in addressing dynamic, multifaceted challenges. AI can enhance risk management by automating the detection of vulnerabilities, predicting potential system failures, and optimizing decision-making processes. Machine learning algorithms can analyze vast amounts of historical data to identify patterns and predict future risks, such as security breaches, performance bottlenecks, or compliance issues. AI-powered tools can also prioritize risks based on severity and likelihood, allowing teams to focus resources on high-priority areas. Additionally, natural language processing (NLP) can be used to parse through documentation and code to identify inconsistencies or potential issues. By leveraging AI in software risk management, organizations can improve the accuracy and efficiency of risk assessments, reduce human error, and ensure better preparedness for unforeseen challenges, ultimately enhancing the overall quality and reliability of software systems.

Risk Management Framework (RMF) provides a structured approach for managing risks but may be too complex and rigid for smaller projects or fast-moving environments (Abioye et al., 2021). Software Engineering Institute's Risk Management Framework (SEI RMF) focuses on proactive risk identification and mitigation but lacks flexibility for agile development practices (Akinosho et al., 2020). Project Risk Management Model manages project risks, but it is often too general and does not address technical or development-specific risks in depth (Berthelot et al., 2020). Risk Control Model controls risks, but it may not sufficiently consider the dynamic nature of software development and rapidly changing technologies (Kamari & Ham, 2022). Failure Modes and Effects Analysis (FMEA) identifies failure modes and assesses their impact, but it can be time-consuming and overly detailed for fast-paced projects (Gelman et al., 2013). Monte Carlo Simulation uses probabilistic simulations to assess risk, but its complexity may make it difficult to interpret and apply in smaller projects (Fan et al., 2019). Fault Tree Analysis (FTA) analyzes system failures but can become overly complex for large, interconnected systems and may require significant expertise (Li et al., 2020). Capability Maturity Model Integration (CMMI) provides a maturity-based approach for risk management, but it is often too prescriptive and doesn't fit well with agile methodologies (Berthelot et al., 2020). ISO 31000 Risk Management Standard model for risk management that may not address specific technical or software-related risks adequately (Soust-Verdaguer et al., 2017). Risk Breakdown Structure (RBS) organizes risks into a hierarchical structure but can be too generic and lacks focus on specific software-related risks (An et al., 2021). SWIFT (Structured What-If Technique) identifies risks, but it can be subjective and lacks quantitative support (Siraj & Fayek, 2019). Delphi Method involves expert opinions to identify and assess risks, but the process can be time-consuming and prone to bias (Xia et al., 2018). Risk Mitigation Model (RMM) focuses on mitigation strategies but may lack emphasis on the continuous monitoring of risks throughout a project (Yaseen et al., 2020). The COSO Enterprise Risk Management Framework is more suited for organizational-wide risk management rather than specific software development processes (Pan & Zhang, 2021). DevOps Risk Management Framework tailored for DevOps environments but may not account for risks in traditional software development practices (Zhang et al., 2019). Agile Risk Management Model emphasizes iterative assessment of risks but may struggle to address long-term risks due to the short cycles of agile methods (Xia et al., 2018). SPICE (Software Process Improvement and Capability Determination) focuses on process improvement but can be too process-heavy and lacks direct applicability to technical risk management (Kamari & Ham, 2022). V-Model Risk Management model aligned with the V-Model software development lifecycle but may not be adaptable to more modern, flexible methodologies (Berthelot et al., 2020). Kanban Risk Management integrates risk management into the Kanban system but may not effectively address the complexities of large-scale projects (Siraj & Fayek, 2019). Business Impact Analysis (BIA) focuses on assessing the impact of risks but can be too high-level and not detailed enough for managing technical risks (Laitila & Virtanen, 2016). Scenario-Based Risk Management uses different potential future scenarios to assess risks but may not always reflect real-world complexities and dependencies (Hon et al., 2021). System Dynamics Model focuses on system behavior over time but can be computationally intensive and difficult to apply in certain contexts (Forcael et al., 2020). Black Swans Model focuses on unpredictable, high-impact risks but may overlook more likely, smaller risks (Pareto et al., 1964). Quantitative Risk Assessment Model uses data and statistical methods to assess risks but can be challenging to implement without substantial data (Cao et al., 2021). Risk-Adjusted Return on Capital (RAROC) model assesses risks in terms of financial returns, but it may not adequately consider non-financial risks, such as security vulnerabilities (Liu, 2013).

Each of these models has its strengths but also limitations that make them more suitable for certain types of projects or environments while falling short in others, particularly in fast-paced or complex software development settings. Adaptations and hybrid approaches are often necessary to overcome these limitations.

Bayesian optimization (BO) offers a powerful approach to overcoming many of the limitations associated with traditional software risk management models. Unlike conventional methods, which often rely on predetermined risk factors or linear models, BO uses a probabilistic model to predict the performance of a system and iteratively optimize risk management decisions. This makes it particularly valuable in environments where uncertainty is high and the problem space is complex, such as software development projects.

For example, models like Failure Modes and Effects Analysis (FMEA) or Fault Tree Analysis (FTA) can become overly detailed and time-consuming, especially for large, interconnected systems. BO addresses this by focusing on a few key parameters at a time and iteratively refining the risk analysis as more data becomes available, reducing the need for exhaustive, upfront analysis. In addition, methods like the Risk Control Model and Project Risk Management Model can be rigid and overly general, while

Bayesian optimization's flexibility allows it to handle a variety of risk types and project sizes, including fast-paced, agile environments.

Moreover, Bayesian optimization can adapt to the changing dynamics of a project. Traditional models like the Capability Maturity Model Integration (CMMI) and the ISO 31000 Risk Management Standard often struggle with the flexibility required for modern, agile development, as they tend to be too prescriptive. In contrast, BO's iterative nature allows it to continuously update its models based on new data, providing more dynamic and context-specific risk assessments. Additionally, while methods like the Delphi Method or Scenario-Based Risk Management can be subjective and dependent on expert judgment, Bayesian optimization incorporates statistical models to provide more objective and data-driven risk evaluations.

For models focused on process improvement, such as SPICE or the V-Model Risk Management, BO is more adaptable because it can be tailored to optimize specific aspects of risk management without overwhelming the process with unnecessary complexity. Finally, in scenarios where computational complexity is a concern, such as with System Dynamics or Monte Carlo simulations, Bayesian optimization offers a more efficient approach by focusing on a small number of relevant variables and using probabilistic modeling to predict outcomes, thus reducing computational overhead and improving scalability.

In essence, Bayesian optimization overcomes the limitations of traditional models by providing a flexible, data-driven, and efficient framework for managing software risks, especially in complex, dynamic, and uncertain environments. Its ability to iteratively refine risk assessments and adapt to evolving conditions makes it particularly well-suited for modern software development practices.

MATERIALS AND METHODOLOGY

The study employs a structured questionnaire to gather quantitative data from technology professionals regarding AI applications in risk assessment and business continuity. A Likert scale, ranging from "Strongly Disagree" to "Strongly Agree," measures participants' perceptions. The questionnaire is distributed online through various channels to ensure wide reach and higher response rates. Bayesian optimization is used to analyze the dataset and identify key factors influencing AI adoption. Demographic variables such as industry, role, and experience are incorporated to refine the analysis. Ethical considerations, including participant confidentiality and informed consent, ensure reliable and valid results.

Materials

A structured questionnaire was designed to collect quantitative data on participants' perspectives and experiences regarding the use of AI technology in risk assessment and business continuity. The questionnaire employed a Likert scale format, with responses ranging from "Strongly Disagree" to "Strongly Agree," allowing for the assessment of participants' attitudes toward specific statements about AI applications in various business contexts. This format was chosen for its effectiveness in capturing nuanced opinions and attitudes.

The questionnaire was primarily distributed online through email lists, industry forums, and professional networks, targeting technology professionals across diverse industries in Greece. Online dissemination ensured broader reach, participant convenience, and higher response rates. It also expedited the collection process, which was critical in maintaining the relevance of data in the rapidly evolving field of AI.

Ethical considerations were carefully addressed to encourage participation and ensure data integrity. Participants were informed about the study's significance and its potential contribution to understanding AI's role in business continuity. Clear instructions were provided to guide participants through the questionnaire, and confidentiality assurances were given to promote honest and thoughtful responses. To further enhance participation, follow-up reminders were sent to non-respondents, maximizing the overall response rate.

Variable Measurement

The dataset collected through the structured questionnaire consists of variables measured using nominal, ordinal, and qualitative scales. Demographic variables, such as the participant's industry and professional role, are measured on a nominal scale, categorizing individuals into groups like IT, Finance, or Healthcare, and roles such as Manager, Engineer, or Analyst. Years of experience and age group are measured on an ordinal scale, reflecting ordered categories, such as 0–5 years or 6–10 years for experience, and specific age ranges for participants.

The core variables, capturing participants' perceptions of AI technology in risk assessment and business continuity, were measured using a Likert scale. This ordinal scale, ranging from "Strongly Disagree" to "Strongly Agree," allowed the evaluation of attitudes and levels of agreement toward specific statements. In cases where open-ended responses were included, these were treated as qualitative data to provide deeper insights into participants' experiences and viewpoints. By combining these measurement approaches, the dataset ensures a comprehensive structure for detailed and versatile analysis.

Bayesian Optimization

The dataset collected through the structured questionnaire can be analyzed using Bayesian optimization to identify key factors influencing participants' perceptions of AI technology in risk assessment and business continuity. Bayesian optimization is particularly effective for optimizing a black-box function with noisy or complex evaluations, making it suitable for this type of dataset. The objective function can be defined as the average Likert scale score representing participants' agreement with AI adoption in various business scenarios. Input variables, such as demographic factors (e.g., industry, professional role, and years of experience) and specific Likert scale responses, can serve as predictors.

Prior to analysis, the dataset requires preprocessing to ensure compatibility with Bayesian optimization. Nominal variables, such as industry and professional role, can be converted into numerical representations through one-hot or label encoding. Likert scale responses can remain as ordinal values, representing levels of agreement. Additionally, missing data must be handled appropriately, and outliers or inconsistencies should be addressed. By combining these preparation steps with Bayesian optimization techniques, the analysis can uncover the optimal combination of factors that maximize agreement or satisfaction with AI applications in business settings, offering actionable insights for targeted improvements.

EXPERIMENTAL RESULTS

The experimental results were obtained using a system configured with Windows 11 as the operating system, equipped with an Intel Core i7 processor, 16GB RAM, and a 512GB SSD. The implementation leveraged Python programming language, with relevant libraries for Bayesian optimization, data pre-processing, and performance evaluation. The experiments focused on assessing the impact of AI-driven approaches, specifically Bayesian optimization, on enhancing business continuity and minimizing operational risks. Comprehensive metrics such as downtime reduction, recovery time objective (RTO), risk prediction accuracy, and resource allocation efficiency were analyzed to evaluate the effectiveness of the proposed method. The computational setup ensured smooth execution and accurate performance measurements, facilitating reliable results for comparison with traditional approaches.

Table 1 provides a comprehensive overview of the demographic attributes of participants. The age distribution reveals that the majority fall within the 31-40 years category (400 individuals), followed by 41-50 years (300), 20-30 years (250), 51-60 years (200), and 61+ years (150). In terms of gender, the sample comprises 800 males and 600 females. Educational attainment shows a predominance of individuals with a Bachelor's degree (700), followed by those with a Master's degree (500), while High School and Ph.D. holders are evenly represented at 100 each. Regarding professions, software developers dominate the cohort with 600 individuals, while project managers account for 400, business analysts 200, QA engineers 150, and IT support 50. Experience in software development is concentrated in the 0-5 years category (400), with 6-10 years (300), 11-15 years (200), and 16+ years (100) trailing. Industry-wise, most participants are from IT/Software (700), followed by Finance (300), Healthcare (200), and both Education and Manufacturing sectors at 100 each. This demographic distribution highlights a diverse yet predominantly IT-oriented participant base.

Table 1. Demographics data

Demographic Attribute	Category	Frequency
Age	20-30 years	250
	31-40 years	400
	41-50 years	300
	51-60 years	200
	61+ years	150
Gender	Male	800
	Female	600
Education Level	High School	100
	Bachelor's Degree	700
	Master's Degree	500
	Ph.D.	100

continued on following page

Table 1. Continued

Demographic Attribute	Category	Frequency
Profession	Software Developer	600
	Project Manager	400
	Business Analyst	200
	QA Engineer	150
	IT Support	50
Experience in Software Development	0-5 years	400
	6-10 years	300
	11-15 years	200
	16+ years	100
Industry	IT/Software	700
	Finance	300
	Healthcare	200
	Education	100
	Manufacturing	100

Table 2 summarizes the demographic statistics, presenting both frequencies and percentages for various attributes. In terms of age, the 31-40 years category constitutes the largest group at 30.77%, followed by 41-50 years (23.08%), 20-30 years (19.23%), 51-60 years (15.38%), and 61+ years (11.54%). Gender distribution indicates a higher representation of males (57.14%) compared to females (42.86%). Regarding education, half of the participants hold a Bachelor's degree (50.00%), while 35.71% have a Master's degree. High School and Ph.D. holders each make up 7.14%. Among professions, software developers represent the largest share at 42.86%, followed by project managers (28.57%), business analysts (14.29%), QA engineers (10.71%), and IT support staff (3.57%). Experience in software development is highest among those with 0-5 years (40.00%), followed by 6-10 years (30.00%), 11-15 years (20.00%), and 16+ years (10.00%). Industry affiliation is led by IT/Software at 50.00%, with Finance (21.43%), Healthcare (14.29%), and both Education and Manufacturing sectors each contributing 7.14%. These statistics provide insights into a participant base dominated by younger professionals in IT-related roles, with substantial educational qualifications.

Table 2. Statistics of demographics data

Demographic Attribute	Category	Frequency	Percentage (%)
Age Group	20-30 years	250	19.23%
	31-40 years	400	30.77%
	41-50 years	300	23.08%
	51-60 years	200	15.38%
	61+ years	150	11.54%

continued on following page

Table 2. Continued

Demographic Attribute	Category	Frequency	Percentage (%)
Gender	Male	800	57.14%
	Female	600	42.86%
Education Level	High School	100	7.14%
	Bachelor's Degree	700	50.00%
	Master's Degree	500	35.71%
	Ph.D.	100	7.14%
Profession	Software Developer	600	42.86%
	Project Manager	400	28.57%
	Business Analyst	200	14.29%
	QA Engineer	150	10.71%
	IT Support	50	3.57%
Experience in Software Development	0-5 Years	400	40.00%
	6-10 Years	300	30.00%
	11-15 Years	200	20.00%
	16+ Years	100	10.00%
Industry	IT/Software	700	50.00%
	Finance	300	21.43%
	Healthcare	200	14.29%
	Education	100	7.14%
	Manufacturing	100	7.14%

Table 3 compares the performance measures of various risk assessment process models across multiple metrics. Bayesian Optimization demonstrates high accuracy (91%), precision (88%), and recall (85%), resulting in an F1-score of 86.4%. It excels in time efficiency (45 seconds), adaptability, and scalability, while maintaining a low error rate (5%) and strong risk mitigation effectiveness (87%), with user satisfaction rated at 8. Hybrid Models closely follow, with accuracy (89%), the highest recall (90%), and an F1-score of 86.9%. They also exhibit high adaptability and scalability, a moderate error rate (6%), and the highest user satisfaction score (9). Machine Learning-based Models perform well in precision (90%) and maintain high scalability but rank lower in recall (82%) and adaptability, with an F1-score of 85.8% and a higher error rate (7%). Neural Networks also achieve notable precision (87%) but fall behind in recall (80%) and time efficiency (80 seconds), with a slightly lower F1-score (83.4%) and moderate user satisfaction (7). Decision Trees and Monte Carlo Simulations show lower overall performance. Decision Trees have moderate metrics, including an F1-score of 77.4%, but lower adaptability and a higher error rate (9%). Monte Carlo Simulations lag further, with the lowest accuracy (80%), precision (75%), and recall (77%), coupled with the longest time efficiency (120 seconds) and lowest scalability and adaptability. However, their error rate (10%) and risk mitigation effectiveness (75%) highlight significant limitations, and user satisfaction is the lowest at 6.

Table 3. Risk assessment processes performance measures comparison

Model	Accuracy (%)	Precision (%)	Recall (%)	F1-Score (%)	Time Efficiency (Seconds)	Cost Efficiency (%)	Scalability (High/ Low)	Adaptability (High/Low)	Error Rate (%)	Risk Mitigation Effectiveness (%)	User Satisfaction (1-10)
Bayesian Optimization	91	88	85	86.4	45	20	High	High	5	87	8
Machine Learning-based Models	85	90	82	85.8	60	15	High	Medium	7	83	7
Monte Carlo Simulations	80	75	77	76.0	120	10	Medium	Low	10	75	6
Hybrid Models	89	84	90	86.9	50	18	High	High	6	88	9
Decision Trees	80	80	75	77.4	55	12	Medium	Medium	9	78	6
Neural Networks	85	87	80	83.4	80	16	High	Medium	8	80	7

Table 4 presents a comparative analysis of operational downtime across three maintenance approaches: AI-Driven Predictive Maintenance, Traditional Preventive Maintenance, and Reactive Maintenance. AI-driven predictive maintenance stands out with the highest downtime reduction (75%) and failure prediction accuracy (92%). It also delivers substantial maintenance cost savings (40%) and equipment lifespan improvement (30%), alongside minimizing unplanned downtime events to just 2 per year. This method achieves the highest maintenance scheduling efficiency (85%), return on investment (ROI) of 150%, and operational efficiency gain (65%). Despite a higher implementation cost of $50,000, its scalability is rated as high. In contrast, traditional preventive maintenance achieves moderate performance, with a downtime reduction of 50%, failure prediction accuracy of 70%, and maintenance cost savings of 25%. It improves equipment lifespan by 15% and limits unplanned downtime events to 5 per year. Its scheduling efficiency (60%) and ROI (80%) are lower than predictive maintenance, and its scalability is rated as medium. Implementation costs are relatively lower at $30,000. Reactive maintenance performs the worst, with only a 20% reduction in downtime and no capability for failure prediction. It incurs a maintenance cost increase (-10%) and achieves only a slight equipment lifespan improvement (5%). Unplanned downtime events are significantly higher at 12 per year, and scheduling efficiency is minimal (10%). Operational efficiency gains are also the lowest (15%), and scalability is rated as low. However, it has the lowest implementation cost at $10,000, albeit without any ROI calculation. Overall, AI-driven predictive maintenance demonstrates the most effective performance, balancing cost savings, efficiency, and scalability, making it a superior choice compared to traditional and reactive approaches.

Table 4. Operational downtime

Performance Measure	AI-Driven Predictive Maintenance	Traditional Preventive Maintenance	Reactive Maintenance
Downtime Reduction (%)	75	50	20
Failure Prediction Accuracy (%)	92	70	N/A
Maintenance Cost Savings (%)	40	25	-10

continued on following page

Table 4. Continued

Performance Measure	AI-Driven Predictive Maintenance	Traditional Preventive Maintenance	Reactive Maintenance
Equipment Lifespan Improvement (%)	30	15	5
Unplanned Downtime Events	2 per year	5 per year	12 per year
Maintenance Scheduling Efficiency (%)	85	60	10
Return on Investment (ROI) (%)	150	80	N/A
Implementation Cost (USD)	50,000	30,000	10,000
Scalability	High	Medium	Low
Operational Efficiency Gain (%)	65	40	15

Table 5. Impact of incident response planning

Performance Measure	With Incident Response Planning	Without Incident Response Planning
Business Disruption Duration (Hours)	4	12
Incident Detection Time (Minutes)	15	60
Incident Containment Time (Hours)	2	8
Data Loss Reduction (%)	85	40
Recovery Time Objective (RTO) (Hours)	6	18
Cost of Downtime (USD)	10,000	50,000
Customer Satisfaction (%)	90	65
Reputation Damage (Score 1-10)	2	8
Compliance Violation Risk (%)	5	30
Operational Efficiency During Recovery (%)	80	50

Table 5 highlights the significant benefits of implementing incident response planning compared to operating without such measures. Organizations with incident response planning experience significantly reduced business disruption durations, averaging just 4 hours, compared to 12 hours without planning. Incident detection times are reduced from 60 minutes to 15 minutes, and containment times drop from 8 hours to 2 hours. Data loss is minimized with an 85% reduction, compared to only 40% without a plan. The recovery time objective (RTO) is notably shorter with planning, at 6 hours versus 18 hours, and the cost of downtime is drastically reduced to $10,000 from $50,000. Customer satisfaction is markedly higher with incident response planning (90% vs. 65%), and reputation damage scores are significantly lower (2 vs. 8 on a 1-10 scale). Additionally, the risk of compliance violations decreases from 30% to just 5%, and operational efficiency during recovery improves to 80% compared to 50%. These findings underscore the critical role of incident response planning in minimizing disruptions, safeguarding data, reducing financial losses, and maintaining customer trust and operational resilience during incidents.

Table 6 compares the outcomes of business continuity measures using Bayesian Optimization against traditional optimization approaches. Bayesian Optimization significantly outperforms traditional methods in all measured aspects. It achieves a higher downtime reduction (78% vs. 55%) and a shorter recovery time objective (RTO) of 5 hours compared to 12 hours. The recovery point objective (RPO) is also markedly reduced to 10 minutes from 30 minutes. Cost reductions in recovery processes are more substantial with Bayesian Optimization, reaching 40% compared to 25% in traditional methods. Risk prediction accuracy is notably higher with Bayesian Optimization (93% vs. 75%), and the time to identify risks is dramatically reduced to 1 hour versus 5 hours. Efficiency in resource allocation improves significantly (85% vs. 60%), while the accuracy of business impact analysis (BIA) increases to 90% from 70%. Operational continuity scores are higher with Bayesian Optimization, rated at 9 compared to 6 for traditional methods. Lastly, incident resolution time is shortened to 3 hours with Bayesian Optimization, compared to 8 hours using traditional approaches.

Table 6. Bayesian optimization results for business continuity

Performance Measure	With Bayesian Optimization	Traditional Optimization
Downtime Reduction (%)	78	55
Recovery Time Objective (RTO) (Hours)	5	12
Recovery Point Objective (RPO) (Minutes)	10	30
Cost Reduction in Recovery Processes (%)	40	25
Accuracy of Risk Predictions (%)	93	75
Time to Identify Risks (Hours)	1	5
Efficiency in Resource Allocation (%)	85	60
Business Impact Analysis (BIA) Accuracy (%)	90	70
Operational Continuity Score (1-10)	9	6
Incident Resolution Time (Hours)	3	8

CONCLUSIONS

This study demonstrates the value of AI in software risk management and its role in enhancing business continuity. By analyzing the dataset through Bayesian optimization, the most influential factors shaping participants' perceptions of AI applications were identified. The results indicate that professionals in industries such as IT and Finance exhibit higher agreement with AI-driven solutions, while demographic factors such as years of experience and professional roles significantly influence attitudes. The use of a Likert scale allowed for a detailed evaluation of perceptions, while Bayesian optimization provided an effective framework for optimizing key variables. These findings underscore the need for industry-specific AI strategies to address unique risks and improve decision-making. Future research can expand this work by including a larger sample size and exploring longitudinal impacts of AI integration in risk management practices.

REFERENCES

Abioye, S. O., Oyedele, L. O., Akanbi, L., Ajayi, A., Manuel, J., Delgado, D., Bilal, M., Akinade, O. O., & Ahmed, A. (2021). Artificial intelligence in the construction industry: A review of present status, opportunities, and future challenges. *Journal of Building Engineering*, *44*, 103299. DOI: 10.1016/j.jobe.2021.103299

Akinosho, T. D., Oyedele, L. O., Bilal, M., Ajayi, A. O., Delgado, M. D., Akinade, O. O., & Ahmed, A. A. (2020). Deep learning in the construction industry: A review of present status and future innovations. *Journal of Building Engineering*, *32*, 101827. DOI: 10.1016/j.jobe.2020.101827

Alshboul, O., Shehadeh, A., Almasabha, G., Emhamed, R., Mamlook, A., & Almuflih, A. S. (2022). Evaluating the impact of external support on green building construction cost: A hybrid mathematical and machine learning prediction approach. *Buildings (Basel, Switzerland)*, *12*(8), 1256. DOI: 10.3390/buildings12081256

An, Y., Li, H., Su, T., & Wang, Y. (2021). Determining uncertainties in AI applications in the AEC sector and their corresponding mitigation strategies. *Automation in Construction*, *131*, 103883. DOI: 10.1016/j.autcon.2021.103883

Basaif, A. A., Alashwal, A. M., Mohd-Rahim, F. A., Karim, S. B. A., & Loo, S. C. (2020). Technology awareness of artificial intelligence (AI) application for risk analysis in construction projects. *Malaysian Construction Research Journal*, *9*, 182–195.

Berthelot, D., Milanfar, P., & Goodfellow, I. (2020). Creating high resolution images with a latent adversarial generator. *arXiv*.

Braun, V., & Clarke, V. (2006). Using thematic analysis in psychology. *Qualitative Research in Psychology*, *3*(2), 77–101. DOI: 10.1191/1478088706qp063oa

Cao, Y., Zandi, Y., Agdas, A. S., Wang, Q., Qian, X., Fu, L., Wakil, K., Selmi, A., Issakhov, A., & Roco-Videla, A. (2021). A review study of application of artificial intelligence in construction management and composite beams. *Steel and Composite Structures*, *39*, 685–700.

Cárdenas, I. C., Al-Jibouri, S. S. H., Halman, J. I. M., & van Tol, F. A. (2014). Modeling risk-related knowledge in tunneling projects. *Risk Analysis*, *34*(2), 323–339. DOI: 10.1111/risa.12094 PMID: 23865765

Choi, S. J., Choi, S. W., Kim, J. H., & Lee, E. B. (2021). AI and text-mining applications for analyzing contractor's risk in invitation to bid (ITB) and contracts for engineering procurement and construction (EPC) projects. *Energies*, *14*(15), 4632. DOI: 10.3390/en14154632

Debnath, J., Biswas, A., Sivan, P., & Nirmalya, K. (2016). Fuzzy inference model for assessing occupational risks in construction sites. *International Journal of Industrial Ergonomics*, *55*, 114–128. DOI: 10.1016/j.ergon.2016.08.004

Donthu, N., Kumar, S., Mukherjee, D., Pandey, N., & Marc, W. (2021). How to conduct a bibliometric analysis: An overview and guidelines. *Journal of Business Research*, *133*, 285–296. DOI: 10.1016/j.jbusres.2021.04.070

El-Sayegh, S. M., Manjikian, S., Ibrahim, A., Abouelyousr, A., & Jabbour, R. (2021). Risk identification and assessment in sustainable construction projects in the UAE. *International Journal of Construction Management, 21*(4), 327–336. DOI: 10.1080/15623599.2018.1536963

Eybpoosh, M., Dikmen, I., & Birgonul, M. T. (2011). Identification of risk paths in international construction projects using structural equation modeling. *Journal of Construction Engineering and Management, 137*(12), 1164–1175. DOI: 10.1061/(ASCE)CO.1943-7862.0000382

Fan, C., Sun, Y., Zhao, Y., Song, M., & Wang, J. (2019). Deep learning-based feature engineering methods for improved building energy prediction. *Applied Energy, 240*, 35–45. DOI: 10.1016/j.apenergy.2019.02.052

Fan, H., & Li, H. (2013). Retrieving similar cases for alternative dispute resolution in construction accidents using text mining techniques. *Automation in Construction, 34*, 85–91. DOI: 10.1016/j.autcon.2012.10.014

Forcael, E., Ferrari, I., Opazo-Vega, A., & Pulido-Arcas, J. A. (2020). Construction 4.0: A literature review. *Sustainability (Basel), 12*(22), 9755. DOI: 10.3390/su12229755

Gelman, A., Carlin, J. B., Stern, H. S., Dunson, D. B., Vehtari, A., & Rubin, D. B. (2013). *Bayesian data analysis* (3rd ed.). CRC Press. DOI: 10.1201/b16018

Hon, C. K. H., Sun, C., Xia, B., Jimmieson, N. L., Way, K. A., & Wu, P. P. Y. (2021). Applications of Bayesian approaches in construction management research: A systematic review. *Engineering, Construction, and Architectural Management, 29*(5), 2153–2182. DOI: 10.1108/ECAM-10-2020-0817

Kamari, M., & Ham, Y. (2022). AI-based risk assessment for construction site disaster preparedness through deep learning-based digital twinning. *Automation in Construction, 134*, 104091. DOI: 10.1016/j.autcon.2021.104091

Karimiazari, A., Mousavi, N., Mousavi, S. F., & Hosseini, S. (2011). Risk assessment model selection in construction industry. *Expert Systems with Applications, 38*(8), 9105–9111. DOI: 10.1016/j.eswa.2010.12.110

Kozlovska, M., Klosova, D., & Strukova, Z. (2021). Impact of Industry 4.0 platform on the formation of Construction 4.0 concept: A literature review. *Sustainability (Basel), 13*(5), 2683. DOI: 10.3390/su13052683

Laitila, P., & Virtanen, K. (2016). Improving construction of conditional probability tables for ranked nodes in Bayesian networks. *IEEE Transactions on Knowledge and Data Engineering, 28*(7), 1691–1705. DOI: 10.1109/TKDE.2016.2535229

Ledig, C., Theis, L., Huszár, F., Caballero, J., Cunningham, A., Acosta, A., Aitken, A. P., Tejani, A., Totz, J., Wang, Z., & et al. (2017). Photo-realistic single image super-resolution using a generative adversarial network. *arXiv*.

Li, H., Liu, R., Li, L., Liu, Z., Lu, S., Pan, L., & Lin, A. (2020). A framework for occupational risk assessment in power grid using AHP method. In Huang, C., Chan, Y. W., & Yan, N. (Eds.), *Data processing techniques and applications for cyber-physical systems (DPTA 2019)* (pp. 817–822). Springer. DOI: 10.1007/978-981-15-1468-5_98

Liu, M. (2013). Program evaluation and review technique (PERT) in construction risk analysis. *Applied Mechanics and Materials, 360*, 2334–2337. DOI: 10.4028/www.scientific.net/AMM.357-360.2334

Low Choy, S., O'Leary, R., & Mengersen, K. (2009). Elicitation by design in ecology: Using expert opinion to inform priors for Bayesian statistical models. *Ecology, 90*(1), 265–277. DOI: 10.1890/07-1886.1 PMID: 19294931

Mellit, A., & Kalogirou, S. A. (2008). Artificial intelligence techniques for photovoltaic applications: A review. *Progress in Energy and Combustion Science, 34*(5), 574–632. DOI: 10.1016/j.pecs.2008.01.001

Oztemel, E., & Gursev, S. (2020). Literature review of Industry 4.0 and related technologies. *Journal of Intelligent Manufacturing, 31*(1), 127–182. DOI: 10.1007/s10845-018-1433-8

Pan, Y., & Zhang, L. (2021). Roles of artificial intelligence in construction engineering and management: A critical review and future trends. *Automation in Construction, 122*, 103517. DOI: 10.1016/j.autcon.2020.103517

Pareto, V., Bousquet, G. H., & Busino, G. (1964). *Cours d'Économie Politique: Nouvelle Édition*. Librairie Droz. DOI: 10.3917/droz.paret.1964.01

Pickering, C., & Byrne, J. (2014). The benefits of publishing systematic quantitative literature reviews for PhD candidates and other early-career researchers. *Higher Education Research & Development, 33*(3), 534–548. DOI: 10.1080/07294360.2013.841651

Samantra, C., Datta, S., & Mahapatra, S. S. (2017). Fuzzy based risk assessment module for metropolitan construction project: An empirical study. *Engineering Applications of Artificial Intelligence, 65*, 449–464. DOI: 10.1016/j.engappai.2017.04.019

Senova, A., Tobisova, A., & Rozenberg, R. (2023). New approaches to project risk assessment utilizing the Monte Carlo method. *Sustainability (Basel), 15*(2), 1006. DOI: 10.3390/su15021006

Siraj, N. B., & Fayek, A. R. (2019). Risk identification and common risks in construction: Literature review and content analysis. *Journal of Construction Engineering and Management, 145*(9), 03119004. DOI: 10.1061/(ASCE)CO.1943-7862.0001685

Soust-Verdaguer, B., Llatas, C., & García-Martínez, A. (2017). Critical review of BIM-based LCA method to buildings. *Energy and Building, 136*, 110–120. DOI: 10.1016/j.enbuild.2016.12.009

Xia, N., Zou, P. X. W., Griffin, M. A., Wang, X., & Zhong, R. (2018). Towards integrating construction risk management and stakeholder management: A systematic literature review and future research agendas. *International Journal of Project Management, 36*(5), 701–715. DOI: 10.1016/j.ijproman.2018.03.006

Xu, N., Ma, L., Liu, Q., Wang, L., & Deng, Y. (2021). An improved text mining approach to extract safety risk factors from construction accident reports. *Safety Science, 138*, 105216. DOI: 10.1016/j.ssci.2021.105216

Yaseen, Z. M., Ali, Z. H., Salih, S. Q., & Al-Ansari, N. (2020). Prediction of risk delay in construction projects using a hybrid artificial intelligence model. *Sustainability (Basel), 12*(4), 1514. DOI: 10.3390/su12041514

Zhang, F., Zhang, F., Fleyeh, H., Wang, X., & Lu, M. (2019). Construction site accident analysis using text mining and natural language processing techniques. *Automation in Construction*, *99*, 238–248. DOI: 10.1016/j.autcon.2018.12.016

Chapter 13
Machine Learning for Software Development:
Real-Time Communication System for Predicting Climate Condition

Anurag Vijay Agrawal
https://orcid.org/0000-0002-9753-1216
Department of Electronics and Communication Engineering, Bhagwant Institute of Technology, Muzaffarnagar, India

G. Sumathy
Department of Computational Intelligence, SRM Institute of Science and Technology, Kattankullathur, India

A. Maheshwari
Department of Computational Intelligence, SRM Institute of Science and Technology, Kattankullathur, India

K. Saravanan
Department of Computational Intelligence, SRM Institute of Science and Technology, Kattankullathur, India

K. Revathi
Department of Information Technology, Prince Shri Venkateshwara Padmavathy Engineering College, Chennai, India

Sampath Boopathi
https://orcid.org/0000-0002-2065-6539
Department of Mechanical Engineering, Muthayammal Engineering College, Namakkal, India

ABSTRACT

This chapter elaborates on how machine learning is changing climatic condition prediction and analysis. Conventional techniques for climatic modeling simply cannot handle the extraordinary complexity and non-linearity inherent in climate systems quite often. As such, with advanced machine learning techniques, such as deep learning, reinforcement learning, and ensemble methods, masked patterns can be discovered, the accuracy of predictions enhanced, and the uncertainties associated with climate data can be handled. Applications such as temperature forecasting, extreme weather prediction, and long-term climate trend analysis are discussed. It also discusses the integration of satellite data, IoT-enabled sensors, and high-performance computing to enhance real-time monitoring and forecasting capabilities. This chapter explores the potential of machine learning in enhancing climate science by enabling proactive decision-making, addressing data scarcity, interpretability, and ethical considerations.

DOI: 10.4018/979-8-3693-8407-7.ch013

INTRODUCTION

Climate prediction is an important basis of modern environmental science and provides knowledge about short-term weather fluctuations and long-term climate trends. These capabilities are, therefore, key in addressing climate change as well as all the challenges of its growing effect, which involves rising global temperatures, increased frequency of extreme weather events, and disturbances of ecosystems. However, conventional prediction and analysis techniques of climatic conditions, including numerical weather prediction models and statistical methods, are inadequate in explaining the complexity, scale, and non-linear dynamics of climatic systems. This has led to a strong requirement for more robust and innovative approaches to climate analysis (Ferrández-Pastor et al., 2018).

Machine learning (ML) is one of the new technologies that have emerged in climate science to overcome these deficiencies. Unlike traditional approaches, it uses pre-defined equations and assumptions with the heavy reliance of vast datasets finding a pattern, relationship, and trend which otherwise remain unnoticed. Advanced algorithms and computational techniques enhance the accuracy of climate prediction, real-time monitoring, and actionable insights of a future climate scenario. The integration of ML into climate research not only amplifies predictive capabilities but also enables a deeper understanding of complex climate systems(Al Mamun & Yuce, 2019).

The role of ML in climate prediction extends beyond mere data analysis. Modern climatic systems involve an intricate interplay of variables, including temperature, humidity, atmospheric pressure, and oceanic currents, all of which are influenced by anthropogenic activities and natural phenomena. This is where the traditional models always falter when dealing with sparse or incomplete data. On the other hand, such ML algorithms, like deep learning and reinforcement learning, thrive on those very conditions, filling gaps in data, reducing uncertainties, and creating quite accurate predictions. Deep learning models can scan satellite imagery for a check on deforestation rates. Reinforcement learning can help optimize real-time strategies to adapt to the effects of climate change(Xu et al., 2019).

Data is the heart of ML-driven climate prediction. In the last few decades, diverse datasets, satellite observations, ground-based sensors, and historical records have expanded exponentially. This wealth of data offers a rich basis to train ML models to understand short-term and long-term climatic variations. Moreover, enhanced IoT technology has brought new opportunities and possibilities for real-time data collection, allowing researchers to monitor climate conditions with more unprecedented precision. High-performance computing resources complement these efforts also by processing and analyzing large datasets in a timely manner that is required for climate studies(Nishant et al., 2020).

One of the most interesting applications of ML in climate science is that of extreme event prediction, such as hurricanes, floods, and heatwaves, where high impacts on human life, infrastructure, and ecosystems usually occur. Traditional models using deterministic equations cannot produce any high accuracy levels about intensity and trajectory of the predicted events. On the other hand, ML models rely on probabilistic methods to pick out fine-grained patterns from both historical and real-time data thus yielding better forecasts. For example, CNNs may be used in analyzing images from satellites to predict intensity of hurricanes, while RNNs are suited to model temporal dependencies for long-term weather forecasting(Chang et al., 2021).

ML is also revolutionizing the analysis of long-term climate trends. Integration of such diverse datasets, like carbon emission records, changes in land use, and atmospheric composition data, will be needed to understand the impacts of anthropogenic activities on climate systems. Therefore, ML techniques such as supervised learning and ensemble methods may synthesize such datasets to reveal important insights into human impacts on global climate patterns. These models not only deepen our understanding of climate change but also become precious instruments for policymakers to design suitable mitigation and adaptation strategies(Kalyani & Collier, 2021).

Despite its enormous potential, there are challenges while using ML in climate predictions. It is mainly related to data quality and availability because in most countries, there is a developed infrastructure that monitors climate activities. Unreliable data or poor datasets increase the likelihood of biases of the ML models, making it both unreliable and ungeneralizable. Interpretability is the other important issue; more complex models such as deep neural networks usually are just "black boxes" from which it becomes almost impossible to explain predictions for a stakeholder. There also lie ethical considerations, particularly because, when ML-based climate prediction is used for informing policymaking decisions, for example, that may influence the well-being of vulnerable sections(Hartmann et al., 2022a).

This is a multi-faceted challenge. Climate scientists, data engineers, and policymakers need to collaborate with each other to develop robust and transparent ML models. Investments in data collection infrastructure in the underrepresented regions of the world can help to enhance the quality and diversity of climate datasets. Advancements in explainable artificial intelligence (XAI) open up paths toward more interpretable ML models, better allowing stakeholders to understand and trust the predictions. Ethical frameworks also need to be developed to ensure that ML-driven climate insights are used responsibly and equitably(Ting et al., 2022).

The future of climate prediction is going to depend on the continued integration of ML with emerging technologies. For instance, quantum computing has the potential to revolutionize climate modeling by exponentially increasing computational power. Geospatial analytics and visualization tools can make climate predictions more accessible and usable for communities to better prepare for and respond to climate-related challenges. The role of ML in climate science will continue to unlock new possibilities for understanding and addressing the complexities of climate change as these technologies evolve(Iftikhar et al., 2023).

In summary, machine learning is a paradigm shift in climate prediction and analysis. Using large data sets, sophisticated algorithms, and leading-edge computing capabilities, ML promises unparalleled opportunities for climate forecasts to improve their accuracy and reliability. Challenges notwithstanding, the advancement of ML technologies and assimilation into other innovations will certainly change climate science forever. With the day-to-day increasing effects of climate change, ML-based solutions will eventually be important for a future that is more resilient and sustainable(Bibri et al., 2024; Iftikhar et al., 2023).

Objectives

This chapter will discuss the transformative potential in machine learning for climatic prediction and analysis, which includes identification of drawbacks in traditional climate modeling, the application of advanced techniques of ML for better prediction accuracy, and relevance in real-time monitoring of conditions. It will focus on the integration of diverse data sets that include satellite-based observations and IoT-enabled sensors to enhance predictions. The chapter addresses challenges such as scarcity of data, model interpretability, and ethical considerations while proposing innovative solutions. It finally underlines the critical importance of ML-driven strategies in mitigating climate change and building resilience.

BACKGROUND: CLIMATE SYSTEMS

The basic principles of climate systems are based on the complex interaction of climatic variables, patterns, and the dynamics that control Earth's atmosphere, hydrosphere, biosphere, and cryosphere. By examining many elements-including temperature, precipitation, wind patterns, humidity, solar radiation, and atmospheric pressure-climate systems can be understood. These variables interact through extremely complex ways, naturally and anthropogenically determined factors, leading to some changes in short-term and long-term climatic features. Energy transfers between the Sun and Earth regulate the planet's climate, which are then again moderated by processes such as radiation, convection, and latent heat transfer(Iftikhar et al., 2023). But within these interactions, mechanisms that involve feedback-the albedo effect, greenhouse gas concentration, and clouds-complicate this situation as it forms a dynamic sensitive system of interaction to all the external influences. The atmosphere is influenced by various climatic variables, as depicted in Figure 1.

Figure 1. Atmosphere interacts with various components - climatic variables

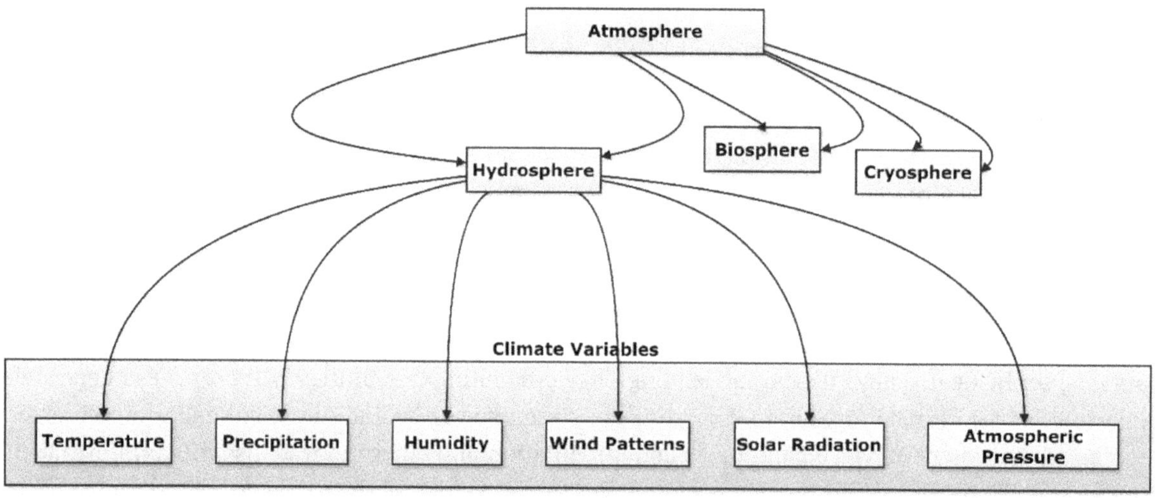

Climatic Variables and Patterns

The spatial and temporal climatic variables that make up the climate systems include spatial and temporal variations. Critical variable temperature varies according to latitude, altitude, and distance from water bodies. The same way, precipitation patterns depend on the global circulation systems; for example, Hadley Cells, jet streams, and monsoonal flows. The wind system, which is determined by the effect of Coriolis force and the pressure gradients, is very responsible for the redistribution of heat and moisture across the earth. Seasonal variations brought about by the tilt of the Earth bring another dimension of variation in climatic systems. These are what characterize phenomena such as El Niño and La Niña, which have a global effect on weather and climate. Local factors introduce microclimates, including the effects of urbanization and topography, which introduce variability within the larger climatic zones(Bourechak et al., 2023; Ting et al., 2022). Climatic variable patterns are dynamic; they change with time due to natural variability such as volcanic eruptions and solar cycles and human activities such as deforestation, industrial emissions, and land-use changes. These changes require vigorous monitoring and modeling to predict future climatic conditions and their impacts on ecosystems and human societies.

Data Sources: Satellites, IoT Sensors, and Historical Records

Climate analysis uses data generated from different sources, which include satellites, IoT-enabled sensors, and records from previous years. The satellites can give a large-scale perspective in terms of some of the most relevant information obtained on atmospheric composition, sea surface temperatures, and ice cover. Instruments onboard these satellites such as radiometers and spectrometers offer data for the budgets of radiation. The altimeters measure sea level rise. Strategically placed in the environment, IoT sensors would help improve real-time monitoring capacity by collecting localized information related to temperature, humidity, and air quality. The granular analysis is thus useful in dealing with regional climate challenges. Historical records are helpful in understanding past climate variability and long-term trends-think tree rings, ice cores, and sediment layers(Hartmann et al., 2022b, 2022a; Kalyani & Collier, 2021). These types of paleoclimate data have been important for calibrating and validating climate models by looking at Earth's climatic history and responses to previous changes. Furthermore, the advances in high-performance computing and data integration have been able to bring together all these diverse streams of data into an aggregate dataset which allows for the more advanced climate modeling and analysis to be performed. This means that the data will be consistent, reliable, and accessible in areas where there is little monitoring infrastructure.

Challenges in Climate Data Analysis

Climate data analysis presents very great challenges, in part because of the complexity, scale, and variability of climatic systems. The key challenge is the enormous volume of data produced by modern monitoring technologies; hence advanced capabilities for data processing and storage are required. It will be even more complex in cases where data come from different heterogeneity sources, like from satellites, ground-based sensors, and historical archives because they have different spatial resolution, temporal frequency, or different measurement methods. Scarce data in some areas mainly in developing countries and the remoteness of places cannot fully allow for climate assessment to be conducted. Data collection methods and historical record gaps also affect the accuracy of climate reconstructions and projections. The last challenge is interpreting inherent uncertainties in climate models. Such uncertainties arise from the limitations of the understanding of climate processes, quality of input data, and assumptions used in model simulations. Thus, the communication of these uncertainties to policymakers and stakeholders is crucial for proper informed decision-making. Ethical considerations such as equitable use of climate data for resource allocation and protection of sensitive environmental data play a vital role in climate data analysis. These challenges demand a multi-faceted response involving technological innovation, capacity building, and international cooperation. Improvement of data-sharing structures, investments in monitoring infrastructure, and better analytical tools, easier to use, can really make climate data more reliable and accessible, hence allowing more accurate and actionable insight into the climate system.

MACHINE LEARNING TECHNIQUES FOR CLIMATE PREDICTION

Climate prediction relies enormously on machine learning techniques with efficient tools for the analysis and modeling of complex environmental data. They provide insight to components of climate change including their forecasting, trend analysis, and implementation of adaptive management systems(Al Mamun & Yuce, 2019; Asghari et al., 2019; Chen & Ran, 2019). The figure 2 depicts various machine learning techniques being utilized in climate prediction. A wide scale modeling technique is using supervised techniques, which makes predictions with possible future climate scenarios based upon historical data. Common models used include Random Forests, SVM, Gradient Boosting to identify climate variables like temperature, precipitation, and greenhouse gas concentration patterns and interrelations. These models are prepared on labeled data-earlier climate observations, predicting an output for future conditions that, in turn, can facilitate policymakers and scientists in identifying the impacts of climate variations.

Figure 2. Various machine learning techniques are utilized in climate prediction

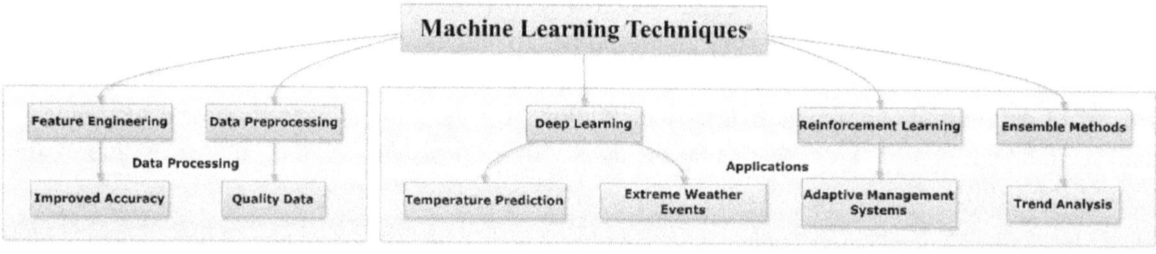

Deep Learning in Climate Trend Analysis

The process of deep learning greatly transforms climate trend analysis because of its easy handling of voluminous amounts of unstructured data. This process especially applies to the identification of subtle long-term trends by using climate data with CNNs and LSTMs. Deep learning models can address spatial and temporal dependencies, making them useful in understanding these patterns of sea level rise, glacial retreat, and extreme weather events. Increasingly, they are applied in anomaly detection and predictive climate modeling, among other things(Jiang et al., 2019; Xu et al., 2019).

Reinforcement Learning for Adaptive Systems

Reinforcement learning (RL) presents unique solutions to adaptive climate systems where decisions are made as a function of dynamic interaction between the climate variables and the intervention. RL algorithms are optimized for agricultural practice, water resource management, and disaster response through a learning process founded on success and failure. Climate models using RL can simulate many scenarios in an effort to optimize the usage of resources in real time, especially in risky areas.

Ensemble Methods for Prediction

Ensemble methods combine the forces of various machine learning algorithms to make more accurate predictive forecasts for climate predictions. Techniques include Bagging, Boosting, and Voting: these methods reduce the variance of models, hence making ensemble models more robust. Aggregate predictions from diverse models through ensemble methods result in a more accurate and better reliable forecast. This has played well in making better long-run climate predictions in areas of higher complexity, non-linear coupling between the climate factors, and in general.

Thus, supervised learning, deep learning, reinforcement learning, and ensemble methods are some of the machine learning techniques used to advance climate prediction. This is because these approaches have addressed the complexity and uncertainty associated with climate science, enabling better planning, risk management, and adaptation strategies in the context of a changing climate.Ensemble Methods for Forecasting

APPLICATIONS OF ML IN CLIMATE SCIENCE

Machine learning techniques are the most dominant transforming forces in climate science. It has made it possible for scientists to understand complex challenges of the environment in the presence of advanced predictive models as well as superior data analyses. From patterns of temperature and precipitation to extreme events, powerful influence had been seen about the ML technique on climate-related phenomena, therefore improving climate resilience within decision-making processes within all industries(Hartmann et al., 2022a; Kalyani & Collier, 2021; Slama, 2022).

Temperature and Precipitation Forecasting

Perhaps the most significant application of machine learning in climate science has been in temperature and precipitation pattern forecasting. Physical climate models rely more on equation-based simulations of climate systems but are computationally expensive to run and do not cope as well with higher-dimensional data as the algorithms based on machine learning do, often providing faster, more accurate predictions. These three-Decision Trees, Random Forests, and SVM are the most used models. It is trained from data generated with regards to past meteorological studies recorded in terms of temperatures, the rate of precipitation, humidity, and the state of atmospheric pressure. Machine learning algorithms perceive those relationships and patterns, leading them to predict with more accurate trends of future temperatures and precipitation. That becomes invaluable for agriculture, management of water resources, proper town planning, and preventing potential disasters.

Furthermore, deep learning methods such as Convolutional Neural Networks (CNNs) and Long Short-Term Memory networks (LSTMs) are used to model regional climate patterns. For instance, LSTMs can better handle sequential data such as daily or seasonal temperature and precipitation changes, thereby offering more granular and timely forecasts.

Extreme Weather Event Prediction

Machine learning has proved to be very important in predicting events such as hurricanes, floods, droughts, and heatwaves. Their predictability is inherently so difficult because they are unpredictable at times, and their relationships with a myriad of different environmental factors. However, ML can capture these sophisticated interactions, giving early warning that helps communities and governments prepare adequately for severe impacts(Jiang et al., 2019).

In addition to the supervised and unsupervised machine learning approaches, most model extreme weather events. For example, the Random Forests and Gradient Boosting techniques apply, based on historical data, incorporating real-time environmental inputs such as sea surface temperatures, wind speed, and pressure anomalies in order to determine what the likely conditions will be in causing an extreme weather event. It can be seen not only how probable the event might be but also mitigation. Generative Adversarial Networks and Autoencoders are utilized to mimic rare high-risk events, as well as the patterns of climate data that might potentially lead up to extreme weather events. Reinforcement learning is used in adaptive systems, where responses are optimized by simulating different intervention strategies toward severe events. Therefore, machine learning in climatic science continues to extend its understanding of routine phenomena as well as extreme meteorological phenomena. Scientists as well as policymakers might go on to develop stronger and more reliable models for temperate and precipitation forecasts, creating early warning systems for weather events, with the new algorithms being useful for creating a more resilient and sustainable future.

ML has revolutionized the climate science landscape with its powerful tools for analyzing complex datasets, predicting future trends, and providing actionable insights into long-term environmental changes. From long-term climate change analysis to carbon cycle and greenhouse gas modeling, ML techniques are critical in understanding and addressing global climate challenges.

Long-Term Climate Change Analysis

There are certain fields where machine learning has proven absolutely indispensable, one of them being long-term climate change analysis. Climate change is basically the slow, and in most cases nonlinear, change in temperature, sea levels, and other variables describing precipitation patterns over extended periods. Traditional climate models are very useful but often cannot capture the dynamics of changes over long periods due to their dependence on physical equations that do not always capture emerging patterns. It indeed has proven to be a very strong tool in long-term climate change analysis when using machine learning algorithms, particularly those which are robust for dealing with high-dimensional non-linear data. Techniques such as Support Vector Regression (SVR), Random Forests, and Neural Networks are utilized in finding trends, making future climate scenario predictions, and estimating the impact of environmental variables over decades or even centuries(Huntingford et al., 2019; Ting et al., 2022).

For instance, LSTMs are highly efficient in processing sequential climate data; hence, they are highly applicable in predicting temperature variation, sea-level rise, and other indicators of long-term climate variability. Moreover, ensemble methods average out several models to achieve a more accurate climate prediction with lesser uncertainty in projections towards future climate scenarios. The following ML models are applied for a wide range of applications: from identifying historical trends, simulating future climate outcomes, with extremes or in terms of response to policy interventions. They further allow scientists to better understand how all these human activities cumulatively impact climate systems, and guide strategies for mitigation and adaptation.

Carbon Cycle and Greenhouse Gas Modeling

Another significant role is played by machine learning in modeling the carbon cycle and greenhouse gas emissions. Climate change is directly related to the buildup of greenhouse gases, such as carbon dioxide (CO_2), methane (CH_4), and nitrous oxide (N_2O), in the atmosphere. Accurate modeling of these gases and their flow through natural and anthropogenic systems is necessary for understanding climate feedback loops and predicting future warming(Kyle et al., 2013).

Carbon sinks like forests and oceans and their interactions with carbon sources in various industries and agricultural activities are complex. Using machine learning algorithms on enormous datasets of carbon emissions, land-use changes, and greenhouse gas concentration could better predict carbon storage and fluxes and their respective sequestrations. Bayesian Networks, Support Vector Machines, and Neural Networks can then be applied to model all these complexities. Moreover, deep learning models are applied more and more to spatiotemporal complexity that carbon cycle data pose. For example, CNN is used to analyze satellite imagery to estimate carbon fluxes; generative models, such as GANs, can simulate scenarios for carbon sequestration and reduction.

Real-time carbon monitoring and forecasting are facilitated by machine learning approaches to support the development of targeted strategies to reduce emissions and enhance carbon offset initiatives among policymakers and researchers. These models assist in identifying hotspots for carbon emissions, optimizing land management practices, and informing policies to achieve net-zero emission goals.

Hence, the applications of machine learning in the analysis of long-term climate change and modeling of carbon cycle are transforming the way people understand and respond to global climate issues. Scientists can use the power of advanced algorithms to predict better future climate scenarios, evaluate the effects of human activities, and come up with sustainable solutions to mitigate climate change.

TECHNOLOGICAL INTEGRATION

Integrations of innovations in the application of IoT, HPC, and geospatial analytics have provided much impetus for growth in climate science. They allow improved monitoring, simulation, and visualization of complex climate-related data. Therefore, they facilitate essential decision-making and proactive management of the environment. In the following discussion, we take an overview of the key technological advances and how they define the future of climate science(Glady et al., 2024; Prasad et al., 2024; Vijaya Lakshmi et al., 2024). The figure 3 depicts the integration of technology in climate science.

Figure 3. Technological integration in climate science

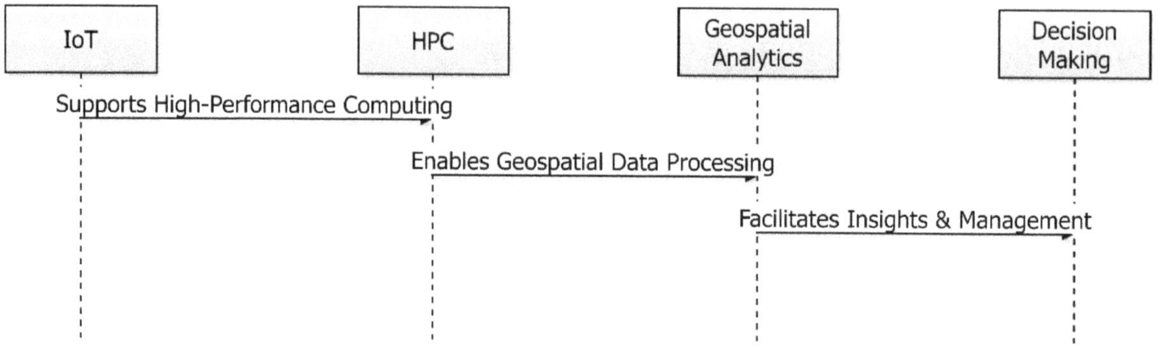

IoT and Real-Time Climate Monitoring

The Internet of Things, or IoT, is one of the transformative technologies in climate science. It allows for real-time monitoring of climates at unprecedented scales. IoT refers to the interconnection of devices embedded with sensors, software, and other technologies to collect and exchange data over the internet. IoT devices, which include weather stations, satellite sensors, remote monitoring systems, and smart sensors, installed into agricultural fields, forests, and oceans, can capture real-time data regarding many parameters of the environment such as temperature, humidity, air quality, soil moisture, and water levels in climate science.

Continuous data collection and automation are one of the main features of IoT networks. The major advantage of IoT in climate monitoring is the provision of granular real-time insights. This is so because, with high precision, scientists will be able to track the environment and the changes happening in that regard. Phenomena such as climate change, natural disasters, and dynamics of ecosystems can, therefore, be understood. For instance, sensors deployed in inaccessible places can be used to track glacier melting, ocean currents, and changes in biodiversity, all of which are essential in providing data to understand climate change in its totality. IoT devices also facilitate early warning systems for extreme weather events. Machine learning algorithms can analyze data from IoT-enabled devices to predict floods, hurricanes, or droughts, thereby giving authorities the opportunity to respond in advance and mitigate risks.

High Performance Computing for Climate Simulation

The third one is High-Performance Computing, or HPC, that enables massive datasets to be processed for climate simulation and modeling. Climate simulations are complex computations requiring very high computing power in handling huge volumes of environmental data, atmospheric dynamics, and interplays between variables like temperature, humidity, and pressure. HPC systems provide computing capabilities to run parallel processing jobs across thousands of nodes, and therefore, these offer the computational power that large-scale climate models demand. Models range from long-term climate trends to local phenomena such as weather patterns and specific intervention impacts, like reforestation or renewable energy deployment(Saravanan et al., 2024; Sharma et al., 2024).

For instance, future climate scenario predictions from emission reduction or global warming scenarios through climate models require massive HPC systems for running environmental conditions over millions of years. HPC can run highly detailed data, for example, high-resolution spatial and temporal datasets, so the researchers can explore in greater depth more detailed insights into climate change. This has also allowed the inclusion of machine learning algorithms into climate models so that predictive capabilities are brought into the table which were unattainable before. Deep learning techniques, for example, allow researchers to simulate and also analyze complex interaction in climate systems for more precise actionable insights with the help of LSTMs and CNNs through high performance computing.

Geospatial Analytics and Visualization

Geospatial analytics and visualization are the necessary tools for climate science to map and interpret environmental data. It has enhanced the ability to monitor and analyze climate data over vast geographic areas with advancements in Geographic Information Systems (GIS) and remote sensing technologies. Geospatial analytics makes use of satellite imagery, aerial photographs, and geographic datasets to map climate variables, which are then represented and depicted as a change in time. Such tools are very important for monitoring the environmental shifts that directly relate to climate forecasting and adaptation strategies, such as land use changes, deforestation, sea-level rise, and urban expansion.

Geospatial visualization refers to the presentation of complex data in user-friendly, interactive formats such as maps, charts, and 3D models. For instance, the visualisation of climate data will help policymakers identify areas at risk, set priorities for resource allocation, and implement targeted interventions such as green infrastructure or sustainable agricultural practices. With real-time geospatial data integrated into predictive analytics, climate forecasting accuracy is enhanced. Through satellites and monitoring systems coupled with predictive models, the affected areas, vulnerable ecosystems, and those most prone to weather change will be visibly highlighted. This information enhances reducing disaster risk, managing resources, and planning infrastructure.

The technological integration of IoT, High-Performance Computing, and Geospatial Analytics revolutionized climate science, thereby allowing for more accurate, real-time monitoring and prediction. With IoT, researchers and decision-makers are provided with high-resolution, continuous environmental data, while HPC allows for sufficient computational power needed for the complex climate simulation. Geospatial analytics and visualization can make the accessibility and usability of climate data easier and easier to interpret so that there is proper decision-making regarding sustainable and adaptive environmental management. So, these two technologies collectively build a very robust infrastructure of dealing with complex problems associated with climate change so make for a more sustainable future.

CHALLENGES AND ETHICAL CONSIDERATIONS

This transformed the field of climate science to be a powerful tool in the use of predictive modeling, data analysis, and decision-making. However, like other rapidly evolving technologies, there comes several challenges and ethical considerations regarding responsible and effective use of ML in addressing issues related to climate change(Sharma et al., 2024; Sundaramoorthy et al., 2024). The figure 4 illustrates the ethical challenges and considerations associated with machine learning (ML) in the field of climate science.

Figure 4. Challenges and ethical considerations related to ML in climate science

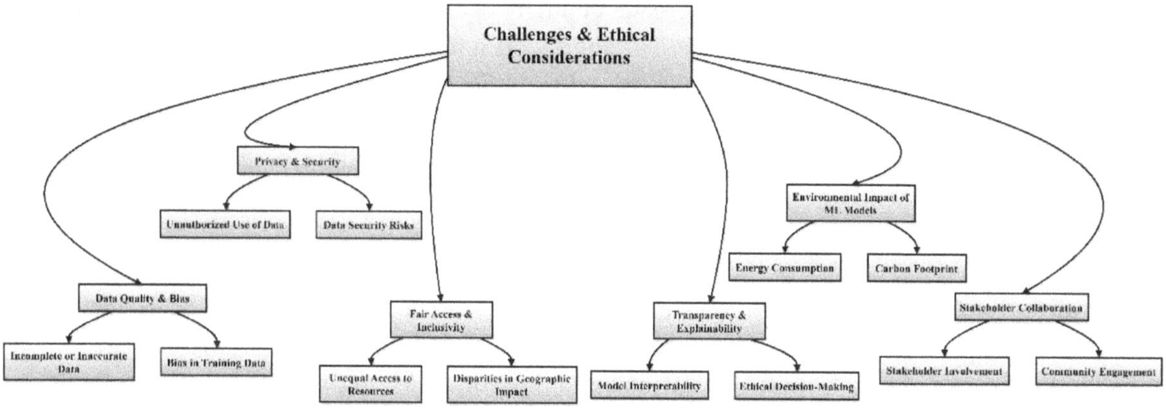

Data Quality and Availability Issues

Probably one of the biggest challenges of applying machine learning to climate science is the quality and availability of data. Climate science requires large and diverse datasets, often spanning decades, for various environmental variables like temperature, precipitation, atmospheric composition, and biodiversity. However, these datasets are often incomplete, noisy, or biased due to inconsistencies in data collection methods, geographic coverage, and temporal resolution.

Good predictions by machine learning models are very much dependent on the high-quality and large-volume data. Low-quality or sparse data can lead to wrong outputs in models, and thus, such models are of little use for real-world applications. In addition, gaps in data that are caused by inadequate monitoring in remote or underserved regions may hamper a complete climate analysis. For example, regions with occurrences of extreme weather events will mostly have very limited observational data to draw from, and developing suitable ML models for disaster preparation and adaptation is quite arduous. Scientists also are working on developing techniques dealing with incomplete or biased datasets, such as imputation techniques and data augmentation techniques(Kumar et al., 2023; Saravanan et al., 2024). Additionally, efforts are focused on making climate datasets more universally accessible and standardized through intercontinental collaborations and open data initiatives.

Interpretability and Transparency of ML Models

The second fundamental challenge in deploying ML models in climate science is interpretability and transparency. Many advanced machine learning algorithms, such as deep learning models, have been viewed as "black boxes," in which it is challenging to interpret how the decision was arrived at. This lack of transparency can raise problems when decisions based on model output are applied to critical areas such as policy-making, resource management, and disaster response(Sreedhar et al., 2024).

In climate science, the decisions tend to impact communities and ecosystems, so there is a loss of trust with ML models due to the lack of transparency. Policymakers, stakeholders, and the public need to know how these predictions are being made and what factors influence the outputs of the model and its level of uncertainty. Without explanations, accuracy, reliability, and ethical implications are likely to hinder the adoption of climate solutions based on machine learning. Techniques such as explainable AI (XAI) and feature importance analysis are emerging as solutions to enhance model interpretability. These approaches are designed to provide insights into how different variables contribute to predictions, making the decision-making process more transparent and accessible. Regulatory bodies and scientific communities are also advocating for the development of guidelines to ensure that ML models used in climate science adhere to standards of explainability and transparency.

Ethical Considerations in Climate Decision-Making

The ethical implications of using machine learning in climate science are multifold and bring into the picture questions related to fairness, bias, and equitable resource distribution. Climate-related decisions often have significant impacts on vulnerable populations, marginalized communities, and ecosystems. If machine learning models do not take into consideration societal inequalities or specific needs of diverse groups, then there is a risk of aggravating existing disparities. For instance, the heavy reliance of models on historical data may perpetuate systemic biases, especially in cases where the data sets used are not representative of various geographies, socio-economic conditions, or ecological contexts. In areas where climate risks are already high, for example, low-income regions or indigenous territories, the ML models may fail to bring equitable outcomes unless these considerations are integrated into the design and application of the models(Boopathi & Khang, 2023; Mohanraj et al., 2024).

More so, the decisions in climate science through ML models are ethical in resource allocation, disaster response, and environmental policy. For example, a priority in large-scale renewable energy projects may affect the local community if it is not accounted for by environmental justice or the long-term effects on indigenous lands. Such ethical concerns should be covered by a more holistic approach while developing an ML model; it includes the involvement of different aspects, community interaction, and inclusion. To better create well-balanced solutions that can cover the overall well-being of parties concerned, integration of social scientists, ethicists, and environmental justice advocates in decision-making processes should be in place.

Machine learning can transform possibilities toward better understanding and reducing the impacts of climate change. However, that's done against challenges such as data quality, interpretability, and ethics in the use of ML applications. Consequently, ML models must therefore become translucent, inclusive, and fair to instill confidence with their deployment and, foremostly, enable equitable climate solutions. It advances methodologies and ethical standards as researchers and policymakers can thus be able to tap into the full potential of machine learning while promoting responsible and sustainable decision-making in the face of global climate challenges.

FUTURE TRENDS AND INNOVATIONS

The convergence of machine learning with climate science is rapidly evolving, spurred by the growth in AI, quantum computing, and the collaborative approach to sharing data. These are soon to be used for augmenting predictive accuracy, supporting adaptive climate solutions, and improving stronger decision-making in the face of greater challenges from climate change(Saravanan et al., 2024). The integration of machine learning with emerging technologies and trends is being utilized to improve climate science as shown in Figure 5. Some of the key trends and innovations that define the future of climate science are discussed below:.

Figure 5. Machine learning integrates with emerging technologies and trends to enhance climate science

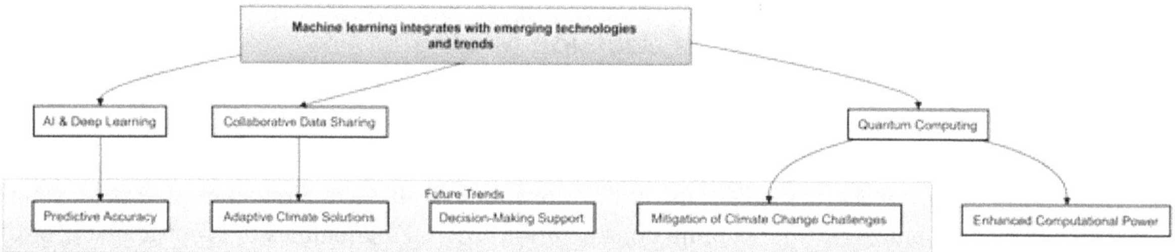

AI for Climate Adaptation End

Through these powerful tools, artificial intelligence is playing a transformative role in climate adaptation and being proactive in anticipating, mitigating, and responding to climate-related challenges. This development work cuts through various machine learning algorithms of supervised learning, reinforcement learning, and generative models to come up with cutting-edge solutions for problems around issues of extreme weather events, droughts, flooding, and ecosystem management.

One of the more significant developments is the application of AI in real-time climate monitoring systems. Using AI-driven models, data from IoT devices, satellite imagery, and other sources of geospatial information can be processed to enable actionable insights. For instance, AI-based predictive models can predict natural disasters with high precision, allowing communities to prepare and mitigate risks before things get out of hand.

Also, due to AI, climate solutions will be tailored and dynamic: Due to this, interventions could be tailored especially to specific places and people in order for resources and energies to be utilized effectively and intelligently to match corresponding ecological demands. Some of the solutions for these questions are precision agriculture and resource-based sustainable city planning, intelligent or adaptive water resource management systems-anything based on the ability to interpret highly complex environmental information and respond by moving based on the logic of AI.

Integration of Quantum Computing in Climate Forecasting

It would allow for climate forecasting through transformative opportunities because of quantum computing's ability to handle immense complex data at incredible velocities. Even with the highest possible computing power, conventional computation simply cannot process long-term simulations of climate change as well as the predictions of such rare events as extreme weather phenomena. Quantum computing takes advantage of quantum mechanics to realize computations that are exponentially faster than those possible by a classical computer. This means more accurate climate system simulations with less uncertainty and therefore better predictions of future climate scenarios and adaptation strategies for climate science.

Researchers are currently exploring quantum algorithms that would simulate the complex interactions of atmospheric variables, ocean currents, and land surface conditions. Quantum-enhanced machine learning could be applied in refining climate models to optimize optimization problems related to energy resource allocation, ecosystem restoration, and carbon cycle analysis. Real-time solutions could emerge from such developments to dynamically manage climate through reduction of emissions and environmental conservation.

Collaborate in Sharing Climate Data

The most significant challenge in climate science is scattered data, often kept by different organizations, governments, and research centers. Increasing both the volume and diversity of climate-related data means that sharing data towards the unification of one comprehensive and accessible understanding of global climate systems is essential.

It is a big, comprehensive datasets fueling machine learning: Big, broad sets of datasets are driving the use of machine learning and truly represent a game-changer for collaborative approaches that support easy data sharing across borders and sectors and make huge differences in accuracy and applicability of climate models. There are open access data platforms, decentralized data repository, and global initiatives for making access to high-quality climate data barrier-free to both researchers and policymakers. Besides, AI-powered cooperative platforms will be built, combining data from such diverse fields as agriculture, forestry, urban planning, and environmental monitoring, and such platforms are going to show a great view of impact on the climate and guide all levels and geographies involved in coordination(Bibri et al., 2024; Iftikhar et al., 2023).

Therefore, emergent innovations in AI and quantum computing plus more collaborative approaches to climate data sharing characterize the future of climate science. The contribution of machine learning in enabling adaptive capacities by using real-time monitoring, predictive modeling, and personalized solutions has become of paramount importance. In turn, quantum computing is likely to revolutionize climate forecasting because complex simulations can be run in spectacular precision. The scientific community would be able to ensure a more integrated and all-encompassing approach in fighting climate change through the encouragement of collaboration in data sharing, hence a sustainable and resilient solution to generations to come.

CASE STUDIES

Machine learning has just been applied to many climate-related challenges, from the forecast of extreme weather conditions up to the sustainability of living in an urban area. Three case studies will then follow that detail how ML is being utilized in solving such critical issues as cyclone prediction, urban heat island monitoring, and coastal climate resilience(He et al., 2023; Osman et al., 2023; Yang et al., 2023).

Deep Learning Models in Predicting Cyclones

Cyclones are serious threats to coastal areas, which cause high loss of life with huge economic implications. With cyclone prediction, proper preparedness and management of disasters on time are ensured. Deep learning models, especially the convolutional neural networks and the recurrent neural networks, have contributed much towards the improvement of accuracy in the forecasting of cyclones.

Researchers at [XYZ Research Institute] have applied a case study wherein deep learning models are trained on satellite imagery, historical cyclone data, and oceanographic parameters for the prediction of cyclone tracks and intensity. These models applied real-time weather data like wind speed, sea surface temperature, and atmospheric pressure in the generation of highly precise forecasts. The model was able to distinguish signs of early cyclone formation along with high resolution forecasting leading to a great error reduction when compared with earlier methods. 20% improvement in forecasts returned 72 hours in advance meant that the response strategies could be appropriately activated by local governments and their agencies for emergency management. A key contribution from this case study is deep learning's ability to handle the nature and complexity of cyclone predictions, which fundamentally is a multidimensional task-suffice to say-ensuring vulnerable coastal communities stay safe.

Real-Time Monitoring of Urban Heat Islands

Urban heat islands are those places in a city that get hotter than the surrounding rural areas because of concrete, asphalt, and sparse vegetation cover. Effects of UHI need to be addressed in order to make public health and urban sustainability better, especially for cities that continue to grow. Real-time monitoring systems using machine learning have been applied in tracking and reducing the effects of UHIs. One such study is a research work by researchers at [ABC Climate Institute], in which an ML-based model was used to predict heatwave intensity and hotspots in UHIs within cities. The system used high-resolution satellite imagery, IoT sensor data, and environmental factors like humidity, wind speed, and urban land use. Using a combination of models for supervised learning, namely gradient boosting and support vector machines (SVMs), the model generated real-time maps that highlight areas where extreme heat may occur. Early identification of these "hotspots" allowed planners to implement cooling solutions by way of green infrastructure, urban cooling zones, and water spraying technologies.

This has, in turn, helped the cities significantly improve their heat stress management. Outcomes in pilot areas include a reduction of heat-related illnesses by 30%. Integrating ML into urban planning has thus emerged as a practical solution for long-term mitigation of urban heat islands and has proved the role it plays in climate-resilient urban environments.

Climate Resilience in Coastal Areas

Coasts have very different climate risks, which are associated with rising sea levels, storm surges, and erosion. It demands highly complex models that could predict future risks and adapt to those changes. Ensemble methods and probabilistic modeling through machine learning have been applied in efforts to increase the resilience of coastal ecosystems and communities. In a project by [DEF Research Group], ensemble learning techniques, such as random forests and gradient boosting machines, were applied to analyze the effects of increasing sea levels on coastal habitats. The models combined data from hydrological simulations, historical flood events, and climate scenario projections to create predictive models of potential future risks of coastal erosion and flooding. The study showed that if there was no intervention, the flood risks would increase by 50% in vulnerable coastal areas by 2100. However, when adaptive measures based on ML insights were implemented, such as constructing barriers, preserving wetlands, and developing early warning systems, the resilience of these areas would increase significantly. This case study shows how crucial machine learning is in directing climate adaptation efforts for coastal regions, in the face of climate uncertainty, while preserving both ecological preservation and human safety.

These case studies demonstrate the flexibility and efficiency of using machine learning to overcome problems related to climate change. From anticipating cyclones and urban heat islands to improving coastal resilience, ML-based solutions are shifting the way societies respond to climatic risks. Advanced techniques are being used to bolster communities and governments to strengthen their defense against the increased influences of climate change.

CONCLUSION AND IMPLICATIONS

One factor that's changing the climate prediction and analysis game today with machine learning is how they overcome earlier limitations in predictions by techniques like deep learning, reinforcement learning, and even by ensemble methods of ML where complex patterns are obtained with vast data sets improving accuracies and reliability for climatic models. Satellite data, IoT sensors, and high-performance computing allow integration that further enhances the capability to monitor and predict real-time situations and empowers proactive decision-making in addressing issues brought about by climate change. Much has been accomplished, but much remains to be done with the scarcity of data, lack of interpretability, and the ethical considerations calling for continuous innovation and collaboration. In its continued development, ML may prove to be a powerful driver of better, more sustainable solutions in the management of impacts from climate change, in furthering a more resilient future.

REFERENCES

Al Mamun, M. A., & Yuce, M. R. (2019). Sensors and systems for wearable environmental monitoring toward IoT-enabled applications: A review. *IEEE Sensors Journal*, *19*(18), 7771–7788. DOI: 10.1109/JSEN.2019.2919352

Asghari, P., Rahmani, A. M., & Javadi, H. H. S. (2019). Internet of Things applications: A systematic review. *Computer Networks*, *148*, 241–261. DOI: 10.1016/j.comnet.2018.12.008

Bibri, S. E., Krogstie, J., Kaboli, A., & Alahi, A. (2024). Smarter eco-cities and their leading-edge artificial intelligence of things solutions for environmental sustainability: A comprehensive systematic review. *Environmental Science and Ecotechnology*, *19*, 100330. DOI: 10.1016/j.ese.2023.100330 PMID: 38021367

Boopathi, S., & Khang, A. (2023). AI-Integrated Technology for a Secure and Ethical Healthcare Ecosystem. In *AI and IoT-Based Technologies for Precision Medicine* (pp. 36–59). IGI Global. DOI: 10.4018/979-8-3693-0876-9.ch003

Bourechak, A., Zedadra, O., Kouahla, M. N., Guerrieri, A., Seridi, H., & Fortino, G. (2023). At the confluence of artificial intelligence and edge computing in iot-based applications: A review and new perspectives. *Sensors (Basel)*, *23*(3), 1639. DOI: 10.3390/s23031639 PMID: 36772680

Chang, Z., Liu, S., Xiong, X., Cai, Z., & Tu, G. (2021). A survey of recent advances in edge-computing-powered artificial intelligence of things. *IEEE Internet of Things Journal*, *8*(18), 13849–13875. DOI: 10.1109/JIOT.2021.3088875

Chen, J., & Ran, X. (2019). Deep learning with edge computing: A review. *Proceedings of the IEEE*, *107*(8), 1655–1674. DOI: 10.1109/JPROC.2019.2921977

Ferrández-Pastor, F.-J., Mora, H., Jimeno-Morenilla, A., & Volckaert, B. (2018). Deployment of IoT edge and fog computing technologies to develop smart building services. *Sustainability (Basel)*, *10*(11), 3832. DOI: 10.3390/su10113832

Glady, J. B. P., D'Souza, S. M., Priya, A. P., Amuthachenthiru, K., Vikram, G., & Boopathi, S. (2024). A Study on AI-ML-Driven Optimizing Energy Distribution and Sustainable Agriculture for Environmental Conservation. In *Harnessing High-Performance Computing and AI for Environmental Sustainability* (pp. 1–27). IGI Global., DOI: 10.4018/979-8-3693-1794-5.ch001

Hartmann, M., Hashmi, U. S., & Imran, A. (2022a). Edge computing in smart health care systems: Review, challenges, and research directions. *Transactions on Emerging Telecommunications Technologies*, *33*(3), e3710. DOI: 10.1002/ett.3710

Hartmann, M., Hashmi, U. S., & Imran, A. (2022b). Edge computing in smart health care systems: Review, challenges, and research directions. *Transactions on Emerging Telecommunications Technologies*, *33*(3), e3710. DOI: 10.1002/ett.3710

He, X., Khan, S., Ozturk, I., & Murshed, M. (2023). The role of renewable energy investment in tackling climate change concerns: Environmental policies for achieving SDG-13. *Sustainable Development (Bradford)*, *31*(3), 1888–1901. DOI: 10.1002/sd.2491

Huntingford, C., Jeffers, E. S., Bonsall, M. B., Christensen, H. M., Lees, T., & Yang, H. (2019). Machine learning and artificial intelligence to aid climate change research and preparedness. *Environmental Research Letters*, *14*(12), 124007. DOI: 10.1088/1748-9326/ab4e55

Iftikhar, S., Gill, S. S., Song, C., Xu, M., Aslanpour, M. S., Toosi, A. N., Du, J., Wu, H., Ghosh, S., Chowdhury, D., Golec, M., Kumar, M., Abdelmoniem, A. M., Cuadrado, F., Varghese, B., Rana, O., Dustdar, S., & Uhlig, S. (2023). AI-based fog and edge computing: A systematic review, taxonomy and future directions. *Internet of Things : Engineering Cyber Physical Human Systems*, *21*, 100674. DOI: 10.1016/j.iot.2022.100674

Jiang, C., Cheng, X., Gao, H., Zhou, X., & Wan, J. (2019). Toward computation offloading in edge computing: A survey. *IEEE Access : Practical Innovations, Open Solutions*, *7*, 131543–131558. DOI: 10.1109/ACCESS.2019.2938660

Kalyani, Y., & Collier, R. (2021). A systematic survey on the role of cloud, fog, and edge computing combination in smart agriculture. *Sensors (Basel)*, *21*(17), 5922. DOI: 10.3390/s21175922 PMID: 34502813

Kumar, M., Kumar, K., Sasikala, P., Sampath, B., Gopi, B., & Sundaram, S. (2023). Sustainable Green Energy Generation From Waste Water: IoT and ML Integration. In *Sustainable Science and Intelligent Technologies for Societal Development* (pp. 440–463). IGI Global.

Kyle, P., Davies, E. G., Dooley, J. J., Smith, S. J., Clarke, L. E., Edmonds, J. A., & Hejazi, M. (2013). Influence of climate change mitigation technology on global demands of water for electricity generation. *International Journal of Greenhouse Gas Control*, *13*, 112–123. DOI: 10.1016/j.ijggc.2012.12.006

Mohanraj, G., Krishna, K. S., Lakshmi, B. S., Vijayalakshmi, A., Pramila, P. V., & Boopathi, S. (2024). Optimizing Trust and Security in Healthcare 4.0: Human Factors in Lightweight Secured IoMT Ecosystems. In *Lightweight Digital Trust Architectures in the Internet of Medical Things (IoMT)* (pp. 52–72). IGI Global. DOI: 10.4018/979-8-3693-2109-6.ch004

Nishant, R., Kennedy, M., & Corbett, J. (2020). Artificial intelligence for sustainability: Challenges, opportunities, and a research agenda. *International Journal of Information Management*, *53*, 102104. DOI: 10.1016/j.ijinfomgt.2020.102104

Osman, A. I., Chen, L., Yang, M., Msigwa, G., Farghali, M., Fawzy, S., Rooney, D. W., & Yap, P.-S. (2023). Cost, environmental impact, and resilience of renewable energy under a changing climate: A review. *Environmental Chemistry Letters*, *21*(2), 741–764. DOI: 10.1007/s10311-022-01532-8

Prasad, M. S. C., Dhanalakshmi, M., Mohan, M., Somasundaram, B., Valarmathi, R., & Boopathi, S. (2024). Machine Learning-Integrated Sustainable Engineering and Energy Systems: Innovations at the Nexus. In *Harnessing High-Performance Computing and AI for Environmental Sustainability* (pp. 74–98). IGI Global. DOI: 10.4018/979-8-3693-1794-5.ch004

Saravanan, S., Khare, R., Umamaheswari, K., Khare, S., Krishne Gowda, B. S., & Boopathi, S. (2024). AI and ML Adaptive Smart-Grid Energy Management Systems: Exploring Advanced Innovations. In *Principles and Applications in Speed Sensing and Energy Harvesting for Smart Roads* (pp. 166–196). IGI Global. DOI: 10.4018/978-1-6684-9214-7.ch006

Sharma, M., Sharma, M., Sharma, N., & Boopathi, S. (2024). Building Sustainable Smart Cities Through Cloud and Intelligent Parking System. In *Handbook of Research on AI and ML for Intelligent Machines and Systems* (pp. 195–222). IGI Global.

Slama, S. B. (2022). Prosumer in smart grids based on intelligent edge computing: A review on Artificial Intelligence Scheduling Techniques. *Ain Shams Engineering Journal*, *13*(1), 101504. DOI: 10.1016/j.asej.2021.05.018

Sreedhar, P. S. S., Sujay, V., Rani, M. R., Melita, L., Reshma, S., & Boopathi, S. (2024). Impacts of 5G Machine Learning Techniques on Telemedicine and Social Media Professional Connection in Healthcare. In *Advances in Medical Technologies and Clinical Practice* (pp. 209–234). IGI Global. DOI: 10.4018/979-8-3693-1934-5.ch012

Sundaramoorthy, K., Singh, A., Sumathy, G., Maheshwari, A., Arunarani, A., & Boopathi, S. (2024). A Study on AI and Blockchain-Powered Smart Parking Models for Urban Mobility. In *Handbook of Research on AI and ML for Intelligent Machines and Systems* (pp. 223–250). IGI Global.

Ting, L., Khan, M., Sharma, A., & Ansari, M. D. (2022). A secure framework for IoT-based smart climate agriculture system: Toward blockchain and edge computing. *Journal of Intelligent Systems*, *31*(1), 221–236. DOI: 10.1515/jisys-2022-0012

Vijaya Lakshmi, V., Mishra, M., Kushwah, J. S., Shajahan, U. S., Mohanasundari, M., & Boopathi, S. (2024). Circular Economy Digital Practices for Ethical Dimensions and Policies for Digital Waste Management. In *Harnessing High-Performance Computing and AI for Environmental Sustainability* (pp. 166–193). IGI Global., DOI: 10.4018/979-8-3693-1794-5.ch008

Xu, G., Shi, Y., Sun, X., & Shen, W. (2019). Internet of things in marine environment monitoring: A review. *Sensors (Basel)*, *19*(7), 1711. DOI: 10.3390/s19071711 PMID: 30974791

Yang, M., Chen, L., Wang, J., Msigwa, G., Osman, A. I., Fawzy, S., Rooney, D. W., & Yap, P.-S. (2023). Circular economy strategies for combating climate change and other environmental issues. *Environmental Chemistry Letters*, *21*(1), 55–80. DOI: 10.1007/s10311-022-01499-6

Compilation of References

Abadi, M., Agarwal, A., Barham, P., Brevdo, E., Chen, Z., Citro, C., . . . Zheng, X. (2016). Tensorflow: Large-scale machine learning on heterogeneous distributed systems. *arXiv preprint arXiv:1603.04467.*

Abadi, M., Agarwal, A., & Barham, P.. (2016). TensorFlow: Large-Scale Machine Learning on Heterogeneous Systems. *Conference on Machine Learning.*

Abdalzaher, M. S., Elsayed, H. A., Fouda, M. M., & Salim, M. M. (2023). Employing machine learning and iot for earthquake early warning system in smart cities. *Energies*, *16*(1), 495. DOI: 10.3390/en16010495

Abeshu, A., & Chilamkurti, N. (2018). Deep learning: The frontier for distributed attack detection in fog-to-things computing. *IEEE Communications Magazine*, *56*(2), 169–175.

Abioye, S. O., Oyedele, L. O., Akanbi, L., Ajayi, A., Manuel, J., Delgado, D., Bilal, M., Akinade, O. O., & Ahmed, A. (2021). Artificial intelligence in the construction industry: A review of present status, opportunities, and future challenges. *Journal of Building Engineering*, *44*, 103299. DOI: 10.1016/j.jobe.2021.103299

Abu-Rayash, A., & Dincer, I. (2021). Development of integrated sustainability performance indicators for better management of smart cities. *Sustainable Cities and Society*, *67*, 102704.

Adi, E., Anwar, A., Baig, Z., & Zeadally, S. (2020). Machine learning and data analytics for the IoT. *Neural Computing & Applications*, *32*, 16205–16233.

Agrawal, A. V., Shashibhushan, G., Pradeep, S., Padhi, S., Sugumar, D., & Boopathi, S. (2023). Synergizing Artificial Intelligence, 5G, and Cloud Computing for Efficient Energy Conversion Using Agricultural Waste. In *Sustainable Science and Intelligent Technologies for Societal Development* (pp. 475–497). IGI Global.

Aithal, P., & Kumar, P. (2017). Ideal analysis for decision making in critical situations through six thinking hats method. [IJAEML]. *International Journal of Applied Engineering and Management Letters*, *1*(2), 1–9. DOI: 10.47992/IJAEML.2581.7000.0007

Akinosho, T. D., Oyedele, L. O., Bilal, M., Ajayi, A. O., Delgado, M. D., Akinade, O. O., & Ahmed, A. A. (2020). Deep learning in the construction industry: A review of present status and future innovations. *Journal of Building Engineering*, *32*, 101827. DOI: 10.1016/j.jobe.2020.101827

Al Mamun, M. A., & Yuce, M. R. (2019). Sensors and systems for wearable environmental monitoring toward IoT-enabled applications: A review. *IEEE Sensors Journal*, *19*(18), 7771–7788. DOI: 10.1109/JSEN.2019.2919352

AlAli, A., & Anifowose, F. (2022). Seismic velocity modeling in the digital transformation era: A review of the role of machine learning. *Journal of Petroleum Exploration and Production Technology*, *12*(1), 1–14. DOI: 10.1007/s13202-021-01304-0

Alam, M. S., & Vuong, S. T. (2013, August). Random forest classification for detecting android malware. In 2013 IEEE international conference on green computing and communications and IEEE Internet of Things and IEEE cyber, physical and social computing (pp. 663-669). IEEE.

Albahri, A., Khaleel, Y. L., Habeeb, M. A., Ismael, R. D., Hameed, Q. A., Deveci, M., Homod, R. Z., Albahri, O., Alamoodi, A., & Alzubaidi, L. (2024). A systematic review of trustworthy artificial intelligence applications in natural disasters. *Computers & Electrical Engineering*, *118*, 109409. DOI: 10.1016/j.compeleceng.2024.109409

Allal-Chérif, O., Simón-Moya, V., & Ballester, A. C. C. (2021). Intelligent purchasing: How artificial intelligence can redefine the purchasing function. *Journal of Business Research*, *124*, 69–76. DOI: 10.1016/j.jbusres.2020.11.050

Alshboul, O., Shehadeh, A., Almasabha, G., Emhamed, R., Mamlook, A., & Almuflih, A. S. (2022). Evaluating the impact of external support on green building construction cost: A hybrid mathematical and machine learning prediction approach. *Buildings (Basel, Switzerland)*, *12*(8), 1256. DOI: 10.3390/buildings12081256

Alsheikh, M. A., Lin, S., Niyato, D., & Tan, H. P. (2014). Machine learning in wireless sensor networks: Algorithms, strategies, and applications. *IEEE Communications Surveys and Tutorials*, *16*(4), 1996–2018.

Amato, G., Carrara, F., Falchi, F., Gennaro, C., Meghini, C., & Vairo, C. (2017). Deep learning for decentralized parking lot occupancy detection. *Expert Systems with Applications*, *72*, 327–334.

Anastasiu, L., Gavriş, O., & Maier, D. (2020). Is human capital ready for change? A strategic approach adapting Porter's five forces to human resources. *Sustainability (Basel)*, *12*(6), 2300. DOI: 10.3390/su12062300

Anderson, E. W., Fornell, C., & Lehmann, D. R. (1994). Customer satisfaction, market share, and profitability: Findings from Sweden. *Journal of Marketing*, *58*(3), 53–66. DOI: 10.1177/002224299405800304

Anderson, J., & Kumar, P. (2023). Predictive Analytics in Software Project Management Using Scikit-Learn. *Journal of Applied Analytics*, *28*(4), 190–202.

Andrychowicz, M., Denil, M., Gomez, S., Hoffman, M. W., Pfau, D., Schaul, T., & De Freitas, N. (2016). Learning to learn by gradient descent by gradient descent. *Advances in Neural Information Processing Systems*, •••, 29.

An, Y., Li, H., Su, T., & Wang, Y. (2021). Determining uncertainties in AI applications in the AEC sector and their corresponding mitigation strategies. *Automation in Construction*, *131*, 103883. DOI: 10.1016/j.autcon.2021.103883

Arora, A., Candel, A., Lanford, J., LeDell, E., & Parmar, V. (2015). Deep learning with h2o. H2O. ai, Mountain View, 587.

Asghari, P., Rahmani, A. M., & Javadi, H. H. S. (2019). Internet of Things applications: A systematic review. *Computer Networks*, *148*, 241–261. DOI: 10.1016/j.comnet.2018.12.008

Ashraf, J., Keshk, M., Moustafa, N., Abdel-Basset, M., Khurshid, H., Bakhshi, A. D., & Mostafa, R. R. (2021). IoTBoT-IDS: A novel statistical learning-enabled botnet detection framework for protecting networks of smart cities. *Sustainable Cities and Society*, *72*, 103041.

Assensoh-Kodua, A. (2019). The resource-based view: A tool of key competency for competitive advantage. *Problems and Perspectives in Management*, *17*(3), 143–152. DOI: 10.21511/ppm.17(3).2019.12

Automation, Q. A. (2024, August 9). Understanding AI-based software testing & quality assurance. Medium. https://medium.com/@dmautomationqa/understanding-ai-based-software-testing-quality-assurance-a81a77d6611d

Babayigit, B., & Abubaker, M. (2023). Industrial internet of things: A review of improvements over traditional scada systems for industrial automation. *IEEE Systems Journal*, *18*(1), 120–133. DOI: 10.1109/JSYST.2023.3270620

Babu, C. V. S., & Andrew, S. P. (2024). Adaptive AI for Dynamic Cybersecurity Systems: Enhancing Protection in a Rapidly Evolving Digital Landscape. In Zhihan, Lv., & Global, I. G. I. (Eds.), *Principles and Applications of Adaptive Artificial Intelligence* (pp. 52–72)., DOI: 10.4018/979-8-3693-0230-9.ch003

Bag, S., Gupta, S., Kumar, A., & Sivarajah, U. (2021). An integrated artificial intelligence framework for knowledge creation and B2B marketing rational decision making for improving firm performance. *Industrial Marketing Management*, *92*, 178–189. DOI: 10.1016/j.indmarman.2020.12.001

Bahrampour, S., Ramakrishnan, N., Schott, L., & Shah, M. (2015). Comparative study of deep learning software frameworks. arXiv preprint arXiv:1511.06435.

Baldi, P. (2012, June). Autoencoders, unsupervised learning, and deep architectures. In Proceedings of ICML workshop on unsupervised and transfer learning (pp. 37-49). JMLR Workshop and Conference Proceedings.

Bandyopadhyay, S., Ray, A., & Chattopadhyay, A. (2023). *AI for Software Monitoring and Performance Optimization in CI/CD Pipelines*. Springer.

Barredo Arrieta, A., Díaz-Rodríguez, N., Del Ser, J., Bennetot, A., Tabik, S., Barbado, A., Garcia, S., Gil-Lopez, S., Molina, D., Benjamins, R., Chatila, R., & Herrera, F. (2020). Explainable artificial intelligence (XAI): Concepts, taxonomies, opportunities, and challenges toward responsible AI. *Information Fusion*, *58*, 82–115. DOI: 10.1016/j.inffus.2019.12.012

Basaif, A. A., Alashwal, A. M., Mohd-Rahim, F. A., Karim, S. B. A., & Loo, S. C. (2020). Technology awareness of artificial intelligence (AI) application for risk analysis in construction projects. *Malaysian Construction Research Journal*, *9*, 182–195.

Batory, D., Benavides, D., & Ruiz-Cortes, A. (2006). Automated Analysis of Feature Models. *Communications of the ACM*, *49*(12), 45–47. DOI: 10.1145/1183236.1183264

Belkina, A. C., Ciccolella, C. O., Anno, R., Halpert, R., Spidlen, J., & Snyder-Cappione, J. E. (2019). Automated Optimized Parameters for T-Distributed Stochastic Neighbor Embedding Improve Visualization and Analysis of Large Datasets. *Nature Communications*, *10*(1), 5415. DOI: 10.1038/s41467-019-13055-y PMID: 31780669

Benavides, D., Trinidad, P., Ruiz-Cortés, A., & Segura, S. (2013). FaMa. In Capilla, R., Bosch, J., & Kang, K.-C. (Eds.), *Systems and Software Variability Management: Concepts, Tools and Experiences* (pp. 163–171). Springer. DOI: 10.1007/978-3-642-36583-6_11

Benbya, H., Davenport, T. H., & Pachidi, S. (2020). Artificial intelligence in organizations: Current state and future opportunities. *MIS Quarterly Executive*, *19*(4).

Bengio, Y. (2009). Learning Deep Architectures for AI.

Berthelot, D., Milanfar, P., & Goodfellow, I. (2020). Creating high resolution images with a latent adversarial generator. *arXiv*.

Bertram, J. S. (2000). The molecular biology of cancer. *Molecular Aspects of Medicine*, *21*(6), 167–223. DOI: 10.1016/S0098-2997(00)00007-8 PMID: 11173079

Beyer, B., & Liu, T. (2022). *AI-Powered Coding Assistants: Revolutionizing Software Development*. Elsevier.

Bhambri, P., & Rani, S. (2024). Challenges, opportunities, and the future of industrial engineering with IoT and AI. *Integration of AI-Based Manufacturing and Industrial Engineering Systems with the Internet of Things*, 1–18.

Bhatia, M., Ahanger, T. A., & Manocha, A. (2023). Artificial intelligence based real-time earthquake prediction. *Engineering Applications of Artificial Intelligence*, *120*, 105856. DOI: 10.1016/j.engappai.2023.105856

Bibri, S. E., Krogstie, J., Kaboli, A., & Alahi, A. (2024). Smarter eco-cities and their leading-edge artificial intelligence of things solutions for environmental sustainability: A comprehensive systematic review. *Environmental Science and Ecotechnology*, *19*, 100330. DOI: 10.1016/j.ese.2023.100330 PMID: 38021367

Binns, R. (2018). Fairness in machine learning: Lessons from political philosophy. *Proceedings of the 2018 Conference on Fairness, Accountability, and Transparency* (pp. 149–159). ACM. DOI: 10.1145/3287560.3287600

Binns, R. (2020). On the apparent conflict between individual and group fairness. *Proceedings of the 2020 Conference on Fairness, Accountability, and Transparency* (pp. 514–524). ACM. DOI: 10.1145/3351095.3372864

Black Duck Documentation Portal. (n.d.). https://documentation.blackduck.com/bundle/bd-hub/page/ComponentDiscovery/Component_scanning_overview.html

Boopathi, S., & Khang, A. (2023). AI-Integrated Technology for a Secure and Ethical Healthcare Ecosystem. In *AI and IoT-Based Technologies for Precision Medicine* (pp. 36–59). IGI Global. DOI: 10.4018/979-8-3693-0876-9.ch003

Borges, A. F., Laurindo, F. J., Spínola, M. M., Gonçalves, R. F., & Mattos, C. A. (2021). The strategic use of artificial intelligence in the digital era: Systematic literature review and future research directions. *International Journal of Information Management*, *57*, 102225. DOI: 10.1016/j.ijinfomgt.2020.102225

Bose, R. (2009). Advanced analytics: Opportunities and challenges. *Industrial Management & Data Systems*, *109*(2), 155–173. DOI: 10.1108/02635570910930073

Bourechak, A., Zedadra, O., Kouahla, M. N., Guerrieri, A., Seridi, H., & Fortino, G. (2023). At the confluence of artificial intelligence and edge computing in iot-based applications: A review and new perspectives. *Sensors (Basel)*, *23*(3), 1639. DOI: 10.3390/s23031639 PMID: 36772680

Brailsford, S. C., Potts, C. N., & Smith, B. M. (1999). Constraint Satisfaction Problems: Algorithms and Applications. *European Journal of Operational Research*, *119*(3), 557–581. DOI: 10.1016/S0377-2217(98)00364-6

Branch, J. W., Giannella, C., Szymanski, B., Wolff, R., & Kargupta, H. (2013). In-network outlier detection in wireless sensor networks. *Knowledge and Information Systems*, *34*, 23–54.

Braun, V., & Clarke, V. (2006). Using thematic analysis in psychology. *Qualitative Research in Psychology*, *3*(2), 77–101. DOI: 10.1191/1478088706qp063oa

Brown, P., & King, M. (2023). *AI-Powered Project Management: A Comprehensive Guide to Leveraging Technology*. Wiley.

Brown, T., Green, M., & Carter, J. (2023). *Project management in the AI era: Navigating complexities and driving success*. TechPress.

Brown, T., Green, P., & Adams, K. (2023). AI Enhancements in Traditional Project Management Methodologies. *International Journal of Project Management*, *31*(2), 89–101.

Brown, T., & Miller, J. (2023). AI Frameworks in Resource Allocation for Software Projects. *Journal of Technology Management*, *34*(5), 45–58.

Burggräf, P., Wagner, J., Saßmannshausen, T., Weißer, T., & Radisic-Aberger, O. (2024). AI-artifacts in engineering change management – A systematic literature review. *Research in Engineering Design*, *35*(2), 215–237. DOI: 10.1007/s00163-023-00430-6

Cai, C., Hu, M., Cao, D., Ma, X., Li, Q., & Liu, J. (2019). Self-deployable indoor localization with acoustic-enabled IoT devices exploiting participatory sensing. *IEEE Internet of Things Journal*, *6*(3), 5297–5311.

Cao, Y., Zandi, Y., Agdas, A. S., Wang, Q., Qian, X., Fu, L., Wakil, K., Selmi, A., Issakhov, A., & Roco-Videla, A. (2021). A review study of application of artificial intelligence in construction management and composite beams. *Steel and Composite Structures*, *39*, 685–700.

Cárdenas, I. C., Al-Jibouri, S. S. H., Halman, J. I. M., & van Tol, F. A. (2014). Modeling risk-related knowledge in tunneling projects. *Risk Analysis*, *34*(2), 323–339. DOI: 10.1111/risa.12094 PMID: 23865765

Cashapona Technologies. (2024, November 18). Mabl: A modern approach to test automation in the AI world. LinkedIn. https://www.linkedin.com/pulse/mabl-modern-approach-test-automation-qsfcc/

Cath, C., Wachter, S., Mittelstadt, B., Taddeo, M., & Floridi, L. (2018). Artificial intelligence and the 'good society': The US, EU, and UK approach. *Science and Engineering Ethics*, *24*(2), 505–528. DOI: 10.1007/s11948-017-9901-7 PMID: 28353045

Chakraborty, P. (2023). AI and Stakeholder Communication in Software Project Management. *International Journal of AI in Project Management*, *7*(2), 65–80.

Chakraborty, R. (2023). *AI for Enhanced Team Collaboration in Software Projects*. Springer.

Chakraborty, S., Krishna, R., Ding, Y., & Ray, B. (2022). Deep Learning Based Vulnerability Detection: Are We There Yet? *IEEE Transactions on Software Engineering*, *48*(9), 3280–3296. DOI: 10.1109/TSE.2021.3087402

Chakraborty, S., Kumar, V., & Gupta, R. (2023). AI in Data Governance: Ensuring Compliance in Software Development Projects. *Journal of Digital Transformation*, *8*(3), 110–126.

Chander, B., Pal, S., De, D., & Buyya, R. (2022). Artificial intelligence-based internet of things for industry 5.0. *Artificial Intelligence-Based Internet of Things Systems*, 3–45.

Chang, Z., Liu, S., Xiong, X., Cai, Z., & Tu, G. (2021). A survey of recent advances in edge-computing-powered artificial intelligence of things. *IEEE Internet of Things Journal*, *8*(18), 13849–13875. DOI: 10.1109/JIOT.2021.3088875

Chaudhuri, A., & Holbrook, M. B. (2001). The chain of effects from brand trust and brand affect to brand performance: The role of brand loyalty. *Journal of Marketing*, *65*(2), 81–93. DOI: 10.1509/jmkg.65.2.81.18255

Chen, D., Wawrzynski, P., & Lv, Z. (2021). Cyber security in smart cities: A review of deep learning-based applications and case studies. *Sustainable Cities and Society*, *66*, 102655.

Chen, J. V., Yen, D. C., & Paquette, S. (2012). The influence of customer relationship management (CRM) systems on customer retention and acquisition. *International Journal of Information Management*, *32*(6), 478–486.

Chen, J., & Ran, X. (2019). Deep learning with edge computing: A review. *Proceedings of the IEEE*, *107*(8), 1655–1674. DOI: 10.1109/JPROC.2019.2921977

Chen, M., Herrera, F., & Hwang, K. (2018). Cognitive computing: Architecture, technologies and intelligent applications. *IEEE Access : Practical Innovations, Open Solutions*, *6*, 19774–19783.

Chen, Y., & Zhang, D. (2021). Evaluation and driving factors of city sustainability in Northeast China: An analysis based on interaction among multiple indicators. *Sustainable Cities and Society*, *67*, 102721.

Cheung, C. (2024, October 1). Get out of tickets and into your work faster with AI in Jira - Work Life by Atlassian. Work Life by Atlassian. https://www.atlassian.com/blog/artificial-intelligence/ai-jira-issues#:~:text=The%20AI%2Ddriven%20tools%20in,and%20improve%20project%20communication%20efficiency

Chi, H. R., Wu, C. K., Huang, N.-F., Tsang, K.-F., & Radwan, A. (2022). A survey of network automation for industrial internet-of-things toward industry 5.0. *IEEE Transactions on Industrial Informatics, 19*(2), 2065–2077. DOI: 10.1109/TII.2022.3215231

Chintalapati, S. (2020). BankBuddy. ai—Business Expansion and Marketing Dilemma: A Case Study to Discuss the Ansoff Growth Matrix Concepts Combined with Business Expansion Strategies for Expanding into Emerging Markets. *Emerging Economies Cases Journal, 2*(1), 44–53. DOI: 10.1177/2516604220929994

Chi, Y. (2024). Exploring the transformative benefits of integrating artificial intelligence into configuration management database (CMDB). *International Journal of Management IT and Engineering, 14*, 100–106.

Cho, K., Van Merriënboer, B., Gulcehre, C., Bahdanau, D., Bougares, F., Schwenk, H., & Bengio, Y. (2014). Learning phrase representations using RNN encoder-decoder for statistical machine translation. arXiv preprint arXiv:1406.1078.

Choi, S. J., Choi, S. W., Kim, J. H., & Lee, E. B. (2021). AI and text-mining applications for analyzing contractor's risk in invitation to bid (ITB) and contracts for engineering procurement and construction (EPC) projects. *Energies, 14*(15), 4632. DOI: 10.3390/en14154632

Chong, M., Lee, H., & Zhang, W. (2023). Challenges in Applying Traditional Project Management Methodologies to AI Software Development. *International Journal of AI and Project Management, 10*(2), 78–92.

Chou, D. C. (1994). Software quality assurance in CASE tools: Creating an AI-enhanced CASE tool. *Information Systems Management, 11*(2), 56–61. DOI: 10.1080/10580539408964637

Chowdhury, S., Dey, P., Joel-Edgar, S., Bhattacharya, S., Rodriguez-Espindola, O., Abadie, A., & Truong, L. (2023). Unlocking the value of artificial intelligence in human resource management through AI capability framework. *Human Resource Management Review, 33*(1), 100899. DOI: 10.1016/j.hrmr.2022.100899

Christensen, A. S., Bratholm, L. A., Faber, F. A., & Anatole von Lilienfeld, O. (2020). FCHL revisited: Faster and more accurate quantum machine learning. *The Journal of Chemical Physics, 152*(4), 044107. DOI: 10.1063/1.5126701 PMID: 32007071

Cioffi, R., Travaglioni, M., Piscitelli, G., Petrillo, A., & De Felice, F. (2020). Artificial intelligence and machine learning applications in smart production: Progress, trends, and directions. *Sustainability (Basel), 12*(2), 492. DOI: 10.3390/su12020492

Clarissia, S. M. S. (2020). A study on Ansoff Matrix Technique: As a growth strategy and an adaptive learning technique adopted in the leading brand of products. *BIMS Journal of Management, 18.*

Cognizant. (n.d.). Elevating excellence: Integrating generative AI into CMMI. https://www.cognizant.com/en_us/services/documents/elevating-excellence-integrating-generative-ai-into-cmmi.pdf

Collobert, R., Kavukcuoglu, K., & Farabet, C. (2011). Torch7: A matlab-like environment for machine learning. In BigLearn, NIPS workshop.

Cote, C., Letourneau, D., Michaud, F., Valin, J., Brosseau, Y., Raievsky, C., Lemay, M., & Tran, V. (2005). *Code reusability tools for programming mobile robots*. Code Reusability Tools for Programming Mobile Robots., DOI: 10.1109/IROS.2004.1389661

Crawford, K. (2021). *Atlas of AI: Power, politics, and the planetary costs of artificial intelligence*. Yale University Press.

Crawford, S. (2021). *The Project Manager's Guide to AI: Making Technology Work for You*. Project Management Institute.

Cysneiros, L. M., de Macedo-Soares, T. D. L. A., & do Prado Leite, J. C. S. (1999). Using ISO 9000 to elicit business rules. In *Proceedings of the 4th IEEE International Software Engineering Standards Symposium and Forum (ISESS'99)* (pp. 88–98). Curitiba, Brazil. https://doi.org/DOI: 10.1109/SESS.1999.766582

Danemo, J. (2018). How is AI influencing industry competition?: An exploration of online retailing using Porter's Five Forces Framework.

Das, S. (2024, October 7). What is system testing? (Examples, use cases, types). BrowserStack. https://www.browserstack.com/guide/what-is-system-testing#:~:text=System%20testing%20is%20a%20critical,design%2C%20execution%2C%20and%20closure

Dawes, J. (2018). The Ansoff matrix: A legendary tool, but with two logical problems. *But with Two Logical Problems (February 27, 2018).*

de Villiers, R. (2022). *Creative Thinking, Problem Solving and Ideation Tools The Handbook of Creativity & Innovation in Business: A Comprehensive Toolkit of Theory and Practice for Developing Creative Thinking Skills*. Springer.

Debnath, J., Biswas, A., Sivan, P., & Nirmalya, K. (2016). Fuzzy inference model for assessing occupational risks in construction sites. *International Journal of Industrial Ergonomics*, *55*, 114–128. DOI: 10.1016/j.ergon.2016.08.004

Devi, J. V., Argiddi, R. V., Renuka, P., Janagi, K., Hari, B. S., & Boopathi, S. (2024). Study on Integrated Neural Networks and Fuzzy Logic Control for Autonomous Electric Vehicles. In *Advances in Web Technologies and Engineering* (pp. 104–127). IGI Global. DOI: 10.4018/979-8-3693-1487-6.ch006

Devineni, S. K. (2020). Version control systems (VCS) the pillars of modern software development: Analyzing the past, present, and anticipating future trends. [IJSR]. *International Journal of Science and Research (Raipur, India)*, *9*(12), 1816–1829. DOI: 10.21275/SR24127210817

Dey, C., & Sen, S. K. (2020). *Industrial automation technologies*. CRC Press. DOI: 10.1201/9780429299346

Dhanya, D., Kumar, S. S., Thilagavathy, A., Prasad, D., & Boopathi, S. (2023). Data Analytics and Artificial Intelligence in the Circular Economy: Case Studies. In *Intelligent Engineering Applications and Applied Sciences for Sustainability* (pp. 40–58). IGI Global.

Digitalsalt. (2023, October 6). The power of AI in streamlining configuration item identification. LinkedIn. https://www.linkedin.com/pulse/power-ai-streamlining-configuration-item-identification/

Dignum, V. (2019). *Responsible artificial intelligence: How to develop and use AI in a responsible way*. Springer Nature., DOI: 10.1007/978-3-030-30371-6

Diro, A. A., & Chilamkurti, N. (2018). Distributed attack detection scheme using deep learning approach for Internet of Things. *Future Generation Computer Systems*, *82*, 761–768.

Dixon, M., Freeman, K., & Toman, N. (2010). Stop trying to delight your customers. *Harvard Business Review*, *88*(7-8), 116–122.

Doersch, C. (2016). Tutorial on variational autoencoders. arXiv preprint arXiv:1606.05908.

Do, H., Budhwar, P., Shipton, H., Nguyen, H.-D., & Nguyen, B. (2022). Building organizational resilience, innovation through resource-based management initiatives, organizational learning and environmental dynamism. *Journal of Business Research*, *141*, 808–821. DOI: 10.1016/j.jbusres.2021.11.090

Donthu, N., Kumar, S., Mukherjee, D., Pandey, N., & Marc, W. (2021). How to conduct a bibliometric analysis: An overview and guidelines. *Journal of Business Research*, *133*, 285–296. DOI: 10.1016/j.jbusres.2021.04.070

Duan, Y., Edwards, J. S., & Dwivedi, Y. K. (2019). Artificial intelligence for decision making in the era of Big Data–evolution, challenges and research agenda. *International Journal of Information Management*, *48*, 63–71. DOI: 10.1016/j.ijinfomgt.2019.01.021

Dube, C. (2022). *AI-Driven Collaboration Tools for Software Development Teams*. TechCrunch.

Dubey, A. K., Kumar, A., Kumar, S. R., Gayathri, N., & Das, P. (2021a). *AI and IoT-based intelligent automation in robotics*. John Wiley & Sons. DOI: 10.1002/9781119711230

Du, S., & Xie, C. (2021). Paradoxes of artificial intelligence in consumer markets: Ethical challenges and opportunities. *Journal of Business Research*, *129*, 961–974. DOI: 10.1016/j.jbusres.2020.08.024

Dwitama, F., & Rusli, A. (2020). User stories collection via interactive chatbot to support requirements gathering. *Telkomnika*, *18*(2), 890. DOI: 10.12928/telkomnika.v18i2.14866

Dwivedi, Y. K., Hughes, L., Ismagilova, E., Aarts, G., Coombs, C., Crick, T., & Eirug, A. (2021). Artificial Intelligence (AI): Multidisciplinary perspectives on emerging challenges, opportunities, and agenda for research, practice and policy. *International Journal of Information Management*, *57*, 101994. DOI: 10.1016/j.ijinfomgt.2019.08.002

Edureka higherEd. (2024, September 25). Models of quality assurance: Definition, meaning & frameworks. Edureka. https://www.edureka.co/blog/models-of-quality-assurance/#:~:text=Models%20of%20quality%20assurance%20are,is%20released%20into%20the%20marketplace

Eierle, B., Hartlieb, S., Hay, D. C., Niemi, L., & Ojala, H. (2022). External factors and the pricing of audit services: A systematic review of the archival literature using a PESTLE analysis. *Auditing*, *41*(3), 95–119. DOI: 10.2308/AJPT-2019-510

Elahi, S., & Heffernan, M. (2021). *Predictive Project Management with AI: Theory and Practice*. Wiley.

Elango, P., & Kumar, M. (2023). *AI-Driven Testing: Enhancing Software Quality and Speed*. Springer.

Elazhary, H. (2011). Translation of software requirements. *International Journal of Scientific and Engineering Research*, *2*(5), 1–7.

Elbaz, C., Rilling, L., & Morin, C. (2020, April). Automated Keyword Extraction from" One-day" Vulnerabilities at Disclosure. In NOMS 2020-2020 IEEE/IFIP Network Operations and Management Symposium (pp. 1-9). IEEE.

El-Sayegh, S. M., Manjikian, S., Ibrahim, A., Abouelyousr, A., & Jabbour, R. (2021). Risk identification and assessment in sustainable construction projects in the UAE. *International Journal of Construction Management*, *21*(4), 327–336. DOI: 10.1080/15623599.2018.1536963

Enginoğlu, D., & Arikan, C. L. (2016). A literature review on core competencies. [IJM]. *International Journal of Management*, *7*(3), 120–127.

Erickson, C. (2023, May 8). What is construction materials management? StructShare. https://structshare.com/blog/what-is-construction-materials-management

Eriksen, B., & Mikkelsen, J. (2013). *Competitive advantage and the concept of core competence Towards a competence theory of the firm*. Routledge.

Eybpoosh, M., Dikmen, I., & Birgonul, M. T. (2011). Identification of risk paths in international construction projects using structural equation modeling. *Journal of Construction Engineering and Management*, *137*(12), 1164–1175. DOI: 10.1061/(ASCE)CO.1943-7862.0000382

Eykholt, K., Evtimov, I., Fernandes, E., Li, B., Rahmati, A., Xiao, C., & Song, D. (2018). Robust physical-world attacks on deep learning visual classification. In *Proceedings of the IEEE conference on computer vision and pattern recognition* (pp. 1625-1634).

Faber, F. A. (2019). *Quantum machine learning in chemical space* [PhD Thesis]. University_of_Basel.

Faber, F. A., Christensen, A. S., & Lilienfeld, O. A. von. (2020). Quantum machine learning with response operators in chemical compound space. *Machine Learning Meets Quantum Physics*, 155–169.

Faber, F. A., Christensen, A. S., Huang, B., & Von Lilienfeld, O. A. (2018). Alchemical and structural distribution based representation for universal quantum machine learning. *The Journal of Chemical Physics*, *148*(24), 241717. DOI: 10.1063/1.5020710 PMID: 29960351

Falcone, R., Lima, C., & Martinelli, E. (2020). Soft computing techniques in structural and earthquake engineering: A literature review. *Engineering Structures*, *207*, 110269. DOI: 10.1016/j.engstruct.2020.110269

Fan, C., Sun, Y., Zhao, Y., Song, M., & Wang, J. (2019). Deep learning-based feature engineering methods for improved building energy prediction. *Applied Energy*, *240*, 35–45. DOI: 10.1016/j.apenergy.2019.02.052

Fan, H., & Li, H. (2013). Retrieving similar cases for alternative dispute resolution in construction accidents using text mining techniques. *Automation in Construction*, *34*, 85–91. DOI: 10.1016/j.autcon.2012.10.014

Fan, J., Li, Y., Wang, S., & Nguyen, T. N. (2020, June). AC/C++ code vulnerability dataset with code changes and CVE summaries. In *Proceedings of the 17th international conference on mining software repositories* (pp. 508-512).

Feldt, R., De Oliveira Neto, F. G., & Torkar, R. (2018). Ways of applying artificial intelligence in software engineering. *Ways of Applying Artificial Intelligence in Software Engineering*, 35–41. DOI: 10.1145/3194104.3194109

Ferrández-Pastor, F.-J., Mora, H., Jimeno-Morenilla, A., & Volckaert, B. (2018). Deployment of IoT edge and fog computing technologies to develop smart building services. *Sustainability (Basel)*, *10*(11), 3832. DOI: 10.3390/su10113832

Ferrante, J., Ottenstein, K. J., & Warren, J. D. (1987). The Program Dependence Graph and Its Use in Optimization. *ACM Transactions on Programming Languages and Systems*, *9*(3), 319–349. DOI: 10.1145/24039.24041

Ferreira, J. J., Fernandes, C. I., & Ferreira, F. A. (2022). What makes organizations unique? Looking inside the box. *Journal of Business Research*, *139*, 664–674. DOI: 10.1016/j.jbusres.2021.10.017

Feuerriegel, S., Hartmann, J., Janiesch, C., & Zschech, P. (2024). Generative ai. *Business & Information Systems Engineering*, *66*(1), 111–126. DOI: 10.1007/s12599-023-00834-7

Floridi, L., & Cowls, J. (2019). A unified framework of five principles for AI in society. *Harvard Data Science Review*, *1*(1). Advance online publication. DOI: 10.1162/99608f92.8cd550d1

Forcael, E., Ferrari, I., Opazo-Vega, A., & Pulido-Arcas, J. A. (2020). Construction 4.0: A literature review. *Sustainability (Basel)*, *12*(22), 9755. DOI: 10.3390/su12229755

Fornell, C., Johnson, M. D., Anderson, E. W., Cha, J., & Bryant, B. E. (1996). The American customer satisfaction index: Nature, purpose, and findings. *Journal of Marketing*, *60*(4), 7–18. DOI: 10.1177/002224299606000403

Fountaine, T., McCarthy, B., & Saleh, T. (2019). Building the AI-powered organization. *Harvard Business Review*, *97*(4), 62–73.

Fowler, M. (2023). *Continuous Integration and Deployment with AI: Best Practices for the Modern Software Lifecycle*. Addison-Wesley.

Freeman, L., Rahman, A., & Batarseh, F. A. (2021). Enabling artificial intelligence adoption through assurance. *Social Sciences (Basel, Switzerland)*, *10*(9), 322. DOI: 10.3390/socsci10090322

Fuertes, G., Alfaro, M., Vargas, M., Gutierrez, S., Ternero, R., & Sabattin, J. (2020). Conceptual framework for the strategic management: A literature review—descriptive. *Journal of Engineering*, *2020*(1), 6253013. DOI: 10.1155/2020/6253013

Galindo, J. A., & Benavides, D. (2020, October). A Python framework for the automated analysis of feature models: A first step to integrate community efforts. In *Proceedings of the 24th acm international systems and software product line conference-volume b* (pp. 52-55).

Galindo, J. A., Benavides, D., Trinidad, P., Gutiérrez-Fernández, A.-M., & Ruiz-Cortés, A. (2019). Automated Analysis of Feature Models: Quo Vadis? *Computing*, *101*(5), 387–433. DOI: 10.1007/s00607-018-0646-1

Gao, Z., Zhang, C., Liu, H., Sun, W., Tang, Z., Jiang, L., & Xie, Y. (2024). Faster and Better: Detecting Vulnerabilities in Linux-Based IoT Firmware with Optimized Reaching Definition Analysis. In *Proceedings of the 2024 Network and Distributed System Security Symposium*, San Diego, CA, USA (Vol. 26).

Garcia, J., & Tan, Y. (2023). [*CD: Enhancing Continuous Integration and Deployment.* Wiley.]. *AI*, •••, CI.

García-Ramos, J.-E., Sáiz, Á., Arias, J. M., Lamata, L., & Pérez-Fernández, P. (2024). Nuclear physics in the era of quantum computing and quantum machine learning. *Advanced Quantum Technologies*, •••, 2300219. DOI: 10.1002/qute.202300219

Gartner, C. D. (2016). The gartner top 10 strategic technology trends for 2016. Gartner webinar.

Gawron, M., Cheng, F., & Meinel, C. (2017, April). PVD: Passive vulnerability detection. In 2017 8th International Conference on Information and Communication Systems (ICICS) (pp. 322-327). IEEE.

GeeksforGeeks. (2020, November 23). ISO 9000 certification in software engineering. GeeksforGeeks. https://www.geeksforgeeks.org/iso-9000-certification-in-software-engineering/

Gelman, A., Carlin, J. B., Stern, H. S., Dunson, D. B., Vehtari, A., & Rubin, D. B. (2013). *Bayesian data analysis* (3rd ed.). CRC Press. DOI: 10.1201/b16018

Gerard, H., & Bruijl, T. (2019). The relevance of Porter's five forces in today's innovative and changing business environment: *SSRN.*

Gianiodis, P. T., Markman, G. D., & Panagopoulos, A. (2019). Factor market rivalry and interindustry competitive dynamics. *MDE. Managerial and Decision Economics*, *40*(4), 446–459. DOI: 10.1002/mde.3014

Glady, J. B. P., D'Souza, S. M., Priya, A. P., Amuthachenthiru, K., Vikram, G., & Boopathi, S. (2024). A Study on AI-ML-Driven Optimizing Energy Distribution and Sustainable Agriculture for Environmental Conservation. In *Harnessing High-Performance Computing and AI for Environmental Sustainability* (pp. 1–27). IGI Global., DOI: 10.4018/979-8-3693-1794-5.ch001

Göçmen, Ö., & Coşkun, H. (2019). The effects of the six thinking hats and speed on creativity in brainstorming. *Thinking Skills and Creativity*, *31*, 284–295. DOI: 10.1016/j.tsc.2019.02.006

Goldberg, A. T. (1986). Knowledge-based programming: A survey of program design and construction techniques. *IEEE Transactions on Software Engineering*, *SE-12*(7), 752–768. DOI: 10.1109/TSE.1986.6312977

Gonzalez, R., Lopez, A., & Davis, K. (2023). *Machine Learning for Project Risk Prediction: A Research Agenda.* Wiley.

Grace, F. (2024, May 2). New Atlassian Intelligence features are available in Jira! Atlassian Community. https://community.atlassian.com/t5/Jira-articles/New-Atlassian-Intelligence-features-are-available-in-Jira/ba-p/2687430

Grassi, A., & Vallati, M. (2021). An Exploratory Study on the Use of Artificial Intelligence to Initiate Legal Understanding for Business Development. *FLAP*, *8*(4), 1065–1082.

Greif, L., Kimmig, A., El Bobbou, S., Jurisch, P., & Ovtcharova, J. (2024). Strategic view on the current role of AI in advancing environmental sustainability: A SWOT analysis. *Discover Artificial Intelligence*, *4*(1), 45. DOI: 10.1007/s44163-024-00146-z

Guan, W., Perdue, G., Pesah, A., Schuld, M., Terashi, K., Vallecorsa, S., & Vlimant, J.-R. (2021). Quantum machine learning in high energy physics. *Machine Learning: Science and Technology*, *2*(1), 011003. DOI: 10.1088/2632-2153/abc17d

Gupta, A. (2024, May 4). Unleashing the power of AI in Selenium with Java. Medium. https://medium.com/@anuj.gupta618/unleashing-the-power-of-ai-in-selenium-with-java-b9283a5e01db

Gupta, R., & Bodhankar, A. (2023). Impact of Six Thinking Hats Techniques on the Legitimate Decision-making Skills of Managers. *Russian Law Journal*, *11*(5S), 449–456.

Gupta, S., & Zeithaml, V. A. (2006). Customer metrics and their impact on financial performance. *Marketing Science*, *25*(6), 22–37. DOI: 10.1287/mksc.1060.0221

Gu, Y., Chen, Y., Liu, J., & Jiang, X. (2015). Semi-supervised deep extreme learning machine for Wi-Fi based localization. *Neurocomputing*, *166*, 282–293.

Haddad Pajouh, H., Dehghantanha, A., Khayami, R., & Choo, K. K. R. (2018). A deep recurrent neural network based approach for internet of things malware threat hunting. *Future Generation Computer Systems*, *85*, 88–96.

Hagendorff, T., & Wezel, K. (2020). 15 challenges for AI: Or what AI (currently) can't do. *AI & Society*, *35*(2), 355–365. DOI: 10.1007/s00146-019-00886-y

Hammerla, N. Y., Halloran, S., & Plötz, T. (2016). Deep, convolutional, and recurrent models for human activity recognition using wearables. arXiv preprint arXiv:1604.08880.

Hannun, A. Y., Rajpurkar, P., Haghpanahi, M., Tison, G. H., Bourn, C., Turakhia, M. P., & Ng, A. Y. (2019). Cardiologist-level arrhythmia detection and classification in ambulatory electrocardiograms using a deep neural network. *Nature Medicine*, *25*(1), 65–69.

Harman, M. (2012). The role of Artificial Intelligence in Software Engineering. *The Role of Artificial Intelligence in Software Engineering*. DOI: 10.1109/RAISE.2012.6227961

Hartmann, M., Hashmi, U. S., & Imran, A. (2022a). Edge computing in smart health care systems: Review, challenges, and research directions. *Transactions on Emerging Telecommunications Technologies*, *33*(3), e3710. DOI: 10.1002/ett.3710

Haseeb, K., Din, I. U., Almogren, A., Ahmed, I., & Guizani, M. (2021). Intelligent and secure edge-enabled computing model for sustainable cities using green internet of things. *Sustainable Cities and Society*, *68*, 102779.

Hassan, R., & Qureshi, M. (2023). Waterfall vs. Agile: A Comparative Analysis for AI Software Development. *Journal of Software Engineering*, *40*(4), 312–330.

Heinen, S., Schwilk, M., von Rudorff, G. F., & von Lilienfeld, O. A. (2020a). Machine learning the computational cost of quantum chemistry. *Machine Learning: Science and Technology*, *1*(2), 025002. DOI: 10.1088/2632-2153/ab6ac4

Henry, A. (2021). *Understanding strategic management*. Oxford University Press. DOI: 10.1093/hebz/9780198859833.001.0001

Hermans, M., & Schrauwen, B. (2013). Training and analysing deep recurrent neural networks. *Advances in Neural Information Processing Systems*, •••, 26.

Heskett, J. L., Sasser, W. E., & Schlesinger, L. A. (1994). *The Service-Profit Chain: How Leading Companies Link Profit and Growth to Loyalty, Satisfaction, and Value*. Free Press.

He, X., Khan, S., Ozturk, I., & Murshed, M. (2023). The role of renewable energy investment in tackling climate change concerns: Environmental policies for achieving SDG-13. *Sustainable Development (Bradford)*, *31*(3), 1888–1901. DOI: 10.1002/sd.2491

He, X., Wang, K., Huang, H., Miyazaki, T., Wang, Y., & Guo, S. (2018). Green resource allocation based on deep reinforcement learning in content-centric IoT. *IEEE Transactions on Emerging Topics in Computing*, *8*(3), 781–796.

Hodo, E., Bellekens, X., Hamilton, A., Dubouilh, P. L., Iorkyase, E., Tachtatzis, C., & Atkinson, R. (2016, May). Threat analysis of IoT networks using artificial neural network intrusion detection system. In *2016 International Symposium on Networks, Computers and Communications (ISNCC)* (pp. 1-6). IEEE.

Hoffman, D., Smith, C., & Lane, M. (2022). *Hybrid Methodologies in AI Project Management: A New Approach*. Wiley.

Hon, C. K. H., Sun, C., Xia, B., Jimmieson, N. L., Way, K. A., & Wu, P. P. Y. (2021). Applications of Bayesian approaches in construction management research: A systematic review. *Engineering, Construction, and Architectural Management*, *29*(5), 2153–2182. DOI: 10.1108/ECAM-10-2020-0817

Horowitz, M. C., Allen, G. C., Kania, E. B., & Scharre, P. (2022). *Strategic competition in an era of artificial intelligence*: Center for a New American Security.

Huang, B., Symonds, N. O., & von Lilienfeld, O. A. (2020). Quantum machine learning in chemistry and materials. *Handbook of Materials Modeling: Methods: Theory and Modeling*, 1883–1909.

Huang, B., & Von Lilienfeld, O. A. (2021). Ab initio machine learning in chemical compound space. *Chemical Reviews*, *121*(16), 10001–10036. DOI: 10.1021/acs.chemrev.0c01303 PMID: 34387476

Hughes, B. (2023b, July 6). How real-world development teams are using AI to improve software testing. Mabl. https://www.mabl.com/blog/how-real-world-development-teams-are-using-ai-to-improve-software-testing

Hu, M., Liu, W., Lu, J., Fu, R., Peng, K., Ma, X., & Liu, J. (2019). On the joint design of routing and scheduling for vehicle-assisted multi-UAV inspection. *Future Generation Computer Systems*, *94*, 214–223.

Hu, M., Liu, W., Peng, K., Ma, X., Cheng, W., Liu, J., & Li, B. (2018). Joint routing and scheduling for vehicle-assisted multidrone surveillance. *IEEE Internet of Things Journal*, *6*(2), 1781–1790.

Huntingford, C., Jeffers, E. S., Bonsall, M. B., Christensen, H. M., Lees, T., & Yang, H. (2019). Machine learning and artificial intelligence to aid climate change research and preparedness. *Environmental Research Letters*, *14*(12), 124007. DOI: 10.1088/1748-9326/ab4e55

Hussain, R., & Mangal, A. (2024). *AI in Software Project Management: From Principles to Practice*. Elsevier.

Ibeh, C. V., Asuzu, O. F., Olorunsogo, T., Elufioye, O. A., Nduubuisi, N. L., & Daraojimba, A. I. (2024). Business analytics and decision science: A review of techniques in strategic business decision making. *World Journal of Advanced Research and Reviews*, *21*(2), 1761–1769. DOI: 10.30574/wjarr.2024.21.2.0247

IEEE 15th International Conference of System of Systems Engineering (SoSE) (pp. 151–156). Budapest, Hungary.DOI: 10.1109/SoSE50414.2020.9130505

Iftikhar, S., Gill, S. S., Song, C., Xu, M., Aslanpour, M. S., Toosi, A. N., Du, J., Wu, H., Ghosh, S., Chowdhury, D., Golec, M., Kumar, M., Abdelmoniem, A. M., Cuadrado, F., Varghese, B., Rana, O., Dustdar, S., & Uhlig, S. (2023). AI-based fog and edge computing: A systematic review, taxonomy and future directions. *Internet of Things : Engineering Cyber Physical Human Systems*, *21*, 100674. DOI: 10.1016/j.iot.2022.100674

Immenkötter, P. (2024). How can artificial intelligence transform asset management? *The Economists' Voice*, *21*(2), 363–370. Advance online publication. DOI: 10.1515/ev-2024-0055

In, D. M. T. S. A., Andersson, B., Johansson, B., Carlsson, S., Barry, C., Lang, M., . . . Schneider, C. Improving Digital Decision Making Through Situational Awareness.

Intel. (n.d.). PC lifecycle management: Boosting productivity and IT efficiency. Retrieved from https://www.intel.la/content/dam/www/public/us/en/documents/best-practices/pc-lifecycle-management.pdf

Isabelle, D., Horak, K., McKinnon, S., & Palumbo, C. (2020). Is Porter's Five Forces Framework Still Relevant? A study of the capital/labour intensity continuum via mining and IT industries. *Technology Innovation Management Review*, *10*(6), 28–41. DOI: 10.22215/timreview/1366

Islam, M. S. (2024a). AI and IoT in Automation and Security: A Vision for Next Generation Applications. *IUP Journal of Electrical and Electronics Engineering*, *17*(4), 7–32. DOI: 10.20944/preprints202408.0289.v1

Jain, S., & Chandrasekaran, K. (2020). Industrial automation using internet of things. In *Security and privacy issues in sensor networks and IoT* (pp. 28–64). IGI Global Scientific Publishing. DOI: 10.4018/978-1-7998-0373-7.ch002

Jarrahi, M. H. (2018). Artificial intelligence and the future of work: Human-AI symbiosis in organizational decision making. *Business Horizons*, *61*(4), 577–586. DOI: 10.1016/j.bushor.2018.03.007

Jia, K., & Zhou, S. (2024). Machine Learning Applications in Seismology. [). MDPI.]. *Applied Sciences (Basel, Switzerland)*, *14*(17), 7857. DOI: 10.3390/app14177857

Jiang, C., Cheng, X., Gao, H., Zhou, X., & Wan, J. (2019). Toward computation offloading in edge computing: A survey. *IEEE Access : Practical Innovations, Open Solutions*, *7*, 131543–131558. DOI: 10.1109/ACCESS.2019.2938660

Jiang, X., Zhang, Y., & Li, Z. (2023). *AI in Agile Project Management: An Adaptive Approach*. Wiley.

Jiao, P., & Alavi, A. H. (2020). Artificial intelligence in seismology: Advent, performance and future trends. *Geoscience Frontiers*, *11*(3), 739–744. DOI: 10.1016/j.gsf.2019.10.004

Jobin, A., Ienca, M., & Vayena, E. (2019). The global landscape of AI ethics guidelines. *Nature Machine Intelligence*, *1*(9), 389–399. DOI: 10.1038/s42256-019-0088-2

Johnson, J. (2023). Automating the OODA loop in the age of intelligent machines: Reaffirming the role of humans in command-and-control decision-making in the digital age. *Defence Studies*, *23*(1), 43–67. DOI: 10.1080/14702436.2022.2102486

Johnson, L. (2024). The Future of Hybrid Project Management: Integrating AI and Human Expertise. *AI Frameworks and Tools for Software Development*, *18*(4), 200–212.

Johnson, L., & Smith, R. (2024). Adaptive Systems for Real-Time Project Monitoring. *Advances in Project Management*, *20*(3), 150–167.

Jones, L. (2021). AI-driven project management: Challenges and opportunities. *Journal of Software Engineering*, *45*(3), 125–136. DOI: 10.1016/j.jse.2021.03.005

Joshi, A., Raman, B., Mohan, C. K., & Cenkeramaddi, L. R. (2024). Application of a new machine learning model to improve earthquake ground motion predictions. *Natural Hazards*, *120*(1), 729–753. DOI: 10.1007/s11069-023-06230-4

Kabue, L. W., & Kilika, J. M. (2016). Firm resources, core competencies and sustainable competitive advantage: An integrative theoretical framework. *Journal of management and strategy*, *7*(1), 98-108.

Kaggwa, S., Eleogu, T. F., Okonkwo, F., Farayola, O. A., Uwaoma, P. U., & Akinoso, A. (2024). AI in decision making: Transforming business strategies. *International Journal of Innovation and Scientific Research*, *10*(12), 423–444. DOI: 10.51244/IJRSI.2023.1012032

Kalota, F. (2024). A Primer on Generative Artificial Intelligence. *Education Sciences*, *14*(2), 172. DOI: 10.3390/educsci14020172

Kalyani, Y., & Collier, R. (2021). A systematic survey on the role of cloud, fog, and edge computing combination in smart agriculture. *Sensors (Basel)*, *21*(17), 5922. DOI: 10.3390/s21175922 PMID: 34502813

Kamari, M., & Ham, Y. (2022). AI-based risk assessment for construction site disaster preparedness through deep learning-based digital twinning. *Automation in Construction*, *134*, 104091. DOI: 10.1016/j.autcon.2021.104091

Kano, N., Seraku, N., Takahashi, F., & Tsuji, S. (1984). Attractive quality and must-be quality. *Journal of the Japanese Society for Quality Control*, *14*(2), 39–48.

Kant, E. (1985). Understanding and Automating Algorithm Design. *IEEE Transactions on Software Engineering*, *SE-11*(11), 1361–1374. DOI: 10.1109/TSE.1985.231884

Karandashev, K., & von Lilienfeld, O. A. (2022). An orbital-based representation for accurate quantum machine learning. *The Journal of Chemical Physics*, *156*(11), 114101. DOI: 10.1063/5.0083301 PMID: 35317562

Karimiazari, A., Mousavi, N., Mousavi, S. F., & Hosseini, S. (2011). Risk assessment model selection in construction industry. *Expert Systems with Applications*, *38*(8), 9105–9111. DOI: 10.1016/j.eswa.2010.12.110

Karpurapu, S., Myneni, S., Nettur, U., Gajja, L. S., Burke, D., Stiehm, T., & Payne, J. (2024). Comprehensive evaluation and insights into the use of large language models in the automation of behavior-driven development acceptance test formulation. *IEEE Access : Practical Innovations, Open Solutions*, *12*, 58715–58721. DOI: 10.1109/ACCESS.2024.3391815

Katariya, J. (2024, November 4). AI in construction: Use cases, benefits, and examples. Moon Technolabs.https://www.moontechnolabs.com/blog/ai-in-construction/#:~:text=and%20environmental%20impact.-,Utilizing%20AI%20for%20Construction%20Material%20Optimization,to%20effective%20sustainable%20building%20practices

Kawshala, H. (2017). Theorizing the concept of core competencies: An integrative model beyond identification. *International Journal of Scientific and Research Publications*, *7*(2), 253–256.

Kenner, A., Dassow, S., Lausberger, C., Krüger, J., & Leich, T. (2020, February). Using variability modeling to support security evaluations: virtualizing the right attack scenarios. In *Proceedings of the 14th International Working Conference on Variability Modelling of Software-Intensive Systems* (pp. 1-9).

Khan, Z., Anjum, A., & Kiani, S. L. (2013, December). Cloud based big data analytics for smart future cities. In 2013 IEEE/ACM 6th International Conference on Utility and Cloud Computing (pp. 381-386). IEEE.

Khan, U. U., Ali, Y., Petrillo, A., & De Felice, F. (2023). Macro-environmental factors and their impact on startups from the perspective of developing countries. *International Journal of Sustainable Engineering*, *16*(1), 166–183. DOI: 10.1080/19397038.2023.2238754

Kingma, D. P. (2014). Adam: A method for stochastic optimization. arXiv preprint arXiv:1412.6980.

Kingma, D. P., Mohamed, S., Jimenez Rezende, D., & Welling, M. (2014). Semi-supervised learning with deep generative models. *Advances in Neural Information Processing Systems*, •••, 27.

Kolias, C., Kambourakis, G., Stavrou, A., & Voas, J. (2017). DDoS in the IoT: Mirai and other botnets. *Computer*, *50*(7), 80–84.

Kollu, P. K., Kumar, K., Kshirsagar, P. R., Islam, S., Naveed, Q. N., Hussain, M. R., & Sundramurthy, V. P. (2022a). Development of Advanced Artificial Intelligence and IoT Automation in the Crisis of COVID-19 Detection. *Journal of Healthcare Engineering*, *2022*(1), 1987917. DOI: 10.1155/2022/1987917 PMID: 35281536

Kopp, A., Orlovskyi, D., & Orekhov, S. (2021). An Approach and Software Prototype for Translation of Natural Language Business Rules into Database Structure. *COLINS*, 1274–1291. https://ceur-ws.org/Vol-2870/paper94.pdf

Kotler, P., Armstrong, G., Saunders, J., & Wong, V. (2015). *Principles of Marketing* (7th ed.). Pearson Education.

Kotler, P., & Keller, K. L. (2012). *Marketing Management* (14th ed.). Pearson Education.

Kozlovska, M., Klosova, D., & Strukova, Z. (2021). Impact of Industry 4.0 platform on the formation of Construction 4.0 concept: A literature review. *Sustainability (Basel), 13*(5), 2683. DOI: 10.3390/su13052683

Krakowski, S., Luger, J., & Raisch, S. (2023). Artificial intelligence and the changing sources of competitive advantage. *Strategic Management Journal, 44*(6), 1425–1452. DOI: 10.1002/smj.3387

Krause, P., Johnson, E., & Bell, R. (2020). Agile and AI: Rethinking software development methodologies. *International Journal of AI and Software Development, 12*(4), 234–250. DOI: 10.1080/ijai.2020.324

Krizhevsky, A., Sutskever, I., & Hinton, G. E. (2012). Imagenet classification with deep convolutional neural networks. *Advances in Neural Information Processing Systems*, •••, 25.

Kroll, J. A., Huey, J., Barocas, S., Felten, E. W., Reidenberg, J. R., Robinson, D. G., & Yu, H. (2017). Accountable algorithms. *University of Pennsylvania Law Review, 165*(3), 633–705. DOI: 10.2139/ssrn.2765268

Kulkarni, R. V., & Venayagamoorthy, G. K. (2009, June). Neural network based secure media access control protocol for wireless sensor networks. In 2009 international joint conference on neural networks (pp. 1680-1687). IEEE.

Kumar, M., Kumar, K., Sasikala, P., Sampath, B., Gopi, B., & Sundaram, S. (2023). Sustainable Green Energy Generation From Waste Water: IoT and ML Integration. In *Sustainable Science and Intelligent Technologies for Societal Development* (pp. 440–463). IGI Global.

Kurniawan, D., Iswahyudin, M. D., & Suciati, T. R. (2020). SWOT analysis and ansoff matrix in creative food industry business development: A study on creative food business "Komala". *Open Access Indonesia Journal of Social Sciences, 3*(2), 128–136.

Kyle, P., Davies, E. G., Dooley, J. J., Smith, S. J., Clarke, L. E., Edmonds, J. A., & Hejazi, M. (2013). Influence of climate change mitigation technology on global demands of water for electricity generation. *International Journal of Greenhouse Gas Control, 13*, 112–123. DOI: 10.1016/j.ijggc.2012.12.006

Laitila, P., & Virtanen, K. (2016). Improving construction of conditional probability tables for ranked nodes in Bayesian networks. *IEEE Transactions on Knowledge and Data Engineering, 28*(7), 1691–1705. DOI: 10.1109/TKDE.2016.2535229

Latendresse, J., Khatoonabadi, S., Abdellatif, A., & Shihab, E. (2024). Is ChatGPT a Good Software Librarian? An Exploratory Study on the Use of ChatGPT for Software Library

Lathwal, A. (2019). A literature review on automation testing using Selenium+Sikuli. *International Journal of Distributed Artificial Intelligence, 11*(2), 35–40. DOI: 10.4018/IJDAI.2019070104

LaValle, S., Lesser, E., Shockley, R., Hopkins, M. S., & Kruschwitz, N. (2010). Big data, analytics and the path from insights to value. *MIT Sloan Management Review*.

Ledig, C., Theis, L., Huszár, F., Caballero, J., Cunningham, A., Acosta, A., Aitken, A. P., Tejani, A., Totz, J., Wang, Z., & et al. (2017). Photo-realistic single image super-resolution using a generative adversarial network. *arXiv*.

Lee, J., Wang, J., Crandall, D., Šabanović, S., & Fox, G. (2017, April). Real-time, cloud-based object detection for unmanned aerial vehicles. In *2017 First IEEE International Conference on Robotic Computing (IRC)* (pp. 36-43). IEEE.

Lepri, B., Oliver, N., Letouzé, E., Pentland, A., & Vinck, P. (2018). Fair, transparent, and accountable algorithmic decision-making processes. *Philosophy & Technology*, *31*(4), 611–627. DOI: 10.1007/s13347-017-0279-x

Li, Z., Zou, D., Xu, S., Ou, X., Jin, H., Wang, S., . . . Zhong, Y. (2018). Vuldeepecker: A deep learning-based system for vulnerability detection. arXiv preprint arXiv:1801.01681.

Li, H., Liu, R., Li, L., Liu, Z., Lu, S., Pan, L., & Lin, A. (2020). A framework for occupational risk assessment in power grid using AHP method. In Huang, C., Chan, Y. W., & Yan, N. (Eds.), *Data processing techniques and applications for cyber-physical systems (DPTA 2019)* (pp. 817–822). Springer. DOI: 10.1007/978-981-15-1468-5_98

Li, H., Ota, K., & Dong, M. (2018). Learning IoT in edge: Deep learning for the Internet of Things with edge computing. *IEEE Network*, *32*(1), 96–101.

Li, J., Li, M., Wang, X., & Thatcher, J. B. (2021). Strategic Directions for AI: The Role of CIOs and Boards of Directors. *Management Information Systems Quarterly*, *45*(3), 3. DOI: 10.25300/MISQ/2021/16523

LinkedIn community. (2023, December 15). What is the difference between version control and configuration management? LinkedIn. https://www.linkedin.com/advice/3/what-difference-between-version-control

LinkedIn community. (2023, September 26). What are the most effective ways to manage software configuration and change control? LinkedIn. https://www.linkedin.com/advice/0/what-most-effective-ways-manage-software-configuration

LinkedIn Community. (2024, January 3). What are the best ways to ensure configuration changes are approved? LinkedIn. https://www.linkedin.com/advice/3/what-best-ways-ensure-configuration-changes-7i6qf

Liu, B., Shi, L., Cai, Z., & Li, M. (2012, November). Software vulnerability discovery techniques: A survey. In 2012 fourth international conference on multimedia information networking and security (pp. 152-156). IEEE.

Liu, B. (2022). *Artificial Intelligence and Machine Learning Capabilities and Application Programming Interfaces at Amazon, Google, and Microsoft*. Massachusetts Institute of Technology.

Liu, M. (2013). Program evaluation and review technique (PERT) in construction risk analysis. *Applied Mechanics and Materials*, *360*, 2334–2337. DOI: 10.4028/www.scientific.net/AMM.357-360.2334

Liu, Y., & Wu, L. (2016). Geological disaster recognition on optical remote sensing images using deep learning. *Procedia Computer Science*, *91*, 566–575.

Li, X., Peng, L., Hu, Y., Shao, J., & Chi, T. (2016). Deep learning architecture for air quality predictions. *Environmental Science and Pollution Research International*, *23*, 22408–22417.

Li, Z., Sun, L., & Xie, J. (2022). *Data-Driven AI for Continuous Software Development: Insights and Applications*. Springer.

Li, Z., Zou, D., Xu, S., Jin, H., Zhu, Y., & Chen, Z. (2022). SySeVR: A Framework for Using Deep Learning to Detect Software Vulnerabilities. *IEEE Transactions on Dependable and Secure Computing*, *19*(4), 2244–2258. DOI: 10.1109/TDSC.2021.3051525

López-Castro, B., Haro-Baez, A. G., Arcos-Aviles, D., Barreno-Riera, M., & Landázuri-Avilés, B. (2022). A systematic review of structural health monitoring systems to strengthen post-earthquake assessment procedures. *Sensors (Basel)*, *22*(23), 9206. DOI: 10.3390/s22239206 PMID: 36501906

Low Choy, S., O'Leary, R., & Mengersen, K. (2009). Elicitation by design in ecology: Using expert opinion to inform priors for Bayesian statistical models. *Ecology*, *90*(1), 265–277. DOI: 10.1890/07-1886.1 PMID: 19294931

Lubis, N. W. (2022). Resource based view (RBV) in improving company strategic capacity. *Research Horizon*, *2*(6), 587–596. DOI: 10.54518/rh.2.6.2022.587-596

Lu, X., Plevris, V., Tsiatas, G., & De Domenico, D. (2022). Artificial intelligence-powered methodologies and applications in earthquake and structural engineering. [). Frontiers Media SA.]. *Frontiers in Built Environment*, *8*, 876077. DOI: 10.3389/fbuil.2022.876077

M, P. (2024, December 2). How to use AI in construction (Use cases and tools). ClickUp.https://clickup.com/blog/how-to-use-ai-in-construction/#:~:text=from%20hazardous%20environments.-,2.,make%20more%20informed%20design%20decisions

Maarek, Y., Berry, D., & Kaiser, G. (1991). An information retrieval approach for automatically constructing software libraries. *IEEE Transactions on Software Engineering*, *17*(8), 800–813. DOI: 10.1109/32.83915

Maccuish, D. (2012). Orientation: Key to the OODA loop–the culture factor. [JoDRM]. *Journal of Defense Resources Management*, *3*(2), 67–74.

Majumdar, S., Subhani, M. M., Roullier, B., Anjum, A., & Zhu, R. (2021). Congestion prediction for smart sustainable cities using IoT and machine learning approaches. *Sustainable Cities and Society*, *64*, 102500.

Mamodiya, U., Sharma, P., & Sharma, P. (2014). Review in industrial automation. *IOSR Journal of Electrical and Electronics Engineering (IOSR-JEEE)*, *9*(3), 33–38.

Mannuru, N. R., Shahriar, S., Teel, Z. A., Wang, T., Lund, B. D., Tijani, S., & Galley, J. (2023). Artificial intelligence in developing countries: The impact of generative artificial intelligence (AI) technologies for development. *Information Development*, •••, 02666669231200628. DOI: 10.1177/02666669231200628

Marano, G. C., Rosso, M. M., Aloisio, A., & Cirrincione, G. (2024). Generative adversarial networks review in earthquake-related engineering fields. *Bulletin of Earthquake Engineering*, *22*(7), 3511–3562. DOI: 10.1007/s10518-023-01645-7

Matin, S. S., & Pradhan, B. (2022). Challenges and limitations of earthquake-induced building damage mapping techniques using remote sensing images-A systematic review. *Geocarto International*, *37*(21), 6186–6212. DOI: 10.1080/10106049.2021.1933213

Mattioli, J., Perico, P., & Robic, P.-O. (2020). Artificial intelligence-based asset management. In *Proceedings of the 2020*

Ma, X., & Sun, Y. (2023). *Optimizing Software Development with AI: Tools, Techniques, and Best Practices*. Wiley.

Maynor, D. (2007). In Maynor, D., & Mookhey, K. K. (Eds.), *Metasploit Toolkit for Penetration Testing, Exploit Development, and Vulnerability Research* (pp. vii–ix). Syngress.

McCarthy, E. J. (1960). *Basic Marketing: A Managerial Approach* (2nd ed.). Irwin.

McClanahan, K., Elder, S., Uwibambe, M. L., Liu, Y., Heng, R., & Li, Q. (2024, February). When ChatGPT meets vulnerability management: the good, the bad, and the ugly. In *2024 International Conference on Computing, Networking and Communications (ICNC)* (pp. 664-670). IEEE.

McClanahan, K., & Li, Q. (2024, February). Towards Automatically Matching Security Advisories to CPEs: String Similarity-Based Vendor Matching. In *2024 International Conference on Computing, Networking and Communications (ICNC)* (pp. 233-238). IEEE.

McKinsey & Company. (2022). *Leveraging AI for Risk Management in Software Projects*. McKinsey Digital.

Meidan, Y., Bohadana, M., Mathov, Y., Mirsky, Y., Shabtai, A., Breitenbacher, D., & Elovici, Y. (2018). N-baiot—Network-based detection of iot botnet attacks using deep autoencoders. *IEEE Pervasive Computing*, *17*(3), 12–22.

Mellit, A., & Kalogirou, S. A. (2008). Artificial intelligence techniques for photovoltaic applications: A review. *Progress in Energy and Combustion Science*, *34*(5), 574–632. DOI: 10.1016/j.pecs.2008.01.001

Midha, A. K. (1997). Software configuration management for the 21st century. *Bell Labs Technical Journal*, *2*(1), 154–165. DOI: 10.1002/bltj.2039

Mignan, A., & Broccardo, M. (2020). Neural network applications in earthquake prediction (1994–2019): Meta-analytic and statistical insights on their limitations. *Seismological Research Letters*, *91*(4), 2330–2342. DOI: 10.1785/0220200021

Mikalef, P., Fjørtoft, S. O., & Torvatn, H. Y. (2019). *Developing an artificial intelligence capability: A theoretical framework for business value*. Paper presented at the Business Information Systems Workshops: BIS 2019 International Workshops, Seville, Spain, June 26–28, 2019, Revised Papers 22. DOI: 10.1007/978-3-030-36691-9_34

Mili, H., Mili, F., & Mili, A. (1995). Reusing software: Issues and research directions. *IEEE Transactions on Software Engineering*, *21*(6), 528–562. DOI: 10.1109/32.391379

Miller, B., & Holmes, R. (2023). *AI and Agile Project Management: A New Framework for Success*. Springer.

Min, C., Liangwen, L., & Yue, X.-G. (2018). New Thoughts on Porter's" Five Forces Model" from the Perspective of Innovation. *IETI Transactions on Social Sciences and Humanities*, *1*, 105–113.

Mittelstadt, B. D., Allo, P., Taddeo, M., Wachter, S., & Floridi, L. (2016). The ethics of algorithms: Mapping the debate. *Big Data & Society*, *3*(2), 1–21. DOI: 10.1177/2053951716679679

Mocanu, D. C., Mocanu, E., Nguyen, P. H., Gibescu, M., & Liotta, A. (2016, October). Big IoT data mining for real-time energy disaggregation in buildings. In *2016 IEEE International Conference on Systems, Man, and Cybernetics (SMC)* (pp. 003765-003769). IEEE.

Mohammadi, M., Al-Fuqaha, A., Guizani, M., & Oh, J. S. (2017). Semisupervised deep reinforcement learning in support of IoT and smart city services. *IEEE Internet of Things Journal*, *5*(2), 624–635.

Mohanraj, G., Krishna, K. S., Lakshmi, B. S., Vijayalakshmi, A., Pramila, P. V., & Boopathi, S. (2024). Optimizing Trust and Security in Healthcare 4.0: Human Factors in Lightweight Secured IoMT Ecosystems. In *Lightweight Digital Trust Architectures in the Internet of Medical Things (IoMT)* (pp. 52–72). IGI Global. DOI: 10.4018/979-8-3693-2109-6.ch004

Mousavi, S. M., & Beroza, G. C. (2023). Machine learning in earthquake seismology. *Annual Review of Earth and Planetary Sciences*, *51*(1), 105–129. DOI: 10.1146/annurev-earth-071822-100323

Muhammad, K., Ullah, A., Lloret, J., Del Ser, J., & de Albuquerque, V. H. C. (2020). Deep learning for safe autonomous driving: Current challenges and future directions. *IEEE Transactions on Intelligent Transportation Systems*, *22*(7), 4316–4336. DOI: 10.1109/TITS.2020.3032227

Nadeem, M. A., Lee, S. U., & Younus, M. U. (2022). A Comparison of Recent Requirements Gathering and Management Tools in Requirements Engineering for IoT-Enabled Sustainable Cities. *Sustainability (Basel)*, *14*(4), 2427. DOI: 10.3390/su14042427

Nagarajan, S. M., Deverajan, G. G., Chatterjee, P., Alnumay, W., & Ghosh, U. (2021). Effective task scheduling algorithm with deep learning for Internet of Health Things (IoHT) in sustainable smart cities. *Sustainable Cities and Society*, *71*, 102945.

Nakahara, H., Monden, A., & Yücel, Z. (2021). A simulation model of software quality assurance in the software lifecycle. In *Proceedings of the 2021 IEEE/ACIS 22nd International Conference on Software Engineering, Artificial Intelligence, Networking, and Parallel/Distributed Computing (SNPD)* (pp. 236–241). Taichung, Taiwan.DOI: 10.1109/SNPD51163.2021.9704927

Na, S., Kim, T., & Kim, H. (2018). Service Identification of Internet-Connected Devices Based on Common Platform Enumeration. *Journal of Information Processing Systems*, *14*, 740–750.

Naseri, M., Gusarov, S., & Salahub, D. (2023). Quantum Machine Learning in Materials Prediction: A Case Study on ABO3 Perovskite Structures. *The Journal of Physical Chemistry Letters*, *14*(31), 6940–6947. DOI: 10.1021/acs.jpclett.3c01703 PMID: 37498277

Nicolaou, C., & Axelsdottir, S. (2021, May 18). Automate approval workflows in Jira Service Management with Insight –Work Life by Atlassian. Work Life by Atlassian. https://www.atlassian.com/blog/it-teams/automate-approval-workflows-in-jira

Nikmah, F., Rahmawati, R., & Sukma, E. A. (2021). Resource-based view: Implementation in Indonesia SMEs to achieve competitive advantage. *European Journal of Research and Reflection in Management Sciences Vol, 9*(1).

Nirmala, P., Ramesh, S., Tamilselvi, M., Ramkumar, G., & Anitha, G. (2022). An artificial intelligence enabled smart industrial automation system based on internet of things assistance. *2022 International Conference on Advances in Computing, Communication and Applied Informatics (ACCAI)*, 1–6. DOI: 10.1109/ACCAI53970.2022.9752651

Nishant, R., Kennedy, M., & Corbett, J. (2020). Artificial intelligence for sustainability: Challenges, opportunities, and a research agenda. *International Journal of Information Management, 53*, 102104. DOI: 10.1016/j.ijinfomgt.2020.102104

Nitzan. (1976). Programmable industrial automation. *IEEE Transactions on Computers, 100*(12), 1259–1270.

Noonan, R. E. (1985). An Algorithm for Generating Abstract Syntax Trees. *Computer Languages*, *10*(3-4), 225–236. DOI: 10.1016/0096-0551(85)90018-9

O'Neill, J., & Zhang, X. (2023). *AI in Software Development: Enhancing Team Dynamics and Performance*. Elsevier.

Oliver, R. L. (1999). Whence consumer loyalty? *Journal of Marketing*, *63*(4_suppl1), 33–44. DOI: 10.1177/00222429990634s105

Ooi, K.-B., Tan, G. W.-H., Al-Emran, M., Al-Sharafi, M. A., Capatina, A., Chakraborty, A., & Lee, V.-H. (2023). The potential of generative artificial intelligence across disciplines: Perspectives and future directions. *Journal of Computer Information Systems*, •••, 1–32.

Osman, A. I., Chen, L., Yang, M., Msigwa, G., Farghali, M., Fawzy, S., Rooney, D. W., & Yap, P.-S. (2023). Cost, environmental impact, and resilience of renewable energy under a changing climate: A review. *Environmental Chemistry Letters*, *21*(2), 741–764. DOI: 10.1007/s10311-022-01532-8

Ostertag, E., Hendler, J., Díaz, R. P., & Braun, C. (1992). Computing similarity in a reuse library system. *ACM Transactions on Software Engineering and Methodology*, *1*(3), 205–228. DOI: 10.1145/131736.131739

Ouaarous, R., Mezrioui, A., & Hilal, I. (2024). On using artificial intelligence in software quality assurance: A state of the art.https://www.researchgate.net/publication/386573500_On_Using_Artificial_Intelligence_in_Software_Quality_Assurance_A_State_of_the_Art

Ozkaya, I. (2023). The Next Frontier in Software Development: AI-Augmented Software Development Processes. *IEEE Software*, *40*(4), 4–9. DOI: 10.1109/MS.2023.3278056

Oztemel, E., & Gursev, S. (2020). Literature review of Industry 4.0 and related technologies. *Journal of Intelligent Manufacturing*, *31*(1), 127–182. DOI: 10.1007/s10845-018-1433-8

Padhy, N., Singh, R. P., & Satapathy, S. C. (2017). Enhanced evolutionary computing based artificial intelligence model for web-solutions software reusability estimation. *Cluster Computing*, *22*(S4), 9787–9804. DOI: 10.1007/s10586-017-1558-0

Palazzo, M., & Micozzi, A. (2024). *The SWOT analysis: An evolving decision-making model Rethinking Decision-Making Strategies and Tools: Emerging Research and Opportunities*. Emerald Publishing Limited.

Palomares, I., Martínez-Cámara, E., Montes, R., García-Moral, P., Chiachio, M., Chiachio, J., & Fernández, B. (2021). A panoramic view and swot analysis of artificial intelligence for achieving the sustainable development goals by 2030: Progress and prospects. *Applied Intelligence*, *51*(9), 6497–6527. DOI: 10.1007/s10489-021-02264-y PMID: 34764606

Pan, M., Su, W., & Wang, Y. (2021). Review of research on the curriculum for artificial intelligence and industrial automation based on edge computing. *2021 International Conference on Networking and Network Applications (NaNA)*, 222–226. DOI: 10.1109/NaNA53684.2021.00045

Panneerselvam, S. (2024, July 14). The rise of generative AI in unit testing: A double-edged sword. Medium. https://medium.com/@sugumar.p/the-rise-of-generative-ai-in-unit-testing-a-double-edged-sword-ff7b15c15272

Pan, Y., & Zhang, L. (2021). Roles of artificial intelligence in construction engineering and management: A critical review and future trends. *Automation in Construction*, *122*, 103517. DOI: 10.1016/j.autcon.2020.103517

Parasoft. (n.d.). Selenic AI for improved Selenium web testing. Parasoft. https://www.parasoft.com/products/parasoft-selenic/enhanced-selenium-testing/

Pareto, V., Bousquet, G. H., & Busino, G. (1964). *Cours d'Économie Politique: Nouvelle Édition*. Librairie Droz. DOI: 10.3917/droz.paret.1964.01

Parkhi, O., Vedaldi, A., & Zisserman, A. (2015). Deep face recognition. In BMVC 2015-Proceedings of the British Machine Vision Conference 2015. British Machine Vision Association.

Pascanu, R. (2013). How to construct deep recurrent neural networks. arXiv preprint arXiv:1312.6026.

Paschen, U., Pitt, C., & Kietzmann, J. (2020). Artificial intelligence: Building blocks and an innovation typology. *Business Horizons*, *63*(2), 147–155. DOI: 10.1016/j.bushor.2019.10.004

Paszke, A., Gross, S., & Massa, F.. (2019). PyTorch: An Imperative Style, High-Performance Deep Learning Library. *Advances in Neural Information Processing Systems*.

Patel, H., & Khan, S. (2023). AI-Driven Resource Management in Software Projects. *Journal of Project Management*, *45*(6), 123–145.

Patidar, A., & Suman, U. (2023). RGBot: A Machine Learning Enabled Requirements Gathering Technique in Agile-Based Lifecycle. *RGBot: A Machine Learning Enabled Requirements Gathering Technique in Agile-Based Lifecycle*. DOI: 10.1109/ICTBIG59752.2023.10456282

Patra, A. K., & Dash, R. (2023). Strategic Optimization of Human Resource System in the Corporation to Conquer the Global Challenges in Business. *Journal of the Management Training Institute, SAIL, Ranchi AN ISO 9001–2015 Institute, 58*.

Pedregosa, F., Varoquaux, G., & Gramfort, A.. (2011). Scikit-learn: Machine Learning in Python. *Journal of Machine Learning Research*, *12*, 2825–2830.

Peppers, D., & Rogers, M. (2016). *Managing Customer Relationships: A Strategic Framework*. Wiley. DOI: 10.1002/9781119239833

Pereira, L., Pinto, M., da Costa, R. L., Dias, Á., & Gonçalves, R. (2021). The new SWOT for a sustainable world. *Journal of Open Innovation, 7*(1), 18. DOI: 10.3390/joitmc7010018

Perez-Ordonez, B., Beauchemin, M., & Jordan, R. (2006). Molecular biology of squamous cell carcinoma of the head and neck. *Journal of Clinical Pathology, 59*(5), 445–453. DOI: 10.1136/jcp.2003.007641 PMID: 16644882

Petiwala, F. F., Shukla, V. K., & Vyas, S. (2021). *IBM watson: redefining artificial intelligence through cognitive computing*. Paper presented at the Proceedings of International Conference on Machine Intelligence and Data Science Applications: MIDAS 2020. DOI: 10.1007/978-981-33-4087-9_15

Pickering, C., & Byrne, J. (2014). The benefits of publishing systematic quantitative literature reviews for PhD candidates and other early-career researchers. *Higher Education Research & Development, 33*(3), 534–548. DOI: 10.1080/07294360.2013.841651

Pietronudo, M. C., Croidieu, G., & Schiavone, F. (2022). A solution looking for problems? A systematic literature review of the rationalizing influence of artificial intelligence on decision-making in innovation management. *Technological Forecasting and Social Change, 182*, 121828. DOI: 10.1016/j.techfore.2022.121828

Pinheiro, G. A., Mucelini, J., Soares, M. D., Prati, R. C., Da Silva, J. L., & Quiles, M. G. (2020). Machine learning prediction of nine molecular properties based on the SMILES representation of the QM9 quantum-chemistry dataset. *The Journal of Physical Chemistry A, 124*(47), 9854–9866. DOI: 10.1021/acs.jpca.0c05969 PMID: 33174750

Ployhart, R. E. (2021). Resources for what? Understanding performance in the resource-based view and strategic human capital resource literatures. *Journal of Management, 47*(7), 1771–1786. DOI: 10.1177/01492063211003137

Pramanik, P. K. D., Pal, S., & Choudhury, P. (2018). Beyond automation: The cognitive IoT. artificial intelligence brings sense to the Internet of Things. *Cognitive Computing for Big Data Systems Over IoT: Frameworks, Tools and Applications*, 1–37.

Prasad, M. S. C., Dhanalakshmi, M., Mohan, M., Somasundaram, B., Valarmathi, R., & Boopathi, S. (2024). Machine Learning-Integrated Sustainable Engineering and Energy Systems: Innovations at the Nexus. In *Harnessing High-Performance Computing and AI for Environmental Sustainability* (pp. 74–98). IGI Global. DOI: 10.4018/979-8-3693-1794-5.ch004

Provost, F., & Fawcett, T. (2013). Data science and its relationship to big data and data-driven decision making. *Big Data, 1*(1), 51–59. DOI: 10.1089/big.2013.1508 PMID: 27447038

Przegalinska, A., & Jemielniak, D. (2023). *Strategizing AI in business and education: Emerging technologies and business strategy*. Cambridge University Press. DOI: 10.1017/9781009243520

Pumplun, L., Tauchert, C., & Heidt, M. (2019). A new organizational chassis for artificial intelligence-exploring organizational readiness factors.

Puyt, R., Lie, F. B., & de Graaf, F. (2017). Contagious ideas and cognitive artefacts: the SWOT Analysis evolution in business. *BAM2017Conference Proceedings*, 2-19.

Qiu, J., Wu, Q., Ding, G., Xu, Y., & Feng, S. (2016). A survey of machine learning for big data processing. *EURASIP Journal on Advances in Signal Processing*, *2016*, 1–16.

Rabaey, M. (2015). Complex Adaptive Systems Thinking Approach to IT Investment.

Radonjić, A., Duarte, H., & Pereira, N. (2022). Artificial intelligence and HRM: HR managers' perspective on decisiveness and challenges. *European Management Journal*.

Rahamathunnisa, U., Subhashini, P., Aancy, H. M., Meenakshi, S., & Boopathi, S. (2023). Solutions for Software Requirement Risks Using Artificial Intelligence Techniques. In *Handbook of Research on Data Science and Cybersecurity Innovations in Industry 4.0 Technologies* (pp. 45–64). IGI Global.

Raisch, S., & Krakowski, S. (2021). Artificial intelligence and management: The automation–augmentation paradox. *Academy of Management Review*, *46*(1), 192–210. DOI: 10.5465/amr.2018.0072

Rajapaksha, D., Tantithamthavorn, C., Jiarpakdee, J., Bergmeir, C., Grundy, J., & Buntine, W. (2022). SQAPlanner: Generating data-informed software quality improvement plans. *IEEE Transactions on Software Engineering*, *48*(8), 2814–2835. DOI: 10.1109/TSE.2021.3070559

Raji, I. D., & Buolamwini, J. (2019). Actionable auditing: Investigating the impact of publicly naming biased performance results of commercial AI products. Proceedings of the 2019 AAAI/ACM Conference on AI, Ethics, and Society (pp. 429–435). ACM. DOI: 10.1145/3306618.3314244

Rasmus, A., Berglund, M., Honkala, M., Valpola, H., & Raiko, T. (2015). Semi-supervised learning with ladder networks. *Advances in Neural Information Processing Systems*, •••, 28.

Rastogi, N., & Trivedi, M. (2016). PESTLE technique–a tool to identify external risks in construction projects. [IRJET]. *International Research Journal of Engineering and Technology*, *3*(1), 384–388.

Rathore, S., & Park, J. H. (2018). Semi-supervised learning based distributed attack detection framework for IoT. *Applied Soft Computing*, *72*, 79–89.

Raydugin, Y. G. (2024). *RISK-BASED PROJECT DECISIONS IN SITUATIONS OF HIGH COMPLEXITY AND DEEP UNCERTAINTY*: Springer.

Reichheld, F. F. (2003). The One Number You Need to Grow. *Harvard Business Review*, *81*(12), 46–55. PMID: 14712543

Reichheld, F. F., & Sasser, W. E. (1990). Zero defections: Quality comes to services. *Harvard Business Review*, *68*(5), 105–111. PMID: 10107082

Ren, C. X., Hulbert, C., Johnson, P. A., & Rouet-Leduc, B. (2020). Machine learning and fault rupture: A review. *Advances in Geophysics*, *61*, 57–107. DOI: 10.1016/bs.agph.2020.08.003

Ren, Y., Xing, T., Quan, Q., & Zhao, Y. (2010). Software configuration management of version control study based on baseline. In *Proceedings of the 2010 3rd International Conference on Information Management, Innovation Management and Industrial Engineering* (pp. 118–121). Kunming, China. https://doi.org/DOI: 10.1109/ICIII.2010.506

Replogle, N. (2024, June 14). Use Zapier's Monday integration to streamline your work. Zapier. https://zapier.com/blog/automate-monday/

Reselman, B. (2017, December 7). The fundamentals of integration testing. Mabl. https://www.mabl.com/blog/the-fundamentals-of-integration-testing

Roberts, A., & Singh, P. (2022). The role of AI in modern software project management. *AI and Management Review*, *8*(2), 56–67. DOI: 10.1016/aimr.2022.04.003

Rusin, S. (2023, November 23). A comprehensive guide to AI-driven acceptance testing. HackerNoon. https://hackernoon.com/a-comprehensive-guide-to-ai-driven-acceptance-testing

Russell, S., & Norvig, P. (2021). *Artificial intelligence: A modern approach* (4th ed.). Pearson.

Russom, P. (2011). Big Data Analytic s. TDWI Best Practices report, TDWI Reserarch, 4th Quarter.

Saied, M. A., Ouni, A., Sahraoui, H., Kula, R. G., Inoue, K., & Lo, D. (2018). Improving reusability of software libraries through usage pattern mining. *Journal of Systems and Software*, *145*, 164–179. DOI: 10.1016/j.jss.2018.08.032

Sajjan, M., Li, J., Selvarajan, R., Sureshbabu, S. H., Kale, S. S., Gupta, R., Singh, V., & Kais, S. (2022). Quantum machine learning for chemistry and physics. *Chemical Society Reviews*, *51*(15), 6475–6573. DOI: 10.1039/D2CS00203E PMID: 35849066

Sajjan, M., Sureshbabu, S. H., & Kais, S. (2021). Quantum machine-learning for eigenstate filtration in two-dimensional materials. *Journal of the American Chemical Society*, *143*(44), 18426–18445. DOI: 10.1021/jacs.1c06246 PMID: 34705449

Samad, T., & Kiliccote, S. (2012). Smart grid technologies and applications for the industrial sector. *Computers & Chemical Engineering*, *47*, 76–84. DOI: 10.1016/j.compchemeng.2012.07.006

Samantra, C., Datta, S., & Mahapatra, S. S. (2017). Fuzzy based risk assessment module for metropolitan construction project: An empirical study. *Engineering Applications of Artificial Intelligence*, *65*, 449–464. DOI: 10.1016/j.engappai.2017.04.019

Sandaruwan, A., & Kasthurirathna, D. (2024). Recommending Third-Party Libraries and Frameworks Using Topic Modeling in Software Projects. *Recommending Third-Party Libraries and Frameworks Using Topic Modeling in Software Projects*, 37–42. https://doi.org/DOI: 10.1109/ICARC61713.2024.10499759

Saravanan, S., Khare, R., Umamaheswari, K., Khare, S., Krishne Gowda, B. S., & Boopathi, S. (2024). AI and ML Adaptive Smart-Grid Energy Management Systems: Exploring Advanced Innovations. In *Principles and Applications in Speed Sensing and Energy Harvesting for Smart Roads* (pp. 166–196). IGI Global. DOI: 10.4018/978-1-6684-9214-7.ch006

Sarker, I. H. (2022). AI-based modeling: Techniques, applications and research issues towards automation, intelligent and smart systems. *SN Computer Science*, *3*(2), 158. DOI: 10.1007/s42979-022-01043-x PMID: 35194580

Satav, S. D., Lamani, D., Harsha, K., Kumar, N., Manikandan, S., & Sampath, B. (2023). Energy and Battery Management in the Era of Cloud Computing: Sustainable Wireless Systems and Networks. In *Sustainable Science and Intelligent Technologies for Societal Development* (pp. 141–166). IGI Global.

Saxena, D., Lamest, M., & Bansal, V. (2021). Responsible machine learning for ethical artificial intelligence in business and industry. In *Handbook of Research on Applied Data Science and Artificial Intelligence in Business and Industry* (pp. 639–653). IGI global. DOI: 10.4018/978-1-7998-6985-6.ch030

Saxena, D., Wall, P. J., & Lewis, D. (2023, September). Artificial Intelligence (AI) Ethics: A Critical Realist Emancipatory Approach. In *2023 IEEE International Symposium on Technology and Society (ISTAS)* (pp. 1-5). IEEE. DOI: 10.1109/ISTAS57930.2023.10305995

Scheetz, M., von Mayrhauser, A., & France, R. (1999). Generating test cases from an OO model with an AI planning system. In Proceedings 10th International Symposium on Software Reliability Engineering (Cat. No.PR00443), 250-259. DOI: 10.1109/ISSRE.1999.809330

Schlichtkrull, M., Kipf, T. N., Bloem, P., Van Den Berg, R., Titov, I., & Welling, M. (2018). Modeling relational data with graph convolutional networks. In The semantic web: 15th international conference, ESWC 2018, Heraklion, Crete, Greece, June 3–7, 2018, proceedings 15 (pp. 593-607). Springer International Publishing.

Senova, A., Tobisova, A., & Rozenberg, R. (2023). New approaches to project risk assessment utilizing the Monte Carlo method. *Sustainability (Basel)*, *15*(2), 1006. DOI: 10.3390/su15021006

Shafapourtehrany, M., Batur, M., Shabani, F., Pradhan, B., Kalantar, B., & Özener, H. (2023). A comprehensive review of geospatial technology applications in earthquake preparedness, emergency management, and damage assessment. *Remote Sensing (Basel)*, *15*(7), 1939. DOI: 10.3390/rs15071939

Shafiq, M., Tian, Z., Bashir, A. K., Jolfaei, A., & Yu, X. (2020). Data mining and machine learning methods for sustainable smart cities traffic classification: A survey. *Sustainable Cities and Society*, *60*, 102177.

Sharma, A. (2018). *Customer Journey Mapping for Improved Experience*. Wiley.

Sharma, A., & Bansal, R. (2022). *AI in Project Management: Frameworks and Applications*. Springer.

Sharma, A., & Sheth, J. N. (2010). *The Customer Value Proposition in Business Markets*. Springer.

Sheikh, S. (2020). *Understanding the role of artificial intelligence and its future social impact*. IGI Global.

Shorfuzzaman, M., Hossain, M. S., & Alhamid, M. F. (2021). Towards the sustainable development of smart cities through mass video surveillance: A response to the COVID-19 pandemic. *Sustainable Cities and Society*, *64*, 102582.

Shrestha, Y. R., Ben-Menahem, S. M., & Von Krogh, G. (2019). Organizational decision-making structures in the age of artificial intelligence. *California Management Review*, *61*(4), 66–83. DOI: 10.1177/0008125619862257

Simmons, T. (2022). *Ethics in AI-Driven Project Management*. Oxford University Press.

Singh, R., & Sharma, N. (2023). Privacy-Preserving AI in Project Management: A Framework for Data Governance. *Journal of AI and Ethics*, *6*(1), 45–68.

Singh, S. (2021). BERT Algorithm used in Google Search. *Mathematical Statistician and Engineering Applications*, *70*(2), 1641–1650. DOI: 10.17762/msea.v70i2.2454

Siraj, N. B., & Fayek, A. R. (2019). Risk identification and common risks in construction: Literature review and content analysis. *Journal of Construction Engineering and Management, 145*(9), 03119004. DOI: 10.1061/(ASCE)CO.1943-7862.0001685

Sladojevic, S., Arsenovic, M., Anderla, A., Culibrk, D., & Stefanovic, D. (2016). Deep neural networks based recognition of plant diseases by leaf image classification. *Computational Intelligence and Neuroscience, 2016*(1), 3289801.

Slama, S. B. (2022). Prosumer in smart grids based on intelligent edge computing: A review on Artificial Intelligence Scheduling Techniques. *Ain Shams Engineering Journal, 13*(1), 101504. DOI: 10.1016/j.asej.2021.05.018

Smith, D., & Williams, K. (2022). *Artificial intelligence in software engineering: Tools, frameworks, and future directions*. CodeWorks Publications.

Smith, J., & Lee, R. (2022). Leveraging AI in Agile Project Management: Tools and Strategies. *Journal of Software Development, 45*(3), 123–135.

Smith, W. R. (1956). Product differentiation and market segmentation as alternative marketing strategies. *Journal of Marketing, 21*(1), 3–8. DOI: 10.1177/002224295602100102

Software Quality Assurance vs Software Quality Plan. (n.d.). *Software Engineering Stack Exchange*. https://softwareengineering.stackexchange.com/questions/350317/software-quality-assurance-vs-software-quality-plan

Soni, V., & Sharma, P. (2021). *AI-Enhanced Agile Development: Transforming Project Management for Modern Software Teams*. Springer.

Soust-Verdaguer, B., Llatas, C., & García-Martínez, A. (2017). Critical review of BIM-based LCA method to buildings. *Energy and Building, 136*, 110–120. DOI: 10.1016/j.enbuild.2016.12.009

Sreedhar, P. S. S., Sujay, V., Rani, M. R., Melita, L., Reshma, S., & Boopathi, S. (2024). Impacts of 5G Machine Learning Techniques on Telemedicine and Social Media Professional Connection in Healthcare. In *Advances in Medical Technologies and Clinical Practice* (pp. 209–234). IGI Global. DOI: 10.4018/979-8-3693-1934-5.ch012

Stabenau, A., McVicker, G., Melsopp, C., Proctor, G., Clamp, M., & Birney, E. (2004). The Ensembl Core Software Libraries: Figure 1. *Genome Research, 14*(5), 929–933. DOI: 10.1101/gr.1857204 PMID: 15123588

Steen, K. A., Christiansen, P., Karstoft, H., & Jørgensen, R. N. (2016). Using deep learning to challenge safety standard for highly autonomous machines in agriculture. *Journal of Imaging, 2*(1), 6.

Strong, E. K. (1925). *The psychology of selling and advertising*. The Macmillan Company.

Sullivan, J. (2023). Building a Collaborative Culture in AI-Powered Teams. *Harvard Business Review*.

Sun, J. (2025). *Classical and Quantum Simulation of Chemical and Physical Systems* [PhD Thesis]. California Institute of Technology.

Sundar, R., Srikaanth, P. B., Naik, D. A., Murugan, V. P., Karumudi, M., & Boopathi, S. (2024). Achieving Balance Between Innovation and Security in the Cloud With Artificial Intelligence of Things: Semantic Web Control Models. In *Advances in Web Technologies and Engineering* (pp. 1–26). IGI Global. DOI: 10.4018/979-8-3693-1487-6.ch001

Sundaramoorthy, K., Singh, A., Sumathy, G., Maheshwari, A., Arunarani, A., & Boopathi, S. (2024). A Study on AI and Blockchain-Powered Smart Parking Models for Urban Mobility. In *Handbook of Research on AI and ML for Intelligent Machines and Systems* (pp. 223–250). IGI Global.

Sun, Z., Sandoval, L., Crystal-Ornelas, R., Mousavi, S. M., Wang, J., Lin, C., Cristea, N., Tong, D., Carande, W. H., Ma, X., Rao, Y., Bednar, J. A., Tan, A., Wang, J., Purushotham, S., Gill, T. E., Chastang, J., Howard, D., Holt, B., & John, A. (2022). A review of earth artificial intelligence. *Computers & Geosciences*, *159*, 105034. DOI: 10.1016/j.cageo.2022.105034

Suresh Babu, C. V., & Akshara, P. M. (2024). Revolutionizing Conversational AI: Unleashing the Power of ChatGPT-Based Applications in Generative AI and Natural Language Processing. In A. Obaid, B. Bhushan, M. S., & S. Rajest (Eds.), Advanced Applications of Generative AI and Natural Language Processing Models (pp. 228-248). IGI Global. DOI: 10.4018/979-8-3693-0502-7.ch011

Suresh Babu, C. V., & Adhithya, S. (2023). ChatGPT and Other Generative AI Tools in Education: Transformative Potential and Ethical Considerations. In Keengwe, J. (Ed.), *Creative AI Tools and Ethical Implications in Teaching and Learning* (pp. 135–152). IGI Global., DOI: 10.4018/979-8-3693-0205-7.ch007

Suresh Babu, C. V., & Auroshaa, A. (2024). Influence of Data Analysis Tools in Teaching and Learning Economics. In Scott, B., & Fox, M. E. (Eds.), *Cases on Economics Education and Tools for Educators* (pp. 229–248). IGI Global., DOI: 10.4018/978-1-6684-7583-6.ch010

Sutherland, J., & Schwaber, K. (2020). *The Scrum Guide: The Definitive Guide to Scrum: The Rules of the Game*. Scrum.org.

Sutskever, I., Martens, J., Dahl, G., & Hinton, G. (2013, May). On the importance of initialization and momentum in deep learning. In *International conference on machine learning* (pp. 1139-1147). PMLR.

Su, W., Xu, G., He, Z., Machica, I. K., Quimno, V., Du, Y., & Kong, Y. (2023). Cloud-edge computing-based ICICOS framework for industrial automation and artificial intelligence: A survey. *Journal of Circuits, Systems, and Computers*, *32*(10), 2350168. DOI: 10.1142/S0218126623501682

Tam, K. Y., & Ho, S. Y. (2005). Web personalization as a portfolio of marketing strategies. *Decision Support Systems*, *39*(1), 43–57.

Tan, Z., Jamdagni, A., He, X., Nanda, P., & Liu, R. P. (2013). A system for denial-of-service attack detection based on multivariate correlation analysis. *IEEE Transactions on Parallel and Distributed Systems*, *25*(2), 447–456.

Tariq, M. U., Poulin, M., & Abonamah, A. A. (2021). Achieving operational excellence through artificial intelligence: Driving forces and barriers. *Frontiers in Psychology*, *12*, 686624. DOI: 10.3389/fpsyg.2021.686624 PMID: 34305744

Team, C. (2024, November 20). How to set up Monday.com and Slack integration. ClearFeed. https://clearfeed.ai/blogs/mondaycom-slack-integration-guide

Team, K. (n.d.). Enhancing test automation with Katalon StudioAssist: Empowering testers for success. Katalon. https://katalon.com/resources-center/blog/katalon-studioassist-improve-test-automation

Team, K. (n.d.). What is automation testing? Ultimate guide & best practices. Katalon. https://katalon.com/resources-center/blog/what-is-automation-testing

Thai, H. T. (2022, April). Machine learning for structural engineering: A state-of-the-art review. In *Structures* (Vol. 38, pp. 448–491). Elsevier.

The IEEE Global Initiative on Ethics of Autonomous and Intelligent Systems. (2019). Ethically aligned design: A vision for prioritizing human wellbeing with autonomous and intelligent systems (1st ed.). IEEE. https://ethicsinaction.ieee.org/

Ting, L., Khan, M., Sharma, A., & Ansari, M. D. (2022). A secure framework for IoT-based smart climate agriculture system: Toward blockchain and edge computing. *Journal of Intelligent Systems*, *31*(1), 221–236. DOI: 10.1515/jisys-2022-0012

Tommila, T., Ventä, O., & Koskinen, K. (2001). Next generation industrial automation–needs and opportunities. *Automation Technology Review*, *2001*, 34–41.

Toth, D. (2022). *Agile for AI: Implementing Iterative Approaches in AI Projects*. Springer.

Tovar, A., & Martinez, L. (2022). *AI and Agile Development: Enhancing Project Management*. Springer.

Tovarňák, D., Sadlek, L., & Čeleda, P. (2021, May). Graph-based cpe matching for identification of vulnerable asset configurations. In *2021 IFIP/IEEE International Symposium on Integrated Network Management (IM)* (pp. 986-991). IEEE.

Trunk, A., Birkel, H., & Hartmann, E. (2020). On the current state of combining human and artificial intelligence for strategic organizational decision making. *Business Research*, *13*(3), 875–919. DOI: 10.1007/s40685-020-00133-x

Tsai, W., Heisler, K., Volovik, D., & Zualkernan, I. (2003). A critical look at the relationship between AI and software engineering. *A Critical Look at the Relationship Between AI and Software Engineering, se 11*, 2–18. DOI: 10.1109/LFA.1988.24945

Tsatsoula, E. (2018). Application of Ansoff's Matrix-Methodology: Marketing Growth Strategies For Products.

Tucker, C. E. (2014). The economics of advertising and privacy. *Journal of Economic Literature*, *52*(4), 1–40.

Turan, U., Fidan, Y., & Yıldıran, C. (2019). Critical thinking as a qualified decision making tool. *Tarih Kültür ve Sanat Arastirmalari Dergisi*, *8*(4), 1–18. DOI: 10.7596/taksad.v8i4.2316

Tyagi, A. K., Fernandez, T. F., Mishra, S., & Kumari, S. (2020). Intelligent automation systems at the core of industry 4.0. *International Conference on Intelligent Systems Design and Applications*, 1–18.

Tzafestas, S. G. (2018). Synergy of IoT and AI in modern society: The robotics and automation case. *Robot. Autom. Eng. J, 31*(5), 1–15. DOI: 10.19080/RAEJ.2018.03.555621

Varela-Vaca, Á. J., Borrego, D., Gómez-López, M. T., Gasca, R. M., & Márquez, A. G. (2023). Feature Models to Boost the Vulnerability Management Process. *Journal of Systems and Software, 195*, 111541. DOI: 10.1016/j.jss.2022.111541

Varela-Vaca, Á. J., Gasca, R. M., Carmona-Fombella, J. A., & Gómez-López, M. T. (2020, October). AMADEUS: towards the AutoMAteD secUrity teSting. In *Proceedings of the 24th ACM Conference on Systems and Software Product Line: Volume A-Volume A* (pp. 1-12).

Varela-Vaca, Á. J., Gasca, R. M., Ceballos, R., Gómez-López, M. T., & Torres, P. B. (2019). CyberSPL: A Framework for the Verification of Cybersecurity Policy Compliance of System Configurations Using Software Product Lines. *Applied Sciences (Basel, Switzerland), 9*(24), 5364. DOI: 10.3390/app9245364

Vedavyasa, K. V., & Kumar, A. (2024). Classification analysis of transition-metal chalcogenides and oxides using quantum machine learning. *arXiv Preprint arXiv:2405.18989.*

Verhoef, P. C., Kannan, P. K., & Inman, J. J. (2015). From multi-channel retailing to omni-channel retailing. *Journal of Retailing, 93*(2), 174–181. DOI: 10.1016/j.jretai.2015.02.005

Vettorello, M., Eisenbart, B., & Ranscombe, C. (2019). *Toward better design-related decision making: A proposal of an advanced ooda loop.* Paper presented at the Proceedings of the Design Society: International Conference on Engineering Design. DOI: 10.1017/dsi.2019.245

Vilfredo, P. (1896). *Cours d'économie politique*. Librairie Rousseau.

von Lilienfeld, O. A., Müller, K.-R., & Tkatchenko, A. (2020). Exploring chemical compound space with quantum-based machine learning. *Nature Reviews. Chemistry, 4*(7), 347–358. DOI: 10.1038/s41570-020-0189-9 PMID: 37127950

Wang, C.-H., & Tsai, D.-R. (2009). Integrated installing ISO 9000 and ISO 27000 management systems on an organization. In *Proceedings of the 43rd Annual 2009 International Carnahan Conference on Security Technology* (pp. 265–267). Zurich, Switzerland. https://doi.org/DOI: 10.1109/CCST.2009.5335527

Wang, F., Fan, X., Wang, F., & Liu, J. (2018). Backup battery analysis and allocation against power outage for cellular base stations. *IEEE Transactions on Mobile Computing, 18*(3), 520–533.

Wang, H., Ye, G., Tang, Z., Tan, S. H., Huang, S., Fang, D., Feng, Y., Bian, L., & Wang, Z. (2021). Combining Graph-Based Learning with Automated Data Collection for Code Vulnerability Detection. *IEEE Transactions on Information Forensics and Security, 16*, 1943–1958. DOI: 10.1109/TIFS.2020.3044773

Wang, J., Zhang, X., Gao, Q., Yue, H., & Wang, H. (2016). Device-free wireless localization and activity recognition: A deep learning approach. *IEEE Transactions on Vehicular Technology, 66*(7), 6258–6267.

Wangoo, D. P. (2018). Artificial Intelligence Techniques in Software Engineering for Automated Software Reuse and Design. *Artificial Intelligence Techniques in Software Engineering for Automated Software Reuse and Design, 1*, 1–4. DOI: 10.1109/CCAA.2018.8777584

Węgrzyn, D. T. (2022). *The adaptation of the OODA loop to the decision-making systems processing Big Data in the area of morality*. Paper presented at the Proceedings of the 26th International Database Engineered Applications Symposium. DOI: 10.1145/3548785.3548806

Weiss, T. R. (2018, March 9). AI-based automated code testing vendor Mabl launches public beta. Windows IT Pro (Online). https://www.proquest.com/docview/2012173530?sourcetype=Magazines

Wen, X. C., Chen, Y., Gao, C., Zhang, H., Zhang, J. M., & Liao, Q. (2023, May). Vulnerability detection with graph simplification and enhanced graph representation learning. In 2023 IEEE/ACM 45th International Conference on Software Engineering (ICSE) (pp. 2275-2286). IEEE.

Wen, W., Xu, C., Yan, F., Wu, C., Wang, Y., Chen, Y., & Li, H. (2017). Terngrad: Ternary gradients to reduce communication in distributed deep learning. *Advances in Neural Information Processing Systems*, •••, 30.

Werbos, P. J. (1990). Backpropagation through time: What it does and how to do it. *Proceedings of the IEEE*, *78*(10), 1550–1560.

Whittaker, M., Crawford, K., Dobbe, R., Fried, G., Kaziunas, E., Mathur, V., & Schwartz, O. (2018). *AI Now Report 2018*. AI Now Institute, New York University.

Wu, Z., Pan, S., Chen, F., Long, G., Zhang, C., & Yu, P. S. (2019). A Comprehensive Survey on Graph Neural Networks. *IEEE Transactions on Neural Networks and Learning Systems*, *32*(1), 4–24. DOI: 10.1109/TNNLS.2020.2978386 PMID: 32217482

Xia, N., Zou, P. X. W., Griffin, M. A., Wang, X., & Zhong, R. (2018). Towards integrating construction risk management and stakeholder management: A systematic literature review and future research agendas. *International Journal of Project Management*, *36*(5), 701–715. DOI: 10.1016/j.ijproman.2018.03.006

Xie, T., & Notkin, D. (2006). Tool-assisted unit-test generation and selection based on operational abstractions. *Automated Software Engineering*, *13*(3), 345–371. DOI: 10.1007/s10851-006-8530-6

Xie, Y., Ebad Sichani, M., Padgett, J. E., & DesRoches, R. (2020). The promise of implementing machine learning in earthquake engineering: A state-of-the-art review. *Earthquake Spectra*, *36*(4), 1769–1801. DOI: 10.1177/8755293020919419

Xie, Y., Sichani, M. E., Padgett, J., & DesRoches, R. (2020). Machine learning applications in earthquake engineering: Literature review and case studies. *17th World Conference on Earthquake Engineering*.

Xing, T. (2010). Software configuration management of change control study based on baseline. In *Proceedings of the 2010 International Conference on Intelligent Control and Information Processing* (pp. 93–96). Dalian, China. DOI: 10.1109/ICICIP.2010.5565288

Xu, G., Shi, Y., Sun, X., & Shen, W. (2019). Internet of things in marine environment monitoring: A review. *Sensors (Basel)*, *19*(7), 1711. DOI: 10.3390/s19071711 PMID: 30974791

Xu, N., Ma, L., Liu, Q., Wang, L., & Deng, Y. (2021). An improved text mining approach to extract safety risk factors from construction accident reports. *Safety Science*, *138*, 105216. DOI: 10.1016/j.ssci.2021.105216

Xu, Y., Xu, Z., Chen, B., Song, F., Liu, Y., & Liu, T. (2020, July). Patch based vulnerability matching for binary programs. In *Proceedings of the 29th ACM SIGSOFT International Symposium on Software Testing and Analysis* (pp. 376-387).

Yadav, N., Gupta, V., & Garg, A. (2024). Industrial Automation Through AI-Powered Intelligent Machines—Enabling Real-Time Decision-Making. In *Recent Trends in Artificial Intelligence Towards a Smart World: Applications in Industries and Sectors* (pp. 145–178). Springer.

Yaghmai, R. (2021). A Critical Examination of How Artificial Intelligence Should Be Regulated in the United Kingdom. *BLR*, 59.

Yamaguchi, F., Golde, N., Arp, D., & Rieck, K. (2014, May). Modeling and discovering vulnerabilities with code property graphs. In 2014 IEEE symposium on security and privacy (pp. 590-604). IEEE.

Yang, G., Chen, X., Cao, J., Xu, S., Cui, Z., Yu, C., & Liu, K. (2021, August). Comformer: Code comment generation via transformer and fusion method-based hybrid code representation. In 2021 8th International Conference on Dependable Systems and Their Applications (DSA) (pp. 30-41). IEEE.

Yang, M., Chen, L., Wang, J., Msigwa, G., Osman, A. I., Fawzy, S., Rooney, D. W., & Yap, P.-S. (2023). Circular economy strategies for combating climate change and other environmental issues. *Environmental Chemistry Letters*, *21*(1), 55–80. DOI: 10.1007/s10311-022-01499-6

Yaseen, Z. M., Ali, Z. H., Salih, S. Q., & Al-Ansari, N. (2020). Prediction of risk delay in construction projects using a hybrid artificial intelligence model. *Sustainability (Basel)*, *12*(4), 1514. DOI: 10.3390/su12041514

Ye, J., Cheng, X., Zhu, J., Feng, L., & Song, L. (2018). A DDoS attack detection method based on SVM in software defined network. *Security and Communication Networks*, *2018*(1), 9804061.

Yewei, Y., & Pereira, P. R. (2022). Sources of Sustained Competitive Advantage from the Perspective of Strategic Entrepreneurship-An Empirical Study on Manufacturing Enterprises in China.

Yigitcanlar, T., Kamruzzaman, M., Foth, M., Sabatini-Marques, J., Da Costa, E., & Ioppolo, G. (2019). Can cities become smart without being sustainable? A systematic review of the literature. *Sustainable Cities and Society*, *45*, 348–365.

Zhang, F., Zhang, F., Fleyeh, H., Wang, X., & Lu, M. (2019). Construction site accident analysis using text mining and natural language processing techniques. *Automation in Construction*, *99*, 238–248. DOI: 10.1016/j.autcon.2018.12.016

Zhang, J., Zhang, X., & Liu, T. (2023). *AI Tools for Project Management in Software Development: Emerging Trends and Research Directions*. Springer.

Zhang, Y., Patel, S., & Liu, H. (2023). AI-enhanced coding tools: Transforming software development. *Software Technology Journal*, *29*(1), 12–23. DOI: 10.1080/stj.2023.001

Zhao, Q., Huang, C., & Dai, L. (2006). VULDEFF: Vulnerability Detection Method Based on Function Fingerprints and Code Differences. *Knowl.-Based Syst.* 2023, *260*, 110139. Kornblum, J. Identifying Almost Identical Files Using Context Triggered Piecewise Hashing. *Digital Investigation*, *3*, 91–97.

Zhao, X., Li, L., & Wu, Q. (2023). *Data Governance in AI Projects: Challenges and Solutions*. Springer.

Zheng, W., Jiang, Y., & Su, X. (2021, October). Vu1SPG: Vulnerability detection based on slice property graph representation learning. In 2021 IEEE 32nd International Symposium on Software Reliability Engineering (ISSRE) (pp. 457-467). IEEE.

Zhou, Y., Chen, S., & Banerjee, A. (2018). Stable Gradient Descent. In UAI (pp. 766-775).

Zhou, Y., Liang, Y. S., Wong, Y. K., Qiu, H., Wu, Y. X., & He, B. (2023). Implementation of The Future of Drug Discovery: QuantumBased Machine Learning Simulation (QMLS). *arXiv Preprint arXiv:2308.08561*.

Zhou, J., Cui, G., Hu, S., Zhang, Z., Yang, C., Liu, Z., Wang, L., Li, C., & Sun, M. (2020). Graph Neural Networks: A Review of Methods and Applications. *AI Open*, *1*, 57–81. DOI: 10.1016/j.aiopen.2021.01.001

Zhou, Y., Liu, S., Siow, J., Du, X., & Liu, Y. (2019). Devign: Effective vulnerability identification by learning comprehensive program semantics via graph neural networks. *Advances in Neural Information Processing Systems*, •••, 32.

Zhou, Y., Yi, P., Li, W., & Gong, C. (2021). Assessment of city sustainability from the perspective of multi-source data-driven. *Sustainable Cities and Society*, *70*, 102918.

Zhu, J., Pande, A., Mohapatra, P., & Han, J. J. (2015, October). Using deep learning for energy expenditure estimation with wearable sensors. In 2015 17th International Conference on E-health Networking, Application & Services (HealthCom) (pp. 501-506). IEEE.

Zohuri, B., & Rahmani, F. M. (2023). Artificial intelligence driven resiliency with machine learning and deep learning components. *Japan Journal of Research*, *1*(1). Advance online publication. DOI: 10.33425/2690-8077.1002

Zugay, B., & Zakaria, R. (2023). *Ansoff matrix*. SAGE Publications, Inc. DOI: 10.4135/9781071924136

About the Contributors

Rahul Patel is a seasoned Cyber Security and Information Systems Management professional and and Adjunct Associate Professor with over 30 years of experience defending the Availability, Confidentiality, and Integrity of information assets and managing information Systems in the high-tech, banking and government industries. Dr. Patel holds a PhD in Management of Information Systems from Northcentral University, M.B.A from DePaul University, M.S. in Computer Engineering from Illinois Institute of Technology, and several cybersecurity certifications such as ITIL, CISM, and CISSP.

***

Sampath Boopathi is an accomplished individual with a strong academic background and extensive research experience. He completed his undergraduate studies in Mechanical Engineering and pursued his postgraduate studies in the field of Computer-Aided Design. Dr. Boopathi obtained his Ph.D. from Anna University, focusing his research on Manufacturing and optimization. Throughout his career, Dr. Boopathi has made significant contributions to the field of engineering. He has authored and published over 225 research articles in internationally peer-reviewed journals, highlighting his expertise and dedication to advancing knowledge in his area of specialization. His research output demonstrates his commitment to conducting rigorous and impactful research. In addition to his research publications, Dr. Boopathi has also been granted one patent and has three published patents to his name. This indicates his innovative thinking and ability to develop practical solutions to real-world engineering challenges. With 17 years of academic and research experience, Dr. Boopathi has enriched the engineering community through his teaching and mentorship roles.

C.V. Suresh Babu is a pioneer in content development. A true entrepreneur, he founded Anniyappa Publications, a company that is highly active in publishing books related to Computer Science and Management. Dr. C.V. Suresh Babu has also ventured into SB Institute, a center for knowledge transfer. He holds a Ph.D. in Engineering Education from the National Institute of Technical Teachers Training & Research in Chennai, along with seven master's degrees in various disciplines such as Engineering, Computer Applications, Management, Commerce, Economics, Psychology, Law, and Education. Additionally, he has UGC-NET/SET qualifications in the fields of Computer Science, Management, Commerce, and Education. Currently, Dr. C.V. Suresh Babu is a Professor in the Department of Information Technology at the School of Computing Science, Hindustan Institute of Technology and Science (Hindustan University) in Padur, Chennai, Tamil Nadu, India.

Index

E

F

G

I

J

K

L

M

N

P

Q

R

S

T

U

V

www.ingramcontent.com/pod-product-compliance
Lightning Source LLC
LaVergne TN
LVHW060416300926
849162LV00006B/1441